Acknowledgments

OUR SPECIAL THANKS TO:

Critical readers

Mitchell Wasserman, Harrison Elementary, Livingston, N.J.

Christine Walker, Mt. Pleasant Elementary, Livingston, N.J.

Our friends, whose encouragement and criticism helped to make this work happen

Dr. Douglas Paul, Profiles Corporation, Iowa City, Iowa

Dr. Lynn Hunter, Lynn Hunter & Associates, Jackson, N.J.

Mary Oates, Livingston, N.J., Public Schools

Dr. Joseph A. Kreskey, Edison, N.J. (retired)

The following teachers critiqued one or more lessons and gave us their advice about what would help real classroom teachers use these materials effectively.

Freddie DiGeronimo	Elizabeth Avenue School, Franklin Township, Somerset, N.J.
Diane Glace	Rutgers Preparatory School, Somerset, N.J.
Ellen Glenn	Ella G. Clarke School, Lakewood, N.J.
Anthony Jenkins	Florence Annex School, Irvington, N.J.
Celine McNally	Lincoln School, New Brunswick, N.J.
Robin Morgan	Parkside Elementary, Camden, N.J.
Claire Passantino	Math Consultant
Elaine Plevier	Memorial School, Union Beach, N.J.
Carolyn Pugh	PS# 2, Paterson, N.J.
Jennifer Saliski	Caruso Elementary, Keansburg, N.J.
Kimberlee Shaw	Ella G. Clarke School, Lakewood, N.J.
Elizabeth Szamreta	Great Meadows Regional Schools, Warren, N.J.
Jacqueline Thompson	Cedarbrook School, Plainfield, N.J.
Katherine Witte	Ridge Avenue School, Neptune, N.J.

And to the many teachers and students who tried out our ideas in the classroom and helped us to learn and to find new ideas and lessons.

abc
123

Good Connections for Testing

Using Children's Books to Maximize Understanding and Achievement in Mathematics and Language Arts!

Ann M. Lawrence
Paul R. Lawrence

LLTeach
Bridgewater, New Jersey

Editorial Services by
Woodglen Publishing Company
Califon, New Jersey

Printed in the United States of America
04 03 02 01 00   9 8 7 6 5 4 3 2 1

ISBN 0-9676545-0-5

Design by Sharon Ferguson
Electronic page production by Debbie Childers
Photographs by Carmen Natale

Distributed by LLTeach
Executive Offices:
709 Country Club Road
Bridgewater, NJ 08807-1601
(908) 575-8830 or (800) 575-7670
Fax (908) 704-1730

LLTeach—Lawrence Learning & Teaching Educational Services focuses on quality education for all students. It provides consulting, staff development and inservice programs in mathematics and English/language arts, K-12, customized to meet the specific needs and goals of participating schools, districts, or consortia. Contact LLTeach for further details.

We would like your comments about the lessons, the books, and your students' responses to the activities. Please write and send your comments to goodconnections@aol.com.

Contents

Overview

Ann and Paul Lawrence, authors of *Good Connections for Testing*, believe that quality instruction is the key for raising test scores for all students.

The elements needed to make high performance an attainable goal are:

- highly motivational lessons;
- proven instructional strategies that emphasize active learning and discovery;
- hands-on activities;
- higher-order thinking questions;
- writing to learn;
- powerful transfer techniques; and
- question formats that reflect state-defined assessments.

To write this teacher's resource, the authors used 18 popular children's books to create 25 lessons that integrate language arts and mathematics within a framework of the expectations and proficiencies underlying most state assessments. The best test preparation is effective teaching of the skills and concepts that students are responsible for knowing. When this teaching is tied to classroom assessments that mirror the high-stakes tests, teachers have a complete, effective test-preparation program. To make this possible, the authors have provided student worksheets and test materials on reproducible masters that can be stored in a three-ring binder.

A typical lesson includes viewing, listening, and writing as well as many hands-on, discovery-based math activities. To assist the teacher in lesson planning, the lessons are cross-matched to specific state standards. The correlations are provided in a separate booklet. Practice questions for assessment are written in the formats found on most state assessments: multiple choice; short, constructed response; extended response; and essay. Answer keys and easy-to-use scoring rubrics are provided.

The mathematics lessons are based on the National Council of Teachers of Mathematics (NCTM) standards, and the language arts lessons draw their inspiration from the National Council of Teachers of English/International Reading Association (NCTE/IRA) standards.

Philosophy

The most important people in the educational community are students and teachers. Our philosophy is that every student can learn and every teacher can present concepts in ways that empower all. We believe the following make the difference in unleashing every student's potential for success: the foundation of instruction; the quality of instruction; strategies that empower all learners; a well-defined curriculum; and teacher commitment and attitude.

As the elementary curriculum becomes more crowded with content to be learned at higher cognitive levels, teachers have more difficulty finding time to make sure all students are prepared for high-stakes assessments. It makes sense to connect concepts, when appropriate, not only because it saves times, but, more importantly, because it helps to integrate "school" learning with the real world. The connections, by giving lessons greater meaning, help learners grasp and apply new concepts. Math and language arts do not occur in segmented units of learning in everyday life. Why then should units of instruction be separated?

Because students should be actively involved in learning, every lesson in *Good Connections for Testing* has been designed to provide high-interest activities with higher-order thinking tasks. Conceptual understanding is established by tapping into techniques that reflect varied learning styles. By experiencing and internalizing essential concepts and practicing question types that are common to statewide assessments and reflect NCTE/IRA standards, students build confidence in their abilities to meet and exceed those expectations that have been established for them.

Flexibility by Design

The lessons in *Good Connections for Testing* are structured in a way that provides teachers with flexibility. Depending on the needs of your class, you can:

- select what you need;
- implement all lessons completely; or
- use the lessons to provide extensive test practice.

While each of the 18 children's stories in this book presents integrated math and language arts activities that reflect much of the content and related assessment questions found on most elementary math/language arts proficiencies, there also are separate activities that isolate math and/or language arts skills. Some teachers use all of the stories and the majority of activities. Other teachers select stories and activities that meet the needs of their students. Some teachers mix and match selected language arts and math activities.

Whether your goal is finding additional student activities, higher-level thinking questions in popular test formats, or ideas to enhance language arts instruction, math instruction, or both, *Good Connections for Testing* becomes an essential aid in empowering you to reach your goal.

Planning Guide: How to Use This Book

There are three parts to *Good Connections for Testing*:

- Twenty-five lessons, activities, questions, answers, and rubrics that accompany each of the stories.
- Reproducible masters that correlate to each of the stories and can be duplicated for the students in one teacher's classroom.
- Correlations to state-specific proficiencies or standards.

Instructional strategies for mathematics are presented within each lesson and are summarized in a section called "Recommended Strategies for Teaching Children to Learn Mathematics," which begins on page *x*. For an overview of information about the teaching of reading and language arts, see "Recommended Strategies for Teaching Reading and Language Arts to Children," page *xii*.

SELECTING AND IMPLEMENTING STORIES

Good Connections for Testing provides two separate charts that show which topics from the standards can be found in specific lessons. Overview matrices on pages *xi–xii* clearly show connections between major topics in mathematics and language arts for each story. State-specific connections are provided in the supplement included with *Good Connections for Testing*. After reviewing these matrices, you may want to choose one of the implementation methods suggested below.

Classroom teachers are the people most aware of the needs of their students. With that knowledge in mind, you can use the information in *Good Connections for Testing* to plan specific lessons and activities that address their students' strengths and weaknesses.

METHOD 1: Use this resource for additional ideas to supplement or assess the topics you are currently teaching from your text and/or district curriculum.

METHOD 2: Select the topics you would like to reteach because the students didn't quite "get it" or that you would like to enhance through integration and high-interest activities. Also use this resource to teach those topics that are not included in your current set of texts and materials.

METHOD 3: Select those children's books that interest you and integrate them throughout the year. Or, use the language arts activities and/or math activities at selected times throughout the year.

IMPLEMENTING STORY CONNECTIONS AND ACTIVITIES

Each lesson in *Good Connections for Testing* has a similar structure.

OVERVIEW OF THE CONNECTIONS. This is a brief description of the story along with a description of the math and language arts concepts that are connected to the story and embedded in the activities.

MATERIALS FOR THE CONNECTIONS. A list of materials that will be needed for the activities is included so that they can be gathered prior to the lesson.

LANGUAGE ARTS: VIEWING CONNECTION. As an anticipation activity, this connection includes a writing activity based on viewing a picture from the book.

LANGUAGE ARTS: LISTENING CONNECTION. Teachers read part or all of the story to the class as a listening activity. They do not show the illustrations or stop to discuss the story. After students listen to the story, they respond to multiple-choice questions and an open-ended listening task. A rubric is provided for scoring the open-ended task. The assessment, which is modeled after the most common elements in various state assessments, mirrors active reading by requiring students to make inferences and recall information from what they have just heard or to make logical predictions about what will happen next. In a few cases, a listening activity was not appropriate for the book, so it was not included in the lesson.

MATHEMATICS: INTRODUCTION AND ACTIVE READING. In this section, students use manipulatives to either act out or investigate concepts related to the story. The thinking processes used as students think about the text being read models the metacognition inherent in active reading.

MATHEMATICS: CONCEPT AND SKILL ACTIVITIES. Activity titles throughout the Math Connections section help teachers clearly identify the skill or concept being presented. Many higher-order think-pair-share activities, often with reproducible masters, are included in these sections.

CONNECTION TO MATHEMATICS ASSESSMENT. This section includes five multiple-choice questions and one open-ended, student-constructed response question on a reproducible master. Answers and a scoring rubric with suggested responses also are included.

COMPOSITION CONNECTION. This connection offers summary or closure activities for either language arts or mathematics. In some cases, both disciplines are included in the activity. Prompts, on reproducible masters, are provided along with scoring rubrics.

EXTENDING THE CONNECTIONS. Additional discovery-based, hands-on math activities that can be easily connected to the story are included in this section. Language arts extensions offer logical links to the lesson, such as vocabulary connections, reading skills, writing revision activities, or additional writing prompts.

PROJECTS. Some lessons contain suggestions for long-term projects that will help students connect and apply many concepts to real-world situations and problems.

ADDITIONAL RESOURCES. Some lessons offer additional sources of activities and cross-reference relevant video segments from *Windows on Math.*

GLOSSARY OF BASIC STRATEGIES

Throughout *Good Connections for Testing*, group work and discussion become key vehicles for reaching conclusions and experiencing alternative approaches and solutions to problems. Several basic discussion techniques are described below.

Think-Pair-Share. When using this strategy, teachers should first have students covertly or overtly think about a solution to a problem or question that is posed. Students should then get in pairs or groups of 3–4 and share and discuss their solutions with others in the group. Finally, a class discussion is held, providing opportunities for all to see varied approaches and solutions to the same problem.

Group Work. Many times when students work in groups, our concern as teachers is that not everyone learns from the experience. Sometimes we observe that three people in a group of four are expecting one person in the group to do the thinking and to supply the answers. To ensure that all members are involved, you may want to assign roles to each student or randomly choose any person in the class to answer a question or supply an explanation, regardless of whether or not they were the originators of the solution. This randomness encourages everyone to be involved and greatly contributes to getting all members of the group to work as a team. "It's everyone's responsibility."

GETTING STARTED

Do I need to use every story?

No, use only those stories that meet the needs of your students or enhance the materials and curriculum you are currently using. Some teachers may want to use only one or two stories, while others may want to use them all.

- **Quick Start:** Use the matrix in the state correlation booklet that comes with *Good Connections for Testing* to help you pinpoint those concepts that your curriculum or text do not cover as thoroughly as you would like. Or, use the matrix to select topics you would like to cover in more detail or for which you would like to have more activity ideas.

Is there any special order in which I should use the stories? What are the major skills in each story?

The literature books appear alphabetically followed by lessons from the Anno's books. Use them in the order that fits your curriculum or meets the needs of your students.

- **Quick Start in Language Arts:** All lessons include short and long writing activities and model active reading. The chart below indicates if the lesson includes a listening activity and highlights additional skills and concepts.

- **Quick Start in Mathematics:** In the chart on the next page, shadings group sets of books sequentially by big ideas in mathematics. Keep in mind that lessons always have cross-strand activities. The books are listed by their major emphasis only.

LANGUAGE ARTS

Title	Listening Activity	Major Emphasis
Alexander, Who Used to Be Rich Last Sunday	✓	speaking
Anno's Hat Tricks		writing as process; point of view; visual literacy
Anno's Math Games (Chapters 1–4)		description in writing; visual literacy
Anno's Math Games II (Chapters 1–5)		description in writing; visual literacy
A Cloak for the Dreamer	✓	story type; vocabulary; journal writing
Counting on Frank	✓	discussion; journal writing
The Doorbell Rang	✓	details in writing; drama; journals
Gator Pie	✓	writing as process; details in writing; discussion; vocabulary; journals
Grandfather Tang's Story	✓	writing as process; story type; vocabulary; journals
The Greedy Triangle	✓	revision; story type; figurative language; journal
How Much, How Many, How Far, How Heavy, How Long, How Tall Is 1000?		developing descriptions
How Much Is a Million?		revision; writing as process; active reading/journals
The King's Commissioners	✓	writing as process; speaking; drawing inferences; vocabulary; specific details; journals
One Hundred Hungry Ants	✓	writing as process; developing descriptions; vocabulary
Pigs Will Be Pigs	✓	vocabulary; figurative language; descriptions
A Remainder of One	✓	specific details; visual literacy; figurative language
Spaghetti and Meatballs for All!	✓	journals; specific details
A Three Hat Day	✓	discussion; writing as process; revision; active reading; vocabulary; journals

MATHEMATICS

Title	Major Emphasis
The King's Commissioners	number sense and estimation
How Much, How Many, How Far, How Heavy, How Long, How Tall Is 1000?	number sense and estimation
How Much Is a Million?	number sense and estimation
Counting on Frank	number sense and estimation; need for standard units of measure
One Hundred Hungry Ants	concepts of multiplication
The Doorbell Rang	concepts of division
A Remainder of One	concepts of division
The Greedy Triangle	identifying and comparing geometric shapes, their properties and relationships
Anno's Math Games: Chapter 2 (Putting Together and Taking Apart)	logic and reasoning; combining and taking apart shapes
Grandfather Tang's Story	concept and operations with fractions; following directions; concepts of similarity and congruence
A Cloak for the Dreamer	concept and operations with fractions; tiling and tessellations; variables
Gator Pie	concepts of fractions and decimals
Spaghetti and Meatballs for All!	concepts of perimeter and area; real-world computation, estimation, and planning applications
Alexander, Who Used to Be Rich Last Sunday	money; variables
Pigs Will Be Pigs	money; problem solving
Anno's Math Games: Chapter 3 (Numbers in Order)	sequencing; concepts of coordinates
Anno's Math Games II: Chapter 4 (Counting With Circles)	variables; number sentences
Anno's Math Games II: Chapter 1 (The Magic Machine)	functions; linear relationships
Anno's Math Games: Chapter 4 (Who's the Tallest?)	representing data effectively
A Three Hat Day	probability; listing possibilities
Anno's Hat Tricks	probability; logic and reasoning
Anno's Math Games: Chapter 1 (What Is Different?)	logic and reasoning; patterns
Anno's Math Games II: Chapter 2 (Compare and Find Out)	logic and reasoning; patterns; spatial sense
Anno's Math Games II: Chapter 3 (Dots, Dots, and More Dots)	density; counting; estimation
Anno's Math Games II: Chapter 5 (Counting With Water)	standard and non-standard measure; capacity

Must I do all the activities in each story? Can I mix and match math and language arts activities?

No, you don't need to do all the activities in each story. Where activities build upon each other, it is noted. Yes, you can mix and math and language arts activities. The key is flexibility in use and meeting the needs of students in your classroom.

- **Quick Start:** Peruse the titles, topics, and activities. Decide on a long-term plan. What experiences are necessary for my students to be prepared for the language arts portion of the test? What experiences are necessary for my students to be prepared for the math portion of the test?

Must I use the questions that accompany each story? Can the questions be used independently?

You don't have to use the questions that accompany each story. It is best, however, not to use the questions independent of the stories. The foundational philosophy of this book is that the best way to increase test scores is through quality instruction that is connected to assessment. Therefore, it is best to use the questions in combination with the stories and lessons, rather than pull them out of context.

Must I use the rubrics that are provided for open-ended questions and writing prompts?

It's best to use the rubrics as frequently as possible. After removing any identifying parameters on student papers, let students evaluate each other's answers so they develop exemplars and have an idea of what makes a good response and a not-so-good response.

How do I correlate my state-defined skills to each lesson or activity?

Use the your state correlation book, which is a supplement that is included as part of *Good Connections for Testing*. There are two ways to correlate: by the big ideas for each story and by individual activities in stories.

An overview chart connects each story to state-defined language arts and math topics. Many times there also is an activity-by-activity correlation to state standards as well.

Do I need all the manipulatives to teach the stories?

It is best to use the manipulatives as recommended. Below is the *ideal* set of manipulatives to have in your classroom if every story is implemented. Often, commercial models of the manipulatives can be replaced by materials that are easy to make. Templates for pattern blocks, base ten blocks, etc., are provided in the reproducible masters.

MANIPULATIVES

- Base ten blocks with an overhead set (one class set)
- Calculators: fraction-capable with an overhead model (at least one for each group of 2–3 students)
- Collectibles: toy animals, dried peas, jellybeans
- Connecting cubes (150 or more per group of 2–3 students)
- Counters (about 20 per group of 2–3 students)
- Containers: Opaque containers, such as plastic tubs, shoe boxes, small and large paper bags, cans, milk cartons, etc., and clear ones, such as jars, bottles, measuring cups, beakers.
- Construction materials: construction paper, markers, poster paper, straws, twist ties, small plastic bags,
- Coordinate grid paper, graph paper, index cards
- Construction tools: scissors, rulers, tape, string, straws and twist ties, pipe cleaners
- 11-x-11 pin geoboards with an overhead model (at least 1 per group of 2–3 students)
- Pattern blocks with overhead sets (at least 1 bucket per 4–6 students)
- Play money: pennies, nickels, dimes, quarters, half dollars, $1 bills
- Random-number generators for 0–9: spinners; 10-sided or 20-sided dice; or playing cards with 10s, queens, and kings removed (one generator per pair of students)
- Response materials: slates, index cards, self-stick notes, scrap pieces of paper (These materials, used to collect data and gather estimations, foster active learning, and increase willingness to guess and take risks.)
- Journals: Should be used to record ideas, responses, and attitudes about mathematics
- Tiles with overhead set (6 of each of the four colors for each group of 2–3 students)
- Tangrams with overhead set (at least one set per 2–3 students)
- Miscellaneous: hats, local maps
- Measurement tools: rulers; eyedropper; containers marked for ounce, cup, pint, quart; kitchen scale

Do I need a copy of the book for each student?

No. It is ideal, however, to have several copies available for situations where students need to look closely at an illustration for a Viewing Connection activity. For *Anno's Math Games* and *Anno's Math Games II*, it is best to have a book for each group of 2–4 students.

Where can I find a list of the books with ISBN numbers, publishers, and authors?

Each lesson identifies the book, author and illustrator, publisher and ISBN. A complete list is provided below. It is best to have a class set of your own, but many times your school librarian will already have the book. You may want to give this list to the librarian.

Title	Author	Paperback ISBN and Publisher	Library and/or Hardcover Edition ISBN and Publisher
Alexander, Who Used to Be Rich Last Sunday	Viorst, Judith	0689711999 Aladdin/Simon & Schuster	0689306024 Atheneum/Simon & Schuster
Anno's Hat Tricks	Nozaki, Akihiro and, Anno, Mitsumasa	0153003499 Harcourt Brace	Out of print
Anno's Math Games	Anno, Mitsumasa	0698116712 PaperStar/Putnam	Out of print
Anno's Math Games II	Anno, Mitsumasa	0698116720 PaperStar/ Putnam	Out of print
A Cloak for the Dreamer	Friedman, Aileen	Not Available	0590489879 Scholastic
Counting on Frank	Clement, Rod	Not Available	0836803582 Gareth Stevens
The Doorbell Rang	Hutchins, Pat	0688092349 Mulberry/Morrow	0688052517 Greenwillow
Gator Pie	Mathews, Louise	0760800057 Sundance	Not Available
Grandfather Tang's Story	Tompert, Ann	0517885581 Crown	051757487X Crown
The Greedy Triangle	Burns, Marilyn	Not Available	0590489917 Scholastic
How Much, How Many, How Far, How Heavy, How Long, How Tall Is 1000?	Nolan, Helen	Not Available	1550741640 Kids Can Press
How Much Is a Million?	Schwartz, David	0688099335 Mulberry/Morrow	0688040497 Lothrop, Lee & Shepard/Morrow
The King's Commissioners	Friedman, Aileen	Not Available	0590489895 Scholastic
One Hundred Hungry Ants	Pinczes, Elinor	Not Available	0395631165 Houghton Mifflin
Pigs Will Be Pigs	Axelrod, Amy	0689812191 Aladdin/Simon & Schuster	002765415X Simon & Schuster
A Remainder of One	Pinczes, Elinor	Not Available	0395694558 Houghton Mifflin
Spaghetti and Meatballs for All!	Burns, Marilyn	Not Available	0590944592 Scholastic
A Three Hat Day	Geringer, Laura	0064431576 HarperCollins	0060219890 HarperCollins

Recommended Strategies for Teaching Children to Understand Mathematics

A Need for Change in the Traditional Approach to Teaching Mathematics

The National Council of Teachers of Mathematics (NCTM) and most state-specific mathematics standards and assessment guidelines emphasize that pedagogy is as important as content in the teaching of mathematics. In fact, many cross-strand, higher-order thinking questions — the foundation of most statewide assessments — are formulated on the assumption that students regularly engage in hands-on, discovery-based, technology-enhanced lessons that offer rich opportunities for communication and problem solving. Success for *all* students cannot be achieved without combining and enhancing traditional teaching methods with the following essential strategies that research has shown empower all students.

The lessons and activities in *Good Connections for Testing* are built on a foundation that includes the essential strategies that follow.

ACTIVE LEARNING

Math is about doing, exploring, and discovering. Passive learning delivered through watch, do, and drill techniques can no longer be the dominant methodology in teaching mathematics. Students that are engaged in active learning have a higher interest in the subject and have more opportunities for long-term retention and conceptual understanding.

HANDS-ON

Ideally students should learn mathematics in three stages: concretely, iconically, and symbolically. Symbol manipulation can be taught, but if students don't have the connection to conceptual understanding and concrete models, it has little meaning and is quickly forgotten.

TECHNOLOGY ENHANCED

Students should not use calculators or computers to recall and apply basic facts. However, calculators should be available at all times so students can extend concepts and solve non-routine problems that they conceptually understand but haven't learned to calculate algorithmically.

GROUP ORIENTED

Students should discuss and defend their mathematical understandings and conclusions with each other to help them solve non-routine problems and internalize concepts. Communication is absolutely essential for conceptual development and understanding, but students should realize that ultimately they are responsible for independent understanding and application.

DISCOVERY ORIENTED

Students who are taught procedures in isolation sometimes do not form sufficient understanding to apply the procedures in the correct situation. Often they apply correct procedures in incorrect situations. Students have more opportunity to understand concepts, procedures, and concepts if they explore concepts, record data, analyze the data, make conjectures about the data, and test them — and then formulate their own procedures and algorithms based on these discoveries.

PROBLEM-SOLVING ORIENTED

Adults have used certain mathematics concepts so often that they sometimes cannot understand why children don't grasp seemingly elementary ideas However, when students are taught only procedures or algorithms, they do not have the opportunity to internalize, retain, and apply the learning over a long period of time. To retain an understanding of the concepts, all learners need to construct their own understanding, not just learn a process. In mathematics, this conceptual base is built through non-routine problem solving.

RICH IN COMMUNICATION

Students must learn to justify their thinking both orally and in writing. Many state assessments include open-ended questions as well as short, constructed-response questions. Students who have little opportunity to write and to discuss their understandings throughout their learning experiences will have a much more difficult time completing these constructed-response questions.

RICH IN CONNECTIONS

Students should experience mathematics as a whole rather than in isolated, disjointed lessons and units. Even though every lesson needs to have a focus and objective, every opportunity should be taken to connect the main concept to other strands in mathematics as well as to other subjects. In life, mathematics does not occur as an isolated skill. It is integrated into problem-solving situations that usually require cross-strand and content applications.

SENSITIVE TO LEARNING STYLES

All students have the potential to understand mathematics and to use it appropriately. However, if lessons do not reflect a learner's preferred learning style — auditory, visual, or kinesthetic — we make it more difficult for all students to learn. If we design lessons that are considerate of all three learning styles, all students will be more likely to be able to internalize the concepts being taught.

HIGH STANDARDS

All students can be successful in mathematics. Very often we create a self-full-filling prophecy. If we believe students can be successful in mathematics, they are. If we believe they cannot be successful, they are not. Henry Ford summarized it by stating that whether we believe we can or believe we can't, we are right! We as professionals must always raise the bar, regardless of past performance and previous low-level expectations.

ADDITIONAL RESOURCE

National Council of Teachers of Mathematics, 1906 Association Drive, Reston, VA 20191-1593, or on the Web at *www.nctm.org*.

Recommended Strategies for Teaching Reading and Language Arts to Children

STANDARDS-BASED READING AND LANGUAGE ARTS

Reading, writing, listening, speaking, and viewing: the language arts. This listing is both familiar and strange to all teachers. We are especially comfortable thinking about reading and writing, the traditional subjects of literacy. Additionally, we have always acknowledged that we need to teach speaking — especially public speaking and group discussion skills — but we usually have spent little time with oral language skills. Listening, the partner of speaking, also is recognized as an important skill, but we probably don't have many strategies in our pedagogical bag of tricks for teaching listening, short of admonitions that our students "listen closely" and "remember what you hear."

Finally, we have probably thought that students need to know how to deal with the messages conveyed in movies and on television, but there has been little on the topic available to us. Somewhere in the K–12 curriculum one can probably find something (most likely dealing with propaganda) that says we need to make students aware of the messages conveyed in visual images. Today, we would call this part of a larger subject: visual literacy. However, with the widespread and growing importance of standards-based, high-stakes testing, it is increasingly urgent that we think about all of these skills and how to teach them more effectively so that all students can succeed.

The high-stakes testing is our immediate motivation, but proficiency in the five language arts is important to our students because they are the foundations of lifelong learning, critical thinking, and economic self-determination. They are at the heart of what citizens of the 21st century will need to be productive.

GOOD CONNECTIONS TO LANGUAGE ARTS INSTRUCTION

The purpose of the language arts activities in *Good Connections for Testing* is to provide some instructional activities and/or materials to assist you in giving your students a foundation and understanding of verbal literacy skills in a context that will enable them to transfer application of the skills to a larger context — not just to use in taking tests, but also to use in everyday school and life activities. Therefore, this chapter about instruction in language arts will merely touch on the tremendously exciting field of teaching literacy skills, one rich in new research and applications. We cannot continue to teach the way we always have without examining our practice, nor do we need to abandon certain trusted practices to wildly embrace the new and unknown. We need to find a balanced and sound approach that will allow us to teach all five of the language arts effectively. Hopefully, you will expand your study to include all that is currently happening in the wider fields of research and practice.

INTEGRATION OF INSTRUCTION

The concept of integration is basic to language arts instruction. While we can talk about certain techniques and strategies that will promote effective learning of a particular skill, such as writing, the actual instruction cannot exist without its interdependence on the other four skills. And whether or not you teach in a self-contained elementary classroom, the other subjects that students learn both depend upon the students' linguistic skills and can be used to enhance them. Likewise, there are some practices that are important to the teaching of all language arts that also can be applied to the teaching of other subjects.

STRUCTURES FOR TEACHING LANGUAGE ARTS

The five language arts skills are not only parts of the communication process, they are most of all methods of making meaning of our world and of our life experiences. Therefore, we must teach the language arts as meaning-making processes — that is, defining and solving problems — as well as ways of sharing our knowledge and ideas and understanding and communicating our most intimate and most public hopes, dreams, and fears. When you look at the mathematics lessons in *Good Connections for Testing*, you will immediately recognize that they are designed to motivate students to think, to problem-solve, to make meaning—the same skills we are teaching in language arts. Teaching the two together helps to strengthen students' thinking skills in all academic disciplines.

The unity of the language arts as ways of finding meaning as well as learning and understanding concepts and knowledge means that there are some basic strategies for teaching the language arts. These are teaching structures that will apply to other subjects, too.

For many years, we have recognized that we promote effective reading by doing pre-reading activities, mid-reading activities, and post-reading activities. We model, explicitly state, and think aloud those things that readers need to do to get ready for reading, how they conduct themselves during reading, and what strategies they can use after reading to promote comprehension, understanding, and retention. Slightly modified, this same basic structure will work for all five language arts and provide us a generic road map for teaching the language arts.

PREPARING FOR LEARNING

The pre-reading activities — writing, speaking, listening, and viewing — are designed to help the learner get ready to learn. They need to access and bring to a conscious level what they know not only about the subject to be considered, but also about what strategies they will use to accomplish the task. The powerful language processor (reader, writer, speaker, listener, and viewer) will eventually move many of these processes to a level of automaticity where they will unconsciously perform these tasks quickly and efficiently. But it is very important for the child who is beginning to establish a repertoire of language skills to understand how to apply the processes of the discipline. Think, for instance, about children who insist that they have "read" a selection but cannot relate to you a single idea or concept from it. Most likely, they have been able to sound out, either aloud or in their own heads, each word, but they have not understood how to transfer those sounds into knowledge and concepts that they can explain or share.

WRITING FROM A PICTURE PROMPT

Each of the lessons in *Good Connections for Testing* provides activities in which students look at a picture and write about what they see prior to the reading of the story. This activity allows them to access prior knowledge, develop questions, and make predictions. Writing is the vehicle used to develop those ideas. In classroom instruction, you can use pairs, small groups, or whole-class discussion to accomplish these goals as well. Instruction can model the process by using a think-aloud, wherein you verbalize a monologue. Consider this example:

> "What do I see here? Well it looks like a(n) **[object]**. Its characteristics are ________, ________, ________, and ________. Those are all things that a(n) **[object]** has. But I also see these things: ________, ________, and ________. Those may or may not apply to **[object]**. I think that in this case, because ________ is happening, that it is **[object]**. Therefore, if it is **[object]**, the thing that is most likely to happen is ________."

Let's use the cover of *Good Connections for Testing* as an example of a pre-learning activity. Here is a sample think-aloud that could be said to the class:

> "OK, what's here? The title is *Good Connections for Testing*. That must mean that it has something to do with tests that kids will have to take. The subtitle is "Using Children's Books to Maximize Understanding and Achievement in Mathematics and Language Arts." Well, that narrows it down to two subjects. So it must be designed to help students get ready for tests. And since it is a textbook, it must be to help them get ready for a certain test or a certain kind of test. I guess I'll find that answer inside when I read the book.
>
> What are these circles here? They have little knobs on them that must fit into something. They can't be tires because the knobs are awfully large in comparison to the circle part of the figure. Oh, I bet they are gears, the gears that help things fit together and run effectively — the connections. The gears mirror the word connections in the title.
>
> What are these kids doing? ..."

In that example, the individual observes the overall picture and then selects certain elements that draw her or his attention. As the observation is made, a hypothesis is developed and considered. Details about the hypothesis may be made explicit, and a way to test the hypothesis may also be devised. As additional details are considered, they are compared to the hypothesis and ideas, and confirmed or rejected. The hypothesis may be revised and the interpretation of what has been read reconsidered in light of the new theory.

In effective instruction, the teacher will model this process over and over with many different items. To emphasize the viewing aspect, the teacher would look at line, shape, and color and try to interpret what they mean. The viewers would think about how the effect would be different if different colors had been chosen or if the picture were in black and white. For speaking or listening, the teacher would think aloud about what in the picture would help the audience develop an understanding of the material. For speaking and writing, concepts of how to convey and explain these ideas to the audience would be considered.

To give variety to the lesson and allow students to do their own thinking, the teacher can ask students to state what they are thinking and guide the group through the process. Eventually, teachers will want to leave students on their own — but even then create opportunities for students to reflect about the steps they are taking at this preparation stage. It is important to note that we have not included a set of questions to ask or steps to follow. There is no recipe for these activities. The questions, the hypotheses or predictions, and the testing and rejecting or accepting of ideas all must come from the subject matter being studied — in this case, the picture itself.

PROCESSING THE IDEAS GENERATED IN THE PREPARATION STAGE

In *Good Connections for Testing*, composing ideas on paper — writing the draft of a composition — is the step in which students make explicit their thinking about the analysis of ideas presented in a visual format. In comparison to talking about the picture, writing takes the process a step further along the path toward literacy. The whole process of writing is discussed separately on pages *xviii–xxv*. As teachers of language arts, using the picture prompt that prepares students for the rest of the lesson gives students interesting and meaningful substance for their writing, while freeing them to be creative and imaginative.

Writing about a picture prompt is a good way to introduce a lesson and can be transferred easily to lessons related to materials not included in this book. But as with all good things, it can be overdone. Lessons will continue to be fresh and new if you maintain the important principles of getting students to access their prior learning, getting them actively involved in thinking and problem solving, keeping them attentive to their own thinking processes, and using interesting and challenging materials that allow for creativity and inventiveness rather than programming them to think a certain way to find a single correct answer.

LESSON ACTIVITIES DESIGNED TO PROMOTE LEARNING

LISTENING AND SPEAKING

Listening and speaking are both "pre-literate" skills that people use almost from birth, so we have commonly spent little time developing them as part of the school program. We have had show-and-tell for younger children and oral reports for older ones. With the advent of instructional strategies that are aimed at making students more responsible for their own learning, however, we have recognized that student interaction can be used as an important learning tool. Furthermore, we now recognize that the ability of an individual to communicate effectively through speaking and listening is an essential skill. Nevertheless, there is little in the literature about the teaching of the aural/oral communications as an integral part of the total language arts curriculum.

This volume includes materials specifically designed for listening assessment, and speaking and listening activities are woven throughout each of the lessons. It is important that the teacher bring to a conscious level strategies that students can use to accomplish various listening and speaking goals. Additionally, the progress of individual students should be observed. As both the teacher and the student monitor individual progress in these areas, they will be able to build on strengths and ameliorate weaknesses.

Listing Strategies

Listening strategies may be arbitrarily divided into pre-listening, listening, and post-listening activities.

Effective pre-listening can included: (1) identifying purposes and goals for the listening activity; (2) developing graphic organizers to use during the listening session; (3) identifying questions to be answered through the listening session, and (4) thinking of the anticipated story grammar of the text to be heard. Students should come to recognize that the pre-listening strategy they select will need to be shaped to the situation they are in. If they are conducting an interview, the pre-listening strategy will be different from what they would do if they were going to listen to the teacher reading a story to the class.

One of the most obvious strategies to be used during the listening activity can include taking notes, but the teacher needs to remember that this is not an easy task. Note taking involves identifying main ideas and supporting details. It is a thinking skill, but students must perform it under time pressure because the speaker moves quickly to new ideas and details. Therefore, the teacher needs to model good note taking and provide meaningful feedback and follow-up for these practice sessions. The student who has prepared a graphic organizer or questions to be answered during the listening session will find these devices to be helpful tools in taking notes and maintaining focus during listening.

A second listening strategy — comparing the pre-listening anticipation predictions to the actual material heard — is similar to active reading. The teacher needs to model this as well. The think-aloud in which the teacher models the active, covert thinking of an effective listener will help students see how the process works. We cannot assume that they will "pick up" active listening unless they see it in good practice.

The strategies used for active listening include confirming predictions made earlier, revising predictions as new information is made apparent, and making new predictions throughout the listening session. Similarly, listeners need to pause occasionally to monitor their own thinking. They need to determine if what they are hearing makes sense, based on what they already know. And if a logic isn't apparent, they need to decide if their comprehension is at fault, or if what the speaker is saying lacks logic. Again, speech, like time, marches on, complicating the listening session, but students who have multiple opportunities to practice active listening will strengthen their memory skills as well.

It is helpful to students if they have opportunities to talk out what they are thinking while listening. While the teacher will want to model the think-aloud for the class and provide some opportunity for the whole class to try out the skills as a group, effective practice may be best accomplished by partners or in small groups. Trying to have one student at a time talking out his or her active listening for the whole class means all the other students are not getting feedback on their own listening.

The speaker's tone, voice inflections, dialect, and other features of spoken language convey powerful meaning to the listener. By providing multiple opportunities with related follow-up to hear text that includes a wide variety of these linguistic features, the teacher will enhance students' ability to interpret these nonverbal listening skills. Students also need to practice visualizing what the speaker is saying, and the dramatic effect produced by the features of spoken language may, in fact, help students develop mental pictures. The stories discussed in *Good Connections for Testing* that particularly lend themselves to these activities include *Alexander, Who Used to Be Rich Last Sunday*, which begins on page 1; *Gator Pie*, page 91; *One Hundred Hungry Ants*, page 159; and *A Remainder of One*, page 189.

Clearly, there needs to be follow-up to the listening activity so that students can monitor their own skills. Answering listening questions like those provided in this text provides one way for both students and teachers to gain information about the students' listening comprehension. Having students prepare summaries or draw illustrations based on the content of the listening activity are additional strategies. Evaluating students' skills in following directions that have been given orally is a valid performance-based assessment of effective listening. The goal is to identify strengths and weaknesses in each individual's listening skill so that additional instruction or practice may be provided to promote continued learning. Ongoing practice with these strategies will help students to move them from a conscious, deliberate level to one in which they are able to automatically select and implement an appropriate strategy for the particular situation in which they find themselves.

Speaking Activities

Informal Communication in Speech: Students will have opportunities to practice their speaking and listening skills as they complete the activities included with every lesson in this volume. The teacher will be able to note numerous opportunities for students to present their ideas to the class, read to the class or a small group, or to develop speeches on topics related to the content of the book or about the mathematics concepts they are learning. Small-group discussion techniques are required by the activities in this book whenever students do think-pair-share or cooperative learning activities — which are in almost every lesson.

Many students will develop informal speaking and listening skills as they complete these activities, but teachers should carefully monitor the groups and pairs to identify those students who are not fully participating. If it is determined that explicit instruction in small-group speaking skills is needed for some students or for the whole class, helping students "see" what these skills look like in practice will be an effective strategy. To accomplish this, give different activities to each cooperative group in the class. Have the class listen while each group, one at a time, completes the activity. Debrief the class regarding the speaking and listening skills students have used to solve their group's problem. Continue to monitor student participation and repeat the demonstration/debriefing model as needed.

Lessons which include specific informal speaking activities are *Alexander, Who Used to Be Rich Last Sunday*, which begins on page 1; *Counting on Frank*, page 33; *The Doorbell Rang*, page 59; *Gator Pie*, page 71; *The King's Commissioners*, page 145; and *A Three Hat Day*, page 213.

Formal Communication in Speech: Although *Good Connections for Testing* doesn't include lessons on formal speaking activities, many of the activities can be easily adapted to a format that will allow students to present formal speeches. The presentations need only be a minute, and a maximum of three minutes for students in the middle elementary grades is sufficient to develop the needed skills and maintain the interest of others in the class. There are, however, some key ideas to keep in mind.

One way to avoid the boredom that is bound to occur if all students present speeches on the same topic is to have all students present the same number of speeches during the year, but space the activities out so that only a few students present speeches at one time and so that they are speaking on different topics. As you think about the full year's instruction, determine how frequently you would like each student to present a formal speech; three or four speeches during one year are probably the maximum to provide the needed practice without taking away time from other important elements of the curriculum. If you have a class of 25 students, and each one gives three speeches, your students will hear approximately 75 speeches per year. That would mean that you would probably need to set aside about 15 to 20 minutes per week for formal speech activities if there are 40 weeks for instruction. And if you wish to have students present a different topic each week, you will need 40 different topics. You can have students draw up a set of topics based on the reading that they are doing. The various writing prompts provided in *Good Connections for Testing* can serve as models for speech topics.

Similarly, the **Rubric for Scoring First Drafts** (Reproducible Master 3) can be a model for developing a rubric for scoring speeches, since both speaking and writing are productive linguistic activities. One element that is different is the use of visual aids. As you have been reading to your class and showing them the illustrations in the books, you have been demonstrating this skill. Most students have been showing science projects and other materials to the class as well, but they may need some instruction in how to create a meaningful visual aid for a speech.

The following process can be used to customize the rubric for speeches. Either show a model speech to the class or have a volunteer student present one. Discuss how speaking and writing are similar and different. Addressing the question of what makes a good speech, attempt to answer it by dealing with the questions of what the speaker is saying and how it is being said. Developing specific statements that answer these questions will help students internalize what they need to do in order to present a good speech. Then when students give speeches, they can use the rubric as a guide in critiquing the work of one another. This practice requires that the teacher provide instruction in how to be a good audience and how to give supportive and helpful comments about the work of another — both valuable skills. Furthermore, it is probably some of the most effective instruction that can be provided.

CONNECTIONS TO MATHEMATICS AND ACTIVE READING

In *Good Connections for Testing,* the next phase of the lessons is based on mathematics, but for the language arts teacher it is important to note that many of the problem-solving activities in mathematics form a bridge to similar kinds of thinking required for active reading. Reading is more than merely decoding words and discovering the ideas a writer has inscribed on the page. Active and effective reading means that the reader constantly monitors her or his progress through the page, comparing what is already known with what they are uncovering in the reading. (That is one of the reasons why pre-reading is so important; it makes explicit what powerful readers will do all of their lives—bring what they already know to bear on the immediate act of creating new meanings.) They need to think about whether or not the words and sentences are making sense, and if they are, to organize the new ideas into appropriate brain-based file folders within the storage bank of their prior knowledge. If the material being read doesn't make sense, the reader needs to have at hand strategies to use to solve the problem.

A major characteristic of poor readers is that they don't understand what reading is. They will insist that they did the reading, but didn't understand a word. (In fact, many teachers will recognize a similar experience from when they first approached the textbook for a difficult and challenging subject in college — perhaps chemistry or philosophy or literature.) The reason the student gives you that blank look as you try to fathom why she can't answer any of your questions about the reading is that she read the words and could pronounce every one of them. But she didn't have the slightest idea what those words meant.

To read powerfully, students need to internalize strategies that help them to monitor their reading as they proceed through the text. If they understand the concept of story grammar — that is, the shape of a particular kind of story — it will help them monitor their own reading. The idea of "once upon a time..." is part of story grammar; the dramatic organization of a story is part as well. The fact that we teach students to write compositions with a beginning, a middle, and an end is part of their developing an understanding of how a written selection works. These understandings enable the reader to know when something is wrong with his comprehension, and it is part of what delights a reader when the skillful writer is able to do something unique with a familiar pattern.

The children's books selected for *Good Connections for Testing* were chosen with a primary focus on the mathematics content they demonstrate. As books designed to develop independent reading skill, they are probably not very challenging for children in the middle elementary grades. However, many of them offer interesting vocabulary and challenging story twists. They are interesting. Even adult audiences enjoy having a story like *Gator Pie* read to them. The illustrations are vivid and offer rich opportunities for teaching students to "read" visual text. They offer equally rich opportunities for teachers to model active reading strategies. Some suggestions for modeling reading are included in lessons.

In fact, all of the lessons in *Good Connections for Testing* demonstrate in a very vivid fashion the active, meaning-making process of reading. We can help students to grow as readers if we point out for them the explicit kinds of thinking they are doing as they translate the words and images presented on the printed page into mathematical knowledge.

IMPLEMENTING WRITING AS PROCESS

The writing activities in *Good Connections for Testing* are designed to assist teachers who are working within a model for teaching writing as process and for helping students produce written products from that process that exemplify their writing skills. The assessment activities — writing from a picture prompt and writing a timed, on-demand composition as a closure activity near the end of the lesson — are designed to provide both the teacher and the student with valuable information about the student's level of writing power and to assist in formulating plans for continued development as a writer.

Although various activities that writers do can be pulled out, examined, and "taught," there is no single sequence. It is not the writing process that we teach. We help students discover the most effective way for them to generate their ideas, formulate them into some kind of cohesive written expression, and then shape that expression into a form that accurately conveys their ideas to an audience. To be effective, the process must center on what the student writers do; not on a formula that helps us shape instruction.

Nevertheless, teachers may find it helpful to divide the elements of what a writer does to accomplish his or her desired goals into five general, overlapping categories: pre-writing, drafting, revising, editing, and publishing. Different sources may divide composing into different elements or name them differently, but whatever the labels, the important principles include common concepts. Powerful writers will have a toolkit of strategies that work for them, and they will be open to learning new strategies. Our goal as teachers is to help student writers find what works for them by getting them to try out many strategies and by keeping the ownership of a piece in the writer's hands, not the teacher's. Both teachers and students need to recognize that writing is a recursive activity and does not proceed in a straight line. Finally, we need to recognize that the use of Standard English is important and that valuing and developing skill in English usage, mechanics, and grammar can be promoted or retarded by what we do as the writer moves through his or her process of writing.

✓ Prewriting

Traditionally, teachers have assigned composition topics. We have discussed methods of developing that topic, both by suggesting form (a paragraph, a five-paragraph theme, a fable, etc.) and possible content. Then we told students to write, urging them to revise and edit their work and to turn it in within a specified time limit, generally no later than the next day. After the work was turned in, we marked and graded it and sometimes allowed students to make changes in it to raise their grade. Frequently, we were disappointed when all the compositions seemed to be cut from the same mold (actually, the one we had programmed them to follow as we discussed topic development), and seldom did students seem enthusiastic about the activity.

This disappointment frequently made us decide to allow students to be more inventive, by telling them to write about whatever interested them. In that case we most frequently heard, "I don't know what to say." or "What do you want me to say?" These two scenarios highlight the opposite poles of topic design. We either said too much and took too much control, or we said to little and gave too little direction. The objective is to help students find something interesting that they have to say and to let the topic give them direction about how the piece should be shaped — a paragraph, an essay, a poem, or a story.

As we prepare students for high-stakes writing assessments, we must recognize that they will be given prompts to get them started on the writing activity and to establish some validity to the testing situation, but there is generally less specificity about methods of development than there are information and reminders about what good writers do. We can follow the lead of the test writers in this area without violating the important principles of effective instruction that promotes the development of individual power for student writers. This same power will be useful to students as they are asked to write on specific topics related to particular school subjects. Most of the writing prompts within *Good Connections for Testing* are general enough to allow students to develop the topic as it interests them in a form that they feel comfortable using.

As part of pre-writing, we need to provide students with many different strategies for thinking of topics, clarifying them, thinking of the various elements of the topic, and so forth. At the same time, we must recognize that those cognitive processes that we think of as pre-writing may occur at any time. It is not as if each step is definitive and that one step must be completed before we can move on to the next one. Some individuals may just sit down and start writing a draft of a topic. Their pre-writing may have occurred before the prompt was given. Other writers will struggle through many kinds of pre-writing before they are ready to draft, and even then they may stop and go back and do some kind of "planning" before they can go on.

Some helpful pre-writing activities include listing, mapping, and brainstorming. Very few young writers find it helpful to develop either an informal or formal outline. Research does seem to indicate that students who do some form of pre-writing for timed, on-demand writing generally produce a composition that earns a higher score. However, more skilled writers may do pre-writing in their head and produce little written evidence of the process.

✓Drafting

It is at the drafting stage when the writer's ideas begin to take shape on the paper. For some, it is a very messy process, and we need to allow or even encourage this messiness. The writers need to recognize that everything they are putting on paper at this point has the potential of being changed later on. While they want to make the composition as good as possible, it is more important that they get their ideas out, rather than struggling to find just the right word or to shape a sentence exactly right.

Not only is drafting a messy process in terms of getting ideas to flow logically, but it also is messy in terms of accuracy. The student who normally never makes a spelling or mechanical error may make one here. This phenomenon is especially true if the topic is new or involves concepts or ideas that the writer has difficulty explaining. The student also may have difficulty with accuracy if the topic is one that evokes strong emotion. Since we know students produce better content in their writing if it is a topic about which they feel strongly, we need to recognize that an emotionally charged piece is likely to have many errors in it. Students need to be aware of this problem as well. They shouldn't spend too much time worrying about how to spell a word or how to handle mechanics properly. The opportunity to correct the selection comes later. At the drafting phase, the goal is to get ideas down on paper.

For the most part, the activities in *Good Connections for Testing* conclude once the drafts have been developed. However, this volume includes some directions to assist students in moving through the process, partly or all the way through publication.

The reason the *Good Connections for Testing* writing activities stop at this point is that most of the formal assessment activities included in high-stakes testing conclude here. In the interest of time, most formal judgments on the ability of students to write are based on drafts that have been produced on-demand, under time pressure, with minimal opportunity for the writer to revise and edit them. Those matters are taken into consideration in the way the selections are scored. These ideas about drafting will be explained in greater detail when we talk later about how to apply the **Rubric for Scoring First Drafts** (Reproducible Master 3), which is included in the discussion on evaluating student writing.

You will also want to notice the section on "Preparing Your Students for High-Stakes Language Arts Assessments," which appears on page *xxiv*.

✓Revising

One of the great challenges to the teacher of language arts comes at this point. The students have finished a draft, and in many cases, they feel it is a finished paper. They are most likely to feel that the task is completed when they have little emotional investment or feel little ownership of a piece. We confirm their opinion if we collect the paper at this point and mark or grade it. It takes great patience to encourage students to move on from the drafting phase of writing to the revising phase.

Sufficient time is the key to good revision. It is best if the draft can be allowed to rest for a significant period of time. In some cases, overnight is a long enough time for a piece to rest. In other cases, a week or a month may be needed. Some pieces may be revised on many occasions over a stretch of several months. Here again, a difficult or an emotionally charged topic can make revision hard to accomplish.

Time provides an opportunity for a selection to cool off. While we are drafting, we put on paper what we think we want to say. Sometimes we accomplish this goal, and sometimes we do not. Our minds play funny tricks on us. When we read the piece while the drafting experience is still in our heads, we see on the page what we *think* we put there, not necessarily what we *actually* put there. And our inability to really read the page makes both editing and revising difficult.

It is helpful in the revising phase for students to let someone else comment on their writing. We need to teach our students how to give and to receive comments about a written selection. These are difficult skills to develop. The teacher who writes with the students and allows them to comment on that writing, eliciting suggestions for improvement that are then considered and accepted, modified, or rejected with reasons, will accomplish a lot by modeling good behavior. Even skilled adults — or perhaps especially skilled adults — find it hard to put their egos aside and concentrate on improving the written word.

Students need to be taught to work on revision of their writing in pairs or small groups. Teachers may find it helpful to develop a list of questions for students to use in revising their writing, but the list needs to be malleable. The class and the teacher working together can revise the list as students acquire new composing strategies and identify new writing techniques throughout the year. As they consider, "What questions do we need to be asking ourselves about our writing so that we can revise it and make it better?" they will be modeling one of the most important skills of powerful writers.

The revising phase is the time when we can change each word or sentence to say exactly what we want it to say. This is a good time to teach students how to develop interesting beginnings and endings for their compositions; to write more complex and mature sentences; and to select just exactly the correct word. It is the time to tighten up sloppy writing and sloppy thinking. This is the time to teach mini-lessons to small groups of students who are experiencing similar challenges in their writing. Giving them an opportunity to see how published writers have conquered these or similar problems will help students begin to generate their own solutions as well. This is also a time to use materials from your English composition or grammar text as a resource for individual, group or class instruction. It is the right time to apply the textbook lessons to real writing situations.

One of the most difficult yet important skills in developing meaningful content in writing is the use specific, appropriate details and vivid descriptions. The lessons on *Anno's Math Games*, which begin on page 249; *One Hundred Hungry Ants*, page 159; and *A Three Hat Day*, page 213 — as well as many others — offer exercises in adding details and specificity to writing. These and other lessons also address vocabulary development. A strong vocabulary is one essential for good writing.

✓Editing

Some authorities see editing and revising as two parts of the same process, and they may be right. However, the classroom teacher may find it more manageable to separate the two processes without abandoning the principle that writing is a recursive process. We make revisions in the content of our compositions as we are doing pre-writing. We start to edit for spelling, grammar, and mechanics at the same time that we start to draft the composition. In fact, for some students, the overwhelming desire to write neatly and to be accurate in spelling, grammar, and mechanics may be a key impediment to fluency in expression. If a student demonstrates an overwhelming desire for accuracy, it may indicate a misperception about what writing really is, just as decoding is misperceived as reading by the student with weak comprehension skills.

Published writing is the most valuable resource for students as they try to identify standard punctuation and usage. If we guide students to books and articles that contain examples of the feature they need to apply in their own writing, they can infer from the text what the standard usage is. The process of making this inference and then applying it to their own writing will help them process the knowledge at the deepest level of understanding. After they have struggled with the principle, direct them to the rule.

Then it will make sense to them; the process of learning will be much faster and they will retain the knowledge longer.

Many of the stories in *Good Connections for Testing* have excellent examples of dialogue and important words that are difficult to spell, and all have good models for accurate punctuation and spelling. Very powerful lessons can be developed by helping students study these models to infer the rules for spelling, grammar, and mechanics. And the best time to present these lessons is when students are actively engaged in editing their own work and have a real, immediate need to know the information.

✓Publishing

The process of "publishing" student writing doesn't necessarily mean that all the finished pieces need to be bound and stored in the classroom library. That step may be appropriate for some very special works, but for the most part the publication step is much simpler than that. Many pieces that a student works on will not go through all the phases of the writing process, however, completed selections that are to be shared with a larger audience should be readied for publication. To do this step, the student needs to consider the needs of the audience. The handwriting needs to be neat and the pages need to be clean. Matters of format are especially important when the selection is to be printed out from a word processor. Students may need to make decisions about illustrations or binding. Writers ready to publish a work feel the selection is finished — they have said what they want to say in the best way they can express themselves; they have reflected on the piece and shaped it; they have attended to matters of accuracy and Standard English. The work can stand on its own.

When students have produced, refined, and polished a work so that it reaches this point, they have a great and justifiable sense of accomplishment. It is one of the strongest sources of motivation they will every have for continuing to face new challenges in writing.

EVALUATING WRITING

The method and standards for evaluating student writing depend upon the context of the activity, primarily the nature of the assignment and the amount of time students were given to complete it. We don't expect elementary students to write an elaborate, polished, multi-page story when they have been given a half hour in which to produce a composition. But if they have had several weeks or months to write a story to present on "Author's Day," our expectations are different.

Rubric for Scoring First Drafts (Reproducible Master 3) is designed to be used to assess students' writing when they have been given a prompt and have written under time pressure with minimal opportunity to revise and edit the piece. Under these conditions, students can reasonably focus on the substance of what they have to say and can be expected to organize the piece in a logical fashion. For example, a more competent writer will have greater control, under these conditions, of how they introduce and conclude the piece. They will tie ideas together with appropriate transitions. They will state generalizations and support them with effective details. They may even say things in fresh and unique ways. Less evidence of effective control of language will be apparent in the product of less-skilled writers.

A very important principle of "writing as process" needs to be kept in mind when we look at spelling, language mechanics, usage, sentence structure, sentence variety, paragraphing, neatness, and handwriting—the surface features of writing that jump out at us when we read something written by someone else. Remember that these are elements that the writer can address during the revising and editing phases, but they are difficult to control when writing under pressure (time, stress of an important test) about a topic that they have had minimal time to rehearse and about which they may have strong feelings. (Many writing prompts are chosen because they will evoke a strong emotional response, personal topics that students are likely to know a great deal about and that, therefore, will produce compelling content.) These topics are exactly the ones that will make it hard for the writer to control the surface features of language. And we know that revising and editing are best done after a selection cools off, perhaps as much as a week or more after the selection was drafted. Therefore, less value should be placed on these elements as we evaluate a timed writing.

When you apply the **Rubric for Scoring First Drafts** as the guide for evaluating student writing produced in the setting that is most common for large-scale writing assessments, the basis of the score should be on those elements at the top of the chart, based on "What the writer has said, the effectiveness of expression." That is what we reasonably can expect students to do under the conditions of the assessment. You might want to lower that score by a point if there are so many mechanical and usage errors on the paper that they really get in the way of reading it. If, however, there are only a few errors, or if the writer makes the same error a number of times (for example, if "ie" words are consistently misspelled or if there are several errors in verb tense or pronoun case), there should be no penalty.

On the other hand, you also can use the use the rubric to score papers that have been produced over a period of time, but the method of application will be different. Think of an occasion when students have had several opportunities to work on revising and editing the selection and others have provided input — implementing all the steps in the writing process. On these occasions, the rubric should be applied in full. Students should be expected, under these conditions, to have strong control of not only content and organization of the writing, but also of all the surface features that they have been taught to use in a selection that is to be read by a larger audience.

As an example of what is intended here, think of a highly trained swimmer. Under normal conditions in the pool where the person regularly swims, you can expect to see the individual swim smoothly with polished form and to be awed by how professional the performance is. In doing the Australian crawl, the swimmer's breathing would be carefully coordinated with arm and leg movements. But if you were to see the same individual attempt to save a child who has been washed overboard in high seas, it is unlikely that you would see careful execution of the fine points of swimming form. What you would look for is whether or not the child was saved. The well-trained, strong swimmer would be much more capable of achieving the goal than would someone who had little swimming skill, but you would be unlikely to criticize the person because arm and breathing motions were not well coordinated.

In a timed, on-demand writing, we're looking for the strong writer who has enough command of the writing craft to achieve the goal of expressing ideas clearly in a well-organized fashion.

WRITING WORKSHOP

Many teachers have found that an excellent way to manage the diverse capabilities of students as they work on composing skills is to implement a writing workshop approach. One of the chief advantages is that it keeps the child in control of his or her own writing — allowing each to find and develop his or her own topics and to develop strategies for all phases of writing as process. This gives students power as writers and motivates them to continue to write. Teachers who are interested in this approach would be well advised to consult the work of Lucy Calkins, Donald Graves, and Reggie Routman. Related articles on writing, as well as reading, are regularly found in *The Reading Teacher*, published by the International Reading Association. Other publications by the National Council of Teachers of English, the American Library Association, and others provide excellent direction and a banquet of ideas from which teachers can choose those elements that suit the needs of their classes and their teaching styles.

As a general description, a writing workshop approach usually includes a number of similar elements. First of all, the classroom is usually a text-rich environment. Students have easy access to resources that both inform and delight. Some of the resources in the class may be books the students themselves have written, either as stories from their imagination or from research on a topic of special interest to the writer. Areas are set aside where students can work on their writing, and they have resources appropriate to their age and developmental level available. These may include the expected references, such as a dictionary, but also the unexpected — a class vocabulary list or a chart of punctuation marks or spelling clues.

A second common element is the use of writing folders and journal writing. In *Good Connections for Testing*, you see many examples of journal writing used as a thinking aid in the learning of mathematics. In the writing workshop classroom, journals may be used for many kinds of personal writing as well as writing to learn. Furthermore, folders may be used for many purposes. One very important use is as the individual "works in progress" folder. Here, each child maintains lists of ideas for writing as well as written pieces in every stage of development — lists of ideas on a topic, drafts written on demand and under timed constraints, topics that they have started and lost interest in, topics that proved to be too large for the time allowed, and so on. It is to this folder that the writer goes to select something to move along in the process. It is from this resource that the teacher will ask students to take a draft to be revised for a particular purpose.

Journals generally are not graded, but they do provide teachers an opportunity to understand a student's thinking on a particular topic. Also, when journal writings are free of the pressure of grades, students feel free to explore ideas and gain valuable practice in thinking on paper. Lessons that include at least one journal writing topic include *Counting on Frank*, which begins on page 33; *The Doorbell Rang*, page 59; *Gator Pie*, page 71; *The Greedy Triangle*, page 103; *Grandfather Tang's Story*, page 87; *A Remainder of One*, page 189; and *A Three Hat Day*, page 213.

A writing workshop gives students time to focus on their own writing, but also provides a structure in which individuals can seek help from a writing group or from a trusted individual. These groups provide a supportive and helpful, but also critical, audience for works in progress. Groups may be formulated in whatever way the teacher desires, but the best size appears to be 3–5 students. In some models, each student in the group is assigned a specific job, such as editing or recorder, but others have a less formal structure. Pairs appear to be too small to work effectively, even though there are times when having a writing partner can be helpful. One practice that shows some promise in providing a wider audience than the students' own group is to have groups switch their writing and offer comments during the revising stage. At times, groups become too comfortable with the writing of their group members. (Classes may also switch and use the **Rubric for Scoring First Drafts** to score each other's papers.)

Finally, the writing workshop also provides a structure within which the class can celebrate the publication of works that are ready for an outside audience. Within this format, students learn to exercise their writing muscles and to learn that the ability to think on paper is a way to communicate and to learn.

TEACHING VOCABULARY

Meaningful repetition and use of words in meaningful contexts are the keys to helping students develop vocabulary skills. Aggressive teaching of vocabulary is essential to the effective teaching of the language arts regardless of the type of reading program being used. Words are the tools we use for thinking, and no reading program by itself will provide all students the with the word experiences they need. To be successful, classroom teachers need to be on the look out for words and ways to use them.

As we use more and more trade books — books for which the vocabulary is not controlled — for teaching reading, the need to attend to vocabulary instruction becomes more critical. New words are not repeated in meaningful contexts often enough for children to learn them. These books facilitate the integration of the curriculum and capitalize on children's variety of interests, assisting the teacher to direct children to books that will be appropriately challenging. However, as children read books for which the vocabulary is not controlled, teachers need to be cognizant of the fact that they need to make conscious and consistent efforts to teach vocabulary for both reading and writing.

Good Connections for Testing offers a few examples of how teachers may use children's books for vocabulary instruction. Students see the word in a meaningful context, learn its definition by discussing the word and its usage with the teacher and/or other classmates, and have meaningful opportunities to use the word in several activities. It is only after this kind of interaction with a word that the child should be sent to the dictionary to look up the dictionary meaning of the word. It is counterproductive to have a child look up the definition of a new word and write it in a sentence because they lack sufficient background to be able to make meaning of the definition. They have no mental file folder prepared to receive the new information.

The process of seeing the word in context, hearing and saying the word, and then discussing at least one definition of the word establishes the foundation for learning that word.

Teachers certainly want to maintain classroom lists of new words. Items should be added to the list as part of a discussion about the word, and at that time, the word should be presented in context. But that is not enough interaction with the word. Therefore, the teacher needs to find opportunities to continue to use the word with students and to enable the students to use the words themselves. In addition, students should keep a word list of their own — new words they have found in their reading or elsewhere. They should use the context to try to discover the meaning of the word, look for its use in other books, and discuss the word with someone else. Such a discussion may or may not lead to the word being added to the class word list. But some activity to grapple with the meaning of the word needs to take place before a formal, dictionary definition is required.

One appropriate occasion to use new words is in the revising phase of writing. Suggest that students take a few moments before a writing workshop session to review both the class word list and their own personal word list. Students can examine their compositions for instances where they could use more forceful words, or they can think of words from their list that they want to use in a composition. Either way, the students are forced to think about what the word means and how it can be used. They have to make decisions about how the word fits into context. And in the process, they are moving the word into their personal vocabulary banks. It works.

PREPARING YOUR STUDENTS FOR HIGH STAKES ASSESSMENTS IN THE LANGUAGE ARTS

The underlying principle of *Good Connections for Testing* is that the best way to prepare your students for a required state or standardized test is to plan and implement on a daily basis a rich variety of meaningful learning activities that focus on students' mastery of the standards for which they are responsible. And even though that is true, there are some factors that impact on these assessments that might not be attended to in the course of normal classroom instruction. It is comforting to know that these activities are not harmful to students and that they will not hinder student learning. In fact, the activities will help students acquire the skills they need to face other challenges in life. It is within this context that these hints for improving student test scores are presented.

(1) Treat classroom assessment activities as if you are the coach preparing your team for a big game. Think about what the coach of any sport does to prepare the team so they can give their best performance when they need to. They learn the elements of the game, and they have many opportunities to practice integrating various skills in high-pressure situations. They scrimmage. They work on a positive, can-win attitude. They take the game seriously and work toward doing their best, even when they know they are up against a powerful opponent. They build up their strength by starting with a challenging but manageable task and gradually increasing the challenge and difficulty until they exceed the requirements. They support one another in achieving the goals of the team.

(2) In the testing and assessment activities for the class, mimic the state or norm-referenced assessment. Get all the information you can about the test and shape your tests so that they look like the state test. That way, students will not be confused by matters of test format.

(3) Think about the kinds of questions that are asked. Do they have true-false or matching items on the test? If not, you may want to avoid them in your own assessments. Well-written multiple-choice items provide a great deal of information about what students know. The wrong answers on multiple choice answers are just as important as the correct ones. Are you careful in writing the wrong answers on your tests?

(4) Use your ongoing class assessments to identify students' strengths and weaknesses in relationship to the standards. Plan your instruction to build on the strengths and correct the weaknesses.

(5) Teach students to understand and use the rubrics that will be used to score their open-ended and written responses. They need to see samples of student work that earn each score point and discuss the qualities they see in the work. It will help them answer for themselves the question, "What do I have to do to improve my work?"

(6) Remember that some of the tried-and-true hints for improving student performance on traditional standardized tests are less likely to be of benefit to

students on contemporary performance assessments. On reading tests, for instance, students have been advised to read the questions first before they read a passage. Most contemporary reading assessments have significantly longer reading passages than we have seen in the past, and the questions require analysis, synthesis, or evaluation. Reading the questions first and skimming for answers will be a poor use of time, at best. Give students a number of practice sessions where they read challenging passages under time pressure and then are asked to respond to challenging questions.

(7) Write, write, write. Read, read, read. Use class time wisely, focusing on important instructional activities.

It used to be said that we learn to read and then we read to learn. Today we know that we must be lifelong learners of all the language arts. It never stops. We also know that we will learn new information and skills as well as mere tidbits of interesting things by applying our linguistic skills throughout our lives. The adventure of continual learning should never stop. The teachers who have helped children to form strong foundations in the elementary grades have acted like the tailor in the inspirational story *A Cloak for the Dreamer* (page 15). They have provided maturing children protection and strength for a lifelong journey. It is a noble task.

ADDITIONAL RESOURCES:

Calkins, Lucy. *The Art of Teaching Writing*. Portsmouth, N.H.: Heineman, 1987.

Graves, Donald. *Writing Teachers and Children at Work. Portsmouth*, N.H.: Heineman, 1983.

Routman, Reggie. *Invitations: Changing as Teachers and Learners*, K–12. Portsmouth, N.H.: Heineman, 1991.

International Reading Association, 800 Barksdale Road, P.O. Box 8139, Newark, DE 19714-8139. www.reading.org

National Council of Teachers of English, 1111 West Kenyon Road, Urbana, IL 61801-1096.

Alexander, Who Used to Be Rich Last Sunday

Written by **Judith Viorst**
Illustrated by **Ray Cruz**

Overview of the Connections

This story is about a boy named Alexander who receives a dollar bill from his grandparents as a gift. Through a series of very humorous events, he manages to spend the entire amount, despite his efforts to save all his money.

In teaching mathematics, the book offers students opportunities to model addition and subtraction with coins and to make appropriate exchanges as money is spent. Some activities provide experiences with finding probability and listing possible outcomes when coins are tossed. Algebraic thinking and problem solving are explored in activities where students use variables and expressions to represent various coin combinations.

In language arts, this book offers an opportunity to practice a longer listening experience, since the story is read to the class in one session. As literature, the story gives students a chance to evaluate character motives and to predict future events. In addition, the viewing and writing activities provide opportunities to exercise these skills.

MATERIALS FOR THE CONNECTIONS

Alexander, Who Used to Be Rich Last Sunday • ISBN 0-689-30602-4 • Written by Judith Viorst. Illustrated by Ray Cruz. New York: Simon & Schuster Children's Publishing Division, Atheneum Books, 1978.

Language Arts

~ One or more copies of the book (Note: In the Viewing Connection, each student will need to see page 5. You may wish to have several copies available.)

~ Optional: **Connection to Viewing Assessment: Writing About a Picture Prompt** (Reproducible Master 1)

~ **Have I...? Checklist** (Reproducible Master 2), a self-monitoring tool for student writers

~ **Rubric for Scoring First Drafts** (Reproducible Master 3)

~ **Connection to Listening Assessment: Listening to a Story** (Reproducible Master 4)

~ **Connection to Writing Assessment: Post-Reading Composition** (Reproducible Master 10)

Mathematics

~ Coins (pennies, nickels, dimes, and quarters)

~ **Keeping Records for Alexander** (Reproducible Master 5)

~ **100 Pennies** (Reproducible Master 6)

~ Overhead coins

~ **Coin Combination Table** (Reproducible Master 7)

~ Pennies (bags of 30 for each group of 2–3 students)

~ Random-number generators for 0–9, such as playing cards with jacks as 0, aces as 1, and kings, queens, and 10s removed; or decahedron (10-sided) die; or icosahedron (20-sided) die with 0–9; or 0–9 spinners

~ Container to hold pennies

~ **Connection to Mathematics Assessment: Check for Understanding I and II** (Reproducible Masters 8–9)

Viewing Connection

INTRODUCING THE LESSON WITH A PICTURE PROMPT AND WRITING

Materials

Copy of the book (page 5), **Connection to Viewing Assessment: Writing About a Picture Prompt** (Reproducible Master 1), **Have I...? Checklist** (Reproducible Master 2), **Rubric for Scoring First Drafts** (Reproducible Master 3)

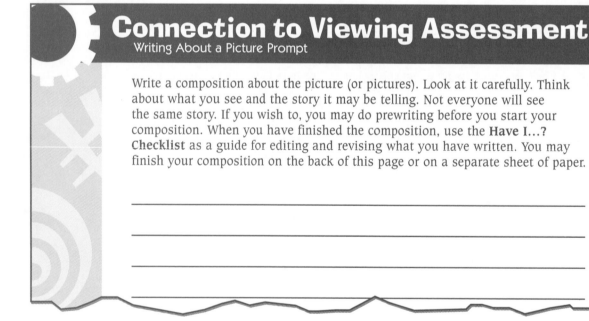

Show the class the picture on page 5 of the book with the text covered. The pages are not numbered, so consider the first page of the story text as page 1. On this page, there is a dream balloon filled with candy, food, and toys above Alexander's head. If possible, allow students to continue to look at the picture throughout the writing session. You may distribute a copy of **Connection to Viewing Assessment: Writing About a Picture Prompt** to each student, or they may use notebook paper for their work. Also distribute copies of the **Have I...? Checklist.**

Read these directions to the class:

"You are going to write a composition about this picture. Look at it carefully. Think about what you see and the story it may be telling. It is OK that not everyone will see the same story. If you wish to, you may do prewriting before you start your composition. When you have finished the composition, use the **Have I...? Checklist** as a guide for editing and revising what you have written."

Give the students 20–30 minutes to write their compositions and do initial editing.

Collect and score the students' compositions using the **Rubric for Scoring First Drafts**. Teach students how to compare their scored compositions to the rubric and to make notes about how to improve their compositions. Students also may be taught to use the rubric to score their own work or that of other students.

Reproducible Master 1

Connection to Viewing Assessment 1

Writing About a Picture Prompt

Write a composition about the picture (or pictures). Look at it carefully. Think about what you see and the story it may be telling. Not everyone will see the same story. If you wish to, you may do prewriting before you start your composition. When you have finished the composition, use the **Have I...? Checklist** as a guide for editing and revising what you have written. You may finish your composition on the back of this page or on a separate sheet of paper.

____

____

____

____

Listening Connection

LISTENING TO A STORY AND ANSWERING QUESTIONS

Materials

Copy of the book (Listening section: entire book, 940 words), **Connection to Listening Assessment: Listening to a Story** (Reproducible Master 4)

This activity will help students develop effective listening skills. As necessary, teach or review some of the effective listening strategies found on page *xv* of this manual.

Tell the class you are going to read them a story. When you are finished, they will answer some questions about what you have read.

Read the entire book aloud to the students. Since you are working on listening, don't stop to discuss the story, show the illustrations, or make predictions as you might do in a reading instructional period.

Distribute the worksheet with multiple-choice and open-ended questions called **Connection to Listening Assessment: Listening to a Story**.

Allow students 15–20 minutes for completing the worksheet.

Collect and score the students' work using the answers and rubric that follow.

Reproducible Master 4 with answers

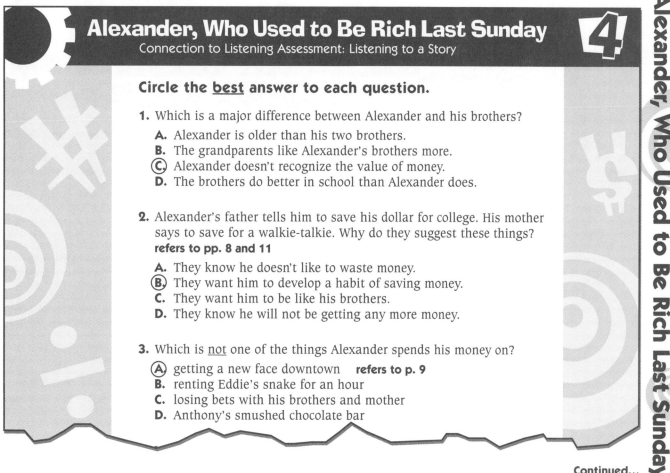

Alexander, Who Used to Be Rich Last Sunday 4

Connection to Listening Assessment: Listening to a Story

Circle the best answer to each question.

1. Which is a major difference between Alexander and his brothers?
   - A. Alexander is older than his two brothers.
   - B. The grandparents like Alexander's brothers more.
   - (C.) Alexander doesn't recognize the value of money.
   - D. The brothers do better in school than Alexander does.

2. Alexander's father tells him to save his dollar for college. His mother says to save for a walkie-talkie. Why do they suggest these things?
   refers to pp. 8 and 11
   - A. They know he doesn't like to waste money.
   - (B.) They want him to develop a habit of saving money.
   - C. They want him to be like his brothers.
   - D. They know he will not be getting any more money.

3. Which is not one of the things Alexander spends his money on?
   - (A.) getting a new face downtown **refers to p. 9**
   - B. renting Eddie's snake for an hour
   - C. losing bets with his brothers and mother
   - D. Anthony's smushed chocolate bar

Continued...

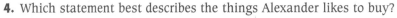

4. Which statement best describes the things Alexander likes to buy?

A. Things his brothers and parents urge him to buy.
B. Things that he will play with in the future.
(C.) Things that catch his imagination.
D. Things for which his parents fine him.

5. When Alexander tells his grandparents to come back soon, what is he hoping for?

A. a visit he will enjoy
B. an invitation to visit them
C. a walkie-talkie as a gift
(D) another dollar as a gift

Open-ended Listening Task: Do you think Alexander and his brothers like each other? Explain why you feel this way. Support your response with details from the story and your own experiences. Write your answer on the paper provided. **see rubric that follows for scoring**

RUBRIC FOR SCORING

Open-ended Listening Task

An effective response will need to:

- reflect knowledge of the story.
- justify ideas from the text.
- be well written with a clear explanation.

POINTS	CRITERIA
4	Writer knows that the brothers fight and use verbal or physical barbs as they argue, but justifies either opinion based on personal experience or observations of interactions between their own siblings.
3	Writer recognizes that the brothers disagree and states an opinion. Provides brief or vague justification for conclusions.
2	Writer doesn't see that the brothers disagree, or doesn't provide an explanation for the conclusion. Or, writer states a conclusion with minimal, inaccurate, or irrelevant justification.
1	Writer makes a conclusion that may or may not be accurate, but provides no elaboration. Shows minimal or no understanding of the selection presented.
0	Doesn't respond or doesn't deal with the task.

Mathematics Connection

INTRODUCTION AND ACTIVE READING

Materials

Copy of the book, **Keeping Records for Alexander** (Reproducible Master 5), **100 Pennies** (Reproducible Master 6), overhead and transparency of **100 Pennies** (optional)

Ask students if they have ever been given money as a present and what they did with it. After a brief discussion, tell the class that you are going to re-read the story of Alexander to them. Then, you will be asking students to remember the ways Alexander spends his money and how much he spends each time.

Read the story again, showing the pictures and discussing the action with the students.

After reading, use a think-pair-share technique to make a class list of the ways in which Alexander spent his money and the amount he spent each time.

Distribute Keeping Records for Alexander and **100 Pennies** to each pair. Have students complete the table. You may wish to follow the procedure suggested below.

Step 1

Tell students to use the first two columns of the table to record the items that Alexander purchased in the story and their cost.

Step 2

Review with the class how to write amounts of money as decimals. Then have students rewrite each of the amounts in the chart as decimals. Students may use the **100 Pennies** reproducible to help them convert the amounts to pennies, then to parts of a hundred, and finally to decimal notation. You may wish to make a transparency of **100 Pennies** and circle the various costs of items, so students can more clearly make the connections.

Step 3

Review the ways various combinations of coins can be used to pay for each item or event. For example, 15¢ could be paid with 1 dime and 1 nickel; with 3 nickels; with 10 pennies and 1 nickel; with 2 nickels and 5 pennies; or with 15 pennies.

Demonstrate how letters and numbers can be used to represent the various combinations of coins. Encourage the students to compare ways each of the amounts can be represented.

P = penny D = dime Q = quarter
N = nickel H = half dollar

EXAMPLE

- 15¢ = 15P
- 15¢ = 1D + 5P
- 15¢ = 10P + 1N
- 15¢ = 2N + 5P

Step 4

After each expenditure, have students calculate the amount of money left from the dollar. You may want to have students mark off the amounts on the **100 Pennies** diagram, so they can see how the solutions can be reached using a model. (Later you may make connections to subtraction of decimals by using the 100 Pennies model.)

Alexander, Who Used to Be Rich Last Sunday

5

Keeping Records for Alexander

Think about these questions as you complete the chart.

- What does Alexander buy or pay for?
- What coin combinations could he use?
- How much does he have left after each purchase?

Item or Event	Cost	Cost as Decimal	Coin Combination	Amount Left from the Dollar
Bubble gum	*15¢*	*$0.15*	*3N*	*$0.85*
Bets	*15¢*	*$0.15*	*2N + 5P*	*$0.70*
Snake rental	*12¢*	*$0.12*	*2P + 1D*	*$0.58*
Fine for bad words	*10¢*	*$0.10*	*2N*	*$0.48*
Lost money	*8¢*	*$0.08*	*1N + 3P*	*$0.40*
Chocolate bar	*11¢*	*$0.11*	*2N + 1P*	*$0.29*
Magic trick	*4¢*	*$0.04*	*4P*	*$0.25*
Fine for kicking	*5¢*	*$0.05*	*1N*	*$0.20*
Garage sale items	*20¢*	*$0.20*	*1D + 1N + 5P*	*$0.00*
Total	*$1.00*	*$1.00*		

Reproducible Master 6 with answer for first expenditure

Alexander, Who Used to Be Rich Last Sunday

100 Pennies

6

Bubble gum costs 15¢.

ACTING OUT THE STORY

Materials

Copy of the book, **Coin Combination Table** (Reproducible Master 7), overhead (optional), coins ($1.00 worth in bags containing either 10 pennies, 4 nickels, and 7 dimes, or 10 nickels, 10 pennies, and 4 dimes; also 20 pennies, 10 nickels, 5 dimes, and 2 quarters)

Distribute a Coin Combination Table to each student. Challenge them to find three different ways they might receive one dollar in coins. You may want to use an overhead of the table to model an example before having students make up their own combinations.

Read the story again, this time pausing to allow students to act it out, using the methods described below.

Page 1

Show the page so everyone can easily see it. Write the amounts using the letter codes from the first activity or write the words on the chalkboard. Ask:

How much money does Anthony have?
[Answer: $3.38]

Page 2

How much money does Nicholas have?
[Answer: $2.28]

Use one of the two methods below to act out the rest of story. The first method requires that students make exchanges; the second does not.

Method 1

Arrange pairs of students. Assign one student to be the banker and the other to be Alexander. Give "Alexander" $1.00 in coins. Give the banker 20 pennies, 10 nickels, 5 dimes, and 2 quarters. As the amounts are paid from the dollar, appropriate exchanges will need to be made with the banker. Have students keep track of the transactions using the empty rows of the **Coin Combination Table**.

Method 2

Give all students $1.00 in coins, so that no exchanges are necessary as they pay for each amount in the story. (Each bag may contain 10 nickels, 10 pennies, and 4 dimes; or 10 pennies, 4 nickels, and 7 dimes.)

Reproducible Master 7

Alexander, Who Used to Be Rich Last Sunday

Coin Combination Table

7

Pennies	Nickels	Dimes	Quarters	Half Dollars	Total

MATHEMATICS ASSESSMENT

Materials

Connection to Mathematics Assessment: Check for Understanding I and II (Reproducible Masters 8–9)

Distribute the worksheets with multiple-choice and open-ended questions called **Connection to Mathematics Assessment: Check for Understanding I and II**. This activity can be used to check students' understanding of the mathematics concepts covered in this lesson.

Collect and **score** the students' work using the answers and rubric that follow.

Reproducible Master 8 with answers

Alexander, Who Used to Be Rich Last Sunday

Connections to Mathematics Assessment: Check for Understanding I

8

Circle the best answer to each question.

Use the information below to answer **Problems 1 and 2.**

- Billy bet that he could hold his breath for 81 seconds.
- Billy bet that he would not watch television for a week.
- Billy bet that he would do his homework within one hour of coming home from school.
- Billy lost all three bets and had to pay a total of 36 cents.

1. If he bet the same amount of money each time, how much was each bet?

A. 6 cents
(B.) 12 cents **36 ÷ 3**
C. 1 dime
D. 36 cents

2. If Billy only had 3 nickels, 1 penny, and 3 dimes in his pocket, how much money would he have left after paying off his bets?

A. 0¢
B. 5¢
(C.) 10¢ **46 – 36**
D. 34¢

3. If Q = 1 quarter, D = 1 dime, N = 1 nickel, and P = 1 penny, which code represents 48¢?

A. 1Q + 2D + 1N + 3P
B. 1Q + 2D + 1N + 2P
C. 1Q + 1D + 3N + 1P
(D.) 1Q + 1D + 2N + 3P **25 + 10 + 10 + 3 = 48**

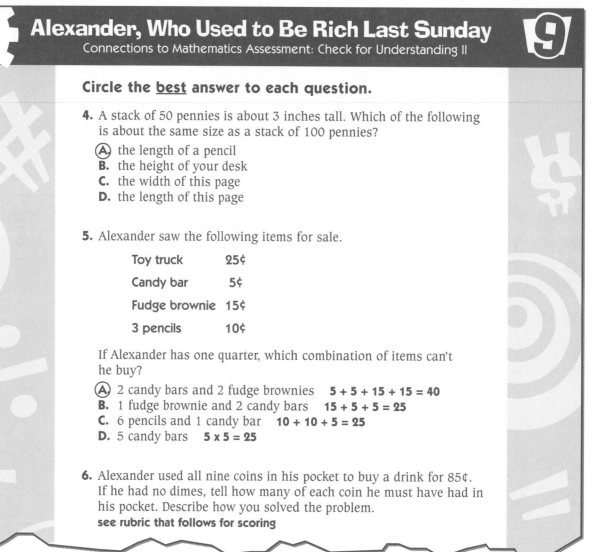

Alexander, Who Used to Be Rich Last Sunday

9

Connections to Mathematics Assessment: Check for Understanding II

Circle the best answer to each question.

4. A stack of 50 pennies is about 3 inches tall. Which of the following is about the same size as a stack of 100 pennies?

(A) the length of a pencil
B. the height of your desk
C. the width of this page
D. the length of this page

5. Alexander saw the following items for sale.

Toy truck	25¢
Candy bar	5¢
Fudge brownie	15¢
3 pencils	10¢

If Alexander has one quarter, which combination of items can't he buy?

(A) 2 candy bars and 2 fudge brownies **5 + 5 + 15 + 15 = 40**
B. 1 fudge brownie and 2 candy bars **15 + 5 + 5 = 25**
C. 6 pencils and 1 candy bar **10 + 10 + 5 = 25**
D. 5 candy bars **5 x 5 = 25**

6. Alexander used all nine coins in his pocket to buy a drink for 85¢. If he had no dimes, tell how many of each coin he must have had in his pocket. Describe how you solved the problem.
see rubric that follows for scoring

RUBRIC FOR SCORING
Problem 6

An effective response will need to:

- show that Alexander had 2 quarters and 7 nickels in his pocket.
- give a clear explanation.
- reflects the use of problem-solving strategies.

POINTS	CRITERIA
3	The student correctly uses nine coins to make 85¢ and provides a clear explanation of how the answer was determined. The solution reflects problem-solving strategies such as making a list, guessing and checking, drawing a diagram, mental math, and/or logic. Suggested response: *He must have had 2 quarters and 7 nickels. I made a table and tried various ways to make 85¢ until I had nine coins that worked.* OR *He must have had 2 quarters and 7 nickels. First, I tried 3 quarters and 2 nickels. It worked but it wasn't 9 coins. Since I could not use dimes, I substituted 5 nickels for one quarter. I still had 85¢, but now it worked.*
2	The student makes the 85¢ with nine coins, but uses dimes in the answer and states that there is no way to make the amount without the dimes. Or, the student makes 85¢ without using dimes, but does not use nine coins and provides a clear explanation of the strategies used to determine the answer. Or, the student uses nine coins but incorrectly adds. For example, an amount is given that is within 15¢ of 85¢, and the student attempts to describe the strategies he or she used to arrive at the answer.
1	The student makes the 85¢, but does not use nine coins and uses dimes as part of the answer. Or, the student makes the 85¢ with nine coins but uses dimes in the answer and provides no explanation or an unclear explanation of strategies.
0	The student shows no understanding. The student gives both the wrong amount of money and the wrong number of coins without any explanation. Or, the student leaves the answer blank.

Composition Connection

WRITING A POST-READING COMPOSITION

Materials

Connection to Writing Assessment: Post-Reading Composition (Reproducible Master 10), **Have I...? Checklist** (Reproducible Master 2), **Rubric for Scoring First Drafts** (Reproducible Master 3)

Give students the **Connection to Writing Assessment: Post-Reading Composition** along with a copy of the **Have I...? Checklist**.

Give students about 20 minutes to write the composition and edit or revise it based on the checklist.

Collect and **score** the students' compositions using the **Rubric for Scoring First Drafts**. Encourage students to put their scored drafts into a folder of "works in progress" so they can be further edited and revised for sharing with an audience at some later date.

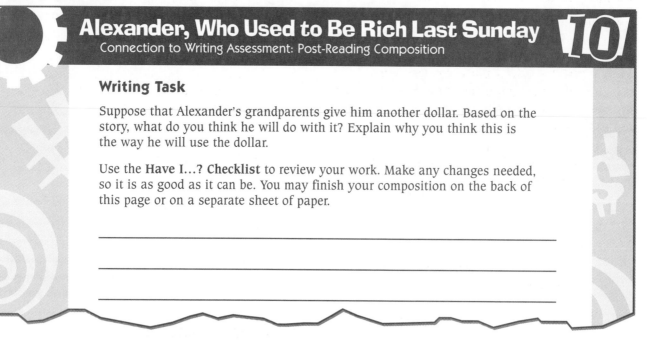

Alexander, Who Used to Be Rich Last Sunday

10

Connection to Writing Assessment: Post-Reading Composition

Writing Task

Suppose that Alexander's grandparents give him another dollar. Based on the story, what do you think he will do with it? Explain why you think this is the way he will use the dollar.

Use the **Have I...? Checklist** to review your work. Make any changes needed, so it is as good as it can be. You may finish your composition on the back of this page or on a separate sheet of paper.

____

____

____

Extending the Connections

WRITING PROJECT

Have students respond to the following prompt:

"Write a story, using your self as a character, about the items that you would buy with $1.00. When you write about yourself, use your name instead of the word I."

PROBABILITY

Materials

10 pennies, container

Place 10 pennies in a container. Ask students the probability of 5 pennies showing heads and 5 pennies showing tails if you spill all the coins out on a table. [Answer: $\frac{5}{10}$ or $\frac{1}{2}$]

Complete several trials by carefully spilling the 10 coins out on a table. Record the results of each trial as a fraction that represents the number of tails.

Have students compare the fractional amounts from the trials with the prediction. Ask:

Which results are smaller? Which are larger?

Discuss why the coins may not always land as half heads and half tails.

EXAMPLE

Spill 1:	H H H H T T H T T T	$\frac{5}{10}$
Spill 2:	T H T H H H H T T H	$\frac{4}{10}$
Spill 3:	H T H H H H H T H H	$\frac{2}{10}$
Spill 4:	T T H H H T T T H T	$\frac{6}{10}$
Spill 5:	H T H H T H H H H T	$\frac{3}{10}$

COMBINATIONS AND ARRANGEMENTS

Materials

Pennies (3 for each student), container

Have each student place three pennies in a container and then spill them on the table. Tell them to record from left to right, whether each coin landed as heads (H) or tails (T).

Ask them to determine how many different ways the coins can fall. [Answer: The coins can fall eight ways: HHH, HHT, HTH, HTT, THH, THT, TTH, and TTT.]

Extend this thinking to discuss how the outcomes can be found by making an organized list using a tree diagram.

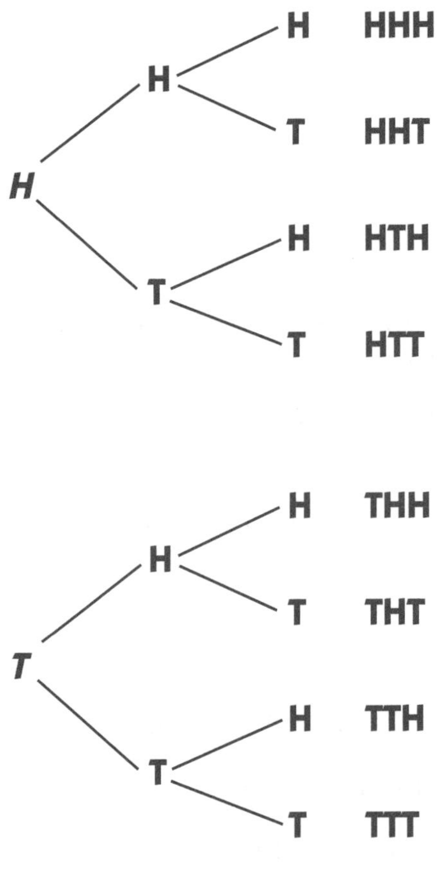

GAME: How Many to Make a Dollar?

Materials

Coins (dimes and pennies); random-number generators for 0–9, such as playing cards with jacks as 0, aces as 1, and kings, queens, and 10s removed; or decahedron (10-sided) die; or icosahedron (20-sided) die with 0–9; or 0–9 spinners

Distribute a random-number generator and coins to small groups. Players take turns generating two digits. The first digit represents the number of dimes a player gets, the second digit represents the number of pennies.

Each player must then calculate how much more money he or she needs to make a dollar. The player who can make a dollar with the fewest coins wins the round and scores a point.

COIN COMBINATIONS

Materials

Random-number generators for 0–9 (playing cards with jacks as 0, aces as 1, and kings, queens, and 10s removed; or decahedron die; or icosahedron die with 0–9; or 0–9 spinners), coins

Distribute a random-number generator and coins to small groups. Students randomly generate two digits. The first digit represents the tens place; the second digit generated represents the ones place. Students use pennies, nickels, dimes, quarters, and half dollars to find up to five combinations of coins that equal the generated number.

DATA ANALYSIS: Penny Collection

Materials

Penny collection

Have students collect a sampling of 25 pennies. Have them organize the pennies by mint date and make a bar graph to represent the data. Ask them to find the median and the range of the dates.

Teacher Notes

A Cloak for the Dreamer

Written by **Aileen Friedman**
Illustrated by **Kim Howard**

Overview of the Connections

A *Cloak for the Dreamer* is a story about a tailor and his three sons. Two of the sons want to be tailors, but the third son dreams of traveling the world. One day the tailor needs help filling an important, order from the Archduke. The tailor seeks the help of his sons. Two of the sons create cloaks by sewing patchworks of shapes that fit together. The third son, however, finds out too late that the cloth circles he cut out and sewed do not make a protective cloak. In the process of helping their father, the sons demonstrate their tailoring skills and their personal dreams. In the end, the father and his two "tailor" sons make a beautiful cloak for the "dreamer" son to wear on his worldly travels.

In teaching mathematics, this story introduces students to tiling and tessellating shapes. Students discover that pattern-block shapes can be tiled to make a "cloak" with no holes or gaps. Students also examine each pattern-block shape to reinforce their understanding of line and rotational symmetry in regular figures. In addition, students use pattern-block shapes to make and price "cloak" designs. As they investigate the symmetry in their designs, students use algebraic, fractional, and decimal representations to calculate sale prices for their "cloaks."

In the study of literature, many stories tell of the frustrated father whose son does not want to follow in his footsteps. As a refreshing change, this story shows a father who recognizes the unique strengths and interests of his children, and ultimately helps them achieve their dreams. The watercolor-and-pencil illustrations are in vivid colors and have designs that support the development of viewing skills.

MATERIALS FOR THE CONNECTIONS

A Cloak for the Dreamer • ISBN 0-590-48987-9
Written by Aileen Friedman. Illustrated by Kim Howard. New York: Scholastic Inc., 1994.

Language Arts

~ One or more copies of the book (Note: In the Viewing Connection, each student will need to see the cover of the book. You may wish to have several copies available.)

~ Optional: **Connection to Viewing Assessment: Writing About a Picture Prompt** (Reproducible Master 1)

~ **Have I ...? Checklist** (Reproducible Master 2), a self-monitoring tool for student writers

~ **Rubric for Scoring First Drafts** (Reproducible Master 3)

~ **Connection to Listening Assessment: Listening to Part of a Story** (Reproducible Master 11)

~ **Connection to Writing Assessment: Post-Reading Composition** (Reproducible Master 18)

Mathematics

~ Buckets of pattern blocks (for each group of students)

~ Construction paper

~ Scissors

~ Rulers

~ Overhead set of pattern blocks

~ String (optional)

~ **Understanding Line Symmetry I and II** (Reproducible Masters 12–13)

~ **Pattern-Block Designs I and II** (Reproducible Masters 14–15)

~ **Connection to Mathematics Assessment: Check for Understanding I and II** (Reproducible Masters 16–17)

~ Dot paper

Viewing Connection

INTRODUCING THE LESSON WITH A PICTURE PROMPT AND WRITING

Materials

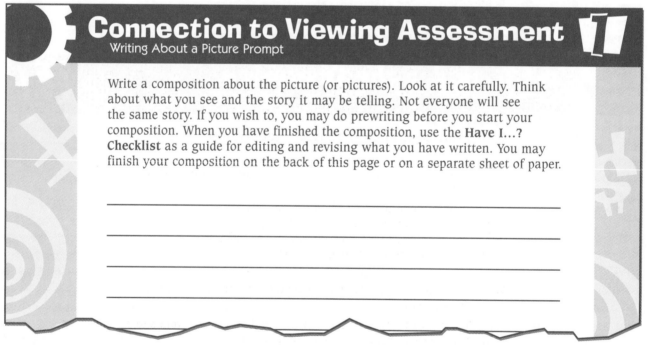

Picture on the book cover, **Connection to Viewing Assessment: Writing About a Picture Prompt** (Reproducible Master 1), **Have I...? Checklist** (Reproducible Master 2), **Rubric for Scoring First Drafts** (Reproducible Master 3)

Show the class the picture on the cover of *A Cloak for the Dreamer*. If possible, allow students to continue to look at the picture throughout the writing session. You may distribute a copy of **Connection to Assessment: Writing About a Picture Prompt** to each student, or they may use notebook paper for their work. Also distribute copies of the **Have I...? Checklist**.

Read these directions to the class:

"You are going to write a composition about this picture. Look at it carefully. Think about what you see and the story it may be telling. It is OK that not everyone will see the same story. If you wish to, you may do prewriting before you start your composition. When you have finished the composition, use the **Have I...? Checklist** as a guide for editing and revising what you have written."

Give the students 20–30 minutes to write their compositions and do initial editing.

Collect and score the students' compositions using the **Rubric for Scoring First Drafts**. Teach students how to compare their scored compositions to the rubric and to make notes about how to improve their compositions. Students also may be taught to use the rubric to score their own work or that of other students.

Reproducible Master 1

Connection to Viewing Assessment 1

Writing About a Picture Prompt

Write a composition about the picture (or pictures). Look at it carefully. Think about what you see and the story it may be telling. Not everyone will see the same story. If you wish to, you may do prewriting before you start your composition. When you have finished the composition, use the **Have I...? Checklist** as a guide for editing and revising what you have written. You may finish your composition on the back of this page or on a separate sheet of paper.

Listening Connection

LISTENING TO PART OF A STORY AND ANSWERING QUESTIONS

Materials

Copy of the book (Listening section: pages 6–13, 588 words), **Connection to Listening Assessment: Listening to Part of a Story** (Reproducible Master 11)

This activity will help students develop effective listening skills. As necessary, teach or review some of the effective listening strategies found on page *xv* of this manual.

Tell the class you are going to read them part of a story. When you are finished, they will answer some questions about what you have read. (The rest of the story will be read in the Mathematics Connection activity.)

Read pages 6–13 aloud to the students. The pages are not numbered, so consider the first page of story text as page 1. The listening section starts with the sentence: *One morning, the tailor gathered his three sons before him.* It ends with the sentence: *Although he worried that the cloak would disappoint his father, Misha completed it in time.*

Since you are working on listening, don't stop to discuss the story, show the illustrations, or make predictions, as you might do in a reading instructional period.

Distribute the worksheet with multiple-choice and open-ended questions called **Connection to Listening Assessment: Listening to Part of a Story.**

Allow students 15–20 minutes for completing the worksheet.

Collect and **score** the students' work using the answers and rubric that follow.

Proceed to the Mathematics Connection for instructions on completing the book.

Reproducible Master 11 with answers

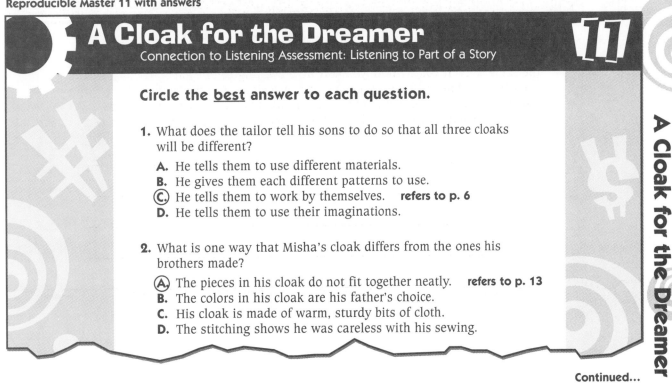

A Cloak for the Dreamer

Connection to Listening Assessment: Listening to Part of a Story

11

Circle the best answer to each question.

1. What does the tailor tell his sons to do so that all three cloaks will be different?
   - **A.** He tells them to use different materials.
   - **B.** He gives them each different patterns to use.
   - **(C.)** He tells them to work by themselves. **refers to p. 6**
   - **D.** He tells them to use their imaginations.

2. What is one way that Misha's cloak differs from the ones his brothers made?
   - **(A.)** The pieces in his cloak do not fit together neatly. **refers to p. 13**
   - **B.** The colors in his cloak are his father's choice.
   - **C.** His cloak is made of warm, sturdy bits of cloth.
   - **D.** The stitching shows he was careless with his sewing.

Continued...

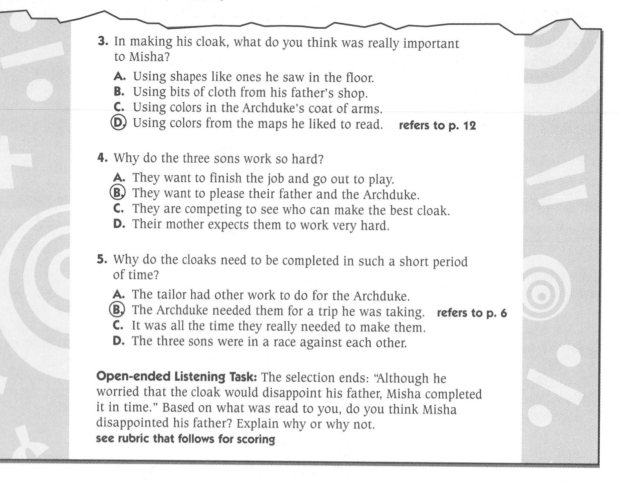

3. In making his cloak, what do you think was really important to Misha?

A. Using shapes like ones he saw in the floor.
B. Using bits of cloth from his father's shop.
C. Using colors in the Archduke's coat of arms.
(D) Using colors from the maps he liked to read. **refers to p. 12**

4. Why do the three sons work so hard?

A. They want to finish the job and go out to play.
(B) They want to please their father and the Archduke.
C. They are competing to see who can make the best cloak.
D. Their mother expects them to work very hard.

5. Why do the cloaks need to be completed in such a short period of time?

A. The tailor had other work to do for the Archduke.
(B) The Archduke needed them for a trip he was taking. **refers to p. 6**
C. It was all the time they really needed to make them.
D. The three sons were in a race against each other.

Open-ended Listening Task: The selection ends: "Although he worried that the cloak would disappoint his father, Misha completed it in time." Based on what was read to you, do you think Misha disappointed his father? Explain why or why not.
see rubric that follows for scoring

RUBRIC FOR SCORING
Open-ended Listening Task

An effective response will need to:
- reflect knowledge of the story.
- justify ideas from the test.
- make logical and reasonable predictions.
- recognize characteristics of sons and fathers, giving examples.
- be well written with a clear explanation.

POINTS	CRITERIA
4	Makes a logical prediction about the father's reaction. Recognizes a significant percentage of the following details and uses them as support. The father wants his sons to: 1. demonstrate skills in tailoring, 2. use creativity through use of shapes and colors, 3. be able to meet a deadline, and 4. make a protective article of clothing. Describes how Misha is similar to or different from his brothers. May recognize either that the father is compassionate or that the father is demanding.
3	Makes a logical prediction about the father's reaction, but bases the answer on a partial understanding of the selection, using some details and ignoring others.
2	Makes a logical prediction about the father's reaction, but bases the answer on a minimum number of details and/or unsupported reasoning. Or, reaches an illogical conclusion, but uses details from the selection to support assertions.
1	Makes a logical prediction about the father's reaction, but it is not based on evidence from the selection, or merely repeats the events in the selection.
0	Addresses personal experience or doesn't address the topic. Shows no understanding of the selection as it was read.

Mathematics Connection

INTRODUCTION AND ACTIVE READING

Tell students that you are going to read the whole story to them.

Before reading, discuss what a *tailor* does and what a *cloak* is. (Instruct students to listen carefully for more information about the shapes that are used to make the cloaks and why one of the shapes does not work.)

Read the story again, this time pausing to show and discuss the illustrations. Encourage discussion about the story.

After you finish reading the story, use a think-pair-share technique to establish which shapes worked well for making a cloak and why the circles did not.

DEVELOPING THE CONCEPT OF TILING THE PLANE

Materials

Buckets of pattern blocks (1 for each group of 3–4 students)

Distribute pattern blocks to groups of 3–4 students. Tell them to investigate whether or not each shape could be used to make a cloak without any gaps or holes.

Have students take a "handful" of one shape and try to completely cover a flat surface (the plane) with them, leaving no gaps or holes. The shapes should be lined up next to each other, fitting together to form a solid pattern on the desk or table. Tell students that this is called "tiling the plane." If a shape can tile the plane, it can be used to make a good cloak.

Students should do this experiment with each of the six pattern-block shapes. Through a question-and-answer technique, establish that all of the pattern-block shapes can, in fact, tile the plane.

Ask:

Why is tiling the plane like making a cloak without any holes? **[Answer: When a shape tiles the plane it leaves no gaps or holes. When making a cloak, the shapes must fit together so there are no holes or gaps through which wind or rain can pass.]**

EXPLORING TILING WITH DIFFERENT SHAPES

Materials

Colored constructions paper, scissors, rulers

Pose the following question to further explore the concept of tiling:

Alex made one of his cloaks using triangles that he made from squares. Do you think any triangles can be used to make a cloak with no holes? In other words, will any triangles tile the plane?

Discuss the questions with students. You may wish to review the different kinds of triangles and their definitions: *isosceles*, *right isosceles*, *equilateral*, and *scalene*.

Distribute colored construction paper, scissors, and rulers to each student. Have students fold their papers in half, then in half again, and then in half again to form eighths. Tell them to use a ruler to draw a triangle of any size and shape on the $\frac{1}{8}$-paper. Then have them cut out the triangle through all of the layers, making 8 triangles that are exactly the same.

You may want to point out that the eight triangles are *congruent* to each other because they are exactly the same shape and size.

Have students try making a cloak, or tile the plane, using their 8 triangles. Point out, if necessary, that they may need to turn or flip over their triangles to get them to tile. Ask:

Are there any gaps? **[Answer: No.]**

- ***Can you make a cloak without holes by combining different size triangles together?*** **[Answer: Usually this is not possible.]**

Distribute another sheet of construction paper to each student. Have them again fold the paper into eighths. This time tell them to draw any quadrilateral (4-sided figure) and cut it out through the layers making 8 shapes. Have them conduct the same experiment as before, trying to tile the plane. Remind students to turn and flip their shapes as they fit them together. (Because of inconsistencies in cutting, students may see tiny holes or gaps in their patterns and think they are not tiling. Tell them you are concerned with larger more obvious gaps.)

Challenge students to create any shape, other than a circle, and try to tile the plane with it. They might try hexagons like the ones used to make the "cloak for the dreamer" in the book. Discuss the fact that any congruent triangles or quadrilaterals will always tile a plane. The only *regular polygons* (all sides and angles equal) that tile a plane are triangles, squares, and hexagons.

UNDERSTANDING LINE SYMMETRY

Materials

For groups of 2–3 students: **Understanding Line Symmetry I and II** (Reproducible Masters 12–13), scissors, pattern blocks, shapes made in the "Exploring Tiling" activity. Optional: overhead pattern blocks; marker or spaghetti

Discuss the concept of line symmetry with students, providing examples as necessary.

1. A shape has line symmetry if it can be folded on a line so that one half lies exactly on top of the other.
2. When a line of symmetry is drawn, the two halves of the shape are mirror images.
3. A shape can have more than one line of symmetry.

Distribute scissors and copies of the enlarged pattern block shapes on **Understanding Line Symmetry I and II** to groups of 2–3 students. Have students cut out and fold each of the shapes to find lines of symmetry. Ask them to find out how many lines of symmetry each shape has.

Use a question-and-answer technique to create a table on the board or overhead that shows their results for each pattern-block shape.

Pattern-Block Shape	Lines of Symmetry
Hexagon	6
Triangle	3
Trapezoid	1
Fat rhombus (blue)	2
Thin rhombus (white)	2
Square	4

As a follow-up, distribute pattern blocks to each group so they can visualize the lines of symmetry for each. You may wish to model the symmetry by drawing dotted lines or placing a piece of spaghetti on overhead pattern blocks to form the lines of symmetry. Relate the dotted lines (or string) to the folds students made with the larger paper figures.

Have students try to find lines of symmetry in the triangles and quadrilaterals they created in the previous "Exploring Tiling" activity. Ask:

Do all the shapes the class made have lines of symmetry? **[Answer: No.]**

- ***What is special about the pattern-block shapes that is not necessarily true for the tiling shapes the class made earlier?*** **[Answer: Except for the trapezoid, all of the pattern-block shapes have sides of equal length. The triangles, squares, and hexagons are *regular polygons*: closed, flat figures that have straight equal sides and equal angles.]**

UNDERSTANDING FRACTIONS USING PATTERN BLOCKS

Materials

Pattern blocks (without the square and white rhombus)

Have students determine the fractional values for the areas of the shapes that are formed from equilateral triangles. Begin by showing a hexagon and tell students that it has a value of 1 unit. (Note: Do not use the squares or white rhombi in these discussions because they are not formed from equilateral triangles.)

Use discussion and modeling techniques to establish that if the hexagon is the unit:

- The trapezoid has a fractional value of $\frac{1}{2}$ because two fit on top of the hexagon.
- The blue rhombus has a fractional value of $\frac{1}{3}$ because three fit on top of the hexagon.
- The triangle has a fractional value of $\frac{1}{6}$ because six fit on top of the hexagon.

Extend thinking by asking questions, such as:

- ***Is the fractional value of the trapezoid always equal to $\frac{1}{2}$?*** **[Answer: No. It depends on what shape has a value of 1 unit.]**

- ***Does the hexagon always have to be the shape assigned to the unit one?*** **[Answer: No.]**

- ***What fractional value would each shape have if two hexagons have a value of 1 unit?***
  [Answer: trapezoid = $\frac{1}{4}$, hexagon = $\frac{1}{2}$, blue rhombus = $\frac{1}{6}$, and triangle = $\frac{1}{12}$.]

- ***What fractional value would each shape have if three hexagons have a value of 1 unit?***
  [Answer: trapezoid = $\frac{1}{6}$, blue rhombus = $\frac{1}{9}$, and triangle = $\frac{1}{18}$]

USING CODES TO REPRESENT PATTERN-BLOCK DESIGNS

Materials

Pattern-Block Designs I and II (Reproducible Masters 14–15), buckets of pattern blocks

Tell students that you know of a business that makes works of art from pattern-block pieces and sells them at flea markets. Explain that they are going to look at the two most popular designs this company makes.

Distribute two copies each of **Pattern-Block Designs I and II** and a bucket of pattern blocks to pairs of students. Have student pairs recreate the designs with pattern blocks.

Tell the students that the company uses a coding system to keep track of the pattern blocks used in the different designs. The code for each design is made up of letters and numbers. The letters represent pattern-block shapes and the numbers tell how many are in a particular design. The pattern-block codes added together represent a complete design.

Write the following letter codes on the chalkboard:

H = hexagon
T = triangle
R = rhombus
Z = trapezoid

Have students write the complete codes for each design.

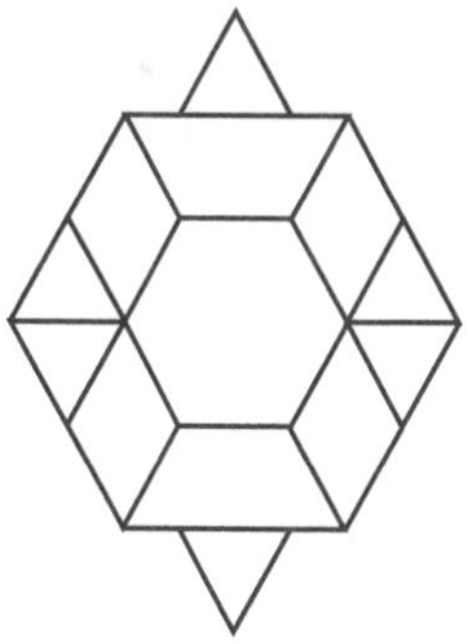

Design I

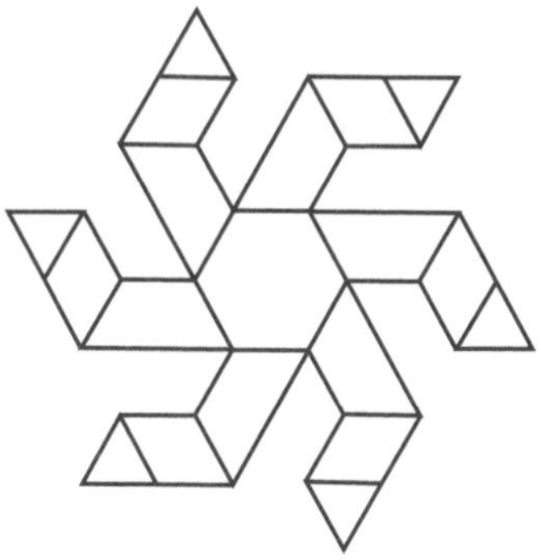

Design II

[Answers: Design I = 1H + 2Z + 4R + 6T; Design II = 1H + 6Z + 6R + 6T.]

Have students take turns making new designs so their partners can write the codes. For example, a design with 8 hexagons, 5 triangles, 4 rhombi, and 3 trapezoids would be recorded as 8H + 5T + 4R + 3Z.

MATHEMATICS ASSESSMENT

Materials

Connection to Mathematics Assessment: Check for Understanding I and II (Reproducible Masters 16–17), pattern blocks

Distribute the worksheets with multiple-choice and open-ended questions called **Connection to Mathematics Assessment: Check for Understanding I and II.** This activity can be used to check students' understanding of the mathematics concepts covered in this lesson.

Collect and score the students' work using the answers and rubric that follow.

Reproducible Master 16 with answers

A Cloak for the Dreamer

Connection to Mathematics Assessment: Check for Understanding I

16

Circle the best answer to each question. Use pattern-block shapes to help you find each answer.

1. A hexagon has a value of 1 unit. What is the fractional value of a trapezoid and blue rhombus that have been glued together on one edge?

A. $\frac{1}{6}$

B. $\frac{1}{3}$

C. $\frac{2}{3}$

(D.) $\frac{5}{6}$ $\frac{1}{2} + \frac{1}{3}$

2. Which can you say is true about the shape shown below?

A. It has one line of symmetry.

(B.) It has two lines of symmetry.

C. It has four lines of symmetry.

D. It has zero lines of symmetry.

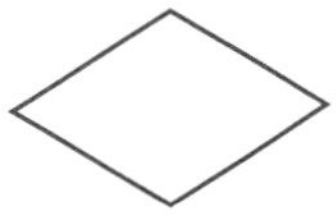

3. A hexagon has a value of 1 unit. You can add only one shape to the design below. Which shape would you add to make a design with a value of $1\frac{1}{6}$ units?

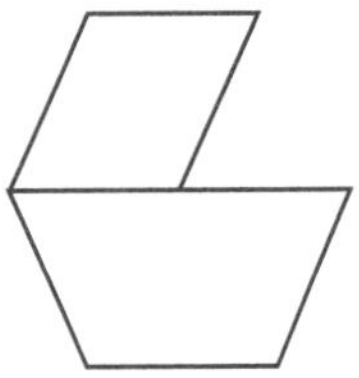

A. triangle

(B.) rhombus $\frac{1}{2} + \frac{1}{3} + \frac{1}{3} = 1\frac{1}{6}$

C. square

D. trapezoid

A Cloak for the Dreamer

Connection to Mathematics Assessment: Check for Understanding II

17

4. Which shape does not form a tiling pattern?

A.

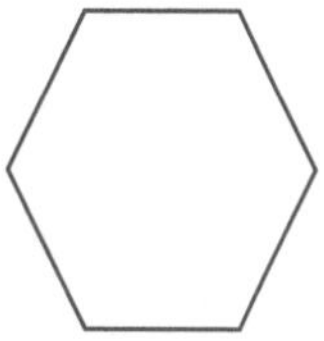

B.

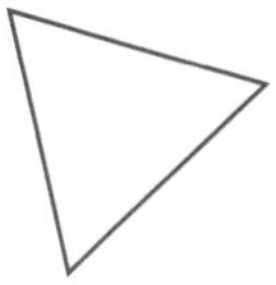

C.

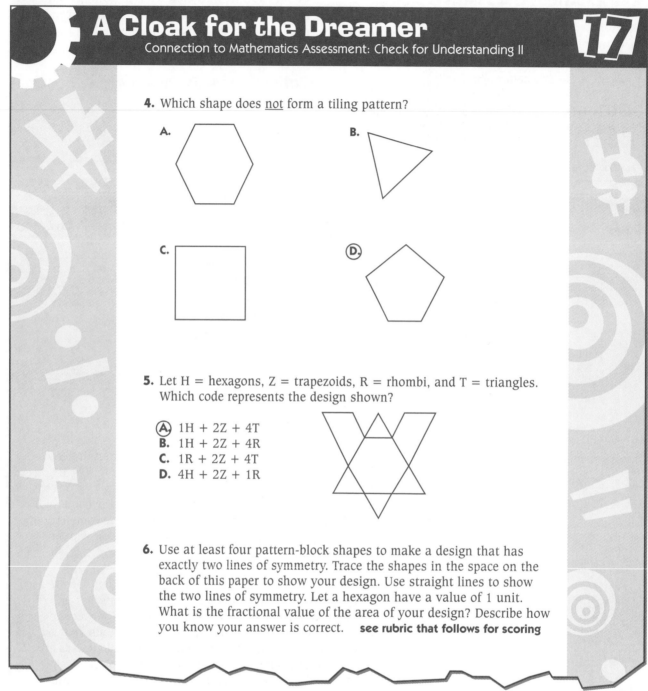

(D.)

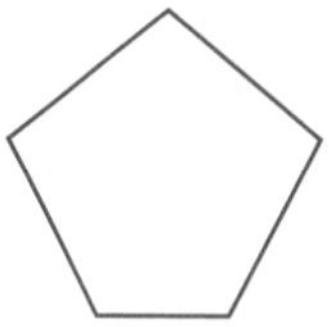

5. Let H = hexagons, Z = trapezoids, R = rhombi, and T = triangles. Which code represents the design shown?

(A.) 1H + 2Z + 4T
B. 1H + 2Z + 4R
C. 1R + 2Z + 4T
D. 4H + 2Z + 1R

6. Use at least four pattern-block shapes to make a design that has exactly two lines of symmetry. Trace the shapes in the space on the back of this paper to show your design. Use straight lines to show the two lines of symmetry. Let a hexagon have a value of 1 unit. What is the fractional value of the area of your design? Describe how you know your answer is correct. **see rubric that follows for scoring**

RUBRIC FOR SCORING
Problem 6

An effective response will need to:
- show a drawing of four pattern-block shapes with two lines of symmetry.
- give the correct fractional value.
- give a clear explanation.

POINTS	CRITERIA
3	The student uses at least four pattern-block shapes to create and draw a design. The drawing clearly shows two lines of symmetry. Students give the correct fractional value of the design and include a clear explanation. Suggested response: 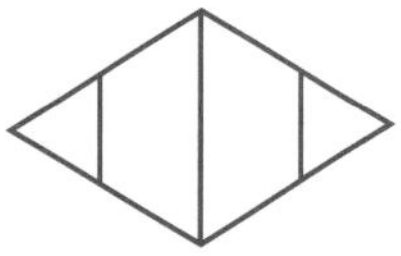 *This figure has a horizontal line of symmetry and a vertical line of symmetry because it can be folded on those lines and only those lines to make one side match the other side exactly. If the value of a hexagon is 1 unit, each trapezoid is $\frac{1}{2}$ a unit because the trapezoid is $\frac{1}{2}$ of the hexagon.* *Each triangle is $\frac{1}{6}$ of a unit because it takes 6 triangles to make a hexagon. Since there are 2 trapezoids and 2 triangles in the drawing, the area of the design is 1 and $\frac{1}{3}$ square units. (The sum of the fractional value of the pieces.)*
2	The student has all parts of the problem correct, but shows a design with less than four shapes. Or, the student makes the design correctly, but does not clearly explain why it has two lines of symmetry yet does explain the area of the figure correctly. Or, the student makes the correct design, explains the lines of symmetry, and shows understanding of computing the area of the figure, but computes it incorrectly. Or, the student uses four pieces, but does not have a design with the appropriate symmetry yet explains the symmetry in the design correctly, and the area given is correct with an appropriate explanation.
1	The student shows the correct design and states the area, but provides no explanation or an explanation that is unclear or has flaws. Or, the student has four or more pieces with one or both of the appropriate explanations, but the design does not meet the criteria. Or, the student uses an inappropriate number of shapes to make a correct design but provides weak or unclear explanations. Or, the student completes only one part of the question but it is correct and has an excellent explanation.
0	The student leaves question blank. Or, the student does not make a correct design and has an explanation with serious errors or no explanation at all.

Composition Connection

WRITING POST-READING COMPOSITIONS

Materials

Copy of the book, Connection to Writing Assessment: Post-Reading Composition (Reproducible Master 18), **Have I...? Checklist** (Reproducible Master 2), **Rubric for Scoring First Drafts** (Reproducible Master 3)

This activity should be completed after the book has been read to the students and discussed with them. If it has been a while since reading the book, you should read it again to students prior to their completing the writing assignment below.

Give students the **Connection to Writing Assessment: Post-Reading Composition** along with a copy of the **Have I...? Checklist**.

Give students about 20 minutes in which to write and revise their compositions based on the checklist.

Collect and **score** the students' compositions using the **Rubric for Scoring First Drafts**.

Reproducible Master 18

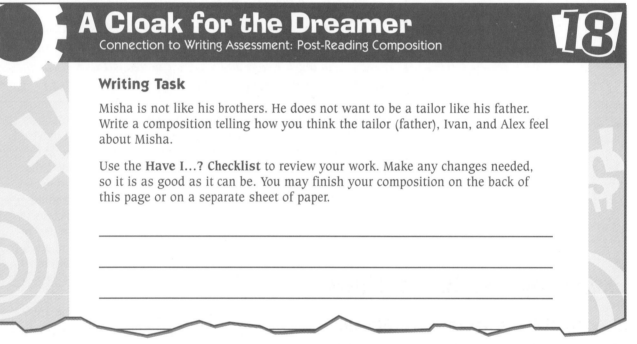

A Cloak for the Dreamer

Connection to Writing Assessment: Post-Reading Composition

18

Writing Task

Misha is not like his brothers. He does not want to be a tailor like his father. Write a composition telling how you think the tailor (father), Ivan, and Alex feel about Misha.

Use the **Have I...? Checklist** to review your work. Make any changes needed, so it is as good as it can be. You may finish your composition on the back of this page or on a separate sheet of paper.

____

____

____

RUBRIC FOR SCORING
Writing Task

An effective response will need to:
- reflect knowledge of the story.
- justify using ideas from the text.
- recognize the affection the tailor and his sons have for Misha.
- be well written with a clear presentation.

POINTS	CRITERIA
4	Ideas are fully developed and supported, describing the actions of father and sons to show their love for Misha. Uses specific details from the story to support ideas, such as the three characters' willingness to work all night to create a special cloak for Misha and the father's willingness to let Misha follow his dreams. Shows insight and understanding. Is well written with a clear presentation.
3	Provides a partial answer by either stating how the tailor and his sons feel about Misha or relating some relevant details from the story, but without the necessary train of thought and support. Shows that the task and the story are understood, but lacks the thoroughness of a well-developed answer.
2	Answer is partially developed. The father's attitude may be discussed, or that of the brothers, but not both. Or, the attitudes of all three are described, but there is no support from the story.
1	Writer may state a conclusion without evidence, or provide details from the selection without explaining the meaning. Or, the writer tells about Misha's feelings without discussing those of the tailor and/or his other sons.
0	Writer shows a lack of understanding of the topic and does not address it in any meaningful way.

Extending the Connections

DEVELOPING AND USING VOCABULARY

As the book is read to the students, you may wish to note and discuss the words listed below. (Note, the pages of the book are not numbered, so consider the first page of story text as page 1.) Follow the general practice you use in your class for recording new vocabulary words, such as listing them on the bulletin board, adding them to a notebook, etc.

Discuss each word as indicated below. Write sample sentences so students can see how the words can be used.

pored read or studied with steady attention or application

p. 5: *There he pored over maps of the world and pictures of faraway places.*

Talk about how this word (verb) helps create a visual image.
- What does it sound like? [homonym is *pour*]
- Have you ever *pored* over anything? Perhaps, your homework or a game you were learning?

nimbly quick and lightly in movement; agile

p.10: *He nimbly stitched the squares together to make one beautiful cloth of the Archdukes' colors, then fashioned the cloth into a sturdy cloak.*

Discuss this descriptive word. Help students find names of actions that could be described using the word *nimbly*. Ask them to name things that they can do *nimbly*.

sturdy strongly built, firm, hardy

p.10: *He nimbly stitched the squares together to make one beautiful cloth of the Archdukes' colors, then fashioned the cloth into a sturdy cloak.*

This is another descriptive word, but it does not describe the same kinds of things that nimbly does.

- What things can you name that are *sturdy*?
- If a person calls someone *sturdy* boy or girl, what does the person mean?
- Do you own anything that can be called *sturdy*?

snipped cut with a small, quick stroke of scissors

p. 27: *Ivan snipped the circles apart, and his father trimmed them into hexagons.*

Snipped is almost onomatopoetic, in that its meaning is suggested by the way it sounds. Children love words that are onomatopoetic and will enjoy using them in speaking, as well as in writing.

fashioned to form or make into something

p.27: *When the cloth was finished, the three tailors fashioned it into a strong and beautiful cloak.*

This word can be a synonym for *make* but with a special connotation. Using different contexts, have students discuss how the words are similar and different.

meanwhile during the same time interval, meantime

p. 10: *Meanwhile, Alex had thought of the colors of the Archduke's carriage and the coat of arms that was painted on its side.*

Students need words to describe the time sequence of events. *Meanwhile* is a useful term in this context. Compare it to "all the while" on page 13. Students can see that things occur simultaneously. Learning to use transitional words and phrases such as these will help students strengthen their writing and help them express complex ideas.

Have the students revise a "work in progress," using one or more of these words to create a more vivid image. When students write new compositions, encourage them to use words from the list to make their writing better.

Periodically, go back to the list and discuss the words again. Praise students when they use words from the list in either their speaking or writing.

UNDERSTANDING ROTATIONAL SYMMETRY

Materials

Overhead pattern blocks

Explain that in addition to line symmetry, there is another type of symmetry called *turn symmetry* or *rotational symmetry*. A figure has turn symmetry if it can be turned through some part of a circle (up to 360 degrees) and look exactly the same as the original shape or design. Note that a figure that must be turned a full circle before it repeats its self does not have rotational or turn symmetry.

EXAMPLE

Place two transparent hexagons on the overhead. Mark each of the hexagons at the same angle and place one of the hexagons on top of the other. Turn the hexagon so that the shape matches the shape below it. Slowly turn the hexagon to establish it can be turned six times before the original mark on the top hexagon matches the original mark on the bottom hexagon. We conclude that a hexagon has one-sixth ($\frac{1}{6}$) turn symmetry.

Continue this procedure for each of the pattern-block figures. Organize the information in a table, by recording the number of lines of symmetry and the fraction of a circle it can be turned through while remaining exactly the same in appearance. (Lines of symmetry were established in the Math Connection activity on page 21 of this manual.)

Shape	Lines of Symmetry	Turn Symmetry
Hexagon	6	$\frac{1}{6}$
Triangle	3	$\frac{1}{3}$
Trapezoid	1	None
Blue rhombus	2	$\frac{1}{2}$
White rhombus	2	$\frac{1}{2}$
Square	4	$\frac{1}{4}$

Ask and discuss the following:

- ***What pattern do you see between the lines of symmetry and turn symmetry for each of the polygons above?*** **[Answer: Except for the trapezoid, the number of lines of symmetry is the number of turns the shape makes; the number of lines of symmetry is the denominator for the turn symmetry fraction.]**

- ***Would the same pattern exist for polygons with unequal sides and/or angles that were not equal?*** **[Answer: No.]**

REVIEWING SYMMETRY: Creating Pattern-Block Designs

Materials

Pattern-Block Designs I and II (Reproducible Masters 14–15), buckets of pattern blocks, scissors, overhead transparencies of **Pattern-Block Designs I and II**

This activity extends the Math Connection activity on page 22 of this manual.

Remind students of the business that makes art from pattern-block pieces and sells them at flea markets. Explain that they are going to look at the two most popular designs again.

Distribute two copies each of **Pattern-Block Designs I and II**, a bucket of pattern blocks, and scissors to pairs of students. Have one student in a pair recreate the designs with pattern blocks, while the other student cuts out each design.

Have students fold and turn the designs to determine whether the figures have line and/or turn symmetry. Discuss and model the results using overhead models of the designs. [Results: Design I has 2 lines of symmetry and $\frac{1}{2}$ turn symmetry. Design II has 0 lines of symmetry and $\frac{1}{6}$ turn symmetry.]

- ***Based on the experiment above, must a design or shape have line symmetry to have turn symmetry?*** **[Answer: No.]**

RELATING FRACTIONS AND MONEY

Materials

Pattern-Block Designs I and II (Reproducible Masters 14–15), buckets of pattern blocks, math journals

Tell students that the designs from the previous activity are priced for sale using a system based on the hexagon. The hexagon has a value of 60 cents. Each of the other shapes is priced according to its area in relation to the hexagon. For example, the area of the trapezoid is $\frac{1}{2}$ of the area of the hexagon. Therefore, it costs $\frac{1}{2}$ of \$0.60, which is \$0.30.

Distribute two copies each of **Pattern-Block Designs I and II** and a bucket of pattern blocks to pairs of students. Have student pairs recreate the designs with pattern blocks.

Have students determine the total price for each design. [Answers: Design I = \$2.60; Design II = \$4.20] You may wish to have students explain the various ways they solved the problems, using overhead models to demonstrate as needed.

Note: Some students will rearrange the pieces to create hexagons. In **Design II**, for example, the trapezoid, rhombus, and triangle of each "arm" can be arranged to make 1 hexagon. There are 6 of these hexagons plus the 1 in the center, so 7 x \$0.60 = \$4.20.

Other students will rearrange the pieces to create hexagons by color. In Design II, the 6 triangles form 1 hexagon, the 6 rhombi form 2 hexagons, and the 6 trapezoids form 3 hexagons. This totals 7 hexagons, including the center hexagon, so 7 x \$0.60 = \$4.20.

Still other students will determine the cost of each shape, count the number of each shape, multiply the number of shapes by the cost, and then add the totals together.

Shape	Cost	Number x Cost	Total
Trapezoids	$\frac{1}{2}$ the hexagon = \$0.30	6 x 0.30	\$1.80
Rhombi	$\frac{1}{3}$ the hexagon = \$0.20	6 x 0.20	\$1.20
Triangles	$\frac{1}{6}$ the hexagon = \$0.10	6 x 0.10	\$0.60
Hexagons		1 x 0.60	\$0.60
		Total	**\$4.20**

Have students write a journal entry describing how they arrived at their answers.

COMBINING AND SUBDIVIDING GEOMETRIC FIGURES

Materials

Pattern-Block Designs I and II (Reproducible Masters 14–15), buckets of pattern blocks, scissors

Using Pattern-Block Designs I and II, have students give the values of the designs in terms of triangles and trapezoids. For example:

- ***If only triangles were used in this design, how many would be needed?*** **[Answers: Design I = 26 triangles; Design II = 42 triangles]**
- ***If as many trapezoids as possible were used in this design, how many would be needed? Would there be any shapes left over?*** **[Answers: Design I = 8 trapezoids + 2 triangles; Design II = 14 trapezoids]**

ADDING FRACTIONS

Materials

Pattern blocks

Distribute pattern blocks to each student. Remind students of the fractional values of each pattern block based on the hexagon being 1 unit.

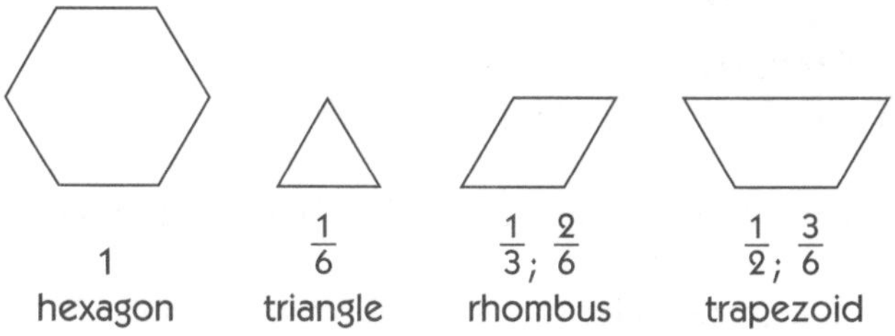

Have students use the pattern blocks to add fractions. Pose problems similar to the following:

- ***What is the fractional value of a rhombus added to a triangle?***

  [Answer: $\frac{1}{3} + \frac{2}{6} = \frac{2}{6} + \frac{1}{6} = \frac{3}{6} = \frac{1}{2}$.

  The rhombus is equal to $\frac{1}{3}$ or 2 triangles, and the triangle is equal to $\frac{1}{6}$ or 1 triangle.

  Altogether there are 3 triangles. This equals is $\frac{3}{6}$ or 1 trapezoid, which has a value of $\frac{1}{2}$.]

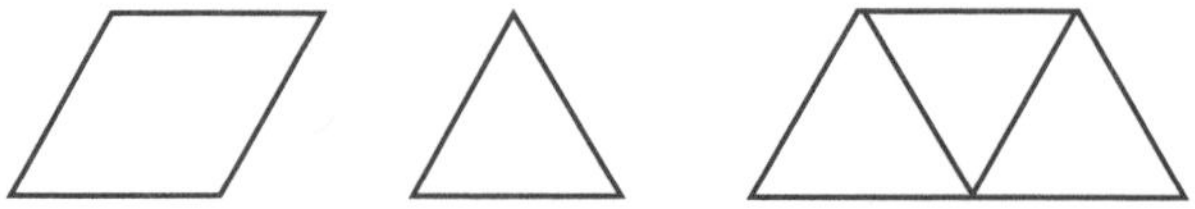

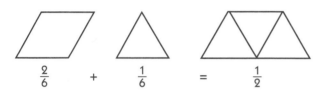

$\frac{2}{6} \quad + \quad \frac{1}{6} \quad = \quad \frac{1}{2}$

- ***What is the fractional value of a trapezoid added to a rhombus?***

  [Answer: $\frac{1}{2} + \frac{2}{6} = \frac{5}{6}$. A trapezoid is equal to $\frac{1}{2}$ or 3 triangles and a rhombus is equal to $\frac{1}{3}$ or 2 triangles. Altogether there are 5 triangles. This equals $\frac{5}{6}$.]

CLOSURE

Materials

Pattern blocks; dot paper, rulers

Have students complete one of the following tasks.

1. Use pattern blocks to see if the combination of a triangle and a square sewn together could be used to make a cloak with no holes. Explain how you arrived at the answer. [Answer: This combination of shapes will tessellate the plane.]
2. Make a combination of shapes that will cover a flat surface without leaving any gaps (tessellate the plane).
3. Use pattern blocks to make a design that has no lines of symmetry but does have turn symmetry. Record a sketch of the design using dot paper and a ruler. (Note, the pinwheel on **Design II** is an example.)

SUGGESTED PROJECTS

Materials

Magazines; pattern blocks; fabric scraps, scissors, needles and thread or sewing machine

Have students complete one of more of the following projects:

1. Find examples of designs from magazines and describe the shapes that are used. Include a discussion of any related line or turn symmetry.
2. Create a design using only hexagons, triangles, trapezoids, and blue rhombi. Record your design on dot paper. Then:
   a. Determine the type of symmetry in your design.
   b. Represent your designs using letters.
   c. Find the cost of your design if the hexagon is worth $0.60.
3. Make your own cloak. Cut scraps of fabric into shapes and then sew them together to make the "cloak." (This activity could be done as a class project to create a "class" cloak, or small groups within the class could each make a cloak.)

EXTENDED COMPOSITIONS

Have students write longer compositions about one or both of the following questions.

1. The book is called *A Cloak for the Dreamer*. Tell why you think this is or is not a good title.

2. Rewrite the story in your own words, but tell it from the point of view of one brother. The story might start with, "I have a brother who…".

Compositions that have been through the complete writing process, including editing and revising, may be ready for "publication." These can be graded with the standard criteria used in your classroom.

ADDITIONAL RESOURCES

Windows on Math, Volume 3, Unit 2 Videodisc, "Symmetry Sleuth." Atlanta: Optical Data Corporation, 1996. Call 1-800-524-2481.

Windows on Math, Volume 4, Unit 2 Videodisc, "Tile Mania." Atlanta: Optical Data Corporation, 1996. Call 1-800-524-2481.

Counting On Frank

Written and illustrated by
Rod Clement

Overview of the Connections

Counting on Frank is a humorous story about a boy who likes to estimate and compare the relative size of things around him, including his dog, Frank. In the story, the boy estimates everything from peas to people, using linear measure, volume, weight, and capacity.

In teaching mathematics, this book provides opportunities for students to consider and verify the boy's statements about the relative sizes of things. Students use their spatial senses, consider the objects used as units of measure, look at details in the book, and then evaluate whether the boy took them into account or ignored them in making his estimates. Activities drawn from the book engage students in fun opportunities to exercise skills in thinking logically. It may be necessary to investigate the concept of volume and capacity as an introduction to the story so students are prepared to discuss solutions to some of the problems presented throughout the book.

In language arts, the story and the comical illustrations are motivational for student writing and effective listening. The study of language arts is enhanced as students discuss and articulate answers to the questions posed in the story.

MATERIALS FOR THE CONNECTIONS

Counting on Frank • ISBN 0-8368-0358-2
Written and illustrated by Rod Clement. Milwaukee: Gareth Stevens Publishing, 1991.

Language Arts

~ One or more copies of the book (Note: In the Viewing Connection, each student will need to see the picture on the very last page of the book. You may wish to have several copies available.)

~ Optional: **Connection to Viewing Assessment: Writing About a Picture Prompt** (Reproducible Master 1)

~ **Have I...? Checklist** (Reproducible Master 2), a self-monitoring tool for student writers

~ **Rubric for Scoring First Drafts** (Reproducible Master 3)

~ **Connection to Listening Assessment: Listening to Part of a Story** (Reproducible Master 19)

~ **Connection to Writing Assessment: Post-Reading Composition** (Reproducible Master 25)

Mathematics

~ Jars (3, each a different size)

~ **Evaluating Estimates I and II** (Reproducible Masters 20–21)

~ Math journals

~ **Checklist for Evaluating Plans and Solutions** (Reproducible Master 23)

~ Calculators

~ Optional: **Research Data** (Reproducible Master 22)

~ **Optional:** materials for verification experiments, including straws; ballpoint pens; water; toy animals or blocks (ideally about 3 in. long x 1 in. in wide x 2 in. high); boxes (ideally about 12 in. long x 10 in. wide x 8 in. high); measuring sticks (centimeter and inch rulers, yardsticks); containers for water; funnels; dried peas; candy jar; bags of jellybeans.

~ Reference sources, such as encyclopedias, science books, and/or the Internet.

~ **Connection to Mathematics Assessment: Check for Understanding** (Reproducible Master 24)

Viewing Connection

INTRODUCING THE LESSON WITH A PICTURE PROMPT AND WRITING

Materials

One or more copies of the book (last page of book), **Connection to Viewing Assessment: Writing About a Picture Prompt** (Reproducible Master 1), **Have I...? Checklist** (Reproducible Master 2), **Rubric for Scoring First Drafts** (Reproducible Master 3)

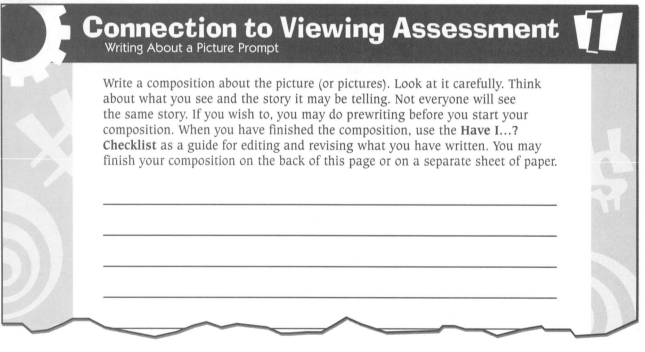

Show the class the picture on the very last page in the book. It is a picture of a boy and a dog with an open jar of items on the floor beside them. If possible, allow students to continue to look at the picture throughout the writing session. You may distribute a copy of **Connection to Viewing Assessment: Writing About a Picture Prompt** to each student, or they may use notebook paper for their work. Also distribute copies of the **Have I...? Checklist**.

Read these directions to the class:

"You are going to write a composition about this picture. Look at it carefully. Think about what you see and the story it may be telling. It is OK that not everyone will see the same story. If you wish to, you may do prewriting before you start your composition. When you have finished the composition, use the **Have I...? Checklist** as a guide for editing and revising what you have written."

Give the students 20–30 minutes to write their compositions and do initial editing.

Collect and score the students' compositions using the **Rubric for Scoring First Drafts**. Teach students how to compare their scored compositions to the rubric and to make notes about how to improve their compositions. Students also may be taught to use the rubric to score their own work or that of other students.

Reproducible Master 1

Connection to Viewing Assessment 1

Writing About a Picture Prompt

Write a composition about the picture (or pictures). Look at it carefully. Think about what you see and the story it may be telling. Not everyone will see the same story. If you wish to, you may do prewriting before you start your composition. When you have finished the composition, use the **Have I...? Checklist** as a guide for editing and revising what you have written. You may finish your composition on the back of this page or on a separate sheet of paper.

____

____

____

____

Listening Connection

LISTENING TO PART OF A STORY AND ANSWERING QUESTIONS

Materials

Copy of the book (Listening section: pages 2–12, 256 words), **Connection to Listening Assessment: Listening to Part of a Story** (Reproducible Master 19)

This activity will help students develop effective listening skills. As necessary, teach or review some of the effective listening strategies found on page *xv* of this manual.

Tell the students you are going to read part of a story. When you have finished, they will answer some questions about what you have read. (The entire story will be read in the Mathematics Connection activity.)

Read pages 2–12 aloud to the students. The pages are not numbered. Count the first illustration of the man asleep on the chair as page 1. The listening section begins on page 2 with the lines: *My dad says, "You have a brain. Use it!" So I do.* It concludes on page 12 with the sentence: *It would take slightly less time to empty, as long as no one opened the door.*

Since you are working on listening, don't stop to discuss the story, show the illustrations, or make predictions as you might do in a reading instructional period.

After reading, distribute the worksheet with multiple-choice and open-ended questions called **Connection to Listening Assessment: Listening to Part of a Story**.

Allow students 15–20 minutes for completing the worksheet.

Collect and score the students' work, using the answers and rubric that follow.

Proceed to the Mathematics Connection for instructions on completing the book.

Reproducible Master 19 with answers

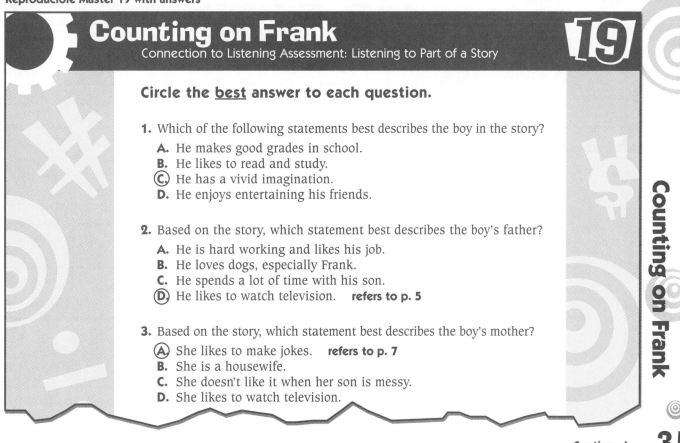

Counting on Frank 19

Connection to Listening Assessment: Listening to Part of a Story

Circle the best answer to each question.

1. Which of the following statements best describes the boy in the story?
   - A. He makes good grades in school.
   - B. He likes to read and study.
   - (C) He has a vivid imagination.
   - D. He enjoys entertaining his friends.

2. Based on the story, which statement best describes the boy's father?
   - A. He is hard working and likes his job.
   - B. He loves dogs, especially Frank.
   - C. He spends a lot of time with his son.
   - (D) He likes to watch television. **refers to p. 5**

3. Based on the story, which statement best describes the boy's mother?
   - (A) She likes to make jokes. **refers to p. 7**
   - B. She is a housewife.
   - C. She doesn't like it when her son is messy.
   - D. She likes to watch television.

Continued...

4. The boy estimated the size of many things, including the items listed below. Which was largest?

(A) the tree in the back yard
B. Frank
C. the father
D. the big television

5. The boy says he thinks it would take twenty-four Franks to fill his bedroom. "But sometimes there isn't even room enough for one." Which statement is the best interpretation of what he means?

A. Frank has eaten a lot and has gotten bigger.
(B) Frank can be very active and annoying.
C. The boy's father wants it quiet in the house.
D. The boy's mother wants Frank outside.

Open-ended Listening Task: Adults may say, "You have a brain. Use it!" when they think a kid has done something that isn't too smart. Other times they say it to encourage a person to do their best. Explain what you think the boy's father means when he says, "You have a brain. Use it!" **see rubric that follows for scoring**

RUBRIC FOR SCORING

Open-ended Listening Task

An effective response will need to:

- reflect knowledge of the story.
- justify ideas from the text.
- interpret figurative language.
- be well written and clearly presented.

POINTS	CRITERIA
4	Response is a logical interpretation with specific supporting details from the story. Shows creativity, depth of thought, and thorough understanding.
3	Response includes logical interpretation and reasoning. Answer may be brief and not thoroughly developed.
2	Response includes either a logical interpretation or reasoning, but probably not both. Some details are included, but they may be irrelevant.
1	The answer is sketchy, providing either an interpretation or reasoning, but not both. Shows minimal understanding of story.
0	Answer is off topic or irrelevant. Shows no understanding of story.

Mathematics Connection

INTRODUCTION AND ACTIVE READING

Materials

A copy of the book, three jars of different sizes, **Evaluating Estimates I and II** (Reproducible Masters 20–21), math journals

Review what the class already has read. Focus on the fact that the boy makes statements about the sizes of things, often using comparisons to make his point.

Display three jars of different sizes. Tell students that later in the story, the boy says that there are 745 jellybeans in the average candy jar. Ask:

Which size do you think the boy is referring to when he talks about an average candy jar?

Tell students that after you read the story, they will be asked to evaluate whether the boy's estimates and comparisons are reasonable and to explain why.

Re-read the story, stopping at appropriate points to model active reading by making predictions, asking thought questions, and monitoring comprehension. Show the illustrations and let students discuss what they see.

Distribute Evaluating Estimates I and II to students. Read the story again, stopping after each two-page spread to have students record whether they think the estimate is reasonably accurate and what, if any, additional information they would like before answering the question.

Emphasize to students that they do not have to try to calculate solutions. Tell them that you just want to know if they think the estimate is reasonably accurate.

Reproducible Master 20

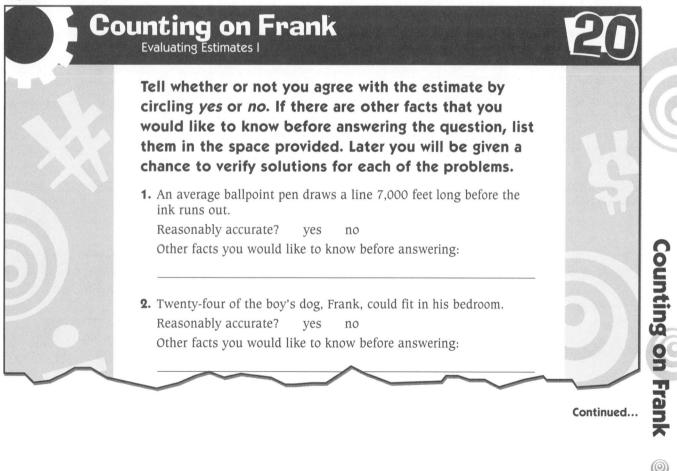

Counting on Frank

Evaluating Estimates I

20

Tell whether or not you agree with the estimate by circling *yes* or *no*. If there are other facts that you would like to know before answering the question, list them in the space provided. Later you will be given a chance to verify solutions for each of the problems.

1. An average ballpoint pen draws a line 7,000 feet long before the ink runs out.
   Reasonably accurate? yes no
   Other facts you would like to know before answering:
   ____

2. Twenty-four of the boy's dog, Frank, could fit in his bedroom.
   Reasonably accurate? yes no
   Other facts you would like to know before answering:
   ____

Continued...

3. Ten humpback whales would fit in the entire house.
Reasonably accurate? yes no
Other facts you would like to know before answering:

____

4. One-tenth of the boy's dad would fit inside a portable television.
Reasonably accurate? yes no
Other facts you would like to know before answering:

____

5. The tree grows about 6 feet every year, and if the boy grew at the same rate he would be almost 50 feet tall.
Reasonably accurate? yes no
Other facts you would like to know before answering:

____

6. It would take 11 hours and 45 minutes to fill the bathroom with water.
Reasonably accurate? yes no
Other facts you would like to know before answering:

____

Counting on Frank

Evaluating Estimates II

21

7. The boy would be 9 feet tall and 6 feet wide wearing all the clothes in his closet.
   Reasonably accurate? yes no
   Other facts you would like to know before answering:
   ____

8. If the boy dropped 15 peas on the floor each night, after 8 years they would reach the tabletop.
   Reasonably accurate? yes no
   Other facts you would like to know before answering:
   ____

9. A mosquito 4 million times bigger than normal would not fit in the boy's ear.
   Reasonably accurate? yes no
   Other facts you would like to know before answering:
   ____

10. If a toaster that shoots toast 3 feet were as big as a house, it would endanger low-flying aircraft.
    Reasonably accurate? yes no
    Other facts you would like to know before answering:
    ____

11. It takes 47 cans of dog food to fill one shopping bag.
    Reasonably accurate? yes no
    Other facts you would like to know before answering:
    ____

12. The average candy jar holds 745 jellybeans.
    Reasonably accurate? yes no
    Other facts you would like to know before answering:
    ____

Have students write a journal entry responding to the following prompt:

"Think about each of the ways the boy tried to describe the sizes of various objects. Do you think the boy is a good estimator? Tell why or why not."

Distribute a slip of paper to each student. Ask the students to write *yes* on the paper if they think the boy is a good estimator and *no* if they think he is not. Collect the papers.

Have students estimate what fraction of the class answered *yes* and what fraction answered *no*.

Tally the *yes* and *no* answers and display the results in a table. Then discuss the results as fractions. Discuss the meaning of each fraction and review its parts.

EXAMPLE

Suppose you have 23 students in your class, and the tallies showed that 12 students think the boy is a good estimator and 11 students think that he is not a good estimator.

Good Estimator	Bad Estimator
~~||||~~ ~~||||~~ ||	~~||||~~ ~~||||~~ |

$\frac{12}{23}$ of the class thinks the boy is a good estimator.

$\frac{11}{23}$ of the class thinks the boy is not a good estimator.

Extend the activity by asking students to compare your class results to halves, quarters, and other fractions by asking questions similar to the following:

Which is more than half, $\frac{12}{23}$ or $\frac{11}{23}$? How do you know? **[$\frac{12}{23}$]**

- ***What would be the denominator of the fraction if there were only 19 students in the class?*** **[19]**
- ***In Mrs. Miller's class, $\frac{11}{14}$ of the students thought the boy was a bad estimator. What does this fraction tell you about the class?*** **[Possible answers: There are 14 students in the class. Most students thought he was a bad estimator.]**

VERIFYING ESTIMATES: General Approaches

Materials

Checklist for Evaluating Plans and Solutions (Reproducible Master 23), calculators, reference sources (e.g., encyclopedia, Internet). **Optional: Research Data** (Reproducible Master 22)

For this activity, students try to confirm their initial reactions to the question of whether or not the boy was a good estimator by trying to verify his estimates for each problem. The overall intent is for students to internalize the necessity of choosing appropriate references when estimating. The first step is for the students to develop and/or evaluate a plan. Next, they list the strengths and weaknesses of the plan. Finally, they use the plan to find a solution and compare the solution to the estimates made by the boy in the book.

The Classroom Management section addresses general approaches to the activities and presents an implementation model for evaluating plans and solving the problems to verify the estimates.

Each of the subsequent activities presents a possible plan, plan evaluation, and solution for the 12 estimation problems in **Evaluating Estimates I and II**. These illustrate just one possible approach to solving each problem.

You and the students will benefit most from these activities if you design and follow your own plans. Don't discourage students who appear to be heading down a path that you think may lead to a dead end or that may not be the most efficient method of arriving at a solution. The greatest value in this lesson is derived from thinking, exploring, and experimenting.

Classroom Management Issues

To manage this activity, you will need to decide how many of the estimations in the book you want the class to investigate.

It is critical that you read the plans and solutions before presenting them to the class so you can determine the materials needed to model the problem and/or additional information needed to solve it.

For questions that require additional research, you can extend the problem-solving experience by having students do the research themselves. In other cases, you may provide the necessary data when students determine that they need it to proceed. Data related to several of the activities appears on the optional **Research Data** reproducible master.

Keep in mind, however, that the sheet does not provide data for all of the questions, and not all of the data on the sheet is relevant to the questions.

For each problem, discuss with students how they arrived at their solutions. If students do their own research, their data and results are likely to differ from those provided in this guide or on the **Research Data** sheet. The information on the **Research Data** sheet is not definitive, but—unlike some of the so-called facts and estimates in the story—it is reasonable!

Reproducible Master 22

Counting on Frank

Research Data

22

Pens

An average ballpoint pen holds about 1 mL of ink. It takes 0.05 mL of ink to draw a line 10-feet long.

Dogs and Dog Food

- Large dogs like a shorthair pointer range from 22 to 28 inches from the ground to shoulder height. Their bodies are about 30 to 45 inches long from nose to rump. And they are probably about a foot or so wide at the middle.
- A can of dog food is about 4 inches tall and weighs about 14 ounces.

Houses and Household Items

- An average one-story house is 1,200 square feet and has an average height of 12 feet.
- An average bedroom is 12 feet long, 10 feet wide, and 8 feet high.
- An average bathroom is 5 feet wide, 7 feet long, and 8 feet high.
- An average dining room is 12 feet long, 9 feet wide, and 8 feet high.
- An average dining room table is about $2\frac{1}{2}$ feet high, 3 feet wide, and 6 feet long.
- Portable television sets range in height from 8 inches to 20 inches.
- A typical toaster is about 6 inches tall.

Humpback Whales

The average humpback whale is about 55 feet in length. It is about 14.5 feet high and 6.3 feet wide.

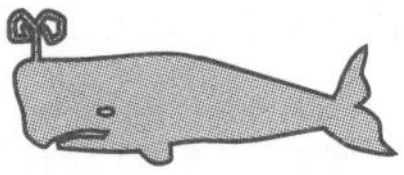

Mosquitoes

There are about 2,000 species of the insects commonly called mosquitoes. Some are less than 1 centimeter long, and some are as long as 5 centimeters long.

People Facts

- Men vary in height. The average height of a man in the United States is about 5 feet 10 inches.
- An average adult ear is about 7 centimeters in length.

Trees

- The tallest tree ever found was an Australian eucalyptus. It was found in 1872. It was 435 feet tall when found, but it was thought to be over 500 feet at one time. The current tallest living tree is a coastal redwood in Humboldt Redwoods State Park in California. Its height is 312 feet.
- Trees grow at different rates. Trees in the deserts may grow 1–4 millimeters a year while other trees can grow up to 0.5 meters a year.

Airplanes

Small airplanes fly at altitudes of about 1,000 to 2,000 feet.

Peas

About 75 dried peas fit in 1 cubic inch.

Shopping Bags

A typical paper grocery bag is about 12 inches long, 7 inches wide, and about 17 inches high. It can hold about 20 pounds.

Some teachers may want to model solutions for a few of the problems in class and then assign some problems for homework and assign others as group problem-solving activities. Groups assigned to different problems can present their solutions to the whole class for further discussion.

When you are modeling solutions for the whole class, describe the plan you are using and have students estimate answers to various parts of the plan before actually gathering the data. For example, for estimating peas, have them estimate the number of peas in 1 cubic inch. For the whale question, ask them to estimate the length of a humpback whale. It may also be helpful to have students formulate a central question that they are trying to answer for each estimation problem. For example, for estimating peas they can ask, "If 15 peas fall on the floor each night for eight years, will they fill a dining room to the height of a tabletop?"

Other teachers may prefer to provide the class with plans to start. With this approach, students can discuss the ability of the plans to verify the estimates in the book, determine possible problems that could occur within each step, and then evaluate the accuracy of the solution. Students can then decide to modify the plans or simply use them to determine the solutions on their own.

Sample Classroom Implementation Plan

1. Teacher and whole class model solutions to estimation problems 2 and 3.
2. Assign estimation problems 1, 5, and 9 as individual questions for homework
3. Form groups of 4–5 students and assign problems as follows:
   - Group A—Problem 4
   - Group B—Problem 6
   - Group C—Problem 7
   - Group D—Problem 8
   - Group E—Problem 10
   - Group F—Problem 11
   - Group G—Problem 12

Alternative: Solve only one problem in class and assign the remaining problems to small groups. Then have the groups present their solutions to the whole class.

As students proceed through the problems, have them refer back to their answers on **Evaluating Estimates I and II**. You also may distribute the **Checklist for Evaluating Plans and Solutions** to help you and the students evaluate plans for and solutions to the situations presented in the story.

Reproducible Master 23

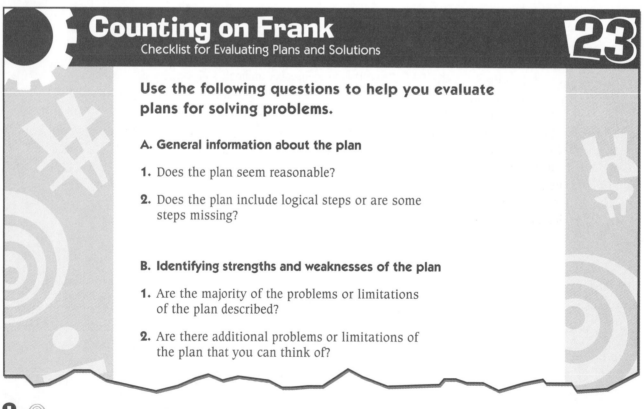

Counting on Frank 23

Checklist for Evaluating Plans and Solutions

Use the following questions to help you evaluate plans for solving problems.

A. General information about the plan

1. Does the plan seem reasonable?
2. Does the plan include logical steps or are some steps missing?

B. Identifying strengths and weaknesses of the plan

1. Are the majority of the problems or limitations of the plan described?
2. Are there additional problems or limitations of the plan that you can think of?

VERIFYING ESTIMATION PROBLEM 1: Ballpoint Pen (pages 1–2)

Reproducible Master 20: Problem 1 on Evaluating Estimates I

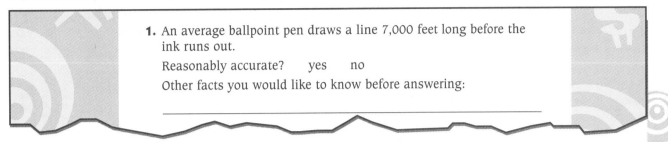

1. An average ballpoint pen draws a line 7,000 feet long before the ink runs out.

Reasonably accurate? yes no

Other facts you would like to know before answering:

____

PROBLEM: Is there enough ink in an average ballpoint pen to draw a line 7,000 feet long?

Step 1: Develop a plan to solve the problem.

a. Determine the amount of ink in the average ballpoint pen.
b. Determine the how much ink is used to draw a line 10 feet long.
c. Determine the number of 10-foot lengths in 7,000 feet.
d. Multiply the amount of ink used to draw a 10-foot line by 700.
e. Compare the answers from *a* and *d* to verify whether the boy's estimate is reasonably accurate.

Step 2: List strengths and weaknesses of the overall plan. Mention specific problems that might occur in each step.

- How could the amount of ink in the average ballpoint pen be determined?
- How could the amount of ink used to draw a line 10 feet long be determined? Would it be helpful to draw a line 100 feet long instead?
- What unit of measurement would be needed to measure the amount of ink in a pen?
- What unit of measurement would be needed to measure the amount of ink in a 10-foot line?

Step 3: Implement the plan and/or determine the accuracy of the answers to each part of the solution.

a. The average ballpoint pen holds about 1 mL of ink. We tested this estimation by measuring the amount of water that could fill a thin straw that is about the same size as the ink-holder in a ballpoint pen.
b. We called a pen company to ask how much ink it takes to draw a line of a specific length. It takes 0.05 mL of ink to draw a line 10-feet long.
c. There are 700 ten-foot lengths in 7,000 feet (7,000 ÷ 10 = 700).
d. 700 x 0.05 = 35 mL
e. Since 35 mL is greater than 1 mL, the pen could not make a line 7,000 feet long. The boy's estimate was not accurate.

If appropriate, ask students how the data in their solution and the approach they took compare with the information in this sample.

- Why might it be difficult to determine how much ink it takes to draw a line?
- What might make it possible to figure out that information yourself? [Possible answer: If you knew how much ink a pen held, you could draw a line until it ran out, measure the line, and divide the length of the line by the total amount of ink the pen held.]

VERIFYING ESTIMATION PROBLEM 2: Frank the Dog (pages 3–4)

Reproducible Master 20: Problem 2 on Evaluating Estimates I

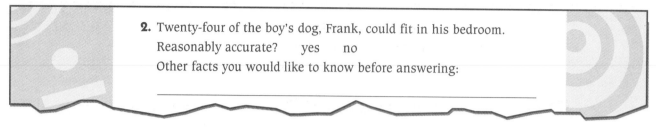

> **2.** Twenty-four of the boy's dog, Frank, could fit in his bedroom.
> Reasonably accurate? yes no
> Other facts you would like to know before answering:
> ______________________________

PROBLEM: Could 24 dogs the size of Frank fit in an average bedroom?

Step 1: Develop a plan to solve the problem.

a. Determine the dimensions of an average bedroom.
b. Find a model that represents the size of an average bedroom.
c. Determine the dimensions of a large dog.
d. Find a model that represents the size of a large dog.
e. Determine about how many dog models fit in the room model.
f. Compare the answer to *e* to 24 dogs to verify if the boy's estimate is reasonably accurate.

Step 2: List strengths and weaknesses of the overall plan. Mention specific problems that might occur in each step.

- Some students might not measure accurately.
- Should meters or feet be used?
- The methods used to find the average dimensions could affect the answer. Were enough sets of data used to determine the average? Were the dimensions given representative of the average size of a bedroom?
- Is there a particular breed of dog that should be used or should all breeds be included? How would these decisions affect the answer?
- Should we determine how many dogs could fit in the room from floor to ceiling or how many can fit standing on the floor?
- The reasonableness of this answer could be challenged even after counting the number of dogs that would fit. That's because the plan doesn't consider other objects taking up space in the room, such as furniture.

Step 3: Implement the plan and/or determine the accuracy of the answers to each part of the solution.

a. By measuring bedrooms or collecting data from outside sources on room size, determine that an average bedroom is 12 feet long, 10 feet wide, and 8 feet high.
b. Use a cardboard box or other container to represent the size of an average bedroom. A box that is 10 inches wide, 12 inches long, and 8 inches high could represent a bedroom that is 10 feet wide, 12 feet long, and 8 feet high. (Scale: 1 inch = 1 foot)
c. Use reference sources or measure a large dog to determine approximate size. An average large dog is about 2 feet tall, about 3 feet long, and probably about a foot wide.
d. A toy animal or block that is about 3 inches long, 1 inch wide, and 2 inches tall could represent one dog in the same way that the box represents the bedroom. (Scale: 1 inch = 1 foot)
e. About 40 toys that are 3 inches by 1 inches at their base would fit on the bottom of a 10-inch by 12-inch box. If each one is 2 inches tall, you could stack 4 in the 8-inch high box. That means 160 would fill the box (40 x 4 = 160). If we were really counting dogs, there might be fewer because there would be space between them.
f. The boy said 24 of his dog, Frank, would fit in his room. Even with some furniture in the room, that would be far fewer than could really fit. His estimate was not reasonably accurate.

If appropriate, ask students how the data in their solution and the approach they took compare with the information in this sample.

- What is another way that you could have done this estimation activity?
- How would the results be different if we considered how many dogs could fit standing on the floor instead of stacked to the ceiling?

VERIFYING ESTIMATION PROBLEM 3: Humpback Whales (pages 5–6)

Reproducible Master 20: Problem 3 on Evaluating Estimates I

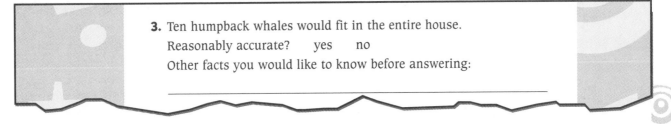

> **3.** Ten humpback whales would fit in the entire house.
> Reasonably accurate? yes no
> Other facts you would like to know before answering:
> ____

PROBLEM: Is an average size house big enough to fit 10 humpback whales?

Step 1: Develop a plan to solve the problem.

a. Determine the dimensions of the average humpback whale.
b. Determine the number of cubic feet in the average humpback whale.
c. Determine the number of cubic feet for 10 average humpback whales.
d. Determine the dimensions of the average house.
e. Determine the number of cubic feet in the average house.
f. Determine about how many humpback whales would fit in a house.
g. Compare the answer to *f* to 10 humpback whales to verify if the boy's estimate is reasonably accurate.

Step 2: List strengths and weaknesses of the overall plan. Mention specific problems that might occur in each step.

- How accurate would the measurements of the average humpback whale be? Should only males be used, or should the data include females and babies? How would changes in the characteristics affect the data?
- Even if the length, width, and height of the average humpback whale were determined, would these measurements give an accurate representation of the number of cubic feet in a whale? The whale is thinner at its tail than its head. How does this affect the calculations for cubic feet of the whale?
- What type of house should be used? What would the result be different if a one-storied house were used vs. a two-storied house or an apartment?
- How should the dimensions of the house be determined? Should the widest and longest lengths be used? Should only the height of the rooms be used or should measurements be taken from the ground to the highest part of the roof?

Step 3: Implement the plan and/or determine the accuracy of the answers to each part of the solution.

a. The average humpback whale is about 55 feet in length. The height is about 14.5 feet, and the width is about 6.3 feet.
b. Each whale is about 5,000 cubic feet (55 x 14.5 x 6.3 = 5,024.25).
c. Ten humpback whales would be about 50,000 cubic feet (5,024 x 10 = 50,240).
d. An average one-story house is about 1,200 square feet and has an average height of 12 feet.
e. The number of cubic feet in the house is 14,400 cubic feet (1,200 x 12 = 14,400).
f. Only 2 humpback whales would completely fit in the house (14,400 ÷ 5,000 = 2.8).
g. That's much less than the 10 that the boy said could fit. His estimate was not reasonable for a one-story house.

If appropriate, ask students how the data in their solution and the approach they took compare with the information in this sample.

VERIFYING ESTIMATION PROBLEM 4: Portable Television (pages 7–8)

Reproducible Master 20: Problem 4 on Evaluating Estimates I

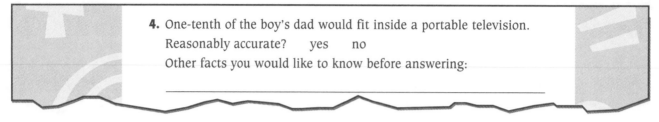

> **4.** One-tenth of the boy's dad would fit inside a portable television.
> Reasonably accurate? yes no
> Other facts you would like to know before answering:
> ____

PROBLEM: Is one-tenth of an average man about the size of a portable TV?

Step 1: Develop a plan to solve the problem.

- **a.** Determine the height of the average dad.
- **b.** Determine the height of the average portable television.
- **c.** Divide the height of the average dad by 10.
- **d.** Compare the answer to *c* to the answer to *b*. If *c* is smaller or they are about the same, it's a good estimate.

Step 2: List strengths and weaknesses of the overall plan. Mention specific problems that might occur in each step.

- Portable televisions vary widely in size.
- Will all the dad heights be measured the same way?
- Should all the measurements be made in inches, feet, centimeters, or meters?

Step 3: Implement the plan and/or determine the accuracy of the answers to each part of the solution.

- **a.** Use inches, centimeters, feet, or meters to measure the heights of 8–10 dads. Find the median height by arranging all the measures in order from the largest to the smallest, and take the one in the middle. (Or use the information from the **Research Data** sheet, which gives an average height of 5 feet 10 inches.)
- **b.** Use inches, centimeters, feet, or meters to measure the heights of 8–10 portable TVs. Find the median height by arranging all the measures in order from the largest to the smallest, and take the one in the middle. (Or use the information from the **Research Data** sheet, which gives a range of 8 inches to 20 inches, which would produce an average height of 14 inches.)
- **c.** Divide 5 feet 10 inches by 10. First convert to inches: 5 x 12 inches + 10 inches = 70 inches. Then divide: 70 inches ÷ 10 = 7 inches.
- **d.** If a portable TV is about 14 inches high and $\frac{1}{10}$ of a dad is 7 inches high, two $\frac{1}{10}$ of a dad, which is the same as $\frac{2}{10}$ or $\frac{1}{5}$ of a dad could fit, in a portable TV. The boy's estimate is not reasonably accurate because it's too low.

If appropriate, ask students how the data in their solution and the approach they took compare with the information in this sample.

VERIFYING ESTIMATION PROBLEM 5: Trees (pages 9–10)

Reproducible Master 20: Problem 5 on Evaluating Estimates I

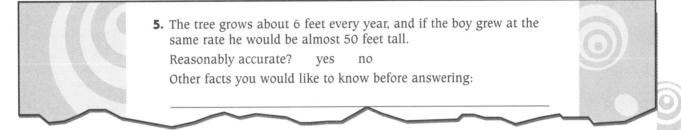

> **5.** The tree grows about 6 feet every year, and if the boy grew at the same rate he would be almost 50 feet tall.
>
> Reasonably accurate? yes no
>
> Other facts you would like to know before answering:
>
> ______________________________

PROBLEMS: Does a tree really grow 6 feet in a year? At that growth rate, how tall would the boy be?

Step 1: Develop a plan to solve the problem.

Part A: Does a tree really grow 6 feet in a year?

a. Determine the height of a tree.
b. Determine its age.
c. Determine the average growth per year by dividing.
d. Compare the answer in *c* to 6 feet.

Part B: At the growth rate of 6 feet per year, would the boy be 50 feet tall?

a. Determine the height of the average student in your class in feet.
b. Determine the average age of students in your class.
c. Multiply the average age of the students in your class by 6.
d. Compare the answer from *c* to 50 feet.

Step 2: List strengths and weaknesses of the overall plan. Mention specific problems that might occur in each step.

Part A:

- Should all trees be used or should only full-grown trees be used?
- Would the species of tree make a difference?
- How could we know the age of a tree?

Part B:

- Are the children in this class the same age as the boy in the book?
- Would the data collected for your class be representative of the data for the all students in your age group?
- What would happen to the data if the two tallest students in the class were absent on the day you computed the average?

Step 3: Implement the plan and/or determine the accuracy of the answers to each part of the solution.

Part A:

a. A tree outside our school is about 20 feet tall.
b. The tree is about 15 years old.
c. Determine the average rate of growth: 20 feet ÷ 15 years = 1.3 feet/year.
d. That's a lot less than the boy's estimate of 6 feet a year. Based on this information, the boy's estimate doesn't seem reasonable. We did research to check. An arborist said trees in a desert may grow 1–4 millimeters a year while other trees can grow up to 0.5 meters a year. Half a meter is a little less than $1\frac{1}{5}$ feet. Based on this information, the tree in the back yard could not grow 6 feet per year.

Part B:

a. Suppose the height of the average fourth grader is 4.1 feet tall.
b. Suppose the age of an average fourth grader is 9 years old.
c. Multiply 6 (the number of feet per year the tree grew in the story) by the age of the average fourth grader to see how tall the average fourth grader would be: 6 feet x 9 years = 54 feet.
d. Using the 6 feet per year growth rate, the boy's estimate that he'd be 50 feet tall by now is reasonable.

If appropriate, ask students how the data in their solution and the approach they took compare with the information in this sample.

- How might the results vary if you considered trees in the redwood forests of California and Oregon vs. trees planted in our neighborhood?
- Do you think each tree grows the same amount each year?

VERIFYING ESTIMATION PROBLEM 6: Water (pages 11–12)

Reproducible Master 20: Problem 6 on Evaluating Estimates I

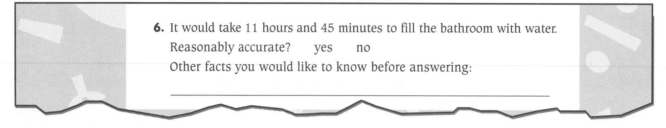

> **6.** It would take 11 hours and 45 minutes to fill the bathroom with water.
> Reasonably accurate? yes no
> Other facts you would like to know before answering:
> ____

PROBLEM: How fast will running water fill up a room the size of an average bathroom?

Step 1: Develop a plan to solve the problem.

a. Measure the dimensions of several bathrooms.
b. Determine the average dimensions.
c. Determine the number of cubic feet in the average bathroom.
d. Determine how fast it would take to fill 1 cubic foot with water.
e. Determine how many cubic feet could be filled in 1 minute.
f. Use this data to determine how long it would take to fill the bathroom.

Step 2: List strengths and weaknesses of the overall plan. Mention specific problems that might occur in each step.

- Is the data collected for the average bathroom representative of the average bathroom? Why or why not?
- Would the data changed by rounding the numbers or taking ballpark figures?

Step 3: Implement the plan and/or determine the accuracy of the answers to each part of the solution.

a. Determine the lengths, widths, and heights of several bathrooms.
b. Determine the average length, width, and height of a bathroom. (You may want to round to nearest foot, such as 5 feet wide, 7 feet long, and 8 feet high.)
c. Determine how much water it would take to fill a bathroom that is 5 feet by 7 feet by 8 feet. Multiply length x width x height: 5 feet x 7 feet x 8 feet = 280 cubic feet.
d. Determine how long it takes to fill 1 cubic foot of water. This can be done through simulation by pouring water from one container through a funnel into another container that measures 1 foot by 1 foot by 1 foot and timing how long it takes.
e. Suppose one class experimented and found that it took 10 seconds to fill half of a container that measured 1 cubic foot. Based on this experiment, it would take 1 minute to fill 3 cubic feet. (If it took 10 seconds to fill $\frac{1}{2}$ cubic foot, it would take twice as long, 20 seconds, to fill 1 cubic foot. One minute is 60 seconds. $60 \div 20 = 3$. Therefore, in 1 minute, 3 cubic feet of water would be filled.)
f. Since there are 280 cubic feet in the average bathroom, it would take $280 \div 3$, or about 90 minutes, to fill the bathroom. The boy estimated 11 hours and 45 minutes. That does not seem reasonable.

If appropriate, ask students how the data in their solution and the approach they took compare with the information in this sample.

- How might the data vary if we took the average size of bathrooms in apartments vs. houses?
- How might the data vary if you used the faucet in the bathtub vs. one in the bathroom sink?

VERIFYING ESTIMATION PROBLEM 7: Clothes (pages 13–14)

Reproducible Master 21: Problem 7 on Evaluating Estimates II

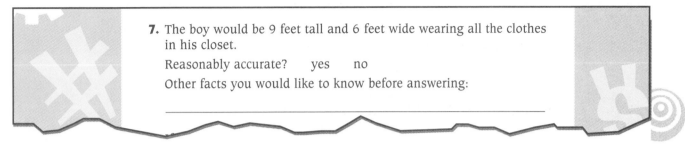

7. The boy would be 9 feet tall and 6 feet wide wearing all the clothes in his closet.

Reasonably accurate? yes no

Other facts you would like to know before answering:

____

Step 1: Develop a plan to solve the problem.
In trying to develop a plan to solve this problem, students may realize how improbable this really is and how difficult it would be to verify. You might have students explain why they think the boy could or could not put on all the clothes in his closet at one time. [Possible answer: The clothes probably wouldn't fit over each other, unless there were few pieces and they were not the same size.]
In addition, to verify you'd need an idea of how many articles of clothing the boy had in his closet.

On page 14, the boy says he would be unable to sit down. Have students suggest why the boy determined that he couldn't sit down with clothes that made him 6 feet wide and 9 feet tall. [Possible answer: He probably couldn't bend his legs with so many layers on.]

If you have a dress-up box of old clothes and coats, allow students to try to put on layers of clothes and coats to see how far they can get.

VERIFYING ESTIMATION PROBLEM 8: Peas (pages 15–16)

Reproducible Master 21: Problem 8 on Evaluating Estimates II

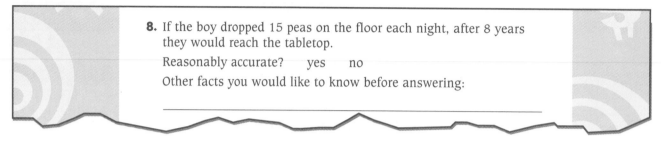

8. If the boy dropped 15 peas on the floor each night, after 8 years they would reach the tabletop.

Reasonably accurate? yes no

Other facts you would like to know before answering:

____

PROBLEM: If 15 peas fall on the floor each night for eight years, will they fill a dining room to the height of a tabletop?

Step 1: Develop a plan to solve the problem.

a. Determine how many peas would have fallen on the floor in 8 years.
b. Determine how many peas are in 1 cubic inch.
c. Determine the height of an average dining room table.
d. Determine the dimensions of the room in which the table and chairs could fit.
e. Determine the number of cubic inches in the room.
f. Based on the data above, determine the number of peas needed to fill the room up to the height of the tabletop.
g. Compare the number of peas in *a* to the number of peas in *f* to verify if the boy's estimate is reasonably accurate.

Step 2: List strengths and weaknesses of the overall plan. Mention specific problems that might occur in each step.

- What is the size of the average dining room table? How tall is it?
- What is the size of the average dining room?
- Would all the peas stack to form straight edges or would the sides be slanted as they spilled on the floor?
- Are all peas the same size?
- What is the average size of a pea?
- How many fit into a cubic inch?

Step 3: Implement the plan and/or determine the accuracy of the answers to each part of the solution.

a. To find out how many peas would have fallen in eight years, multiply 15 per night by 365 days in a year, and then multiply by 8 years: 15 x 365 = 5,475. In 8 years that would be 43,800 peas.
b. You could figure out different ways to determine the number of peas in a cubic inch. One way is to use a three-dimensional net for a cube to make a box that is 1 cubic inch, then see how many peas would fit. If you use dry peas, the number is about 75.
c. Measure several dining room tables, or look at catalogs with tables, to get an average size: $2\frac{1}{2}$ feet high, 3 feet wide, and 6 feet long.
d. Measure several dining rooms, or call a real-estate agent or builder, to get an average size: 12 feet long, 9 feet wide, and 8 feet high.
e. Since the peas are measured in a cubic inch, find the number of cubic inches in the room. One way is to convert each of the dimensions to inches: 9 feet x 12 inches = 108 inches; 12 feet x 12 inches = 144 inches; 8 feet x 12 inches = 96 inches. To calculate cubic inches, multiply length by width by height: 144 x 108 x 96 = 1,492,992 cubic inches. But the peas in the problem reach the height of the tabletop, not the ceiling. So the calculation should use the height of the table, which is $2\frac{1}{2}$ feet or 30 inches: 144 x 108 x 30 = 466,560 cubic inches, or about 500,000 cubic inches.
f. Multiply the number of peas in a cubic inch by the number of cubic inches in the room up to the height of the tabletop: 75 x 500,000 = 37,500 peas would fill the room to the table.
g. The boy's estimate was way off because only 43,800 peas would have fallen, and it would take at least 35 million peas to fill a dining room up to the tabletop.

If appropriate, ask students how the data in their solution and the approach they took compare with the information in this sample.

VERIFYING ESTIMATION PROBLEM 9: Mosquito (pages 17–18)

Reproducible Master 21: Problem 9 on Evaluating Estimates II

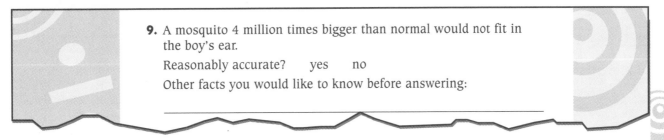

9. A mosquito 4 million times bigger than normal would not fit in the boy's ear.

Reasonably accurate? yes no

Other facts you would like to know before answering:

____

PROBLEM: Would a mosquito 4 million times bigger than normal be bigger than a boy's ear?

Step 1: Develop a plan to solve the problem.

a. Determine the length of a mosquito.
b. Determine the length of a mosquito that is 4 million times as long.
c. Determine the length of your ear.
d. Compare the answers to *b* and *c*.

Step 2: List strengths and weaknesses of the overall plan. Mention specific problems that might occur in each step.

- Which species of mosquito would be used? Could you catch them and measure them? How could you gather the data?
- What part of the ear should be measured? The whole ear? The opening in the ear?

Step 3: Implement the plan and/or determine the accuracy of the answers to each part in of the solution.

a. Suppose an average mosquito is 3 centimeters long.
b. Multiply to find the length of a mosquito that is 4 million times as long: 4,000,000 x 3 centimeters = 12,000,000 centimeters. 12,000,000 centimeters ÷ 100 = 120,000 meters. That's 120 kilometers!
c. An average *adult* ear is about 7 centimeters in length, and the opening is even smaller.
d. The boy is correct. The mosquito would not fit in his ear. A normal mosquito might fit in someone's ear, but a mosquito 4 million times as long never would!

If appropriate, ask students how the data in their solution and the approach they took compare with the information in this sample.

VERIFYING ESTIMATION PROBLEM 10: Toaster (pages 19–20)

Reproducible Master 21: Problem 10 on Evaluating Estimates II

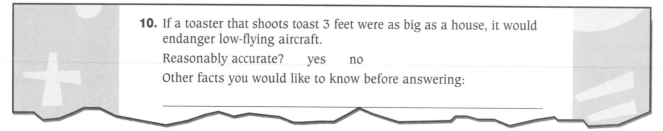

10. If a toaster that shoots toast 3 feet were as big as a house, it would endanger low-flying aircraft.

Reasonably accurate? yes no

Other facts you would like to know before answering:

____

PROBLEM: If a toaster that shoots toast 3 feet in the air were as big as a house, how high would it shoot toast? Would it shoot it as high as an airplane flies?

Step 1: Develop a plan to solve the problem.

a. Determine the height of the average toaster.
b. Determine the height of the average house.
c. Determine how many "toasters" high the house is.
d. Determine how high low-flying airplanes fly.
e. Multiply the height of the house in "toasters" by 3 to find out how high the toast would fly.
f. Compare answer *d* to answer *e*.

Step 2: List strengths and weaknesses of the overall plan. Mention specific problems that might occur in each step.

- Are all toasters about the same height?
- How could the height of the house be determined? Should the heights of the rooms be used or should measurements be taken from the ground to the peak of the highest roof?
- How do you determine how high low-flying airplanes fly? Is it when they are coming in a for a landing or flying steady?

Step 3: Implement the plan and/or determine the accuracy of the answers to each part in of the solution.

a. An average toaster is 6 inches high, or 0.5 feet.
b. A typical house is 12 feet high.
c. Two toasters are 1 foot high (2 x 0.5 feet), so if you multiply by the height of the house (12 feet), you determine the house is 24 toasters high.
d. A low-flying airplane flies at about 1,000 feet.
e. If the half-foot tall toaster shoots toast 3 feet, multiply 24 toasters by 3 feet to get the height at which a toaster the size of the house would shoot toast: 24 x 3 feet = 72 feet.
f. Low-flying airplanes fly at 1,000 feet, so 72 feet is way too low. The boy was wrong. The toast wouldn't hit low-flying aircraft.

If appropriate, ask students how the data in their solution and the approach they took compare with the information in this sample.

VERIFYING ESTIMATION PROBLEM 11: Dog Food Cans (pages 21–22)

Reproducible Master 21: Problem 11 on Evaluating Estimates II

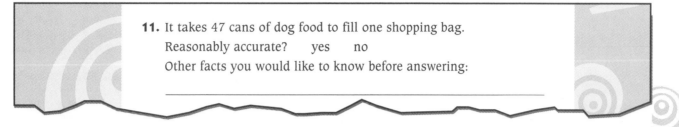

> **11.** It takes 47 cans of dog food to fill one shopping bag.
> Reasonably accurate? yes no
> Other facts you would like to know before answering:
> ____

PROBLEM: How many cans of dog food could you carry in one shopping bag?

Step 1: Develop a plan to solve the problem.

Part A: Would 47 cans of dog food be too heavy for one shopping bag?

a. Determine the average weight of one can of dog food.
b. Determine the total weight of 47 cans of dog food.
c. Determine how much weight the average shopping bag could hold before breaking.
d. Compare answer *b* to answer *c*.

Part B: Would 47 cans of dog food fit in one shopping bag?

a. Determine the dimensions of a typical shopping bag.
b. Determine how many cans could fit in one layer on the bottom of the shopping bag.
c. Determine the height of a can of dog food.
d. Determine how many layers of cans could fit in a typical shopping bag.
e. Multiply the number of cans in one layer by the number of layers.
f. Compare *e* to the boy's estimate of 47.

Step 2: List strengths and weaknesses of the overall plan. Mention specific problems that might occur in each step.

- What is an average size can of dog food?
- What brand should be used?
- What is the average size shopping bag?
- Can shopping bags made from different materials carry different amounts of weight?

Step 3: Implement the plan and/or determine the accuracy of the answers to each part of the solution.

Part A:

a. Suppose an average can of dog food weighs about 14 ounces.
b. The 47 cans of dog food would weigh 658 ounces (47 x 16 = 658). That's about 41 pounds (658 ÷ 16 = 41).
c. Suppose the average size shopping bag holds about 20 pounds.
d. It would be impossible for the average size shopping bag to hold the weight of all the dog food without breaking.

Part B:

a. A typical paper shopping bag is about 12 inches long, 7 inches wide, and 17 inches high.
b. About 8 cans could be arranged in an array to cover the bottom of the shopping bag.
c. A can of dog food is about 4 inches tall.
d. About 4 layers of cans could fit in a bag that is 17 inches tall (17 ÷ 4 = 4 R1).
e. About 32 cans could fit in a bag (8 cans/layer x 4 layers = 32 cans).
f. The boy's estimate was not reasonably accurate because the paper bag could hold only 32 cans, not 47.

If appropriate, ask students how the data in their solution and the approach they took compare with the information in this sample.

VERIFYING ESTIMATION PROBLEM 12: Jellybeans (pages 23–24)

Reproducible Master 21: Problem 12 on Evaluating Estimates II

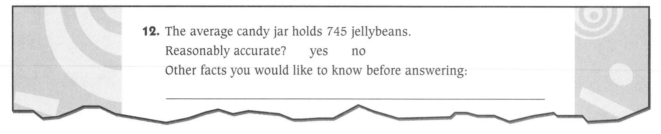

> **12.** The average candy jar holds 745 jellybeans.
> Reasonably accurate? yes no
> Other facts you would like to know before answering:
> ____

PROBLEM: How many jellybeans will fit in an average size candy jar?

Step 1: Develop a plan to solve the problem.

- **a.** Use an average size candy jar.
- **b.** Count out how many jellybeans it takes to fill a small container.
- **c.** See how many containers it takes to fill the jar.
- **d.** Multiply the number of jellybeans in the small container by the number of containers it takes to fill the jar.
- **e.** Compare answer *d* with 745.

Step 2: List strengths and weaknesses of the overall plan. Mention specific problems that might occur in each step.

- What's a candy jar? What's the size of an average size candy jar?
- Do jellybeans vary in size?
- How would the results differ if we used a different size candy jar?

Step 3: Implement the plan and/or determine the accuracy of the answers to each part of the solution.

- **a.** We used a candy jar that measures 4 inches by 4 inches at the bottom and is 7 inches tall.
- **b.** We counted jellybeans until we filled a small container. We fit 75 in the container.
- **c.** We were able to empty the small container into the candy jar 8 times.
- **d.** The candy jar holds about 600 jellybeans ($8 \times 75 = 600$).
- **e.** Our answer is less than 745, but the boy could have estimated for a larger jar.

If appropriate, ask students how the data in their solution and the approach they took compare with the information in this sample.

DEVELOPING UNDERSTANDING

After you have completed some or all of the estimation/verification activities, have the whole class discuss **Evaluating Estimates I and II**, the reproducible that the students completed as an introduction to the problem-solving activities.

Review each of their initial answers about whether the boy's estimate was reasonable. Help them articulate what a good estimate is and some of the principles they can use in making good estimates.

MATHEMATICS ASSESSMENT

Materials

Connection to Mathematics Assessment: Check for Understanding (Reproducible Master 24)

Distribute the worksheet with multiple-choice and open-ended questions called **Connection to Mathematics Assessment: Check for Understanding**.

Collect and **score** the students' work using the answers and rubric that follow.

Reproducible Master 24 with answers

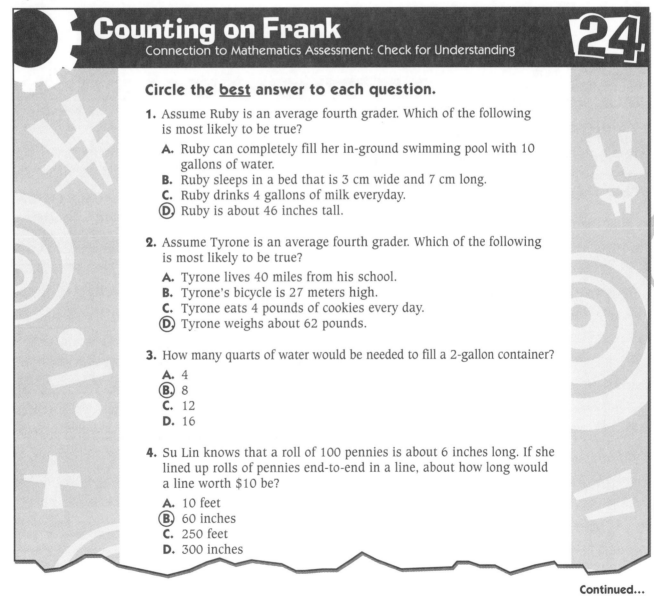

Counting on Frank

Connection to Mathematics Assessment: Check for Understanding

24

Circle the best answer to each question.

1. Assume Ruby is an average fourth grader. Which of the following is most likely to be true?
   - A. Ruby can completely fill her in-ground swimming pool with 10 gallons of water.
   - B. Ruby sleeps in a bed that is 3 cm wide and 7 cm long.
   - C. Ruby drinks 4 gallons of milk everyday.
   - (D.) Ruby is about 46 inches tall.

2. Assume Tyrone is an average fourth grader. Which of the following is most likely to be true?
   - A. Tyrone lives 40 miles from his school.
   - B. Tyrone's bicycle is 27 meters high.
   - C. Tyrone eats 4 pounds of cookies every day.
   - (D.) Tyrone weighs about 62 pounds.

3. How many quarts of water would be needed to fill a 2-gallon container?
   - A. 4
   - (B.) 8
   - C. 12
   - D. 16

4. Su Lin knows that a roll of 100 pennies is about 6 inches long. If she lined up rolls of pennies end-to-end in a line, about how long would a line worth $10 be?
   - A. 10 feet
   - (B.) 60 inches
   - C. 250 feet
   - D. 300 inches

Continued...

D. 3

5. Mark knows that a can of Good for Dog's Gourmet Dog Food weighs 8 ounces. About how much would a case of 24 cans of this dog food weigh?

A. 3 pounds
B. 6 pounds
(C.) 12 pounds
D. 18 pounds

6. Ben said that instead of mowing his lawn, he would buy 3 sheep to keep the lawn cut because they can do it faster than he can. Do you think Ben's statement is reasonable or not? Support your answer.
see rubric that follows for scoring

RUBRIC FOR SCORING
Problem 6

An effective response will need to:
- provide a reasonable explanation for any conclusion.
- provide several reasons to support the conclusion.

POINTS	CRITERIA
3	The student gives a reasonable explanation to support the conclusion that is reached. Possible response: *It does not seem reasonable. Sheep eat grass, but they probably don't eat it evenly, and it wouldn't look like a mowed lawn. Even if they did, we'd have to know how much grass they eat in a given amount of time and how big the lawn is to know how long it would take them. Then we'd have to compare that to how long it takes Ben.*
2	The student states that it is unreasonable or reasonable, but does not provide a thorough explanation of why, or one of the reasons makes no sense.
1	The student states that it is unreasonable or reasonable, but only gives one or two reasons why, or several of the reasons make no sense.
0	The student states that it is unreasonable or reasonable, but has no supporting statements or leaves the question blank.

Composition Connection

WRITING A POST-READING COMPOSITION

Materials

Connection to Writing Assessment: Post-Reading Composition (Reproducible Master 25), **Have I...? Checklist** (Reproducible Master 2), **Rubric for Scoring First Drafts** (Reproducible Master 3)

Distribute a copy of **Connection to Writing Assessment: Post-Reading Composition** to each student along with the **Have I...? Checklist**.

Allow students 25 minutes for writing and reviewing their compositions.

Collect and **score** the compositions using the **Rubric for Scoring First Drafts**. You may wish to encourage students to put their scored drafts into a folder of "works in progress" and to edit and revise it further to be shared with an audience at some later date.

Reproducible Master 25

Counting on Frank

25

Connection to Writing Assessment: Post-Reading Composition

Writing Task

Write a composition telling why you would or would not like to have this boy in your class. Use details from the book and/or examples from your own experience to support your ideas.

Be sure to use the **Have I...? Checklist** to review your work and make it the best it can be. You may finish your composition on the back of this page or on a separate sheet of paper.

Extending the Connections

THINKING ABOUT MEASUREMENT

Materials
Math journals, calculators

The following prompts may be used for class discussion or for journal entries/writing activities.

Option 1

Many times during the story the boy does not use standard units of measure to indicate the size of something. Tell why you think using a dog to measure a room is an accurate or inaccurate way to describe the size of a room. [Possible response: Using a dog to measure the size of a room is not accurate. The size of the dog would need to be accurately given, and the estimator would need to know how the dogs were to be arranged in the room. Were they in straight lines or jumbled all together? The estimator would also need to have excellent spatial sense. The answer also would be difficult to verify.]

Option 2

Many times we hear statements that are exaggerations of facts. Here is one such statement: "I have asked you a million times to clean up your room, and you still haven't done it." Do you think you were actually asked a million times to clean up your room? Why or why not? [Possible response: I was probably not told a million times to clean my room. I am 8 years old, or about 3,000 days old (8 years x 365 days/year = 2,920 days). To be told a million times, I would have to be asked to clean my room 333 times a day (1,000,000 ÷ 3,000 = 333). That's about 14 times an hour (333 times/day ÷ 24 hours = 13.85 times/hour) all day long. That's about once every 5 minutes all day long since I was born (60 minutes/hour ÷ 14 times/hour = 4.28 minutes).]

Have students give another example of exaggerations of facts and explain why it is an exaggeration, or have them make up an exaggeration and explain it.

Option 3

Why do you think standard units of measure such as inches, feet, gallons, quarts, ounces, and pounds are used? After reading this story, what must you consider when making an estimate? Use examples from the book to justify your answer. [Possible response: Without standard measures there would be no way to compare because everyone would be measuring using different size units. When making estimations, common sense and reasoning must be used.]

The Doorbell Rang

Written and illustrated by
Pat Hutchins

Overview of the Connections

In *The Doorbell Rang,* Ma made cookies for Victoria and Sam. Just as they sit down to eat the cookies, the doorbell rings and two friends arrive. Victoria and Sam figure out how to share the cookies fairly. The doorbell rings again and more children arrive, first two brothers and then six cousins. As each group arrives, Sam and Victoria say how many cookies each child will get. At the end of the story, when each child has just one cookie, the doorbell rings again. This time it's Grandma with a tray filled with more cookies!

For teaching mathematics, this story vividly illustrates the division concept of sharing fairly and provides the opportunity for powerful connections between symbolic interpretations of division and the actual meaning of division.

Through a well-sequenced set of activities that connect to the story, students investigate the relationship between the divisor and the quotient. They begin to realize that if the dividend remains constant, the quotient gets smaller as the divisor increases. The concept of sharing fairly is extended with activities that change the details in the story and invite exploration of remainders.

An optional project that involves making cookies provides opportunities for connections to estimation, following directions, and fractions.

For language arts instruction, the story offers an opportunity to study dialogue and to act out a story through dramatic reading. It engages readers and promotes active reading through the use of predictability. The illustrations add meaning to the story and are a valuable source of viewing and writing activities.

MATERIALS FOR THE CONNECTIONS

The Doorbell Rang • ISBN 0-688-05251-7
Written and illustrated by Pat Hutchins. New York: Greenwillow Books, 1986.

Language Arts

~ One or more copies of the book (Note: In the Viewing Connection, each student will need to see the picture on the cover of the book. You may wish to have several copies available.)

~ **Optional: Connection to Viewing Assessment: Writing About a Picture Prompt** (Reproducible Master 1)

~ **Have I...? Checklist** (Reproducible Master 2), a self-monitoring tool for student writers

~ **Rubric for Scoring First Drafts** (Reproducible Master 3)

~ **Connection to Listening Assessment: Listening to Part of a Story** (Reproducible Master 26)

~ **Connection to Writing Assessment: Post-Reading Composition** (Reproducible Master 31)

Mathematics

~ Slates

~ Chocolate chip and/or other type of cookies (enough for the class for the Listening Connection; 36 or more for Math Connections)

~ Opaque container to hold cookies (such as a box or bag)

~ Paper bags

~ Tablecloth

~ Trays (2)

~ Construction paper in 9-inch-by-18-inch sheets (brown for acting out the story; any color for making a tray)

~ Math journals

~ Optional: **Circles** (Reproducible Master 27)

~ Optional: **Fraction Circles** (Reproducible Master 28)

~ Scissors

Mathematics materials continued...

Mathematics materials (continued)

~ Markers

~ Nametags (alternative: index cards and paper clips)

~ **Base ten blocks or Models of Base Ten Blocks** (Reproducible Master 29)

~ Tape

~ Rulers

~ **Optional:** Cubes or tiles in 4 colors (6 of each color for each group of students)

~ **Optional:** Materials and ingredients for your favorite cookie recipe.

~ Optional materials for making flour-and-salt cookies (for each group of 2–4 students):

- Large sheet of aluminum foil
- Bowl (may be plastic or paper)
- Spoon for mixing ingredients
- Measuring spoons (tablespoon and teaspoon)
- Flour (a little more than 4 tablespoons)
- Salt (1 tablespoon plus a bit more than a teaspoon)
- Water (a plastic cupful)

~ **Connection to Mathematics Assessment: Check for Understanding** (Reproducible Master 30)

Viewing Connection

INTRODUCING THE LESSON WITH A PICTURE PROMPT AND WRITING

Materials

One or more copies of the book (cover), **Connection to Viewing Assessment: Writing About a Picture Prompt** (Reproducible Master 1), **Have I...? Checklist** (Reproducible Master 2), **Rubric for Scoring First Drafts** (Reproducible Master 3)

Show the class the picture on the cover of *The Doorbell Rang*. If possible, allow students to continue to look at the picture throughout the writing session. You may distribute a copy of **Connection to Viewing Assessment: Writing About a Picture Prompt** to each student, or they may use notebook paper for their work. Also distribute copies of the **Have I...? Checklist**.

Read these directions to the class:

"You are going to write a composition about this picture. Look at it carefully. Think about what you see and the story it may be telling. It is OK that not everyone will see the same story. If you wish to, you may do prewriting before you start your composition. When you have finished the composition, use the **Have I...? Checklist** as a guide for editing and revising what you have written."

Give the students 20–30 minutes to write their compositions and do initial editing.

Collect the compositions and score them using the **Rubric for Scoring First Drafts**. Teach students how to compare their scored compositions to the rubric and to make notes about how to improve their compositions. Students also may be taught to use the rubric to score their own work or that of other students.

Reproducible Master 1

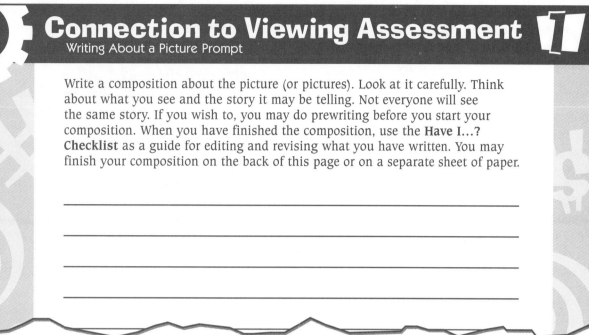

Connection to Viewing Assessment 1

Writing About a Picture Prompt

Write a composition about the picture (or pictures). Look at it carefully. Think about what you see and the story it may be telling. Not everyone will see the same story. If you wish to, you may do prewriting before you start your composition. When you have finished the composition, use the **Have I...? Checklist** as a guide for editing and revising what you have written. You may finish your composition on the back of this page or on a separate sheet of paper.

____

____

____

____

Listening Connection

LISTENING TO PART OF A STORY AND ANSWERING QUESTIONS

Materials

Copy of the book (Listening section: pages 1–11, 157 words), chocolate chip or other kind of cookies, opaque container to hold cookies (such as a box or bag), slates or scrap paper, **Connection to Listening Assessment: Listening to Part of a Story** (Reproducible Master 26)

This activity will help students develop effective listening skills. As necessary, teach or review some of the effective listening strategies found on page *xv* of this manual.

Preparation: Before class, place enough cookies for the class in an opaque bag or box so students cannot determine the contents.

Tell students that before you start reading *The Doorbell Rang* to the class, you want to play a guessing game about something in the story.

Display the box or bag. Tell students you want them to ask questions that will help them determine what is inside. The questions must be in a form that yields a *yes* or *no* answer.

To help them get started, suggest that they ask questions about the size, purpose, color, and number of items in the bag or box. You might write the words *size*, *purpose*, *color*, and *number* on the board to help keep the questions focused.

After they guess that there are cookies in the bag, don't yet show them the contents.

Have students record their favorite kind of cookies on slates or scrap paper.

Collect the data, and create an informal chart of the cookies they mention. Decide which is the class's favorite kind of cookie, based on the data.

Ask them to guess what type of cookie you placed in the bag or box. Then open the box to reveal the contents.

Give each student a cookie. Complete the listening selection as they snack.

Tell the class you are now going to read part of the story and that when you are finished, they will answer some questions about what you have read. (The rest of the story will be read in the Mathematics Connection activity.)

Read pages 1–11 of the book. The pages are unnumbered, so page references count from the first page of story text. The listening section begins on page 1 with the sentence: *"I've made some cookies for tea," said Ma.* It ends on page 11 with the sentence: *"Nobody makes cookies like Grandma," said Ma as the doorbell rang.*

Since you are working on listening, don't stop to discuss the story, show the illustrations, or make predictions as you might do in a reading instructional period.

The Doorbell Rang offers unique opportunities for listening activities. It has both dialogue and predictable repetition. It is important to read the selection dramatically.

Distribute the worksheet with multiple-choice and open-ended questions called **Connection to Listening Assessment: Listening to Part of a Story**.

Allow students 15–20 minutes for completing the worksheet.

Collect and score the students' work using the answers and rubric that follow.

Proceed to the Mathematics Connection for instructions on completing the book.

Reproducible Master 26 with answers

The Doorbell Rang

Connection to Listening Assessment: Listening to Part of a Story

26

Circle the best answer to each question.

1. Who made the cookies for tea?
   - **A.** Grandma
   - **(B.)** Ma **refers to p. 1**
   - **C.** Sam
   - **D.** Victoria

2. Which word best describes Sam, Victoria, and Ma in this story?
   - **A.** selfish
   - **B.** tired
   - **(C.)** generous
   - **D.** energetic

3. Ma tells the friends who arrive that they can *share* the cookies. What is another way to say what she means?
   - **(A.)** Everyone can have the same number of cookies.
   - **B.** Everyone can have at least one cookie.
   - **C.** Everyone can have as many cookies as they want.
   - **D.** Everyone who likes the cookies will get some of them.

Open-ended Listening Task: Tell what you think will happen next in the story and explain why. **see rubric that follows for scoring**

RUBRIC FOR SCORING
Open-ended Listening Task

An effective response will need to:
- reflect knowledge of the story.
- justify ideas from the text.
- recognize the repetitive nature of the story and use it to make a prediction.
- be clearly presented and well written.

POINTS	CRITERIA
4	The student accurately recognizes the repetitive pattern of the story and predicts the next events. Explanation is detailed, recognizing that they soon will run out of cookies. May or may not predict that someone will provide more cookies.
3	The student accurately recognizes the pattern of the story, but misses one or more significant details or provides only some details to justify reasoning. Probably does not predict that there will be more cookies.
2	The response is accurate in the main details, but sketchy and/or poorly supported. Prediction probably does not go beyond the next ringing of the doorbell.
1	The response is minimal and/or inaccurate in one or more significant points.
0	The student doesn't respond or doesn't address the task.

Mathematics Connection

INTRODUCTION AND ACTIVE READING

This story will be read several times, each time with a different emphasis and activity.

Review the section you read for the Listening Connection activity, this time showing students the illustrations and discussing what they already have heard.

In some classes, you may find it worthwhile to go back to the beginning and re-read the entire selection (pages 1–11). This is a good way to help students confirm the answers they gave in the listening activity. If necessary, explore the rationale behind some of the answers.

Read the rest of the story. Continue to point out the illustrations, make predictions, and discuss the events as you read. In this way, you model active reading and help students to internalize the practices that effective readers use to make meaning from the words on the page.

ACTING OUT THE STORY AS A CLASS

Materials

Copy of the book, tablecloth, 2 trays, 36 or more cookies, paper bag, 14 nametags (each labeled with the name or description of a character in the story). Alternative: Make name tags from index cards and secure them with paper clips.

Tell students they will be acting out the story. Talk about the props and the characters that will be needed.

Props should include a desk or table covered with a tablecloth, one tray with 12 cookies, and another tray with 24 or more cookies. Display the props in an area where everyone can see them.

Choose students to play the parts in the story by randomly drawing names from a bag. Place nametags or index cards, each labeled with a different story character, in a paper bag. There should be 14 in all, including four unnamed "cousins." Ask:

What is the probability of drawing a particular character? **[Answer: At the start, the probability of drawing any of the named characters is $\frac{1}{14}$. The probability of drawing one of the four unnamed cousins is $\frac{4}{14}$.]**

Have volunteers draw character names from the bag and attach the tags to their clothes.

Encourage students to gather in a group for the "performance" of *The Doorbell Rang*. Have the students playing Victoria, Sam, and Ma stand in front of the group near the props. Set aside the tray with 24 cookies for the student playing "Grandma" to carry in at the end of the story.

Re-read the story, stopping each time to allow new characters to enter and to observe how the cookies are being shared equally.

ACTING OUT THE STORY: Transferring to Symbols

Materials

Copy of the book. For each group of 3–4 students: paper lunch bag, brown construction paper (9-inch-by-18-inch sheet) or **Circles** (Reproducible Master 27), scissors, markers.

Arrange students in groups of 3–4, and give each group materials for making "cookies": a sheet of brown construction paper or **Circles**, scissors, and markers.

Have each group cut 12 "cookies" from the brown construction paper or reproducible. Tell students to come up with a plan to ensure that the cookies are about equal in size. Encourage them to use markers to decorate their cookies with "chocolate chips."

As the students make their cookies, you might cut some extra for use in the next activity. Each group should store its cookies in a paper lunch bag labeled with the names of the students in the group.

Implement each of the following steps as you re-read the story to the class.

1. Have groups use their sets of paper cookies to act out the sharing situations in the story as the visitors enter the house.
2. Connect each of these models to the traditional mathematical symbols for division.
3. Emphasize what the symbols on the board mean in relation to the actual cookies that are being shared among the children.

Note: If you wish, introduce alternative forms of the division format:

$12 \div 2 = 6$ $\qquad 4\overline{)12}$ with 3 above $\qquad 12 \div 6 = 2$ $\qquad 12\overline{)12}$ with 1 above

For closure, ask:

***When grandma appears with a tray of 24 cookies, how many more would each child get?* [2] *Explain how you know. Write a problem using symbols.* [24 ÷ 12]**

- ***What does 15 ÷ 5 mean?***

Conduct a class discussion emphasizing that ÷ is a symbol that is used to indicate division or equal sharing.

Write other problems on the board. Have students "picture" what the problems would look like in terms of sharing cookies.

DEVELOPING THE CONCEPT OF REMAINDERS

Materials

Copy of the book; paper cookies from the previous activity, plus some extra for each group; scissors. Optional: **Fraction Circles** (Reproducible Master 28)

Adapt the situations in *The Doorbell Rang* so that they involve a remainder. Do this by changing the number of people who visit so that 12 whole cookies cannot be shared fairly.

Have groups of students model the new problems with 12 paper cookies. You might distribute one or more copies of **Fraction Circles** to help them more easily cut the cookies into parts.

EXAMPLE

Change the situation on page 4 of the story by adding more people at the door. For example: *It was Tom, Hannah, and Kendra from next door.* Then ask:

***How could Sam and Victoria share the cookies fairly with their three friends?* [Answer: $12 \div 5 = 2$ R2 or $2\frac{2}{5}$]**

Students may approach the problem in different ways. Some might distribute 2 cookies to each student, and set the remaining 2 aside. Or, they might cut each of the remaining 2 cookies into five pieces and distribute them fairly.

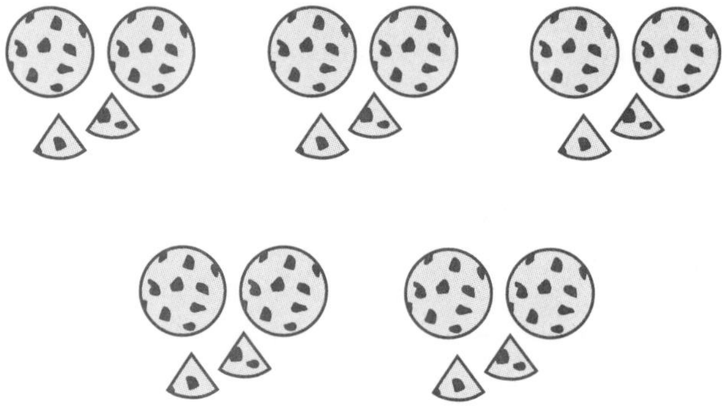

Before proceeding with subsequent problems, have students set aside any cut up cookies and start again with 12 whole ones.

MATHEMATICS ASSESSMENT

Materials

Connection to Mathematics Assessment: Check for Understanding (Reproducible Master 30). Optional: Base ten blocks or **Models of Base Ten Blocks** (Reproducible Master 29)

Distribute the worksheet with multiple-choice and open-ended questions called **Connection to Mathematics Assessment: Check for Understanding.** You might wish to distribute base ten blocks or models to represent the $100 bills, $10 bills, and $1 bills for Problem 6.

Collect and score the students' work using the answers and rubric that follow.

Reproducible Master 30 with answers

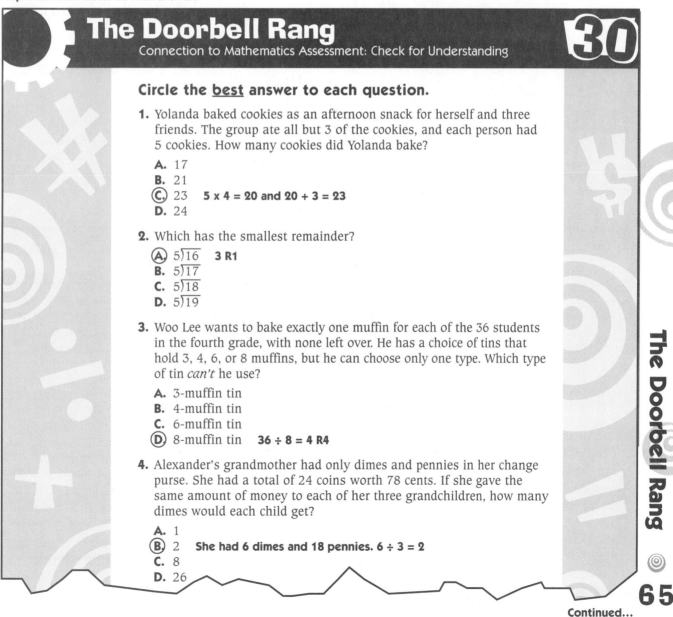

The Doorbell Rang

Connection to Mathematics Assessment: Check for Understanding

30

Circle the best answer to each question.

1. Yolanda baked cookies as an afternoon snack for herself and three friends. The group ate all but 3 of the cookies, and each person had 5 cookies. How many cookies did Yolanda bake?

   A. 17
   B. 21
   (C.) 23 **5 x 4 = 20 and 20 + 3 = 23**
   D. 24

2. Which has the smallest remainder?

   (A.) $5\overline{)16}$ **3 R1**
   B. $5\overline{)17}$
   C. $5\overline{)18}$
   D. $5\overline{)19}$

3. Woo Lee wants to bake exactly one muffin for each of the 36 students in the fourth grade, with none left over. He has a choice of tins that hold 3, 4, 6, or 8 muffins, but he can choose only one type. Which type of tin *can't* he use?

   A. 3-muffin tin
   B. 4-muffin tin
   C. 6-muffin tin
   (D.) 8-muffin tin **36 ÷ 8 = 4 R4**

4. Alexander's grandmother had only dimes and pennies in her change purse. She had a total of 24 coins worth 78 cents. If she gave the same amount of money to each of her three grandchildren, how many dimes would each child get?

   A. 1
   (B.) 2 **She had 6 dimes and 18 pennies. 6 ÷ 3 = 2**
   C. 8
   D. 26

Continued...

5. Sarah made 36 chocolate chip cookies and 12 oatmeal cookies. Her 6 friends shared the cookies equally. How many cookies did each friend get?

   A. 2
   B. 6
   (C.) 8 **48 ÷ 6 = 8**
   D. 48

6. Four people shared $648 fairly. The total consisted of $100 bills, $10 bills, and $1 bills. Each person received the least number of bills possible. How many $100, $10, and $1 bills did each person receive? Give the solution and explain how you determined the answer.
   see the following rubric for scoring

RUBRIC FOR SCORING

Problem 6

An effective response will need to:

- give the correct answer of one $100 bill, six $10 bills, and two $1 bills.
- explains how the answer was reached.

POINTS	CRITERIA
3	The student gives the correct answer and explains, if necessary, the concept of exchanging two $100 bills for twenty $10 bills so the money can be shared fairly. Or, the student gets the correct answer by dividing algorithmically and explains why 162 yields one $100 bill, six $10 bills and two $1 bills. Suggested responses: *Each person will get one $100, six $10 bills, and two $1 bills. If there are six $100 bills to start with, after each person gets one $100 bill, only two are left, so they can't be given out. You can exchange them for twenty $10 bills and combine those with the four $10 bills already there. Each person then gets six $10 bills. There are eight $1 bills, so each person gets two of them.* OR *I divided 648 by 4. That equals 162 so each person would have one $100, six $10 bills, and two $1 bills.*
2	The student provides the correct number of bills for each person, but the explanation is not clear. Or, the student has the incorrect answer for 648 divided by 4, but provides a correct explanation of how many $100 bills, $10 bills, and $1 bills each person would receive based on the answer provided.
1	The student divides 648 by 4 and gives the correct answer of 162, but does not explain how many $100 bills, $10 bills, and $1 bills each person would receive. Or, the student calculates the wrong amount each person would receive and has an explanation that has flaws and/or is unclear.
0	The student divides 648 by 4 incorrectly and provides no explanation for the distribution of the money. Or, the student shows no understanding of the concept of division or sharing fairly or leaves the answer blank.

Composition Connection

WRITING A POST-READING COMPOSITION

Materials

Connection to Writing Assessment: Post-Reading Composition (Reproducible Master 31), **Have I...? Checklist** (Reproducible Master 2), **Rubric for Scoring First Drafts** (Reproducible Master 3)

The following writing activity will help students internalize the literary theme of sharing.

Distribute a copy of **Connection to Writing Assessment: Post-Reading Composition** to each student along with the **Have I...? Checklist.**

Allow students 25 minutes for writing and reviewing their compositions.

Collect and **score** the compositions using the **Rubric for Scoring First Drafts.**

You may wish to encourage students to put the scored drafts into a folder of "works in progress" and to edit and revise them further so they can be shared with an audience at some later date.

Reproducible Master 31

The Doorbell Rang 31

Connection to Writing Assessment: Post-Reading Composition

Writing Task

Think of a time when you had to share something, but you didn't want to. Write about what happened and tell how you felt. Tell why you think you were right or wrong in not wanting to share.

Be sure to use the **Have I...? Checklist** to review your composition and make it the best it can be. You may finish your composition on the back of this page or on a separate sheet of paper.

____

____

____

Extending the Connections

CONNECTING WORDS TO ILLUSTRATIONS

Materials
One or more copies of the book

Review the story, this time focusing on the illustrations. Have students look for details. They might notice:

- the pattern of the tablecloth. (checkered)
- the pattern of the floor. (squares)
- facial expressions. (The children look happy at the beginning, but as more children arrive they look less so.)
- the fact that Ma is cleaning the floor, and more people show up, there are more footprints.
- the fact that Ma starts taking the children's sweaters and coats, and then the collection in the corner of the kitchen grows to include bikes, baby carriages, etc.

Ask them to think about what the illustrations add to the story.

This activity will give you an opportunity to discuss the importance of details in adding interest to a story or composition.

Remind students of this activity when they are revising compositions. Discuss how they can create "word pictures" in their writing to help their readers "see" what they are saying.

As an optional writing activity, you can have the class work in groups to write descriptions of the illustrations on pages 16–17 or 18–19, when the doorbell rings for the last time. Have the groups compare their compositions and talk about what they described and what they left out.

DRAMATIC READING

Materials
One or more copies of the book

This is an ideal story to have the students read parts as they would in a play and to act out the story. Assign parts to students in advance of the reading.

Parts include the narrator, Ma, Victoria, Sam, Tom, Hannah, Peter, and others. (The narrator will read the lines that are not quotes, such as: *It was Tom and Hannah from next door.*) You may want a device to serve as the doorbell, or assign a student to make the sound.

The "actors" will need to be taught about cues and to avoid reading the speaker tags, such as: *..., said Ma.*

It will be important for students to practice reading their parts until they are comfortable with them, but they should not have to memorize their lines.

Allow the students to study the illustrations in preparation for the dramatic reading.

JOURNAL ENTRY

Materials
Journals

In the following writing activity, students are asked to do some fairly sophisticated analysis, and they will need time to think about the answer and explore their reasoning. It is important that they not be under a lot of pressure for a grade or score, particularly in the early drafting stages. Later, you might encourage students to go back to this journal entry and revise it. Then it could be prepared to submit for evaluation.

Have students write a journal entry that responds to the following prompt, or a variation that addresses the ways you shared the story with the class:

> At first, the class heard just part of the story and concentrated on listening. Then, the class used props to follow along and act out the math concepts. Another time, the class looked at the illustrations while the story was read. Finally, class members acted out the roles of characters in the story. How were these experiences different, and which one did you like best? Why did you like it?

CREATING A TRAY

Materials

Construction paper (9-inch-by-18-inch sheets), scissors, tape, rulers, math journals

Have students use construction paper, rulers, and tape to make cookie trays. The diagram below indicates one method, in which students cut out the corners of the paper, fold up the sides, and tape the corners.

This activity helps students develop an understanding of what happens when a 2-dimensional object is turned into a 3-dimensional one.

Have them complete a journal entry describing how they made the tray.

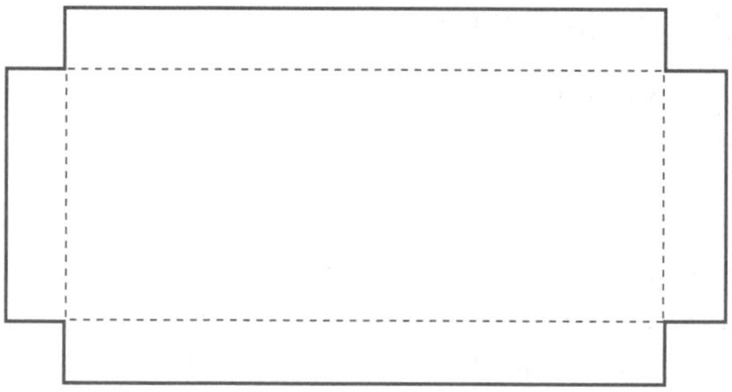

AVERAGES

Materials

Chocolate chip cookies

Conduct a sampling of chocolate chip cookies to determine the average number of chips in each cookie. Based on the average, predict how many chips will be in the next 3–4 cookies. Then take apart 3–4 new cookies and see if the prediction is accurate.

COMBINATIONS AND ARRANGEMENTS

Materials

cubes or tiles in 4 colors (6 of each color for each group)

Have students find all the ways that one oatmeal cookie, one chocolate chip cookie, one peanut butter cookie, and one sugar cookie can be arranged in a row. Allow them to use cubes or tiles to help determine the answer. (Forming some type of pattern helps. Pattern recognition is an important skill.)

O = Oatmeal, C = Chocolate Chip,
P = Peanut Butter, S = Sugar

OCPS	COPS	PSOC	SPOC
OCSP	COSP	PSCO	SPCO
OPCS	CPSO	POCS	SOPC
OPSC	CPOS	POSC	SOCP
OSCP	CSOP	PCSO	SCPO
OSPC	CSPO	PCOS	SCOP

PROJECT: Making Flour-and-Salt Cookies

Materials

For each group of 2–4 students: large sheet of aluminum foil, bowl (may be plastic or paper), spoon for mixing ingredients, measuring spoons (tablespoon and teaspoon), flour (a little more than 4 tablespoons), salt (1 tablespoon plus a bit more than a teaspoon), water (a plastic cupful)

These cookies are made from a flour and salt recipe. They are not meant to be eaten.

Give students these instructions for making cookie dough:

> Mix 4 tablespoons of all-purpose flour with 1 tablespoon and 1 teaspoon of salt. Then add 1 tablespoon and 2 teaspoons of water. Knead the dough until it can be easily worked with the hands. Place the dough on a piece of aluminum foil. Divide it as evenly as possible to make 12 individual cookies.

Observe how students divide their dough. Some will divide the quantity in half and in half again so there are four equal sets. Then they will divide each of the four pieces into three equal parts. A few will divide the quantity into three parts and then each of the three parts into fourths.

Have students make predictions.

What will happen to the cookies as they bake?

- ***Will they get larger or smaller?***
- ***How else might they change?***

Bake cookies in an oven at 300°F for 45 minutes. They can be decorated with paints and saved for other activities.

CLOSURE

Have students write a journal entry responding to the following prompt. Encourage them to give conceptual or concrete interpretations of the problem.

Explain to someone who doesn't understand division how to find the answer to $3\overline{)18}$. [Possible answers: Take 18 cookies and 3 plates and put one cookie at a time on the plates until they are all gone or until they cannot be shared fairly. Or, skip count by 3s and keep track of how many numbers it takes to get to 18.]

ADDITIONAL RESOURCES

Windows on Math, Volume 4 Videodisc, Unit 1, "Lemma's Dilemma." Atlanta: Optical Data Corporation, 1996. Call 1-800-524-2481.

Windows on Math, Volume 4 Videodisc, Unit 1, "Manny Makes Muffins." Atlanta: Optical Data Corporation, 1996. Call 1-800-524-2481.

Lawrence, Paul. *ESPA*^{3} *Mathematics: Daily Activities for Math Success, Book 5, Base-Ten Block Month*. Iowa City, Iowa: Tutor Tools, Inc., 1998. Call 1-800-776-3454. ISBN 0-7836-1758-5

Gator Pie

Written by **Louise Mathews**
Illustrated by **Jeni Bassett**

Overview of the Connections

This story is about two alligators, Alice and Alvin, who find a pie and decide to split it into two equal parts. When a third alligator shows up, they decide to share the pie equally by dividing it into thirds. More and more alligators arrive, eventually leading Alice and Alvin to divide the pie into 100 pieces. Before the pie gets eaten, Alvin cleverly says a few words that make it possible for him to share the pie with Alice alone.

As the pie is cut into smaller and smaller slices, the story provides a mathematically powerful lesson. Students gain a deeper understanding of the meaning of denominators and the comparison and ordering of fractions. When the pie is cut into hundredths, the story offers the opportunity to relate and compare fractions and decimal equivalencies. The exploration of equivalencies is extended through hands-on activities. Students create polygons with construction paper and 100-square grids or 11-x-11-pin geoboards to verify common fraction and decimal equivalencies. The concepts are extended further through connections to coordinates and calculators.

In teaching language arts, the book provides opportunities for enhancing skills in viewing, writing on demand, and listening. Students gain practice writing a friendly letter. They also study vocabulary, the use of descriptive language, and revision as part of the writing process and then apply them to development of their own writing.

MATERIALS FOR THE CONNECTIONS

Gator Pie • ISBN 0-7608-0005-7
Written by Louise Mathews. Illustrated by Jeni Bassett. Littleton, MA: Sundance Publishing, 1995.

Language Arts

~ One or more copies of the book (Note: In the Viewing Connection, each student will need to see the cover of the book. You may wish to have several copies available.)

~ Optional: **Connection to Viewing Assessment: Writing About a Picture Prompt** (Reproducible Master 1)

~ **Have I...? Checklist** (Reproducible Master 2), a self-monitoring tool for student writers

~ **Rubric for Scoring First Drafts** (Reproducible Master 3)

~ **Connection to Listening Assessment: Listening to Part of a Story** (Reproducible Master 32)

~ **Connection to Writing Assessment: Post-Reading Composition** (Reproducible Master 36)

Mathematics

~ Math journals

~ Slates or index cards

~ Overhead projector

~ Transparencies of circles or rectangles

~ 11-x-11-pin geoboards and geobands for every 1–2 students. Alternative: **Hundredths Grid** (Reproducible Master 33)

~ Construction paper in various colors cut into 6-inch-by-6 inch squares to match the dimensions of the geoboards and hundredths grids

~ Scissors

~ Calculators

~ **Connection to Mathematics Assessment: Check for Understanding I and II** (Reproducible Masters 34–35)

Viewing Connection

INTRODUCING THE LESSON WITH A PICTURE PROMPT AND WRITING

Materials

One or more copies of the book (front cover), Have I...? Checklist (Reproducible Master 2), **Rubric for Scoring First Drafts** (Reproducible Master 3), **Connection to Viewing Assessment: Writing About a Picture Prompt** (Reproducible Master 1)

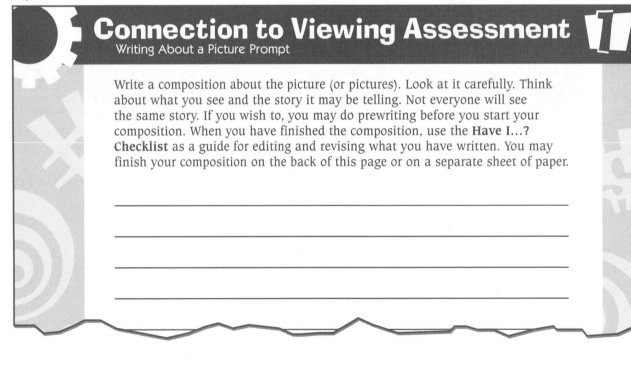

Show the class the picture on the cover of *Gator Pie*. If possible, allow students to continue to look at the picture throughout the writing session. You may distribute a copy of **Connection to Viewing Assessment: Writing About a Picture Prompt** to each student, or they may use notebook paper for their work. Also distribute copies of the **Have I...? Checklist**.

Read these directions to the class:

"You are going to write a composition about this picture. Look at it carefully. Think about what you see and the story it may be telling. It is OK that not everyone will see the same story. If you wish to, you may do prewriting before you start your composition. When you have finished the composition, use the **Have I...? Checklist** as a guide for editing and revising what you have written."

Give the students 20–30 minutes to write their compositions and do initial editing.

Collect and score the students' compositions using the **Rubric for Scoring First Drafts**. Teach students how to compare their scored composition to the rubric and to make notes about how to improve their compositions. Students may also be taught to use the rubric to score their own work or that of other students.

Reproducible Master 1

Connection to Viewing Assessment 1

Writing About a Picture Prompt

Write a composition about the picture (or pictures). Look at it carefully. Think about what you see and the story it may be telling. Not everyone will see the same story. If you wish to, you may do prewriting before you start your composition. When you have finished the composition, use the **Have I...? Checklist** as a guide for editing and revising what you have written. You may finish your composition on the back of this page or on a separate sheet of paper.

Listening Connection

LISTENING TO PART OF A STORY AND ANSWERING QUESTIONS

Materials

Copy of the book (Listening section: pages 1–23, about 440 words), **Connection to Listening Assessment: Listening to Part of a Story** (Reproducible Master 32)

This activity will help students develop effective listening skills. As necessary, teach or review some of the effective listening strategies found on page *xv* of this manual.

Tell the students you are going to read them part of a story that features two alligators named Alice and Alvin. When you are finished, they will answer some questions about what you have read. (The rest of the story will be read in the Mathematics Connection activity.)

Read pages 1–23 aloud to the students. The pages are not numbered. Count the first page of text, opposite the copyright page, as page 1. The listening section begins on page 1 with the sentence: *This is Alvin and this is Alice.* It concludes on page 23 with the sentence: *But Alvin winked at her.*

Since you are working on listening, don't stop to discuss the story, show the illustrations, or make predictions as you might do in a reading instructional period.

It is important to read the story with effective oral expression, especially since the class will not be seeing the book's illustrations during the listening section and students will be asked to infer the emotions and attitudes of characters in the story.

Distribute the worksheet with multiple-choice and open-ended questions called **Connection to Listening Assessment: Listening to Part of a Story**.

Allow 15–20 minutes for students to complete the worksheet.

Collect and score the students' work using the answers and rubric that follow.

Proceed to the Mathematics Connection for instructions on completing the book.

Reproducible Master 32 with answers

Gator Pie

Connection to Listening Assessment: Listening to Part of a Story

32

Circle the best answer to each question.

1. When four gators show up, they are "swaggering like gangsters," and they talk with a sneer. Based on the story, which statement best describes them? **refers to p. 10**

A. These gators haven't eaten in a long time and are hungry.
B. These gators are good friends of Alvin and Alice.
(C.) These gators are scary and perhaps dangerous characters.
D. These gators are polite and wait to be invited to eat.

2. How does Alice seem to feel as new alligators show up and demand pie?

(A.) Alice is frightened by the way they act and look.
B. Alice is frustrated that she can't just cut and serve the pie.
C. Alice is glad to have visitors and is happy to entertain them.
D. Alice is afraid they will run away with the whole pie.

3. Which statement best describes the way that Alice and Alvin try to divide up the pie when each new group arrives?

A. They want to keep the biggest part of the pie for themselves.
B. They decide to keep none of the pie for themselves.
C. They don't know what to do as each new alligator arrives.
(D.) They always want to give everyone a fair share.

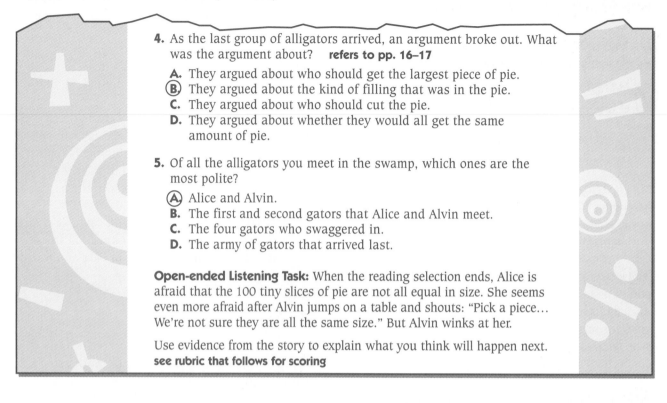

4. As the last group of alligators arrived, an argument broke out. What was the argument about? **refers to pp. 16–17**

   A. They argued about who should get the largest piece of pie.
   (B.) They argued about the kind of filling that was in the pie.
   C. They argued about who should cut the pie.
   D. They argued about whether they would all get the same amount of pie.

5. Of all the alligators you meet in the swamp, which ones are the most polite?

   (A.) Alice and Alvin.
   B. The first and second gators that Alice and Alvin meet.
   C. The four gators who swaggered in.
   D. The army of gators that arrived last.

Open-ended Listening Task: When the reading selection ends, Alice is afraid that the 100 tiny slices of pie are not all equal in size. She seems even more afraid after Alvin jumps on a table and shouts: "Pick a piece… We're not sure they are all the same size." But Alvin winks at her.

Use evidence from the story to explain what you think will happen next.
see rubric that follows for scoring

RUBRIC FOR SCORING

Open-ended Listening Task

An effective response will need to:

- reflect knowledge of the story.
- justify ideas from the text.
- identify a logical result of Alvin's actions.
- recognize Alvin's growing dissatisfaction as each new group of alligators arrives.
- recognize the qualities in the alligators that would lead them to fight.

POINTS	CRITERIA
4	Answer is logical and takes into account Alvin's ongoing reaction as new gators arrive, as well as Alvin's understanding of the combative nature of the gators. Alvin is seen as a problem solver who chooses a different way to solve the problem than Alice would. Response is well-written in terms of content and organization.
3	Answer is logical and recognizes most, if not all, of the content elements present in a 4-point response, but it may lack elements of effective writing. Or, the response may be well-written, but miss major points—such as a failure to recognize why Alvin signals Alice with a wink.
2	Response is either poorly written or misses several significant elements of the content. The answer may focus on Alice or the other alligators more than on Alvin and his ability to deal with a difficult situation in a creative way.
1	The response is sketchy and poorly written. It misses the main points or merely retells the prompt or the story. It lacks insight and linguistic control.
0	Answer is incorrect or student does not respond to the task.

Mathematics Connection

INTRODUCTION AND ACTIVE READING: Graphing Survey Results

Materials
Copy of the book, slates or index cards

When students have finished the listening activity, conduct a class survey, as described in the activity below, then finish reading the story to the class.

Remind the class that in the first part of *Gator Pie*, the alligators wonder what kind of pie they have found. Tell the class that before you finish reading the story to them, you want to find out what the class's favorite pie is.

Have students record their favorite pies on slates or index cards. Collect the data and make a bar graph or picture graph to represent it. Discuss the data and ask questions similar to the following:

About what part or portion of the class likes apple pie best?

- ***Which pie is the class favorite? Which pie or pies are liked by about half the class? How do you know?***
- ***Which pie or pies are liked by about a quarter of the class? How do you know?***

Re-read the section of the story you already read and complete the book, this time showing the illustrations as you read. Ask students to compare their mental pictures of the story to the author's and illustrator's.

FORMING FRACTIONS: Equal parts

Materials
Math journals; overhead projector and transparencies of circles or rectangles

Have the class to write a journal entry responding to the following question:

Why was Alice so worried about having equal parts? **[Answer: Because she wanted to make sure each alligator got a fair share. If they didn't, they might argue.]**

Model the difference between cutting the pie into two parts and cutting the pie into halves by showing a rectangle or circle on the overhead projector, dividing it into two unequal parts, and discussing the fairness of sharing the pieces. Then demonstrate halves as two equal parts.

Model the same concept by making four parts into fourths and three parts into thirds.

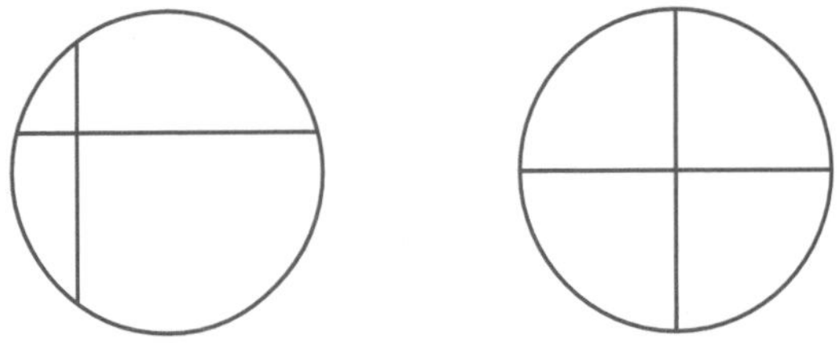

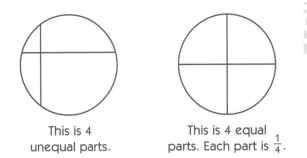

This is 4 unequal parts.

This is 4 equal parts. Each part is $\frac{1}{4}$.

Connect each of the problems you have done to symbols by writing $\frac{1}{2}$, $\frac{1}{3}$, and $\frac{1}{4}$ on the board. Also have students think of the story to visualize the fractions that are being investigated.

Introduce the meaning of the denominator by asking students what they think the bottom number in a fraction means.

Through questions and answers, establish that the denominator tells how many equal parts the whole is to be divided into.

Ask students to describe what $\frac{1}{5}$, $\frac{1}{8}$, $\frac{1}{10}$, $\frac{1}{30}$, $\frac{1}{50}$, or $\frac{1}{100}$ would look like.

Have students make a journal entry responding to the following questions:

Why do the fractional parts of any whole have to be equal parts? **[Answer: So the parts are shared fairly.]**

- ***What does the denominator tell us about forming fractions?*** **[Answer: It tells us how many equal parts are in the whole.]**

COMPARING FRACTIONS

Discuss the following questions with the class:

Why were Alice and Alvin so concerned when there were three of them altogether, then four altogether, and then eight altogether? **[Answer: The pieces were getting smaller and smaller.]**

- ***Based on the book and other experiences you have had, how do you know that $\frac{1}{49}$ is larger than $\frac{1}{50}$?*** **[Answer: Because each of the 49 pieces would be larger than each of the 50 pieces.]**

Each day have students answer similar questions using different denominators.

MODELING HUNDREDTHS

Materials

Math journals; 11-x-11-pin geoboards and geobands (for every 1–2 students). Alternative: **Hundredths Grid** (Reproducible Master 33)

Distribute the geoboards and geobands or copies of **Hundredths Grid** and have students make a journal entry responding to the following:

"Think of this square as your favorite cake. Show and then explain what part of the 'cake' each alligator would get if 100 alligators were to share it." [Students should indicate one of the squares on the model.]

To continue developing an understanding of the symbolism of each of the small squares representing $\frac{1}{100}$, ask the class to use geobands or to draw rectangles or figures that are $\frac{3}{100}$, $\frac{5}{100}$, $\frac{9}{100}$, $\frac{13}{100}$, etc., of the area of the board or grid.

Eventually have the class only visualize—without using the grid or other device—what $\frac{7}{100}$ or $\frac{12}{100}$ or $\frac{78}{100}$ would look like.

Write pairs of fractions on the chalkboard and have the class compare the size of the fractions by indicating whether the fraction on the left is larger or smaller than the fraction on the right.

Connect these problems to the story by letting the children visualize the pieces of pie that are being named.

Establish the meaning of numerator and denominator by having students respond to the following questions:

What does the fraction $\frac{31}{100}$ mean to you?

- ***What does the 31 tell us in the fraction $\frac{31}{100}$?*** **[Answer: 31 of 100 equal parts]**
- ***What does the 100 tell us in the fraction $\frac{31}{100}$?*** **[Answer: The whole is divided in 100 equal parts.]**
- ***What does the numerator of any fraction always mean?*** **[Answer: how many of the whole]**
- ***What does the denominator of any fraction always mean?*** **[Answer: how many equal parts this whole is divided into]**

DECIMAL NOTATION

Materials

11-x-11-pin geoboards and geobands (for every 1–2 students). Alternative: **Hundredths Grid** (Reproducible Master 33)

Establish the concept that fractions can also be written as decimals by discussing how there can be two or more ways to show the same thing.

You might ask the students if they always wear the same clothes to school each day. Even though they are the same person they can look very different depending on whether they are playing, are in school, or are eating lunch. Tell them that fractions work the same way.

Show $\frac{25}{100}$ on the geoboard or grid. Tell students that another way to show exactly the same fraction is to write it in decimal form as 0.25.

Tell them that 0.25 is read as *twenty-five hundredths*. Show other examples to make the point, such as $\frac{3}{100}$ and 0.03; $\frac{9}{100}$ and 0.09.

Once the class understands the concept, present decimals and have students show you various hundredths on the geoboard or grid.

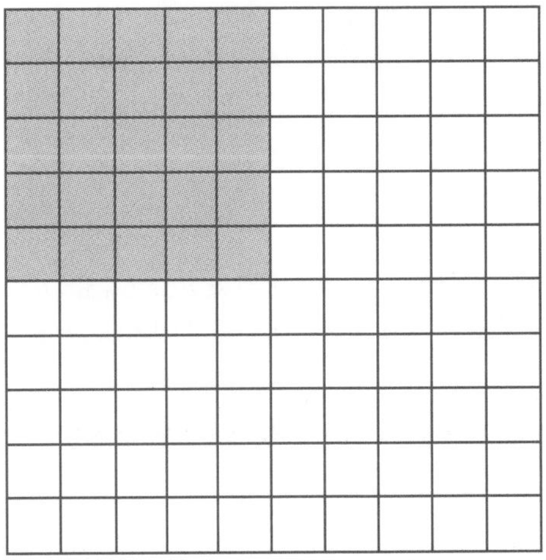

The shaded area is $\frac{25}{100}$ or 0.25.

DECIMAL AND FRACTION EQUIVALENCE

Materials

11-x-11-pin geoboards and bands (for every 1–2 students), construction paper in various colors cut to the same dimensions as geoboards (6-inch-by-6-inch squares), scissors, math journals. Alternative to geoboards: **Hundredths Grid** (Reproducible Master 33)

After discussing the answer, distribute 11-x-11-pin geoboards or copies of the grid. Also distribute square pieces of construction paper that are the same size as the boards or grid you will be using. Have students imagine that the square pieces of paper are cakes.

Discuss why the geoboards and grids can be described as hundredths models.

Have students fold the paper in half and cut the paper so they have two halves of the square.

Tell students to place the papers on top of their grids or geoboards. Discuss how the two halves cover the entire geoboard or grid.

Have them lift one of the halves and count the number of hundredths under it. Then have them replace that half and lift the other half and count the number of hundredths under it.

Through discussion, establish that $\frac{50}{100} = \frac{1}{2} = 0.50$.

To check for understanding, have students respond to the following journal prompt:

Why did Alice and Alvin each get 50 slices of pie when the two of them shared the pie equally? **[Answer: Because Alice already had cut the pie into 100 pieces and each of them had half.]**

Tell the students that they are going to complete an experiment that will help them see what would happen if more than two alligators had to share 100 pieces of cake.

By building on the foundation of the boards and construction paper, ask the students to use geoboards and bands, or to draw on their grids, what $\frac{25}{100}$ of the cake would look like. Ask:

How many $\frac{25}{100}$ could be made on the board if none of the parts overlapped? **[4]**

- ***If there were 4 alligators, what part of this cake would each of them get?*** **[Answer: $\frac{1}{4}$ or $\frac{25}{100}$ or 0.25 of the cake.]**

To confirm their answers, distribute additional square pieces of construction paper that are the same size as the geoboard or grid.

Have the students fold the paper into quarters and form fourths by cutting it. Have them place each fourth on top of the geoboard or grid so they can see that $\frac{1}{4} = \frac{25}{100}$, which equals 0.25.

Have students work in pairs or small groups to determine other fractional names for $\frac{20}{100}$. They do this by making as many non-overlapping rectangles as possible, each with an area that is $\frac{20}{100}$ of the board or grid.

When they have finished, have students count the number of rectangles formed. [Answer: There are 5 congruent rectangles, which means that $\frac{20}{100}$ has divided the board into fifths so $\frac{1}{5} = \frac{20}{100} = 0.20$.]

Continue this type of experiment for $\frac{10}{100}$, $\frac{5}{100}$, and $\frac{4}{100}$.

(See Extending the Connections exercises on p. 84 to establish $\frac{1}{3} = 0.33$ and $\frac{1}{8} = 0.125$.)

MAKING CONNECTIONS TO SYMBOLS

Materials

Hundredths models, such as 11-x-11-pin geoboards with bands or **Hundredths Grid** (Reproducible Master 33)

Each day, complete a series of problems that lets you assess student understanding. Write a fraction and a decimal on the board and have students verify whether they are equal to, less than, or greater than each other.

For example, write $\frac{1}{4}$ and 0.08 on the board. Have students place a >, <, or = sign between the numbers to show how they compare. Have students use a model to show why they are correct.

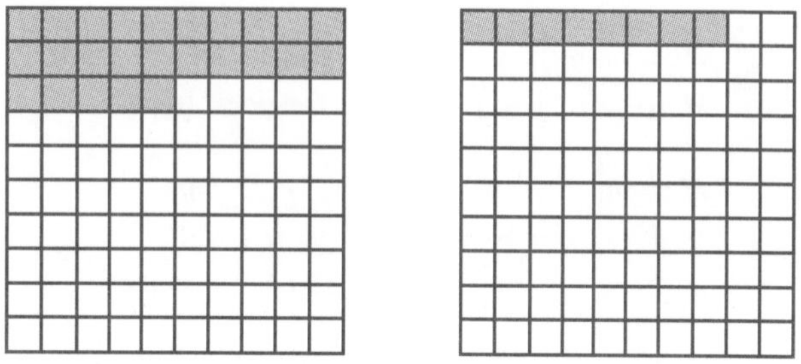

$\frac{1}{4} > 0.08$ because $\frac{1}{4} = 0.25 = \frac{25}{100}$ and $0.08 = \frac{8}{100}$.

SHOW WHAT YOU KNOW ABOUT FRACTIONS AND DECIMALS

Use the following questions as writing/discussion prompts to assess students' conceptual understanding of fractions and fraction-decimal equivalencies.

Bonita bought a 10-inch pizza and a 9-inch pizza to feed 16 children at a party. Bonita planned to give each child a slice of pizza, so she divided each of the pies into eighths. Bonita's friend Bruno realized without even looking at the pizzas that not everyone would get the same amount of pizza. Explain how Bruno knew this.

[Answer: Bruno knew that because each pie was a different size, the eighths would be different. He knew that $\frac{1}{8}$ of the 10-inch pie would be bigger than $\frac{1}{8}$ of the 9-inch pie.]

Megan and Sean's mother made two 9-inch chocolate marshmallow pies. She cut one pie into quarters and the other pie into fifths. If Megan ate $\frac{1}{4}$ and Sean ate $\frac{1}{5}$, who had the most chocolate marshmallow pie? Explain how you know.

[Answer: Megan had more pie because $\frac{1}{4}$ is larger than $\frac{1}{5}$.]

- ***Gail made a Tennessee-Style Swamp-Mud Pie. Ginny ate $\frac{1}{2}$ the pie and Lindsay ate 0.47 of the pie. Determine who ate the most pie and explain how you know you are correct.*** **[Answer: Ginny ate the most pie because $\frac{1}{2} = \frac{50}{100}$ and $0.47 = \frac{47}{100}$. $\frac{50}{100}$ is greater.]**

- ***How much pie was left over when Ginny and Lindsay each took their slices?*** **[Answer: If each of the pieces were shown on a hundredth grid, there would be 3 squares left over, which is the same as $\frac{3}{100}$ or 0.03 of the pie.]**

COORDINATES

Materials

11-x-11-pin geoboards and bands (for every 1–2 students). Alternative: **Hundredths Grid** (Reproducible Master 33)

If students are using the **Hundredths Grid**, have them label both the vertical and horizontal axes by numbering each from 0–10, starting with 0 in the bottom left corner.

Have students build rectangles and other figures to show $\frac{4}{100}$, $\frac{8}{100}$, etc., on their geoboards or grids. For each figure that they build, have them give the coordinates of the vertices. The following examples illustrate different techniques for relating decimals, area, and coordinates.

EXAMPLE 1

Tell students to show a rectangle that is $\frac{5}{100}$ of the board or grid.

Are all the rectangles each student made congruent? **[Answer: Yes]** ***How do you know?*** **[Answer: Because they are all the same size and the same shape.]**

Are they all in the same location on the boards? **[Answer: No.]**

- ***What decimal describes the area of your rectangle?*** **[Answer: 0.05]**

Have students use coordinates to describe the location of their rectangles.

Extend these problems by giving similar fractions. When the numerators are larger than 10, use *figure* or *polygon* instead of *rectangle* to describe what you want them to build. That is because some of the areas cannot be made as rectangles ($\frac{11}{100}$, for example). Keep in mind that polygons with the same area are not necessarily congruent.

EXAMPLE 2

Tell students to show a figure that is 0.16 of the board or grid.

Are the figures made by every student congruent? **[Answer: Probably not. Even though they are the same size, they might not be the same shape.]**

Take this opportunity to promote discussion about the meaning of congruence. Then ask:

Are the figures in same location on the boards? **[Answer: Probably not.]**

Have students give the coordinates of the vertices in their figures. Tell them to provide the coordinates in clockwise or counterclockwise order so someone else could make the exact same figure in the same location.

EXAMPLE 3

Tell students to show a rectangle whose vertices have the following coordinates: (4,1), (4,7), (5,7), and (5,1).

Are all the rectangles on the board congruent? **[Answer: Yes. They are all the same size and the same shape.]**

- ***Are they all in the same location on the board?*** **[Answer: Yes, because they have the same coordinates.]**

- ***What part of the board is the area of this rectangle?*** **[Answer: $\frac{6}{100}$ or 0.06]**

MATHEMATICS ASSESSMENT

Materials

Connection to Mathematics Assessment: Check for Understanding I and II (Reproducible Masters 34–35)

Distribute the multiple-choice and open-ended questions called **Connection to Mathematics Assessment: Check for Understanding I and II.** Use this activity to check students' understanding of the mathematics concepts covered in this lesson.

Collect and score the students' work using the answers and rubric that follow.

Gator Pie

Connection to Mathematics Assessment: Check for Understanding I

34

Circle the best answer to each question.

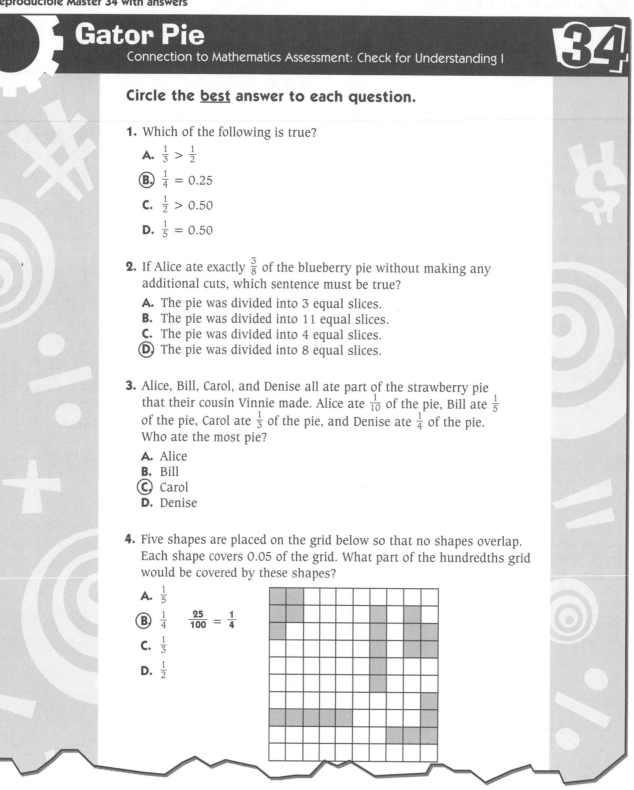

1. Which of the following is true?

A. $\frac{1}{3} > \frac{1}{2}$

(B.) $\frac{1}{4} = 0.25$

C. $\frac{1}{2} > 0.50$

D. $\frac{1}{5} = 0.50$

2. If Alice ate exactly $\frac{3}{8}$ of the blueberry pie without making any additional cuts, which sentence must be true?

A. The pie was divided into 3 equal slices.
B. The pie was divided into 11 equal slices.
C. The pie was divided into 4 equal slices.
(D.) The pie was divided into 8 equal slices.

3. Alice, Bill, Carol, and Denise all ate part of the strawberry pie that their cousin Vinnie made. Alice ate $\frac{1}{10}$ of the pie, Bill ate $\frac{1}{5}$ of the pie, Carol ate $\frac{1}{3}$ of the pie, and Denise ate $\frac{1}{4}$ of the pie. Who ate the most pie?

A. Alice
B. Bill
(C.) Carol
D. Denise

4. Five shapes are placed on the grid below so that no shapes overlap. Each shape covers 0.05 of the grid. What part of the hundredths grid would be covered by these shapes?

A. $\frac{1}{5}$

(B.) $\frac{1}{4}$ $\quad \frac{25}{100} = \frac{1}{4}$

C. $\frac{1}{3}$

D. $\frac{1}{2}$

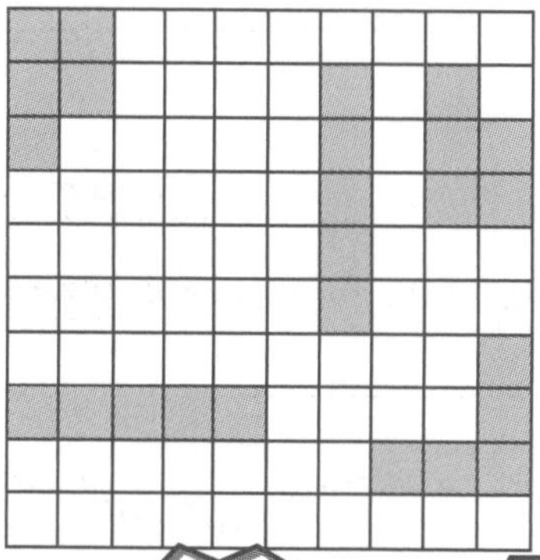

Gator Pie

Connection to Mathematics Assessment: Check for Understanding II

35

5. Mr. Adam's fourth grade class calculated that 0.50 of the class liked oatmeal cookies best. Based on this information, which statement is the most accurate?

   A. $\frac{1}{3}$ of the students voted for oatmeal cookies as their favorite.

   B. $\frac{1}{4}$ of the students voted for oatmeal cookies as their favorite.

   (C.) $\frac{1}{2}$ of the students voted for oatmeal cookies as their favorite.

   D. The majority of the class liked oatmeal cookies.

6. Draw a shape on the grid below that has an area that is $\frac{1}{5}$ of the grid and explain how you know you are correct. Tell the name of the shape. Then give the coordinates of its vertices so that a friend could form the same figure by connecting the vertices in the order that you give them.

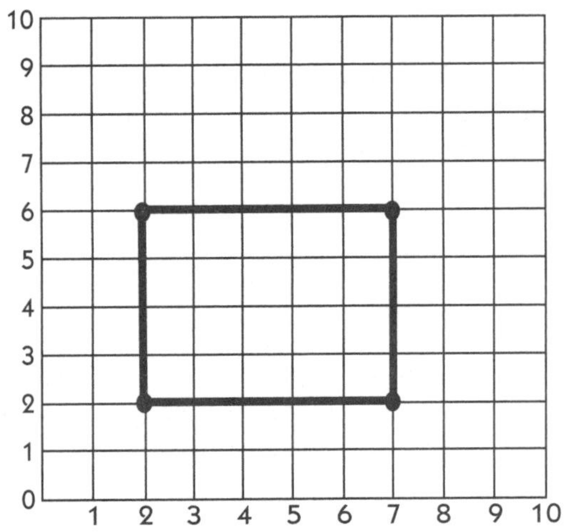

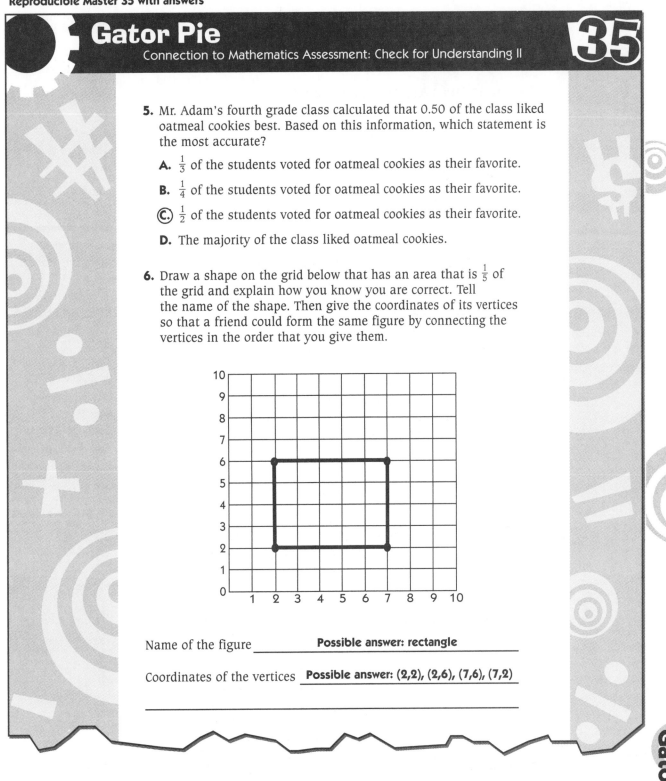

Name of the figure **Possible answer: rectangle**

Coordinates of the vertices **Possible answer: (2,2), (2,6), (7,6), (7,2)**

RUBRIC FOR SCORING
Problem 6

An effective response will need to:

- show any figure whose area is 20 squares and verify that 20 squares on a 100-square grid is $\frac{1}{5}$.
- correctly name the figure drawn.
- correctly list coordinates.

POINTS	CRITERIA
3	The student draws a figure whose area is 0.20, correctly names the figure drawn, and correctly lists the coordinates of its vertices so that they will yield the figure if connected in the order given. The student also clearly and logically explains how he or she knows that the figure is $\frac{1}{5}$ of the grid, such as: *The area of the figure I drew is 20 squares, which is $\frac{20}{100}$ of the grid. $\frac{20}{100}$ is the same as $\frac{1}{5}$.* *I drew a rectangle with the coordinates (2,2), (2,6), (7,6), and (7,2).*
2	The student addresses 2 of the 3 criteria correctly and has minor errors in one of the answers. For example, the student names the coordinates out of order or names the figure incorrectly or fails to verify why $\frac{1}{5}$ of the grid is 20 squares.
1	The student answers 1 of the 3 criteria correctly or with minor error and leaves out or incorrectly answers the other parts of the problem.
0	The students answers all three parts incorrectly or indicates no understanding of any of the parts of the question or leaves the question blank.

Composition Connection

WRITING A POST-READING COMPOSITION

Materials

Connection to Writing Assessment: Post-Reading Composition (Reproducible Master 36), **Have I...? Checklist** (Reproducible Master 2), **Rubric for Scoring First Drafts** (Reproducible Master 3)

Use the composition activity described below as a summary/closure activity for the book.

Distribute a copy of **Connection to Writing Assessment: Post-Reading Composition** to each student along with the **Have I...? Checklist**.

Allow students 25 minutes for writing and reviewing their letters.

Collect and score the students' work using the answers and rubric that follow.

You also may encourage students to put the scored drafts into a folder of "works in progress" and to further revise and edit it so it can be shared with an audience at a later date.

Reproducible Master 36

Gator Pie

Connection to Writing Assessment: Post-Reading Composition

36

Writing Task

Pretend that you are Alice. Write a letter to your mother that describes what happened when you and your friend Alvin found a pie in the swamp. Use details from the story and from your experience to make the story real. Remember to use the style of a friendly letter.

Be sure to use the **Have I...? Checklist** to review your letter and make it the best it can be. You may finish your composition on the back of this page or on a separate sheet of paper.

Extending the Connections

ESTABLISHING THIRDS AND EIGHTHS AS HUNDREDTHS

Materials

11-x-11-pin geoboards (for every 1–2 students), construction paper in various colors cut to the same dimensions as geoboards (6-inch-by-6-inch squares), scissors. Alternative to geoboards: **Hundredths Grid** (Reproducible Master 33)

Distribute a geoboard or grid and two squares of construction paper to each student or pair of students.

Have students fold and then cut the square into thirds then have them place the thirds on top of the board or grid.

Discuss how the three thirds cover the entire geoboard or grid.

Have them lift one of the thirds and count the number of hundredths under it. Have them do the same for each of the other thirds.

Through discussion, establish that each piece of paper is equal to $33\frac{1}{3}$ hundredths of the board and that it's estimated decimal value is written as 0.33.

Use a similar method to establish eighths as hundredths.

Have students fold and then cut the other construction paper square into eighths, then have them place the eighths on top of the board or grid.

Discuss how the eight eighths cover the entire geoboard or grid.

Have them lift each of the eighths in turn and count the number of hundredths under it.

Through discussion, establish that the paper is equal to $12\frac{1}{2}$ hundredths of the board and that it's estimated decimal value is written as 0.125.

CALCULATOR APPLICATIONS

Materials

Calculators, **Hundredths Grid** (Reproducible Master 33)

After the experiments with geoboards and construction paper, connections can be made to calculators that have "fraction/decimal" buttons.

Ask the class to visualize what each of the following fractions would look like on a geoboard or grid: $\frac{1}{4}$, $\frac{1}{2}$, $\frac{1}{5}$, $\frac{1}{10}$, $\frac{1}{20}$, and $\frac{1}{25}$. Establish the equivalent decimal for each one.

During this process have the students enter each of the fractions into a calculator using the / key and press the F/D key to see what happens.

After finishing these examples, enter $\frac{1}{25}$ and press F/D. Ask students to explain what the display 0.04 means. [Answer: It means that $\frac{1}{25} = 0.04$.]

Have students enter fractions such as $\frac{3}{4}$, $\frac{7}{20}$, and $\frac{4}{5}$ and have them use models to explain why the decimal displays of their fractions are correct.

Ask students to respond to the following prompt, without using their own calculators:

> Sally entered $\frac{45}{60}$ in her calculator. When she pressed the F/D button, the calculator displayed 0.75. Explain what this must mean. [Possible response: This must mean that $\frac{45}{60}$ is about the same as $\frac{75}{100}$.]

MODELING ADDITION OF DECIMALS

Materials

11-x-11-pin geoboards and bands (for every 1–2 students). Alternative: **Hundredths Grid** (Reproducible Master 33)

Have students create non-overlapping rectangles equal to 0.05, 0.03, and 0.01 of a grid or geoboard. Ask:

What part of the board would be covered if all the rectangles were placed together? **[Answer: 0.09 or $\frac{9}{100}$]**

Pose similar problems with rectangles of different sizes, such as 0.10, 0.05, and 0.24.

Connect these models to symbolic interpretations. For example, have them write the problems above as:

0.04 + 0.01 + 0.11 = ?   0.10 + 0.05 + 0.24 = ?

VOCABULARY

Materials

Copy of the book or one for each writing group

The story *Gator Pie* offers a rich opportunity to help students expand their vocabulary and to see how new words can be used in their writing. They may also notice that a word can be used in many ways. Informally, they can discern that a word can be used as different parts of speech, but a discussion of language instruction is not a necessary part of the lesson.

Re-read the entire story, asking students to note specific words that they find interesting.

As you read, create a chart of new words, classifying them by the "kinds" of words they are.

The chart below provides examples of how you might classify words, but it is preferable for the class to agree on its own categories.

Discuss each word and write it in the appropriate category on the chart without inflections (e.g., verb endings such as *-ed* and *-ing*, initial capital letters). Removing the inflections allows students to learn the word in its base form without tense or case.

Help students see that some words might function in other ways. For example:

- ***How is*** **sputter** ***a "walking" word?*** **[Possible response: The alligators sputter as they walk out of the swamp.]** ***Could it also be a "saying" word?*** **[Possible response: Yes, because it also means spitting while you talk.]**
- ***Where else might*** **squeak** ***go on the chart if it had been used differently in the story?*** **[Answer: describing word]**

Discuss how many of the "saying" words and "moving" words could also be "acting" words. This discussion will help students develop a knowledge base for learning more vivid ways to write phrases, such as "he said..." or "he went... ."

Students also should develop a sense of the fine distinctions in some of the words. For example, how are *mutter* and *murmur* different? Which is stronger, *sigh* or *groan*?

If you teach more traditional terms for parts of speech, you may choose to use these words in addition to the labels suggested above.

Acting Words	Walking or Moving Words	Describing Words	Saying Words (Speaker Tags)
slap	stomp	nasty	mutter
wink	slither	sneer	murmur
nudge	swagger	warty	grumble
snarl	splash	clickety-clack	gasp
chomp	sputter		sigh
	flash		groan
	skitter		squeak
			snarl
			growl

INSTRUCTION IN REVISION

To promote effective revision strategies and to give students an opportunity to process and use the vivid words in the previous chart, have them select a draft composition from their "works in progress" folder—or the writing task from the Composition Connection—and revise it by substituting some of the words from the chart for words they had already used. Have them explain to their writing group or to the class why they chose to use the word and how its use changes or enhances the meaning of the selection.

ADDITIONAL RESOURCES

Windows on Math, Volume 3, Unit 7 Videodisc, "Fraction Action." Atlanta: Optical Data Corporation, 1996. Call 1-800-524-2481.

Windows on Math, Volume 3, Unit 7 Videodisc, "Morning Swamp: Squeeze Me, I'm Fresh!" Atlanta: Optical Data Corporation, 1996. Call 1-800-524-2481.

Lawrence, Paul. *ESPA^3 Mathematics, Daily Activities for Math Success, Book 7, Penny, Dime, and Dollar Month*. Iowa City, Iowa: Tutor Tools Inc., 1998. Call 1-800-776-3454.

Lawrence, Paul. *ESPA^3 Mathematics, Daily Activities for Math Success, Book 8, Geoboard Month*. Iowa City, Iowa: Tutor Tools Inc., 1998. Call 1-800-776-3454.

Grandfather Tang's Story

Written by **Ann Tompert**
Illustrated by **Robert Andrew Parker**

Overview of the Connections

This book is about a grandfather who uses tangram shapes to tell a story to his granddaughter. The story he tells is about "fox fairies," mythical characters from Chinese folklore. These foxes have magical powers , enabling them to change their shapes into the forms of other creatures, and often getting them into mischief. As Grandfather Tang tells the story, he uses seven tangram shapes to illustrate the foxes and the creatures they become.

For mathematics instruction, this lesson leads students into an investigation of the geometric concepts of area, perimeter, congruency, and similarity. By making and reconstructing their own tangram squares, students use discovery to develop a conceptual understanding of fractions and decimals, as well as the addition and subtraction of common fractions. The instruction may be extended to include coordinates and three-dimensional tangram shapes.

Language arts concepts that can be taught using this book include fable and frame story, as well as development of character. There are rich examples of dialogue through which students can develop an understanding of the appropriate of punctuation. By viewing and analyzing the various illustrations, students gain experience interpreting visual text and using symbols.

MATERIALS FOR THE CONNECTIONS

Grandfather Tang's Story • ISBN 0-517-57487-X
Written by Ann Tompert. Illustrated by Robert Andrew Parker. New York: Crown Publishers, Inc., 1990.

Language Arts

~ One or more copies of the book (Note: In the Viewing Connection, each student will need to see pages 21–22. You may wish to have several copies available.)

~ **Optional: Connection to Viewing Assessment: Writing About a Picture Prompt** (Reproducible Master 1)

~ **Have I...? Checklist** (Reproducible Master 2), a self-monitoring tool for student writers

~ **Rubric for Scoring First Drafts** (Reproducible Master 3)

~ **Connection to Listening Assessment: Listening to Part of a Story** (Reproducible Master 37)

~ **Connection to Writing Assessment: Post-Reading Composition** (Reproducible Master 40)

Mathematics

~ Plastic tangram shapes (one set for each student)

~ **Optional:** overhead tangram shapes

~ Optional: **Paper Tangram Set** (Reproducible Master 38)

~ Construction paper (various colors; one 6-inch-by-6-inch square for each student)

~ **Optional:** scissors

~ 11-x-11-pin geoboards and geobands or coordinate grid paper

~ Math journals

~ **Connection to Mathematics Assessment: Check for Understanding** (Reproducible Master 39)

~ Centimeter rulers

Viewing Connection

INTRODUCING THE LESSON WITH A PICTURE PROMPT AND WRITING

Materials

Copy of the book (pages 22–23), **Connection to Viewing Assessment: Writing About a Picture Prompt** (Reproducible Master 1), **Have I...? Checklist** (Reproducible Master 2), **Rubric for Scoring First Drafts** (Reproducible Master 3)

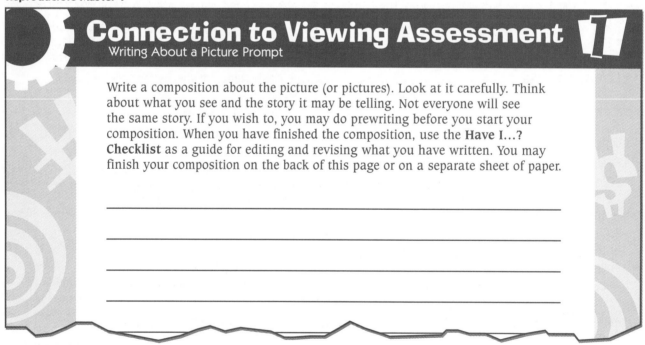

Show the class the picture on pages 22–23 of the book with the text covered. Pages are not numbered, so consider the first page of the story's text as page 1. This is a double-page spread showing a hunter on the left, a lion in the center, and an injured goose on the right. If possible, allow students to continue to look at the picture throughout the writing session. You may distribute a copy of **Connection to Viewing Assessment: Writing About a Picture Prompt** to each student, or they may use notebook paper for their work. Also distribute copies of the **Have I...? Checklist**.

Read these directions to the class:

"You are going to write a composition about this picture. Look at it carefully. Think about what you see and the story it may be telling. It is OK that not everyone will see the same story. If you wish to, you may do prewriting before you start your composition. When you have finished the composition, use the **Have I...? Checklist** as a guide for editing and revising what you have written."

Give the students 20–30 minutes to write their compositions and do initial editing.

Collect and score the student's compositions using the **Rubric for Scoring First Drafts**. Teach students how to compare their scored compositions to the rubric and to make notes about how to improve their compositions. Students may also be taught to use the rubric to score their own work or that of other students.

Reproducible Master 1

Connection to Viewing Assessment 1

Writing About a Picture Prompt

Write a composition about the picture (or pictures). Look at it carefully. Think about what you see and the story it may be telling. Not everyone will see the same story. If you wish to, you may do prewriting before you start your composition. When you have finished the composition, use the **Have I...? Checklist** as a guide for editing and revising what you have written. You may finish your composition on the back of this page or on a separate sheet of paper.

____

____

____

____

Listening Connection

LISTENING TO PART OF A STORY AND ANSWERING QUESTIONS

Materials

Copy of the book (Listening section: pages 2–6, 390 words), **Connection to Listening Assessment: Listening to Part of a Story** (Reproducible Master 37)

This activity will help students develop effective listening skills. As necessary, teach or review some of the effective listening strategies found on page *xv* of this manual.

Tell the class you are going to read them part of a story. When you are finished, they will answer some questions about what you have read. (The rest of the story will be read in the Mathematics Connection activity.)

Read pages 2–6 to the students. The listening section starts with the rabbit tangram and the phrase: *Although Chou and Wu Ling were best friends, they were always trying to outdo each other.* It ends with the hawk tangram and the phrase: *Round and round Chou circled the willow tree until he spied Wu Ling.*

Since you are working on listening, don't stop to discuss the story, show the illustrations, or make predictions as you might do in a reading instructional period.

Distribute the worksheet with multiple-choice and open-ended questions called **Connection to Listening Assessment: Listening to Part of a Story**.

Allow students 15–20 minutes for completing the worksheet.

Collect and score the students' work using the answers and rubric that follow.

Proceed to the Mathematics Connection for instructions on completing the book.

Reproducible Master 37 with answers

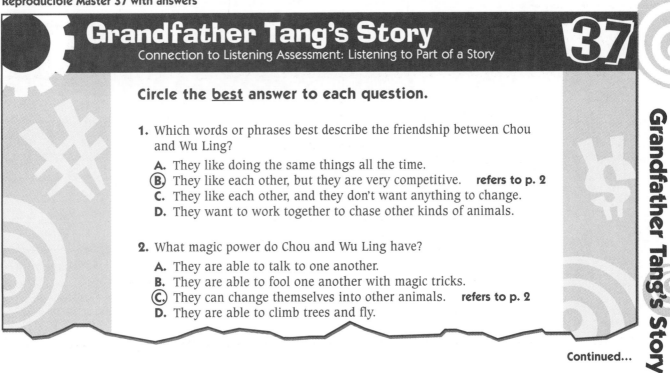

Grandfather Tang's Story

37

Connection to Listening Assessment: Listening to Part of a Story

Circle the best answer to each question.

1. Which words or phrases best describe the friendship between Chou and Wu Ling?
   - **A.** They like doing the same things all the time.
   - **(B.)** They like each other, but they are very competitive. **refers to p. 2**
   - **C.** They like each other, and they don't want anything to change.
   - **D.** They want to work together to chase other kinds of animals.

2. What magic power do Chou and Wu Ling have?
   - **A.** They are able to talk to one another.
   - **B.** They are able to fool one another with magic tricks.
   - **(C.)** They can change themselves into other animals. **refers to p. 2**
   - **D.** They are able to climb trees and fly.

Continued...

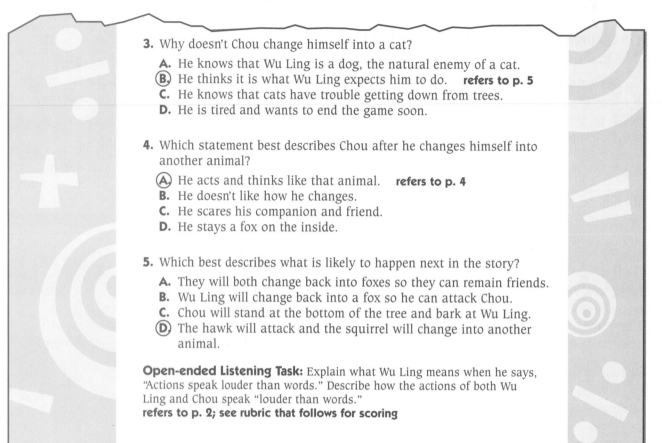

3. Why doesn't Chou change himself into a cat?

- **A.** He knows that Wu Ling is a dog, the natural enemy of a cat.
- **(B)** He thinks it is what Wu Ling expects him to do. **refers to p. 5**
- **C.** He knows that cats have trouble getting down from trees.
- **D.** He is tired and wants to end the game soon.

4. Which statement best describes Chou after he changes himself into another animal?

- **(A)** He acts and thinks like that animal. **refers to p. 4**
- **B.** He doesn't like how he changes.
- **C.** He scares his companion and friend.
- **D.** He stays a fox on the inside.

5. Which best describes what is likely to happen next in the story?

- **A.** They will both change back into foxes so they can remain friends.
- **B.** Wu Ling will change back into a fox so he can attack Chou.
- **C.** Chou will stand at the bottom of the tree and bark at Wu Ling.
- **(D)** The hawk will attack and the squirrel will change into another animal.

Open-ended Listening Task: Explain what Wu Ling means when he says, "Actions speak louder than words." Describe how the actions of both Wu Ling and Chou speak "louder than words."
refers to p. 2; see rubric that follows for scoring

RUBRIC FOR SCORING
Open-ended Listening Task

An effective response will need to:
- reflect knowledge of the story.
- justify ideas from the text.
- interpret figurative language.
- be well written with a clear presentation.

POINTS	CRITERIA
4	Correctly defines the figurative language and gives accurate and appropriate examples from the selection. Ideas are clearly expressed.
3	Correctly defines the figurative language and gives a minimal example.
2	Either correctly defines the figurative language or gives one or more good examples, but not both.
1	Gives an incorrect definition of the figurative language with examples that are not relevant.
0	Response is off the point or nonexistent.

Mathematics Connection

INTRODUCTION AND ACTIVE READING

Materials

Copy of the book, two sets of plastic tangrams or **Paper Tangram Set** (Reproducible Master 38), overhead tangrams (optional)

Before reading the entire story, you may wish to discuss the origins of tangrams to provide some background. Tell students that today we have televisions, radios, computers, and video games to entertain us. However, long before those inventions people spent their leisure time reading and telling stories. Sometimes storytellers illustrated their stories with puppets, drawings, and even geometric shapes called tangrams.

A tangram is made up of seven geometric shapes that form a square. The shapes that make up a tangram are 2 large, 1 medium, and 2 small isosceles right triangles; 1 square; and 1 parallelogram. These shapes can be rearranged in different ways to create many different figures. You may want to show the seven shapes to the class and demonstrate by making the foxes on page 1 of the story.

Tell students that after the story they will make these seven shapes from construction paper and use them to form their own tangram squares. They will also use the shapes to study fractions, congruency (figures of the same shape and size), and similarity.

Read the entire story to the class. Be sure to show and discuss the illustrations on each page. Use the tangrams to make each animal shape as it occurs in the story. Or, you might have volunteers come to the front and form the animal shapes for you. Encourage students to make predictions and discuss what is happening, thus creating an active reading environment.

DEVELOPING UNDERSTANDING: Making the Tangram Shapes

Materials

Construction paper (various colors; one 6-inch-by-6-inch square for each student), scissors (optional)

Distribute a 6-inch-by-6-inch square of colored construction paper to each student. Discuss the characteristics that make the figure a square. Mention that a square is a quadrilateral; it has four equal sides, four vertices (corners), and four right angles.

Create the tangram shapes as a class. For each step, model the procedure first, then have students follow suit. Be sure students have made the correct shapes before moving on to each subsequent step. After each step, have the students "mess up" the figures and reconstruct the square. (Several examples of this technique are shown.)

Step 1: Create two large right triangles.
Fold the square along one of its diagonals. To make the paper easier to tear, fold it back and forth along the original fold line several times. Tear or cut carefully along the fold.

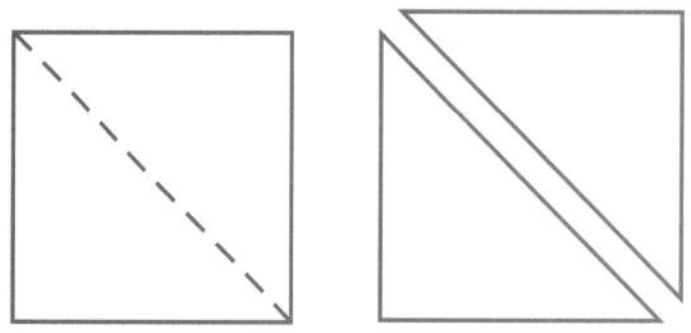

After the two triangles are formed, discuss the characteristics of the triangles. Point out that the right angles mean these are *right triangles*. Rotate the triangles so students realize that right triangles can be in many positions. Establish that these right triangles are *isosceles right triangles* because two of the sides have equal measures.

You also might point out the *hypotenuse* and *legs* of the triangles, as well as the *acute* angles. Have them arrange the triangles to form the original square.

Step 2: Create two medium right triangles.
Select one of the large right triangles made in the Step 1. Find the acute angles (or base angles) and fold the triangle so the vertices (corners) of the acute angles overlay each other. Form a crease down the center of the triangle. Fold it back and forth along the original fold line several times. Tear or cut carefully along the fold.

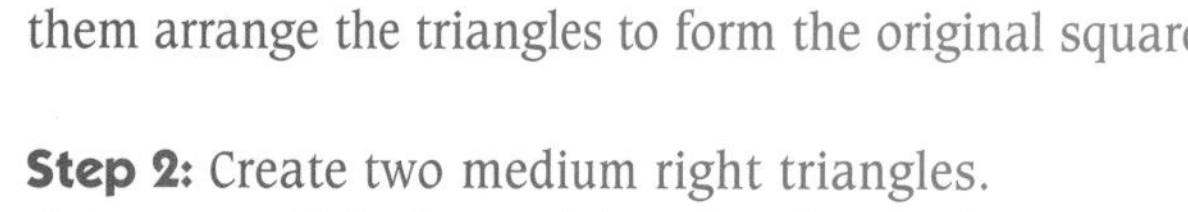

Discuss the characteristics of these right triangles. Point out the congruency between the two and their *similarity* to the remaining larger right triangle. Have the students reconstruct the original square using these three triangles.

Step 3: Create a triangle and a trapezoid.
Create a triangle and a trapezoid from the remaining large right triangle. Bend the triangle so the vertices (corners) of the two acute angles are on top of each other just as you did in the previous step. This time, <u>do not</u> make a fold along the entire length; simply crimp the bottom to mark the midpoint of the side (hypotenuse).

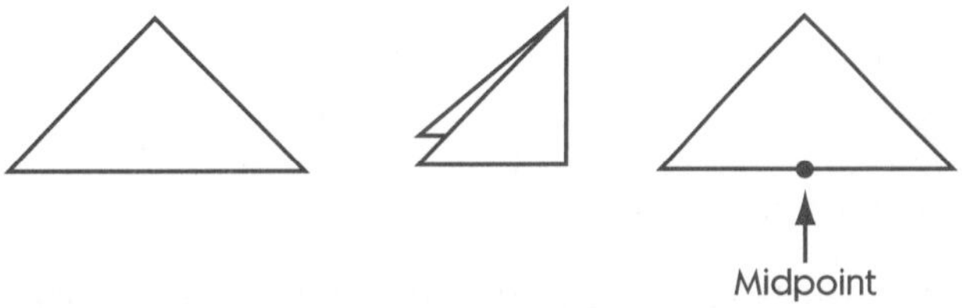

With the triangle open, fold the vertex (corner) of the right angle down so that it meets the midpoint mark on the opposite side. Make a crease so that it forms a trapezoid and a smaller triangle. Fold it back and forth along the original fold line several times. Tear or cut carefully along the fold, separating the trapezoid and smaller triangle.

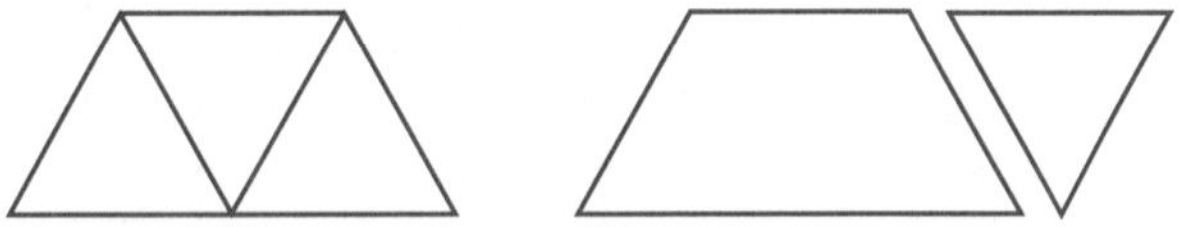

Discuss the characteristics of the trapezoid. Point out that it is a quadrilateral, but that it is special because it has exactly one pair of parallel sides. You might mention that this is an isosceles trapezoid because the measures of its two non-parallel sides are equal.

Have students "mess up" the four existing pieces and then reconstruct the original square.

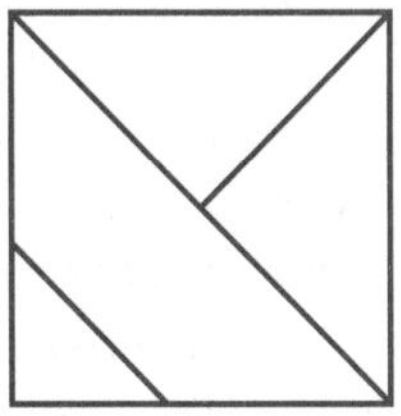

Step 4: Create two right trapezoids.
Select the trapezoid from Step 3 and fold it so the vertices (corners) of the base angles (acute) overlay each other. Crease the paper so there is a *line of symmetry* between the two halves of the trapezoid. Fold it back and forth along the original fold line several times. Tear or cut carefully along the fold forming two smaller right trapezoids.

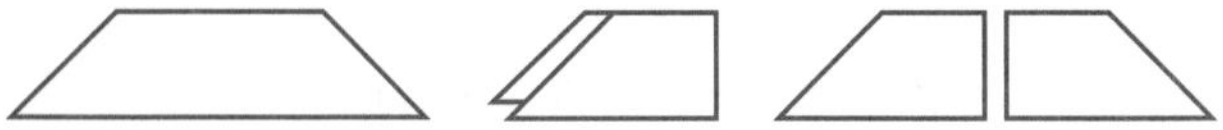

Discuss the characteristics of these two trapezoids. Ask:

Are they congruent? [Answer: Yes.]

- **_What makes them trapezoids?_ [Answer: They are quadrilaterals with exactly one pair of parallel sides.]**
- **_Are they isosceles trapezoids?_ [Answer: No, they are right trapezoids.]**
- **_Why are they right trapezoids?_ [Answer: They contain right angles.]**

Step 5: Create a square and a small triangle.
Select one of the right trapezoids made in Step 4. Fold the figure so the vertex of the acute angle touches the vertex of the *adjacent* right angle. This will form a triangle and a square. Crease and tear the figures apart.

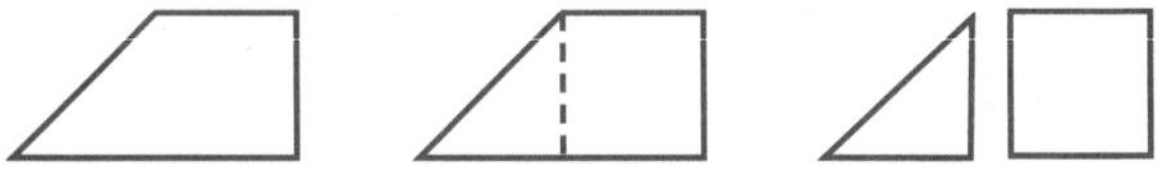

Discuss the characteristics of the two new shapes. Ask:

Why is this a square? [Answer: It is a quadrilateral that has four right angles and four equal sides.]

- **_Why is this a triangle?_ [Answer: It has three sides.]**
- **_Is it congruent or similar to any of the other right triangles we have made?_ [Answer: Yes, it is similar.]**

Have students "mess up" the six existing pieces and then reconstruct the original square.

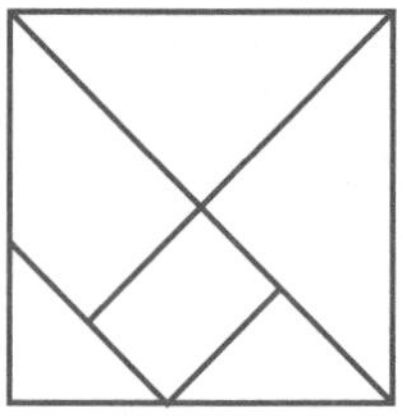

Step 6: Create a triangle and a parallelogram. Select the other right trapezoid made in Step 4. Fold it so the vertex of the *obtuse* angle overlays the vertex of the right angle diagonally opposite it. When the crease is made, a triangle and a parallelogram are formed. Tear or cut the figure to create the two new shapes.

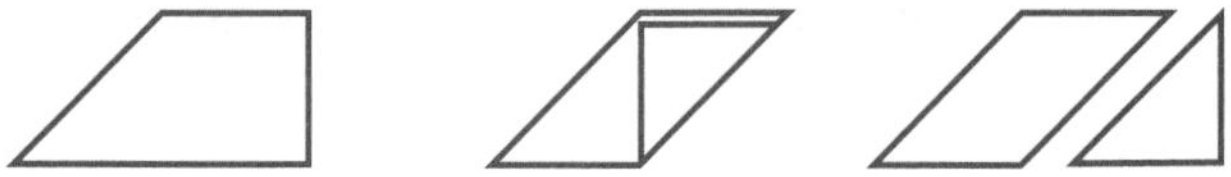

Discuss the attributes of the parallelogram. It is a parallelogram because it is a quadrilateral that has two pairs of parallel sides and because its opposite sides have equal measures. You may want to point out the pairs of obtuse and acute angles in the parallelogram. Ask:

- ***Is this triangle congruent to any other triangle we've created?* [Answer: Yes, it is congruent to the other small right triangle.]**
- ***Is it similar to any others?* [Answer: Yes, it is similar to the two large right triangles and the medium right triangle.]**

Have students "mess up" the seven existing pieces and then reconstruct them to form the tangram square.

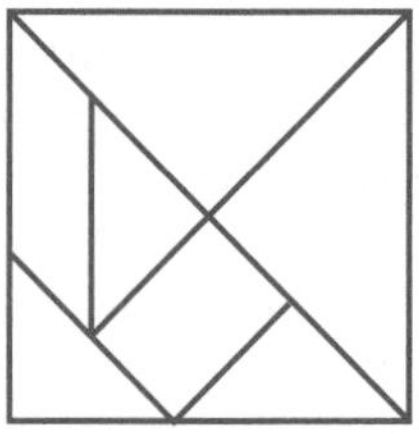

Tangram Square

As an additional activity, you may want the students to use their tangram pieces to make some of the animal shapes from the story.

DEVELOPING UNDERSTANDING: Modeling Area

Materials

Math journals. For each small group: tangram sets or **Paper Tangram Set** (Reproducible Master 38)

Arrange students into small groups and provide either a set of the paper or plastic tangrams to each.

Have them determine the money value of the tangram square's area. Tell them that the area of each of the smallest triangles has a value of 1¢. Based on this information, they should find the value of each shape and then the total value of the entire tangram square. Tell them to present their findings in a chart.

Tangram Shape	Value	Number of Shapes	Total Value
Small Right Isosceles Triangle	1¢	2	2¢
Medium Right Isosceles Triangle	2¢	1	2¢
Square	2¢	1	2¢
Parallelogram	2¢	1	2¢
Large Right Isosceles Triangle	4¢	2	8¢
Total		**7**	**16¢**

Ask students to write a journal entry describing how they arrived at each shape's value.

Responses should focus on comparing pieces, finding equivalencies, and combining shapes to form other shapes. Suggested journal response:

If the smallest triangles are each 1¢, then the parallelogram, square, and medium right triangle are each worth 2¢ because placing two small triangles together can form them. The largest triangles are worth 4¢ each because each large triangle can be made by combining the square and two small triangles or by combining four small triangles. The total value is 16¢.

DEVELOPING UNDERSTANDING: Modeling Fractions

Materials

Chart from previous activity, overhead tangrams (optional). For each small group: tangram sets or **Paper Tangram Set** (Reproducible Master 38)

Arrange students into small groups and provide either a set of the paper or plastic tangrams to each.

Have students use the chart from the previous activity to determine the fractional value of each of the tangram shapes, assuming that the area of the entire tangram square is one unit. Have the students place the pieces in order from the largest to the smallest fractional part.

[Answer: Two large triangles are each $\frac{1}{4}$, the square, parallelogram, and middle triangle are each $\frac{1}{8}$, and the small triangles are each $\frac{1}{16}$ of the whole.]

If students have trouble determining the answers, model the original square on the overhead and place the pieces on top of each other to form the various fractions. Or, you may use the information in the chart from the previous activity to form fractions. For example, if the whole square is worth 16¢, then the small triangles are each $\frac{1}{16}$. The square, parallelogram, and medium triangles are each $\frac{2}{16}$, and the large triangles are each $\frac{4}{16}$.

Ask questions, such as the following. (Assume the area of the tangram is one unit.)

How can you use tangrams to show why $\frac{1}{16} + \frac{1}{16} = \frac{1}{8}$? **[Answer: Place two small triangles on top of the square.]**

- ***How can you use tangrams to show why $\frac{1}{4} + \frac{1}{8} = \frac{3}{8}$?*** **[Answer: Place two medium triangles on top of the large triangle and add one more medium triangle.]**

- ***How much is the fractional area of 1 large triangle plus 1 square?*** **[$\frac{2}{8} + \frac{1}{8} = \frac{3}{8}$]**

How much is the fractional area of 1 medium triangle plus 1 small triangle? **[$\frac{2}{16} + \frac{1}{16} = \frac{3}{16}$]**

- ***How can you use tangrams to make a trapezoid with an area that is $\frac{1}{4}$ of the tangram square? Explain.*** **[Answer: Use two small triangles and the square.]**

- ***How can use your tangram pieces to explain how you know that $\frac{1}{4}$ is less than $\frac{1}{2}$?***

  [Possible answer: The largest triangle is $\frac{1}{4}$ the area of the tangram square; two of these triangles take up $\frac{1}{2}$ the area.]

- ***How do you know that $\frac{1}{16}$ is smaller than $\frac{1}{8}$?***

  [Possible answer: The small triangle represents $\frac{1}{16}$ and the square is $\frac{1}{8}$; two triangles fit in the square.]

- ***Which three shapes have the same area?*** **[Answer: square, medium triangle, and parallelogram]**

- ***How do you know?*** **[Answer: Use the two small triangles arranged to make each of the shapes.]**

- ***If they have the same area, why aren't they congruent?*** **[Answer: They do not have the same shape.]**

THREE-DIMENSIONAL TANGRAMS

Materials

For each small group: tangram sets or **Paper Tangram Set** (Reproducible Master 38)

Form small groups or work as a class to stack congruent tangram shapes on top of each other. Tell students to imagine that the shapes are all glued together to form a three-dimensional shape. For each tangram, make a shape, discuss it, and ask questions similar to the example shown.

EXAMPLE

"Stack a handful of the small triangle tangram shapes on top of each other. Imagine that they are glued together."

What is the name of this shape? **[Answer: triangular prism]**

- ***How do you know this shape is a prism rather than a pyramid?*** **[Answer: A prism has equal slices; a pyramid does not.]**
- ***How many faces are there?*** **[5]**
- ***What are the geometric names of the faces?*** **[Answer: There are three rectangles and two triangles.]**
- ***How many edges are there?*** **[9]**
- ***How many vertices are there?*** **[6]**

The table below presents answers for the other tangram shapes.

SUMMARY

What shapes could be stacked on top of each other to make a cylinder? **[Answer: circles]**

- ***What shapes could be stacked on top of each other to make a trapezoidal prism?*** **[Answer: trapezoids]**

Shapes Stacked	Three-Dimensional Shape Formed	Faces	Edges	Vertices
squares	rectangular prism	6	12	8
parallelograms	parallelogram prism	6	12	8

MATHEMATICS ASSESSMENT

Materials

Connection to Mathematics Assessment: Check for Understanding (Reproducible Master 39), tangram sets or **Paper Tangram Set** (Reproducible Master 38)

Distribute the worksheet with multiple-choice and open-ended questions called **Connection to Mathematics Assessment: Check for Understanding**. This activity can be used to check students' understanding of the mathematics concepts covered in this lesson.

Collect and score the students' work using the answers and rubric that follow.

Grandfather Tang's Story

Connections to Mathematics Assessment: Check for Understanding

39

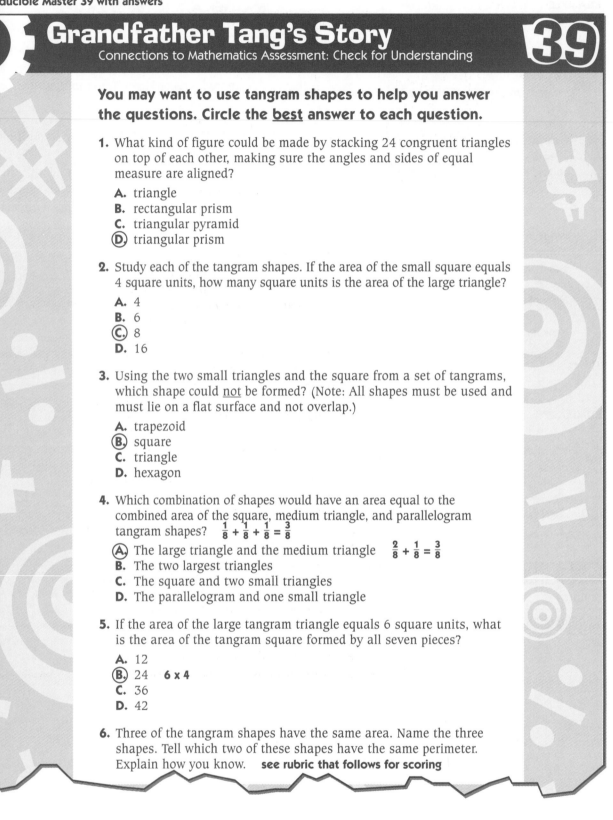

You may want to use tangram shapes to help you answer the questions. Circle the best answer to each question.

1. What kind of figure could be made by stacking 24 congruent triangles on top of each other, making sure the angles and sides of equal measure are aligned?
   - A. triangle
   - B. rectangular prism
   - C. triangular pyramid
   - (D.) triangular prism

2. Study each of the tangram shapes. If the area of the small square equals 4 square units, how many square units is the area of the large triangle?
   - A. 4
   - B. 6
   - (C.) 8
   - D. 16

3. Using the two small triangles and the square from a set of tangrams, which shape could not be formed? (Note: All shapes must be used and must lie on a flat surface and not overlap.)
   - A. trapezoid
   - (B.) square
   - C. triangle
   - D. hexagon

4. Which combination of shapes would have an area equal to the combined area of the square, medium triangle, and parallelogram tangram shapes? **$\frac{1}{8} + \frac{1}{8} + \frac{1}{8} = \frac{3}{8}$**
   - (A.) The large triangle and the medium triangle **$\frac{2}{8} + \frac{1}{8} = \frac{3}{8}$**
   - B. The two largest triangles
   - C. The square and two small triangles
   - D. The parallelogram and one small triangle

5. If the area of the large tangram triangle equals 6 square units, what is the area of the tangram square formed by all seven pieces?
   - A. 12
   - (B.) 24 **6 x 4**
   - C. 36
   - D. 42

6. Three of the tangram shapes have the same area. Name the three shapes. Tell which two of these shapes have the same perimeter. Explain how you know. **see rubric that follows for scoring**

RUBRIC FOR SCORING
Problem 6

An effective response will need to:
- name the medium right triangle, square, and parallelogram as equal in area.
- name the parallelogram and medium triangle as equal in perimeter.
- give a clear explanation.

POINTS	CRITERIA
3	The student correctly names, sketches, and labels the three shapes that are equal in area and gives a clear explanation of why they are equal in area. The student also correctly names the shapes that are equal in perimeter and gives a clear explanation through sketches and/or descriptions of why they are equal in perimeter. Suggested response: *The medium triangle, square, and parallelogram are equal in area because they all can be formed from the two small triangles. The parallelogram and the medium triangle have equal perimeters because I measured the sides and found the perimeter of each one, and they are equal.* OR *The medium triangle, square, and parallelogram are equal in area because each has an area that is equal to* $\frac{1}{8}$ *the area of the larger tangram square. The parallelogram and the medium triangle have equal perimeters because each of the larger bases of the parallelogram is the same length as the equal sides of the triangle. The remaining side of the triangle is equal to the two small bases of the parallelogram.*
2	The student correctly names the three shapes of equal area, but gives an incomplete explanation. The student correctly names the two shapes with the same perimeter but gives an explanation that contains some unclear statements. OR The student has a correct answer for both parts of the question, but fails to clearly explain.
1	The student answers both parts of the questions correctly but provides no explanations. OR The student shows some indication of understanding the concept of area and perimeter, but the names of the shapes are missing, incorrect, or misidentified.
0	The student leaves both parts unanswered or indicates no understanding of shape recognition, area, and/or perimeter.

Composition Connection

WRITING A POST-READING COMPOSITION

Materials

Connection to Writing Assessment: Post-Reading Composition (Reproducible Master 40), **Have I...? Checklist** (Reproducible Master 2), **Rubric for Scoring First Drafts** (Reproducible Master 3)

Give students the **Connection to Writing Assessment: Post-Reading Composition** along with a copy of the **Have I...? Checklist**.

Allow students about 30 minutes in which to plan, write, review, and edit the composition.

Collect and score the students' compositions using the **Rubric for Scoring First Drafts**. If you wish, this draft may be further revised and edited so it can be shared with a wider audience. The draft also may go into a "works in progress" folder that the students may use as a resource for additional ideas or pieces to revise at a later date.

VOCABULARY DEVELOPMENT: Journal Entry

Present the following prompt for a journal entry. You may wish to add the phrases discussed to the class vocabulary chart or list.

The story says that when Chou changed himself into a dog, he "bared his teeth" and "lashed his tail." What do those phrases mean?

Reproducible Master 40

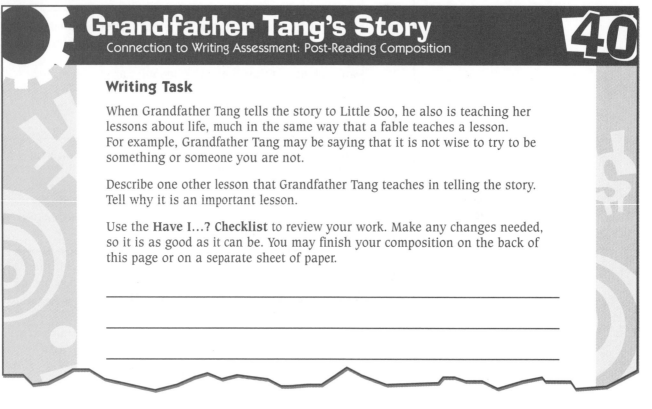

Grandfather Tang's Story

Connection to Writing Assessment: Post-Reading Composition

40

Writing Task

When Grandfather Tang tells the story to Little Soo, he also is teaching her lessons about life, much in the same way that a fable teaches a lesson. For example, Grandfather Tang may be saying that it is not wise to try to be something or someone you are not.

Describe one other lesson that Grandfather Tang teaches in telling the story. Tell why it is an important lesson.

Use the **Have I...? Checklist** to review your work. Make any changes needed, so it is as good as it can be. You may finish your composition on the back of this page or on a separate sheet of paper.

___

___

___

Extending the Connections

ENRICHMENT: WRITING/REVISING SKILLS

This story has many examples of rich descriptions, especially in animal behavior. Every time a character becomes a new animal, it adopts all of that animal's characteristics.

Read some of these examples to the class and discuss them. Discuss how the descriptions help the reader visualize the animal and add interest to the writing. Have students select from "works in progress" and attempt to add this kind of specific description, as appropriate, to their work, thus strengthen their writing skills.

MEASUREMENT AND PERIMETER

Materials

For each group: tangram sets or **Paper Tangram Set** (Reproducible Master 38). For each student: centimeter rulers

Review or establish the concept of perimeter through a question and answer session. Ask:

If the paper tangram set is made from a square that is 6 in. by 6 in., what is its perimeter? **[Answer: 4 x 6 = 24 in.]**

Use centimeter rulers to measure all sides of each tangram shape and compute the perimeter for each. You may want to have the students label each side and record the data in a chart.

EXAMPLE

Note: Measures shown are based on sizes of typical commercial tangram sets.

Shape	Side *A*	Side *B*	Side *C*	Side *D*	Perimeter
Large Triangle	7.1 cm	7.1 cm	10 cm		24.2 cm
Medium Triangle	4.9 cm	4.9 cm	7 cm		16.8 cm
Small Triangle	3.5 cm	3.5 cm	4.9 cm		11.9 cm
Square	3.5 cm	3.5 cm	3.5 cm	3.5 cm	14 cm
Parallelogram	3.5 cm	4.9 cm	3.5 cm	4.9 cm	16.8 cm

Ask questions about the chart, such as:

What information from the chart verifies that all of the triangles are isosceles? **[Answer: Two of the sides of the triangle are equal in length.]**

- ***What information from the chart verifies that the square has four equal sides?*** **[Answer: The four measurements are equal.]**
- ***Based on the data from the chart, what might you conclude about the opposite sides of a parallelogram?*** **[Answer: They are equal in measure.]**
- ***Which two figures have the same perimeter? Why do you think this happens?*** **[Answer: The medium triangle and the parallelogram have the same perimeter because sides *A* and *B* on the triangle are equal to sides *B* and *D* on the parallelogram and the sum of sides *A* and *C* on the parallelogram equals the length of side C on the triangle.]**

COORDINATES AND GEOBOARDS

Materials

11-x-11-pin geoboards and geobands or coordinate grid paper

Lead a class discussion similar to the one below for each of the tangram shapes. After modeling one or two shapes, you may want to have students work independently.

EXAMPLE

"Use one geoband to make a right triangle on the geoboard." Ask:

Do you think all of the triangles that the class made are congruent? **[Answer: No.]** ***Why or why not?*** **[Answers will vary, but in order to be congruent any two triangles must fit exactly on top of each other. They must be the same size and shape.]**

- ***Are all of the triangles in the same location?*** **[Answer: No.]**
- ***What characteristics make them right triangles?*** **[Answer: They have right angles.]**
- ***Does everyone have an isosceles right triangle?*** **[Answer: No.]** ***How can you tell?*** **[Answer: Not everyone's triangles have two sides that are equal.]**
- ***What are the coordinates of each of the vertices in the triangles?*** **[Answers will vary.]**
- ***Is it still a right triangle if I turn the board a quarter of a turn?*** **[Answer: Yes.]** ***What if I hold the board upside down?*** **[Answer: Yes.]**
- ***What directions could be given to make sure everyone makes congruent right triangles?*** **[Answer: Give the dimensions by telling the length of each side and the position of the right angle.]**
- ***Would the directions be different if the triangles needed to be isosceles right triangles?*** **[Answer: Yes. Two of the three sides also would need to be equal in measure.]**

Would the directions be different if the triangles needed to be in exactly the same place on the geoboard and still be congruent? **[Answer: Yes. The coordinates of the vertices, or corners, also would need to be given.]**

This last problem provides an excellent segue into naming coordinates. Remind students that when they name coordinates the column value, or vertical coordinate (x coordinate), is always first and the row value, or horizontal coordinate (y coordinate), is always second.

Have pairs take turns creating a shape and then announcing the coordinates of the shape's vertices, so their partner can recreate it.

To check for understanding, give the vertex coordinates for a shape and have students make the shapes on their boards. Create or have students create additional figures using this method.

EXAMPLE

"Use one geoband to make the quadrilateral formed by connecting the following vertices in the order given: (3,5), (6,5), (6,1), and (3,1)."

What shape did you make? **[Answer: a rectangle with dimensions of 4 x 3 units]**

To summarize this activity, have the class use geoboards to make an isosceles right triangle with an area of 8 square units. (Hint: The sides of equal lengths should be four units each.)

Follow up by asking questions similar to the following:

Are all the triangles in the class congruent? **[Answer: Yes, because the two equal sides must be four units each.]**

Note: If students disagree with the answer, remind them that the diagonal unit lengths on the board do not equal the vertical or horizontal unit lengths.

***Are they all in the same place on the board?* [Answer: No.]**

Have students record the coordinates of the vertices for their triangles. Verify results by having one student make another's triangle on their geoboard, using the given coordinates.

EXAMPLE

"Use one geoband to make a triangle whose vertices are (8,6), (4,6), and (8,2). Compare this triangle to the isosceles right triangle you created. Is it in the same place?" [Answers will vary.] "Is it congruent to the one you created?" [Answer: Yes.]

CLOSURE

Have students respond to the following in a discussion or journal entry.

"Margarita said that all right triangles are congruent because they all have right angles and they all have the same shape. Tell why you agree or disagree with Margarita." [Possible answer: I disagree. They do have the same shape, but they are not all the same size.]

SUGGESTED PROJECTS

- Recreate each of the tangram shapes on a geoboard so that the area of the whole tangram square equals 64 square units. Find the area of each shape and explain how you found it. (As an alternative, you may want to assign 16 square units as the area of the whole tangram square.)

- Determine the number of shapes with even vs. odd vertices in a whole tangram. [Answer: 5 shapes are odd; 2 are even] Could the tangram square be "traveled"? Meaning, could you trace along the sides and never go over any side more than once? [Answer: No.]

ADDITIONAL RESOURCES

Available from Creative Publications.
Call 1-888-MATH FUN:
~ *Moving On with Tangrams* (Grades 4–6)
~ *Tangram Job Cards* (Primary and Intermediate)
~ *Cooperative Problem Solving with Tangrams* (Grades 4–6)
~ *Tangram Patterns* (Grades K–12)

Teacher Notes

The Greedy Triangle

Written by **Marilyn Burns**
Illustrated by **Gordon Silveria**

Overview of the Connections

This is a story about a triangle that gets bored with its various jobs, such as catching wind for sailboats, holding up roofs for houses, and other "triangular" tasks. The triangle seeks help from a "shapeshifter," who transforms it into different shapes. At each visit, the shapeshifter adds a new side and angle to form a new shape. First, the triangle becomes a square, then a quadrilateral, a pentagon, a hexagon, and so on. But the shape is never satisfied with its new form for long. Eventually, it realizes it was happiest as a triangle.

The Greedy Triangle offers an interesting twist on a common theme in the genre of fables, developing self-acceptance. Although the shape has its every request granted, it is never truly happy until it realizes that its original shape was best. The story offers students opportunities to develop listening and writing skills, especially when making comparisons.

In teaching mathematics, this story provides a vehicle for identifying shapes and connecting those shapes to objects in real life. This connection gives students opportunities to recognize the shapes in contexts, as well as by definitions. As the shapeshifter adds more sides and angles, students model the shapes and discuss the similarities and differences. Through this exploration, they develop an understanding of the relationship between shape formation and the number of sides and angles.

Additional activities have students classifying various polygons, such as types of quadrilaterals. Connections are also made between shapes, vertices, and the coordinate plane. An informal exploration of limits is suggested as well.

MATERIALS FOR THE CONNECTIONS

The Greedy Triangle • ISBN 0-590-48991-7
Written by Marilyn Burns. Illustrated by Gordon Silveria. New York: Scholastic, Inc., 1994.

Language Arts

One or more copies of the book (Note: In the Viewing Connection, each student will need to see the pictures on pages 4 and 28. Pages are not numbered, so consider the title page that is facing the credits as page 1. You may wish to have several copies available.)

~ Optional: **Connection to Viewing Assessment: Writing About a Picture Prompt** (Reproducible Master 1)

~ **Have I...? Checklist** (Reproducible Master 2), a self-monitoring tool for student writers

~ **Rubric for Scoring First Drafts** (Reproducible Master 3)

~ **Connection to Listening Assessment: Listening to a Story** (Reproducible Master 41)

~ **Connection to Writing Assessment: Post-Reading Composition** (Reproducible Master 44)

Mathematics

~ Straws cut into equal lengths (10 for each student)

~ Scissors

~ Connectors, such as garbage-bag twist ties or pipe cleaners

~ Math journals

~ Geoboards with geobands (an 11-x-11-pin board and bands for each student or pair)

~ Overhead geoboard and overhead projector

~ Pattern blocks (1 bucket for each group of 3-4 students)

~ **Connection to Mathematics Assessment: Check for Understanding I and II** (Reproducible Masters 42–43)

~ Straightedges or rulers

Viewing Connection

INTRODUCING THE LESSON WITH A PICTURE PROMPT AND WRITING

Materials

Copies of the book (pages 4 and 28), Have I...? Checklist (Reproducible Master 2), **Rubric for Scoring First Drafts** (Reproducible Master 3). Optional: **Connection to Viewing Assessment: Writing About a Picture Prompt** (Reproducible Master 1).

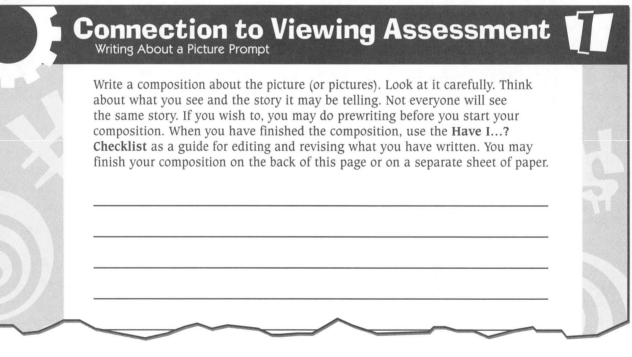

Show the class the pictures on pages 4 and 28 of *The Greedy Triangle* with the text covered up. On these two pages, triangles are formed by the spaces created when people put their hands on their hips. If possible, allow students to continue to look at the pictures throughout the writing session. You may distribute a copy of **Connection to Assessment: Writing About a Picture Prompt** to each student, or they may use notebook paper for their work.

Read these directions to the class:

"You are going to write a composition about these two pictures. Look at them carefully. Think about what you see and the story they may be telling. It is OK that not everyone will see the same story. You may write about either one or both of the pictures. If you wish to, you may do prewriting before you start your composition. When you have finished the composition, use the **Have I...? Checklist** as a guide for editing and revising what you have written."

Give the students 20–30 minutes to write their compositions and do initial editing.

Collect and score the student's compositions using the **Rubric for Scoring First Drafts**. Teach students how to compare their scored composition to the rubric and to make notes about how to improve their compositions. Students may also be taught to use the rubric to score their own work or that of other students.

Reproducible Master 1

Connection to Viewing Assessment 1

Writing About a Picture Prompt

Write a composition about the picture (or pictures). Look at it carefully. Think about what you see and the story it may be telling. Not everyone will see the same story. If you wish to, you may do prewriting before you start your composition. When you have finished the composition, use the **Have I...? Checklist** as a guide for editing and revising what you have written. You may finish your composition on the back of this page or on a separate sheet of paper.

____

____

____

____

Listening Connection

LISTENING TO A STORY AND ANSWERING QUESTIONS

Materials

Copy of the book (Listening section: the whole book, 966 words), **Connection to Listening Assessment: Listening to a Story** (Reproducible Master 41)

This activity will help students develop effective listening skills. As necessary, teach or review some of the effective listening strategies found on page *xv* of this manual.

Tell the students you are going to read them a story. When you are finished, they will answer some questions about what you have read.

Read the entire story to the class. Since you are working on listening, don't stop to discuss the story, show the illustrations, or make predictions as you might do in a reading instructional period.

Distribute the worksheet with multiple-choice and open-ended questions called **Connection to Listening Assessment: Listening to a Story**.

Allow students 15–20 minutes for completing the worksheet.

Collect and score the students' work using the answers and rubric that follow.

Reproducible Master 41 with answers

The Greedy Triangle

Connection to Listening Assessment: Listening to a Story

41

Circle the best answer to each question.

1. Why does the triangle like to slip into place when people put their hands on their hips?

- **A.** In this way, it feels very useful.
- **B.** It is a shape that is more unique than any other shape.
- **C.** In this way, it can to be as busy as a bee.
- **(D.)** In this way, it gets to hear what people are talking about.
  refers to pages 4 and 28

2. Which person has a job that is most similar to that of the "shapeshifter"?

- **(A.)** A person who does magic tricks.
- **B.** A person who builds houses.
- **C.** A person who tells you what will happen in the future.
- **D.** A person who bakes cakes and pies.

3. Which statement best explains how the greedy shape felt after it changed into a new shape?

- **(A.)** At first it was very happy, but then it became bored.
- **B.** It was always happy being useful.
- **C.** It was always happy to be able to share new things with its friends.
- **D.** It never thought the shapeshifter did a good job.

Continued...

4. What does the shapeshifter add to the shape to change it into a new shape?

A. One side.
(B.) One side and one angle.
C. One angle.
D. Many sides and many angles.

5. What problem does the shape have when it is a hexagon?

A. It has so many sides that it loses its balance.
B. It is kicked around a lot.
(C.) It is too busy to spend time with its friends. **answer on page 19**
D. People play games with it.

Open-ended Listening Task: Explain what you think would have happened if the shapeshifter had refused to grant the shape's wishes. Use details from the story and from your experience to support your answer.
see rubric that follows for scoring

RUBRIC FOR SCORING
Open-ended Listening Task

An effective response will need to:
- reflect knowledge of story.
- justify ideas using the text.
- make logical predictions.
- be well written with a clear presentation.

POINTS	CRITERIA
4	Response is well written, logical, and thorough. Supporting details are provided from the story and from the writer's personal experience to create a convincing argument.
3	Response is generally well written, but lacking in depth or in one or more elements that would make it deserving of 4 points. Answer is logical, but the reference to the book may be weak or the personal experience poorly related. Or, there may be minor deficiencies in writing content and organization.
2	Response is generally well written, but lacking in logic or supporting details. Or, it may be poorly written, but sound in content. It may be a surface treatment rather than one that shows depth.
1	Response is illogical and/or unsupported and generally poorly written. It is sketchy and lacking in substance.
0	Response is inaccurate, or question was not answered.

Mathematics Connection

INTRODUCTION AND ACTIVE READING: Naming Polygons

Tell students that before you read the story again, you want to discuss some concepts that will help them understand the material more fully. Ask students to write the names of as many shapes as they can remember.

List the names on the board and hold a brief discussion about each one.

Use a think-pair-share technique to have students add information to the list of shapes. Tell them to record the number of sides for each shape, along with several examples of where each shape can be found in real life. Discuss the list and the various objects they named.

ACTING OUT THE STORY: Creating Polygons

Materials

Straws, each cut into 3 equal lengths (10 for each student); scissors; connectors, such as garbage-bag twist ties or pipe cleaners

Distribute 6 of the same size straws, scissors, and connectors to each student. Demonstrate for students how to build a shape using the straws and connectors. Slip a connector into the end of one straw and then into the end of another. (This works best with straws that are not too wide, so the twist-tie or pipe cleaner fits snugly into the straw.) This creates a "joint" at the corner where two sides meet. Use the same technique to connect one more straw to the two sides, forming a triangle. The result should be a slightly flexible shape.

Read the story and have students act it out using their shape-building materials. Have them pretend to be the shapeshifter as they change the triangle into new shapes by adding a side (straw) and angle (connector) each time. Students will change:

- the triangle into a quadrilateral
- the quadrilateral into a pentagon
- the pentagon into a hexagon
- the hexagon into a heptagon
- the heptagon into an octagon
- the octagon into a nonagon
- the nonagon into a decagon

Ask questions to prompt thinking.

- ***What happens to the angles as the shapes are changed?*** **[Answer: The angles get larger in measure. You may want to use acute, obtuse and right angle terminology.]**
- ***Why does adding a side mean adding an angle?*** **[Answer: When a new side connects to an existing side, it forms a new angle.]**
- ***What do all the shapes have in common?*** **[Answer: Every shape the class made has equal sides.]**

Introduce the term *polygon* as a word to describe all shapes that form a closed flat figure made of line segments. Then discuss the concept of *regular* polygons. Point out that the triangles, pentagons, and hexagons they made are called regular polygons because they have equal sides and equal angles. The quadrilateral they made is also a regular polygon because it is a square (all straws are equal in length).

Ask students how they think they could make triangles, quadrilaterals, pentagons, and hexagons that are *irregular*, or not regular, polygons. Be sure they understand that the sides in the shapes could not all be equal in measure.

Challenge students to make irregular triangles, quadrilaterals, pentagons, and hexagons. Have them cut their straws to make different lengths and connect them together to create polygons with sides of different sizes.

Discuss the illustrations of the shapes in the book. Ask students if they are all regular polygons. [Answer: No they are not.]

CLASSIFYING POLYGONS

Materials

Straw models of various triangles (equilateral, isosceles, scalene) and quadrilaterals (parallelograms, trapezoids); math journals

Triangles

In preparation, you may wish to have some triangle models pre-made for this activity to ensure you have an assortment of equilateral, isosceles, and scalene triangles. In addition, you should gather all the various triangles the class made in the activity above.

Tell the class that you are going to hold up each of the triangles they made. Then you are going to sort them by placing each triangle into one of three piles.

Without telling the class, you should place all of the equilateral triangles (three sides equal) into one pile, all of the isosceles triangles (exactly two sides equal) into another, and all of the scalene triangles (no equal sides) into a third.

After several classifications, hold up a triangle and ask volunteers to tell which pile they think it should be placed into and why. Lead the class to evaluate each triangle by comparing the lengths of its sides. (You may want to classify right triangles as well.)

When finished, ask students to write a journal entry describing the rules you used to sort the triangles into the various piles.

As an extension, have students use rulers to find the perimeters of each of the triangles they made.

Quadrilaterals

In preparation, you may wish to have different types of quadrilateral models pre-made for this activity. In addition, you should gather all the various quadrilaterals the class made in the activity above.

Tell the class that you are going to hold up each of the quadrilaterals they made. Then you are going to sort them by placing each quadrilateral into one of three piles.

Without telling the class, you should place all of the parallelograms (with two pair of parallel sides) into one pile, all of the trapezoids (with exactly one pair of parallel sides) in another, and all of the others (no sides parallel) into a third.

Name each kind of quadrilateral, defining *parallelogram* and *trapezoid*. Discuss the differences between the various parallelograms, thus establishing definitions for *rectangle* (parallelogram with four right angles), *square* (parallelogram with four right angles and four equal sides), *rhombus* (parallelogram with four equal sides, like a diamond) and all other parallelograms.

You may want to continue the discussion to include definitions for *isosceles trapezoids* (with two equal non-parallel sides) and *right trapezoids* (with two right angles).

As an extension, have students use rulers to find the perimeter of each of the quadrilaterals they made.

MAKING CONNECTIONS: Polygons and Geoboards

Materials

Geoboards with geobands (an 11-x-11-pin board and bands for each student or pair). Optional: overhead geoboard and overhead projector

Distribute 11-x-11-pin geoboards (with 100 squares) and geobands to each student. Check students' understanding of the definitions for various quadrilaterals by having them complete exercises similar to the following. (This activity also establishes a foundation for the understanding of coordinates.)

1. Direct students to use one geoband to make a quadrilateral on their geoboards. Tell them to hold up their geoboards if they've made a trapezoid. Choose examples of trapezoids from the class to further classify them into isosceles and right trapezoids.

   Turn the boards and ask students if the figures are still trapezoids when the board is turned. [Answer: Yes they are, but this gives students an opportunity to understand the definition, not just the picture of the shape.]

2. Direct students to use one geoband to make a parallelogram that is a rectangle on their geoboards. Before asking them to hold up the boards, ask if they think all the rectangles are the same size.

   Keeping in mind that squares are rectangles, have students show squares and then rectangles that are not squares. Ask:

Why are these figures rectangles?
[Answer: They both have four right angles.]

3. Direct students to use one geoband to make a square. Before asking the students to hold up their geoboards, ask:

Do you think that all the squares are congruent? **[Answer: They probably are not all the same size and shape, so they are not congruent.]**

- ***Do you think that all the squares similar?*** **[Answer: Yes, they are. They have corresponding equal angles and proportional sides.]**

MAKING CONNECTIONS: Polygons and Coordinates

Materials
Geoboards with geobands (an 11-x-11-pin board and bands for each student or pair), overhead geoboard and overhead projector

Distribute 11-x-11-pin geoboards (with 100 squares) and geobands to each student. Most 11-x-11-pin geoboards have numbers on the borders that can be used as coordinates.

Use an overhead 11-x-11-pin geoboard with a square or other figure on it to model reading the coordinates of the vertices (corners). Name the x coordinate (column; vertical) first and the y coordinate (row; horizontal) second. The picture below shows a rectangle with vertices at coordinates (2,2), (5,2), (5,7), and (2,7).

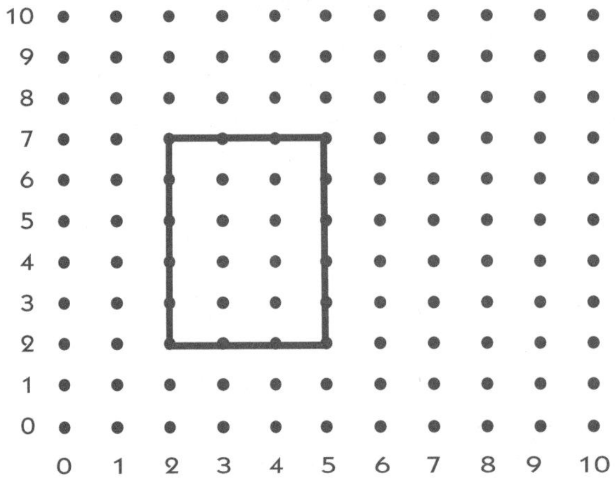

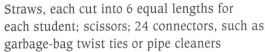

After demonstrating several examples, ask students to make their own shapes and record the coordinates. Students then take turns reading their coordinates aloud so the entire class can make the figure. Discuss why all the polygons made from the same coordinates would be congruent and in the same location. (They are congruent because they were all constructed in exactly the same way and are all the same size and shape. They are in the same position because they all have the same vertices.)

MAKING CONNECTIONS: Developing Underpinnings for Calculus

Materials
Straws, each cut into 6 equal lengths for each student; scissors; 24 connectors, such as garbage-bag twist ties or pipe cleaners

Provide pre-made hexagons or have students build hexagons using 6 straws and connectors. Discuss the hexagon shape, then have students take them apart.

Tell students to cut each of the straws exactly in half to make 12 pieces. They can then use all 12 pieces to construct a dodecagon (12-sided polygon).

Next, have them take the dodecagon apart and cut each of the 12 sides in half again, making 24 smaller pieces. Now, they should reconstruct the pieces to form a 24-sided polygon. Hold a discussion about what they think the shape will begin to look like if they continue to halve the sides and build the new shapes.

What shape is it starting to look like? **[Answer: a circle]**

- ***Will it ever become a circle if you keeping cutting the sides in half?*** **[Answer: No.]**

MAKING CONNECTIONS: Pattern Blocks

Materials

Pattern blocks (1 bucket for each group of 3–4 students)

Distribute a bucket of pattern blocks to each group of 3–4 students. Have students list similarities and differences that exist between the pattern blocks and the shapes in *The Greedy Triangle*. Almost all of the regular shapes in the story—except the pentagons —are also pattern-block shapes. The pattern blocks also contain other quadrilaterals.

Discuss the differences between a rhombus (a quadrilateral with four equal sides, but no right angles) and a square (a quadrilateral with four equal sides and four right angles). Also discuss why a trapezoid is not a "regular" polygon. [Answer: A trapezoid is not a regular polygon because it does not have all of its sides equal in measure.]

EXTENDING TO SOLIDS: Pattern Blocks and Prisms

Materials

Pattern blocks (1 bucket for each group of 3–4 students); Optional: straws and connectors

Use pattern blocks to create stacks of triangles, trapezoids, squares, rhombi, and hexagons, so that they form various types of prisms. Hold up one of the stacks and ask the children to imagine that all the pieces are glued together and cannot come apart. Tell the students that when the pieces are all "glued" together they model a solid, or three-dimensional, figure known as a *prism*.

Discuss the faces of the prism formed by the various pattern-block shapes. Point out that the two faces at each end of the prism are identical and can help determine the name of the prism. These "end faces" are called *bases*. Hold up each of the three-dimensional figures formed with the pattern blocks and give their correct names: *triangular prism*, *rhomboidal prism*, *trapezoidal prism*, and *hexagonal prism*.

After identifying the solids in this manner, use a question-and-answer-technique to lead students to understand that all of the side faces on the prisms are rectangles. Discuss the pictures of the pyramids on page 26 of *The Greedy Triangle*. Ask:

How are the pyramids like prisms?
How are the pyramids different from prisms?
[Answers: They are alike because they are solids. They are different because most of the faces of a pyramid are triangles rather than rectangles, as in a prism.]

If time permits, distribute straws and connectors and have the students build selected solids, such as: rectangular, hexagonal, triangular, and pentagonal prisms; and rectangular, hexagonal, and triangular pyramids. Discuss the similarities and differences among the models.

MATHEMATICS ASSESSMENT

Materials

Individual copies of **Connection to Mathematics Assessment: Check for Understanding I and II** (Reproducible Masters 42–43)

Distribute the worksheet with multiple-choice and open-ended questions called **Connection to Mathematics Assessment: Check for Understanding I and II**. This activity can be used to check students' understanding of the mathematics concepts covered in this lesson.

Collect and score the students' work using the answers and rubric that follow.

The Greedy Triangle

Connection to Mathematics Assessment: Check for Understanding I

42

Circle the best possible answer for each problem.

1. Pedro wants to use some straws that are all the same size and not bent to make a cube. How many of these straws does he need?

A. 6
(B.) 12   **4 for the top, 4 for the bottom, 4 to connect them**
C. 24
D. 72

2. Penelope wants to make separate models of an equilateral triangle, a regular hexagon, and a regular decagon, using straws of the same size that are not bent. How many straws does she need so there are none left over?

A. 17
(B.) 19   **3 + 6 + 10**
C. 21
D. 25

3. Use the grid below to draw a figure with the vertices given by the coordinates: (3,2), (3,8), (9,8), and (9,2).

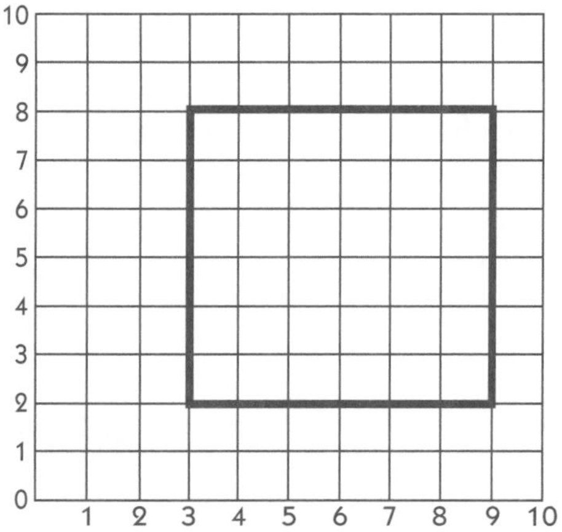

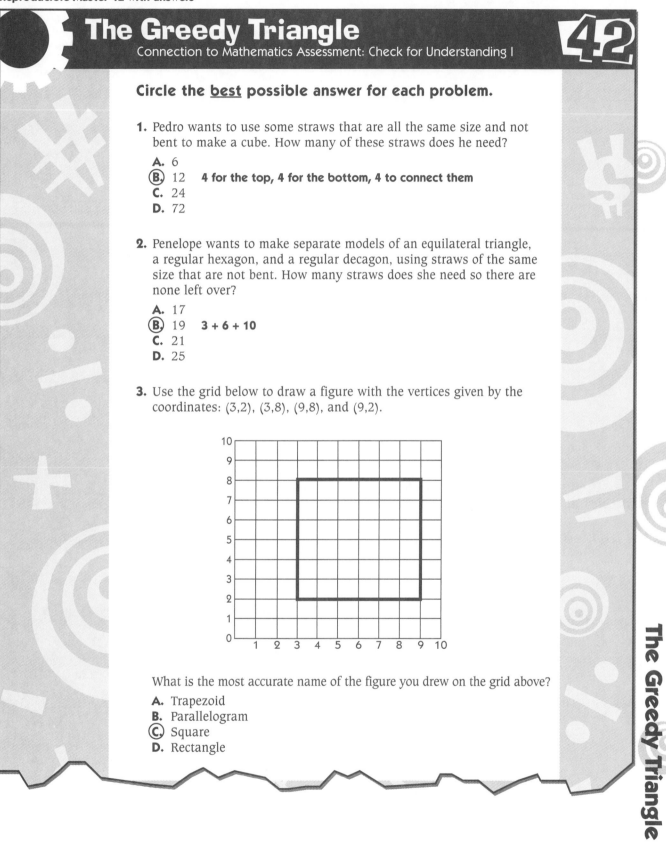

What is the most accurate name of the figure you drew on the grid above?

A. Trapezoid
B. Parallelogram
(C.) Square
D. Rectangle

The Greedy Triangle

Connection to Mathematics Assessment: Check for Understanding II

43

Circle the best possible answer for each problem.

4. How many rectangular faces does a hexagonal prism have?

A. 2
B. 4
(C.) 6
D. 8

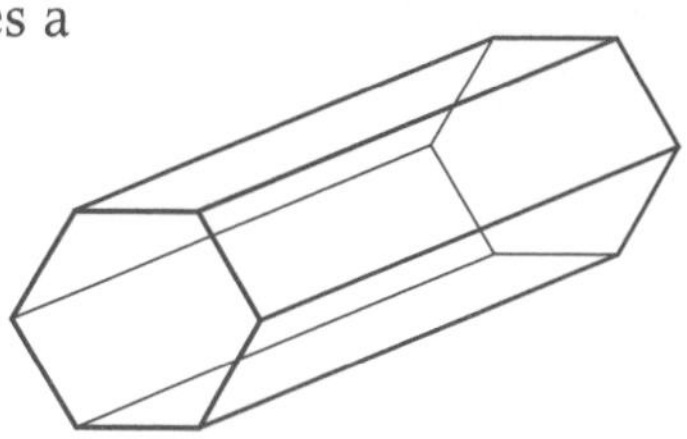

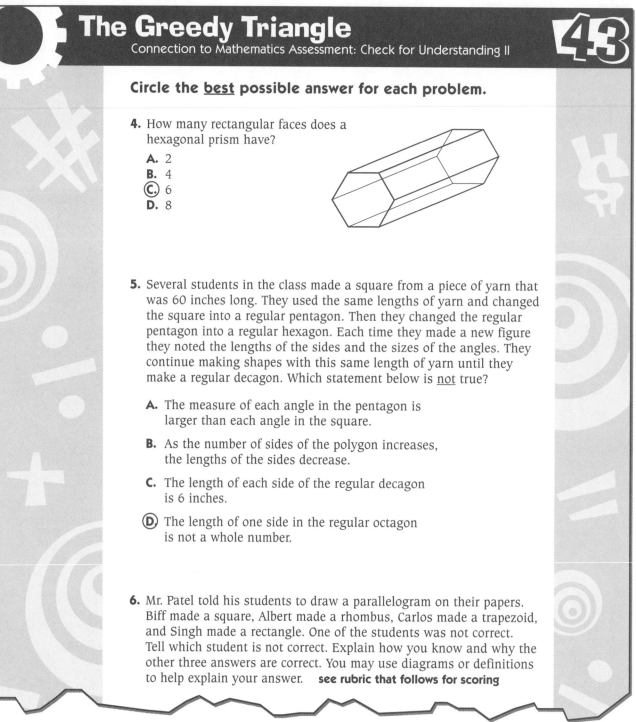

5. Several students in the class made a square from a piece of yarn that was 60 inches long. They used the same lengths of yarn and changed the square into a regular pentagon. Then they changed the regular pentagon into a regular hexagon. Each time they made a new figure they noted the lengths of the sides and the sizes of the angles. They continue making shapes with this same length of yarn until they make a regular decagon. Which statement below is not true?

A. The measure of each angle in the pentagon is larger than each angle in the square.

B. As the number of sides of the polygon increases, the lengths of the sides decrease.

C. The length of each side of the regular decagon is 6 inches.

(D.) The length of one side in the regular octagon is not a whole number.

6. Mr. Patel told his students to draw a parallelogram on their papers. Biff made a square, Albert made a rhombus, Carlos made a trapezoid, and Singh made a rectangle. One of the students was not correct. Tell which student is not correct. Explain how you know and why the other three answers are correct. You may use diagrams or definitions to help explain your answer. **see rubric that follows for scoring**

RUBRIC FOR SCORING
Problem 6

An effective response will need to:
- show that Carlos and his trapezoid are incorrect.
- give a clear explanation of the difference. between a trapezoid and a parallelogram.
- explain why a rhombus, square, and rectangle are parallelograms.

POINTS	CRITERIA
3	The student states that Carlos' trapezoid is not a parallelogram. The student provides a clear explanation, verbally and/or pictorially, stating the difference between parallelograms and trapezoids and includes reference to the number of parallel sides. The student also indicates why the rhombus, square, and rectangle are parallelograms. Possible responses: *"Parallelograms must have two pairs of opposite sides that are parallel. Since the square, rhombus, and rectangle have parallel opposite sides, they are parallelograms. Since a trapezoid has exactly one pair of parallel sides, it cannot be a parallelogram."* OR *"Carlos is not correct because a trapezoid has only one pair of parallel sides. A parallelogram must have two pairs of parallel sides. The other answers are correct because each of those figures has two pairs of parallel sides."*
2	The student states that the trapezoid is not a parallelogram and that the other shapes are, but the explanations are not clear. Or, the explanation of the difference between a parallelogram and trapezoid is clear but the student fails to explain why each of the other figures is correct.
1	The student correctly classifies each of the figures to be parallelograms or non-parallelograms, but provides no explanation, or an explanation that is unclear and difficult to follow. Or, the student provides appropriate descriptions of parallelograms and trapezoids but classifies one or more of the figures incorrectly.
0	The student names the wrong figures and provides no explanation or leaves the problem blank.

Composition Connection

WRITING A POST-READING COMPOSITION

Materials

Copy of the book (focus on illustrations on pages 29–30), **Connection to Writing Assessment: Post-Reading Composition** (Reproducible Master 44), **Have I...? Checklist** (Reproducible Master 2), **Rubric for Scoring First Drafts** (Reproducible Master 1)

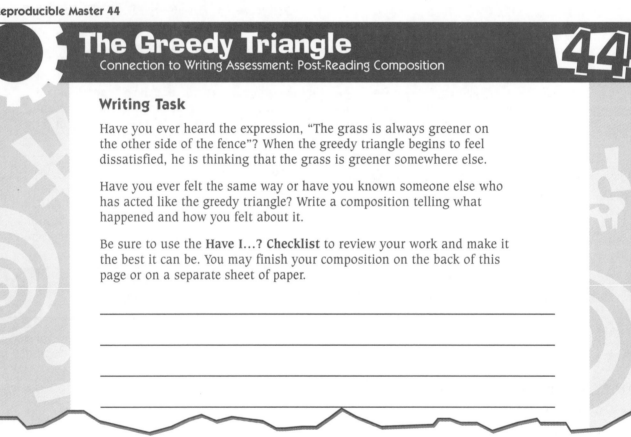

Give students the **Connection to Writing Assessment: Post-Reading Composition** along with a copy of the **Have I...? Checklist**.

Give students about 25 minutes in which to write the composition and revise/edit it based on the checklist.

Collect and score the students' compositions using the **Rubric for Scoring First Drafts**.

See Extending the Connections for ideas that practice skills in using writing to interpret meaning of text.

Reproducible Master 44

The Greedy Triangle

Connection to Writing Assessment: Post-Reading Composition

44

Writing Task

Have you ever heard the expression, "The grass is always greener on the other side of the fence"? When the greedy triangle begins to feel dissatisfied, he is thinking that the grass is greener somewhere else.

Have you ever felt the same way or have you known someone else who has acted like the greedy triangle? Write a composition telling what happened and how you felt about it.

Be sure to use the **Have I...? Checklist** to review your work and make it the best it can be. You may finish your composition on the back of this page or on a separate sheet of paper.

Extending the Connections

INTERPRETING FIGURATIVE LANGUAGE

Divide the class into discussion groups. Assign each group one of the underlined figures of speech from the list below. (You may have more than one group work on a particular figure of speech.)

Expressions:

- I have an angle on something.
- It's a top secret file.
- I have trouble keeping my balance.
- Which side are you on?
- I don't know which side is up.
- Quit taking sides.
- He's always changing sides.

Have each group prepare a definition of their assigned expression. They may use whatever resources are available—their families, dictionaries, the book, encyclopedia, or the Internet. Once they have determined an appropriate definition, they can prepare a poster illustrating the meaning of the expression. The poster should include the expression and a written definition of it. Have groups present their posters to the class and display them around the room.

As a follow-up, have students discuss why the use of figures of speech makes writing more vivid. They can select a draft composition they have in their works-in-progress folder and add one or more figures of speech to it to make the composition more effective.

PARTITIONING POLYGONS: Looking for Patterns

Materials
Straightedges or rulers

Conduct the following series of exercises to help students discover the number of non-overlapping triangles that can be made by connecting vertices in various polygons.

Then ask them to form non-overlapping triangles by connecting various vertices. They should form as many as possible without intersecting another line. Then have them count the number of triangles.

Use a question-and-answer-technique to establish that if you connect the vertices, all quadrilaterals contain exactly two triangles, all pentagons have exactly three, and all hexagons have exactly four. Continue this discussion by having them guess how many triangles could be formed inside an octagon or decagon. [Answer: Octagon has six triangles and a decagon has eight.] Some students may discover that there are always two fewer triangles than the number of sides of the polygon.

EXAMPLE

Draw a quadrilateral on your paper. Connect the vertices to make as many triangles as possible without allowing any part of one triangle to cross over or intersect any other part of another.

How many triangles do you have?

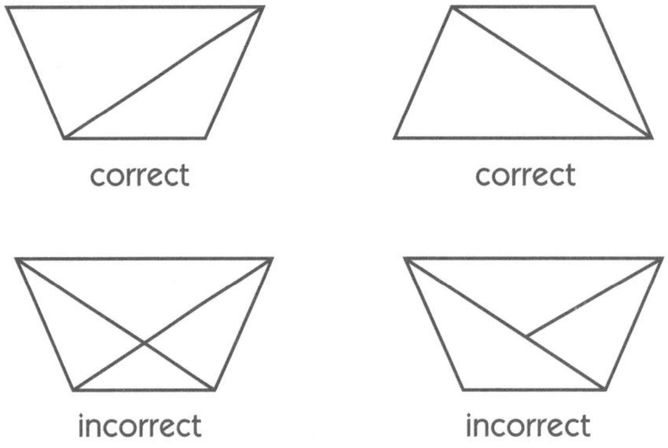

Note: There are many other quadrilaterals of various sizes and classifications that could be drawn, but they all must have exactly two non-overlapping triangles.

CLOSURE

Ask students to make a journal entry describing why a polygon with 50 sides is like a circle but is not actually a circle.

[Suggested response: A polygon with 50 sides is like a circle because its sides are so small the straight lines begin looking like curves. It is not a circle because the figure is made from line segments.]

Have students make a journal entry responding to the following:

If you could be a polygon, how many sides would you have? Name the polygon and explain why you decided to be that shape.

ADDITIONAL RESOURCES

Windows on Math, Volume 3, Unit 2 Videodisc, **"Marty McShape."** Atlanta: Optical Data Corporation, 1996. Call 1-800-524-2481.

Windows on Math, Volume 4 Unit 8 Videodisc, **"Shapes in Sand."** Atlanta: Optical Data Corporation, 1996. Call 1-800-524-2481.

How Much, How Many, How Far, How Heavy, How Long, How Tall Is 1000?

Written by **Helen Nolan**
Illustrated by **Tracy Walker**

Overview of the Connections

Ever wonder what 1,000 really means? This book illustrates the meaning of 1,000 in, well, less than 1,000 ways.

In teaching mathematics, this lesson helps students develop skills in estimation and build a deep understanding of number sense and place value related to the concept of 1,000. In addition to being important concepts on their own, these conceptual understandings are also essential foundations for comprehending larger numbers.

In language arts, the vivid illustrations provide multiple opportunities for writing and help students develop skills in "reading" visual text.

MATERIALS FOR THE CONNECTIONS

How Much, How Many, How Far, How Heavy, How Long, How Tall Is 1000? • ISBN 1-55074-164-0
Written by Helen Nolan. Illustrated by Tracy Walker. Toronto: Kids Can Press Ltd., 1995.

Language Arts

~ One or more copies of the book (Note: In the Viewing Connection and for group work, each student will need to look closely at particular illustrations. You may wish to have several copies available.)

~ Optional: **Connection to Viewing Assessment: Writing About a Picture Prompt** (Reproducible Master 1)

~ **Have I...? Checklist** (Reproducible Master 2), a self-monitoring tool for student writers

~ **Rubric for Scoring First Drafts** (Reproducible Master 3)

Mathematics

~ **A Thousand Through My Eyes** (Reproducible Master 45)

~ Self-stick notes or index cards

~ Six bags or shoe boxes

~ **Finalizing 'A Thousand Through My Eyes' I and II** (Reproducible Masters 46–47)

~ Calculators

~ Optional: pennies; dimes; scales; rulers; yardsticks or tape measures; Oreo® cookies; oatmeal-raisin cookies; clocks or clock faces

~ Math journals

~ Overhead projector

~ Overhead base ten blocks

~ Base ten blocks or **Models of Base Ten Blocks** (Reproducible Master 48)

~ Masking and/or other tape

~ Scissors

~ Random-number generators for the digits from 0–9. Icosahedron (20-sided) dice work well, as do decks of playing cards with the aces used as one; the jacks as zero; and the 10s, queens, and kings removed.

~ **Connection to Mathematics Assessment: Check for Understanding** (Reproducible Master 49)

For optional project: collectibles (macaroni, peas, beans, stickers, paper clips, etc.); plastic sandwich bags; tag paper or poster board

Viewing Connection

INTRODUCING THE LESSON WITH A PICTURE PROMPT AND WRITING

Materials

One or more copies of the book (first page), **Connection to Viewing Assessment: Writing About a Picture Prompt** (Reproducible Master 1), **Have I...? Checklist** (Reproducible Master 2), **Rubric for Scoring First Drafts** (Reproducible Master 3)

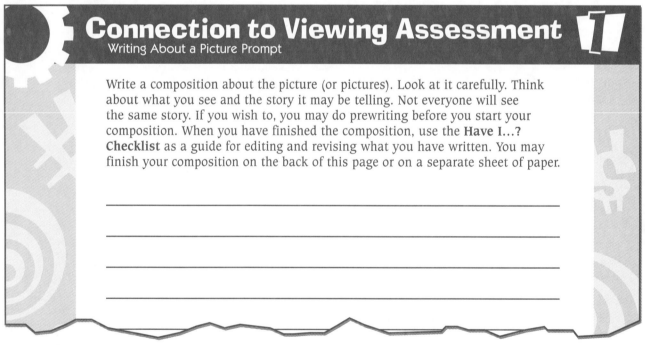

Show the class the picture on the first page of *How Much, How Many, How Far, How Heavy, How Long, How Tall Is 1000?* (The pages are unnumbered, so all page references count from the first page of story text, which is opposite the copyright page.) It shows a boy, a girl, and a dog. If possible, allow students to continue to look at the picture throughout the writing session. You may distribute a copy of **Connection to Viewing Assessment: Writing About a Picture Prompt** to each student, or they may use notebook paper for their work. Also distribute copies of the **Have I...? Checklist**.

Read these directions to the class:

"You are going to write a composition about this picture. Look at it carefully. Think about what you see and the story it may be telling. It is OK that not everyone will see the same story. If you wish to, you may do prewriting before you start your composition. When you have finished the composition, use the **Have I...? Checklist** as a guide for editing and revising what you have written."

Give the students 20–30 minutes to write their compositions and do initial editing.

Collect and score the students' compositions using the **Rubric for Scoring First Drafts**. Teach students how to compare their scored compositions to the rubric and to make notes about how to improve their writing. Students also may be taught to use the rubric to score their own work or that of other students.

Reproducible Master 1

Connection to Viewing Assessment 1

Writing About a Picture Prompt

Write a composition about the picture (or pictures). Look at it carefully. Think about what you see and the story it may be telling. Not everyone will see the same story. If you wish to, you may do prewriting before you start your composition. When you have finished the composition, use the **Have I...? Checklist** as a guide for editing and revising what you have written. You may finish your composition on the back of this page or on a separate sheet of paper.

____

____

____

____

Mathematics Connection

Choose the mathematics activities that suit the needs of your students. Before using this lesson, review the book and the estimation activities below. You can complete just one activity or do them all. The choice depends on how much time you want to devote to number sense and estimation.

INTRODUCING A THOUSAND

Materials

Copy of the book, **A Thousand Through My Eyes** (Reproducible Master 45), index cards or self-stick notes, six bags or shoe boxes

This activity begins with a series of questions to introduce the book and prompt students' thinking about 1,000. The purpose of this activity is to first have the students make estimates, and then have them display and discuss the estimates as a set of class data.

In subsequent activities, students develop plans for finding a solution to problems involving 1,000, and then they calculate answers based on their plans. They evaluate the reasonableness of their plans and their answers, and then they compare their calculations to their original estimates.

Introduce the book *How Much, How Many, How Far, How Heavy, How Long, How Tall Is 1000?* Tell students that before you read it to them, you want them to make some estimates about 1,000. (Ensure that they understand that the estimates will not be graded, but that you want to see each student's ideas about 1,000.)

There are several options for completing the **A Thousand Through My Eyes** estimation sheet. (The master is shown on the next page.)

Choose one of the following options:

- Distribute copies of **A Thousand Through My Eyes** to students, and have them fill in their estimates in the spaces provided on the sheet.
- Read the problems from **A Thousand Through My Eyes** to the class, and have students record their estimates for each problem on a self-stick note or index card. Remind them to record the question number on each note or card for easy sorting later. (Using this method makes the arrangement and display of data much easier. It also encourages risk-taking because no one knows the estimate that each person recorded.)
- Distribute copies of **A Thousand Through My Eyes** to the class, and have students record their estimate for each question on an index card or self-stick note. Remind them to record the question number on each note or card.

In this part of the activity, students make quick estimates or guesses. Allow just 3–5 minutes for them to complete the entire sheet.

Collect the students' estimates. You might set up a shoe box or bag for each question and have students sort their index cards or self-stick notes into the appropriate boxes.

Proceed to the next step, which provides options for displaying and discussing data.

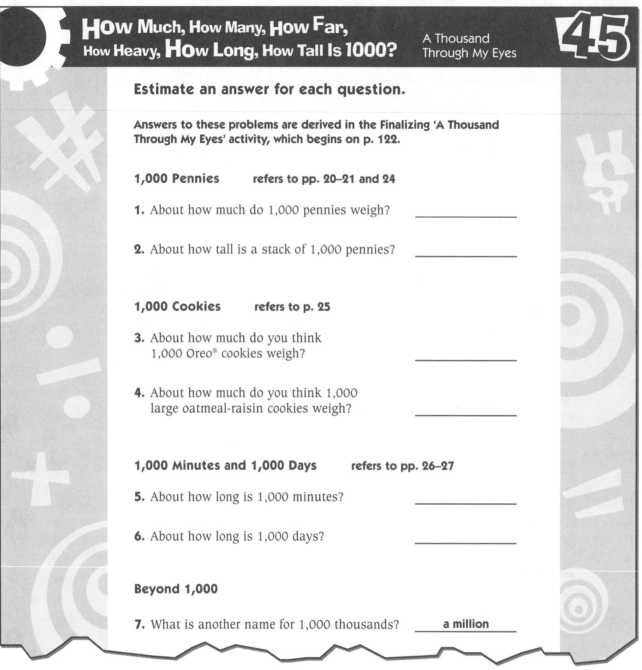

How Much, How Many, How Far, How Heavy, How Long, How Tall Is 1000?

A Thousand Through My Eyes

45

Estimate an answer for each question.

Answers to these problems are derived in the Finalizing 'A Thousand Through My Eyes' activity, which begins on p. 122.

1,000 Pennies **refers to pp. 20–21 and 24**

1. About how much do 1,000 pennies weigh? ____________

2. About how tall is a stack of 1,000 pennies? ____________

1,000 Cookies **refers to p. 25**

3. About how much do you think 1,000 Oreo® cookies weigh? ____________

4. About how much do you think 1,000 large oatmeal-raisin cookies weigh? ____________

1,000 Minutes and 1,000 Days **refers to pp. 26–27**

5. About how long is 1,000 minutes? ____________

6. About how long is 1,000 days? ____________

Beyond 1,000

7. What is another name for 1,000 thousands? **a million**

Choose one of the following options for displaying the students' estimates in a graph.

- If students wrote their answers directly on the sheet: Select one of the questions to investigate and display. Then read each response and record it on a self-stick note. Arrange the responses in some type of graph on the board as you read them. Discuss the median, mode, and range for the data.
- If students wrote their estimates on cards or notes: Arrange students into six groups. Distribute the data from one of the estimation questions to each group, and have the groups create a graph to show the data for their assigned question. Have each group report its findings to the class, making sure to discuss the median, mode, and range of the data. Encourage students to practice good speaking skills as part of this activity.

MODELING ACTIVE READING

Materials

Copy of the book

Read the book to the class, showing the illustrations and pausing after each page to model active reading.

Either "think aloud" the questions skilled readers unconsciously ask themselves or pose those questions to the class so students will think about them.

Tell the students that you don't want them to give an answer. Encourage them to think silently about the estimates they already have made.

ILLUSTRATION OF METACOGNITIVE THINKING

The following is an example of how you might model active reading throughout the book. It is not intended to be an exhaustive script. The methodology recommended is to read the text and then do the activity suggested and/or pose questions. It is important that students see the illustrations as you read to them. (The pages of the book are not numbered, so all page references count from the first page of story text, which is opposite the copyright page.)

Page 1. Read the text: *How much, how many, how far, how heavy, how long, how tall is 1,000?* Think aloud:

> "These characters look as if they are actually wondering, and the dog looks like he is happy. They are eager to learn the answers to these questions."

Pages 2–3. Read the text. Think aloud:

> "I know they are out camping because they have a tent and a campfire. The sky is full of stars, and even the bear is wondering how many stars there are. I wonder if there are more than a thousand or less than a thousand stars. The girl has a pair of binoculars. I wonder if they would help her count the stars?"

Pages 4–5. Read the text. Study the picture without comment.

Pages 6–7. Read the first sentence: *If you collect 1,000 acorns and put them in a pile, the pile won't be very big.* Then think aloud:

> "In this picture the pile of acorns is about the size of a big dog, but the pile spreads out a bit more than the dog does."

Read the second sentence: *But if the 1,000 acorns grow into oak trees, they'll make a whole forest.* Then think aloud:

> "The 1,000 big oak trees that grow from the 1,000 small acorns certainly would take up more space than the pile of acorns."

Pages 8–9. Read the text, then think aloud:

> "If the sheets of paper blew around, they would cover more space than when they were stacked neatly together. But is that the same as small acorns growing into large oak trees?"

Pages 10–11. Read the text and study the illustration. Then think aloud:

> "That's about 1,000 people in a small arena. How many 1,000s would fit into a large arena?"

Pages 12–13. Read the text, then think aloud:

> "That would be a really long line, but it is still the same number of people."

Pages 14–15. Read the text and study the illustrations. Then think aloud:

> "I wonder if I have more than 1,000 hairs on my head. I bet I have a lot more than 1,000."

Pages 16–17. Read the text, then think aloud:

> "I wonder if all of my stuff would fit into a small room built of just 1,000 bricks. How many bricks would be needed to build my house?"

Pages 18–19. Read the text and study the illustration without comment.

Pages 20–21. Read the text and remind the students that a question like this appeared on the **A Thousand Through My Eyes** estimation sheet. Encourage them to mentally compare their estimates to the information in the book.

Pages 22–23. Read the text, then think aloud:
"I wonder if I walk 1,000 steps during a day."

Pages 24–27. Read the text and study the illustrations without comment, except to encourage mental comparisons with their earlier estimates.

Pages 28–29: Read the text and study the illustration. Then proceed to the journal writing activity below.

DEVELOPING THE CONCEPT OF A THOUSAND

After reading the story, ask the students to make a journal entry responding to the following:

"Think about the pile of acorns and then the oak trees. Think of the people in the hockey rink and then the line of people waiting to get into the game. Think of the papers neatly stacked and then spread all over the room. Think of the pile of bricks and then the bricks used in the room. What makes these thousands look so different?" [Possible response: Thousands look different because they take up different amounts of space depending on the size of the objects and how they are arranged.]

Use a pair-share technique to discuss the responses. Through questioning, establish that the same quantity of objects can look different because they take up different amounts of space depending on the size of the objects and how they are arranged.

FINALIZING 'A THOUSAND THROUGH MY EYES'

Materials

Finalizing 'A Thousand Through My Eyes' I and II (Reproducible Masters 46–47) for each group, calculators. Optional: pennies; dimes; scales; rulers, yardsticks or tape measures; Oreo® cookies; oatmeal-raisin cookies; clocks or clock faces

In this activity, students work in groups to design plans to help them calculate answers to the estimation questions presented in the introductory activity and other problems in the book.

Each estimation problem extends the original question to help students reach conclusions and make further conjectures. To maximize time, you may want to assign different problems or sets of problems to different groups and have them present their plans and solutions to the class.

For the problems that ask students to estimate weights or heights, you might wish to provide scales (such as a postage scale for weighing coins and cookies) and/or rulers, yardsticks, or tape measures.

As a time-saving alternative, you might provide the following weights and heights to students. The ideal time for providing the data is after students have established a plan for solving a problem and realize they need additional information to calculate the solution. Emphasize that these are averages, and that the heights and weights of children can vary widely.

- Ten pennies weigh about 1 ounce.
- A stack of 100 pennies is about 6 inches tall.
- A stack of 20 dimes is about an inch.
- One Oreo® cookie weighs about a $\frac{1}{2}$ ounce.
- One oatmeal-raisin cookie weighs about 1 ounce.
- An average 2-year-old child weighs about 28 pounds.
- An average 7-year-old child is about 4 feet tall.
- An average 8-year-old child weighs about 55 pounds.
- An average 11-year-old child is between 4 $\frac{1}{2}$ and 5 feet tall.

Distribute Finalizing 'A Thousand Through My Eyes' I and/or II to groups and have students complete selected questions.

Students may copy or revise their original estimates from **'A Thousand Through My Eyes'** (Reproducible Master 45) for the problems in this activity.

Note: The plans and the calculations presented as possible solutions on the following page provide only one of many approaches that students might use to solve the problems. Accept any plans and calculations that are reasonable and make sense.

How Much, How Many, How Far, How Heavy, How Long, How Tall Is 1000?

Finalizing 'A Thousand Through My Eyes' I

46

1. A Thousand Pennies

a. Estimate about how much you think 1,000 pennies would weigh. ______________

b. Describe a plan for estimating the weight of 1,000 pennies without having that many pennies. Use your plan to calculate a reasonable estimate.
Possible response: Weigh 10 pennies and multiply that weight by 100 because there are 100 tens in 1,000. Calculate: 10 pennies weigh about 1 oz, so 1,000 pennies would weigh about 100 oz [(1,000 ÷ 10) x 1]. That's about $6\frac{1}{4}$ lb (100 oz ÷ 16 lb/oz = 6.25 lb).

c. Based on your calculation, explain why you could or could not put 1,000 pennies in one student's pockets.
Possible response: One person could probably carry the weight of that many pennies, but there wouldn't be room to fit them all in one person's pockets.

d. Why isn't a stack of 50 pennies the same height as a stack of 50 dimes? Which is taller?
Answer: Dimes are thinner, so the stack of pennies is taller.

e. Do you think that a stack of 1,000 pennies would be as tall as an 11-year-old child? Describe a plan that you could use to find out. Use your plan to calculate an answer.
Possible response: Yes, a stack of 1,000 pennies would be as tall as an 11-year-old child. Plan: To find out, we would measure the height of 100 pennies, then multiply by 10 to calculate the height of 1,000 pennies. We would then measure an 11-year-old and compare the heights. Calculate: 100 pennies are 6 in. tall. So 1,000 pennies would be 60 in. tall (6 in. x 10 = 60). That's the same as 5 ft (60 ÷ 12 = 5). An 11-year-old child is about 5 ft, so a stack of 1,000 pennies would be as tall as an 11-year-old.

f. Do you think a stack of 1,000 dimes would be as tall as a 7-year-old child? Describe a plan you could use to find out. Use your plan to calculate an answer.
Possible response: Yes, we think a stack of 1,000 dimes would be as tall as a 7-year-old child. Plan: To find out, we'd measure the height of 100 dimes then we would multiply by 10 because 1,000 dimes would be the same as 10 stacks of 100 dimes. Calculate: It's too hard to stack 100 dimes, so we can measure a stack of 20 dimes. That's about 1 in. There are 5 sets of 20 in 100, so 100 dimes would be 5 in. (100 ÷ 20 = 5 and 5 x 1 in. = 5 in.). To get the height of 1,000, we multiply the height of 100 dimes by 10 to get 50 in. (5 in. x 10 = 50). That's the sames as about 4 ft (50 ÷ 12 = 4 R2). An average 7-year-old child is about 4 ft tall.

How Much, How Many, How Far, How Heavy, How Long, How Tall Is 1000?

Finalizing 'A Thousand Through My Eyes' II

47

2. A Thousand Cookies

a. About how much do you think 1,000 Oreo® cookies weigh? ________

b. About how much do you think 1,000 oatmeal-raisin cookies weigh? _____

c. Describe a plan for estimating the weight of 1,000 Oreo® cookies without having that many cookies. Use your plan to calculate a reasonable estimate.

Possible response: Weigh 1 Oreo cookie. Multiply that weight by 1,000 to determine the weight of 1,000 cookies. Calculate: An Oreo cookie weighs about a $\frac{1}{2}$ oz. Multiply $\frac{1}{2}$ oz by 1,000 to get a total estimated weight of 500 oz (1,000 x $\frac{1}{2}$ oz = 500 oz). That's the same as 31 $\frac{1}{4}$ lbs (500 oz ÷ 16 oz/lb = 31.25 lbs).

d. Based on your calculation, which do you think would be heavier: 1,000 Oreo® cookies or a 2-year-old child? Explain your answer.

Possible response: Their weights would be very close. An average 2-year-old weighs about 28 lbs, so 1,000 Oreo cookies would be a little bit heavier.

e. Do you think 1,000 oatmeal-raisin cookies would be as heavy as an 8-year old child? Explain why.

Possible response: An oatmeal-raisin cookie weighs about 1 oz, so 1,000 oatmeal-raisin cookies would weigh about 1,000 oz. That's the same as 62 $\frac{1}{2}$ lbs (1,000 oz ÷ 16 oz/lb = 62.5 lbs). An average 8-year-old child weighs about 55 lbs, so the cookies would be a little heavier.

3. Time

a. About how long is 1,000 minutes? ________ **b.** 1,000 days? ________

c. Describe how you would calculate about how long 1,000 minutes and 1,000 days are and then use your plan to find a solution.

Possible solution: There are 60 minutes in an hour, so divide 1,000 by 60 to find out how many hours there are in 1,000 minutes. (1,000 min ÷ 60 min/hr = 16.67 hours) There are 365 days in a year, so divide 1,000 by 365 to find out about how many years there are in 1,000 days. (1,000 ÷ 365 = 2.73 years)

d. What time would it be exactly 1,000 minutes after 6:00 A.M.? Make an estimate, write a plan, then calculate the time.

Possible solution: Calculate how many hours and minutes there are in 1,000 minutes and add that answer to 6:00 A.M. Calculate: 1,000 min ÷ 60 min/hr = 16 hr with a remainder of 40 minutes. Counting from 6:00 A.M., it will be 6:00 P.M. in 12 hours and 10:00 P.M. 4 hours after that. Add another 40 minutes to get 10:40 P.M.

e. How old will Joe be 1,000 days after his seventh birthday?

Possible solution: We estimated that if there were only 300 days in a year, it would be 900 days in 3 years so Joe would be about 3 years older than 7, which is 10. To check, we divided 1,000 by 365 because there are 365 days in a year. The answer is 2.73. That's a little less than 3, so Joe would be older than 9 $\frac{1}{2}$ by not yet 10.

MAKING A MODEL OF A THOUSAND

Materials

Collectibles (macaroni, peas, beans, stickers, paper clips, etc.), plastic sandwich bags, tag paper or poster board, math journals

In this activity, pairs of students design a plan to create a model of 1,000 and then build it by displaying a collection of small items.

Explain to the class that each pair of students will have 10 days to collect items to create a model of 1,000. Brainstorm possible items to collect.

The most common items are macaroni, beans, stickers, and paper clips, all of which are reasonable to collect and display. This is an excellent opportunity to counsel children who choose items that would be impractical to collect or display. Don't tell them their choice is unreasonable; rather, ask questions that lead them to reach that conclusion.

Have students create a plan for making their model, and require that students get your final approval before starting their collections.

Ensure that their plans address the following questions:

Where will the 1,000 objects will come from?

- ***What is the best way to group the objects and display them to easily show that there are 1,000?***

Note: Most students use small plastic bags to hold 100 of each item and then staple the bags to tag paper or poster board.

After the models have been completed and displayed, have students respond to the following prompts in a journal entry and/or class discussion. The questions promote the concept of number sense because they require children think about 1,000 in context. As in the story, they realize that sometimes 1,000 is big, while other times it can be quite small.

If every display has 1,000 items, would they weigh the same? Why or why not? **[Answer: No. The weights of the various objects in different models would not be the same.]**

- ***Would your models of 1,000 be the same length if the objects were placed end-to-end? Why or why not?*** **[Answer: No. The sizes of the objects in different models would not be the same.]**

- ***If these differences exist, how can each display represent 1,000?*** **[Answer: Because there are 1,000 objects in each set.]**

USING BASE TEN BLOCKS TO MODEL A THOUSAND

Materials

Overhead projector, overhead base ten blocks (units and 10 flats) or several copies of **Models of Base Ten Blocks** (Reproducible Master 48), masking or other tape, scissors

Note: The following activities help students relate the models of 1,000 that they created to symbolic displays. These activities use an area model of 1,000 rather than the large cube model of 1,000 commonly found in commercial sets of base ten blocks. The area model, which is made with 10 base ten flats, helps students with perceptual problems to see the 1,000 more clearly.

Place a base ten unit on the overhead projector. Ask the students to imagine that the unit block is one of the objects that they collected and displayed in their own models of 1,000. Discuss the fact that for some students, the unit square will stand for one macaroni; for others, it stands for one bean, etc.

Place a base ten flat, which represents 100, on the overhead projector and have students relate their own bags of 100 items to the flat.

Continue the discussion by having students further connect the ideas that, just as their 10 bags of 100 items represented 1,000, so too do 10 base ten flats represent 1,000.

Arrange 10 base ten flats into a rectangle to show 1,000. Use either a 10 x 1 or a 2 x 5 arrangement of flats as shown below.

If you are using cutouts of paper base ten flats, tape them together and display the model of 1,000 on the chalkboard or bulletin board. For base ten blocks, place masking tape on the back of each flat to secure it to the board for all students to see.

USE A 1,000 STRIP...

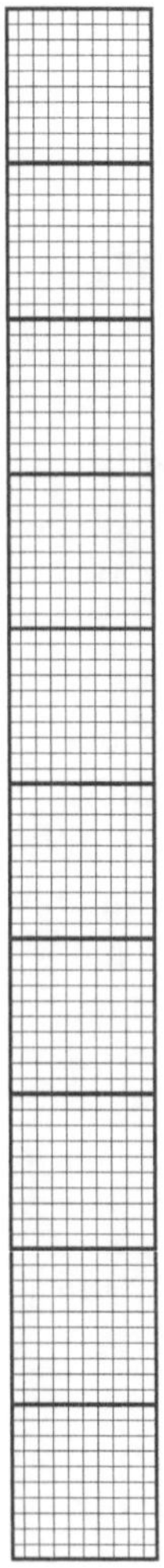

OR

... A 2 X 5 ARRANGEMENT OF FLATS.

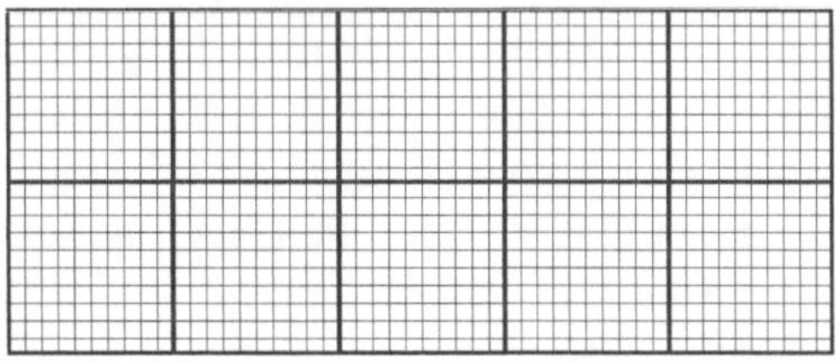

COMPARING NUMBERS

Materials

Area model of 1,000 from previous activity made into a transparency, random-number generators for the digits from 0–9 (icosahedron dice or decks of playing cards with the aces used as one; the jacks as zero; and the 10s, queens, and kings removed), overhead projector

Use random-number generators to create three-digit numbers. Ask students to visualize each number using the area model of 1,000.

To help students visualize the answer, project the model of 1,000 onto the board, then use chalk to circle or shade the numbers.

Use visual representations to compare various numbers.

EXAMPLE

Which is greater: 349 or 34? 999 or 99? Why?
[Possible responses: 349 is greater because it takes up almost 3 $\frac{1}{2}$ flats and 34 takes up less than 1 flat; 999 is greater because it covers almost the whole 1,000 model, but 99 takes up less than 1 flat.]

Students should be able to compare the numbers visually rather than by the standard method of comparing place values.

MATHEMATICS ASSESSMENT

Materials

Connection to Mathematics Assessment: Check for Understanding (Reproducible Master 49)

Distribute the worksheet with multiple-choice and open-ended questions called **Connection to Mathematics Assessment: Check for Understanding**.

Collect and score the students' work using the answers and rubric that follow.

How Much, How Many, How Far, How Heavy, How Long, How Tall Is 1000?

Connection to Mathematics Assessment: Check for Understanding

49

Circle the best answer to each question.

1. How many 100s are in 4,300?
   - A. 4300
   - B. 430
   - (C.) 43
   - D. 4.3

2. How many $100 bills would it take to model the sum of the following numbers?

   $4,000 + $300 + $800

   - A. 41
   - (B.) 51 **$5,100 ÷ $100**
   - C. 510
   - D. 5,100

3. Alicia, Bonita, Carlos, and Desiree were playing a game. Each student randomly generated four digits and tried to make the largest possible number from any three of those digits. The chart shows the digits each of them had to work with. Who should have been able to create the largest number?
   - A. Alicia
   - B. Bonita
   - (C.) Carlos
   - D. Desiree

Student	Digits generated	Answers:
Alicia	4, 7, 1, 0	**741**
Bonita	3, 5, 1, 8	**853**
Carlos	4, 9, 1, 5	**954**
Desiree	8, 0, 1, 1	**811**

4. If 100 pennies weigh about 10 ounces, then about how much would 1,000 pennies weigh?
   - A. 20 ounces
   - (B.) 100 ounces **1,000 ÷ 100 = 10 and 10 x 10 oz = 100 oz**
   - C. 500 ounces
   - D. 1,000 ounces

5. Which of the following sets would be the shortest?
   - A. 1,000 pennies stacked on top of each other
   - B. 1,000 dimes stacked on top of each other
   - (C.) 1,000 pieces of paper stacked on top of each other
   - D. 1,000 computer floppy disks stacked on top of each other

6. Latisha's teacher gave the class 10 days to collect and display 1,000 objects. Latisha decided to collect and display 1,000 baseball cards. Do you think Latisha made a good choice or a bad choice? Explain your answer.
   see rubric that follows for scoring

RUBRIC FOR SCORING
Problem 6

An effective response will need to:

- provide a clear and reasonable explanation to support either answer.
- reflect an understanding of 1,000.

POINTS	CRITERIA
3	The student can agree or disagree, but must provide a clear and reasonable explanation to support his or her answer. Possible responses: *Latisha did not make a good choice. To collect 1,000 baseball cards in 10 days would mean collecting about 100 cards a day, which seems almost impossible.* OR *Latisha made a good choice because lots of people could lend her baseball cards for the project. There are more than 100 kids in her school, and if each kid lent her 10 cards, she would have 1,000 cards. Her display of 1,000 would be fun to look at.*
2	The student states an opinion, but the explanation has minor flaws.
1	The student answer indicates an opinion, but the explanation does not show reasonableness or number sense.
0	The student indicates the choice, but provides no explanation at all or leaves the problem blank.

Composition Connection

WRITING A POST-READING COMPOSITION

Materials

One or more copies of the book, ideally one for each writing group

Note: See "Implementing Writing As Process" on page *xviii* of this manual for more information about writing groups and how to conduct and extend this writing assignment.

Have each writing group select a different illustration from *How Much, How Many, How Far, How Heavy, How Long, How Tall Is 1000?* Arrange it so that no two groups are using the same illustration.

Have each student in the group write his or her own composition that tells a story about what is happening in the illustration. The story can go well beyond the illustration, both before and after the moment caught in the picture. Make this a composition that can lead students to implement all major elements of a full writing process cycle from pre-writing to publishing.

Extending the Connections

To extend the concepts in this lesson, you may wish to do the activities and extensions in the lesson based on the book *How Much Is a Million?* which begins on page 129.

How Much Is a Million?

Written by **David M. Schwartz**
Illustrated by **Steven Kellogg**

Overview of the Connections

In this book, vivid descriptions and illustrations help readers develop number sense and the magnitude of a million, a billion, and even a trillion.

In teaching mathematics, *How Much Is a Million?* helps students estimate and visualize a million and other very large numbers. Activities that involve visualizing, comparing, and ordering numbers to a million are connected to building a model of million by displaying 100 ten-thousand squares. Additional projects and questions about a million provide more practice and opportunities to extend thinking about a million and a billion.

In teaching language arts, the book's vivid illustrations are excellent for interpretation and for helping children to read visual "text." Its descriptions provide a starting point for creative compositions.

Note: It is recommended that you teach the lesson that focuses on the concept of thousands before you introduce *How Much Is a Million?* That lesson, which begins on p. 117 of this manual, is based on the book *How Much, How Many, How Far, How Heavy, How Long, How Tall Is 1000?*

MATERIALS FOR THE CONNECTIONS

How Much Is a Million? • ISBN 0-688-04049-7 Written by David M. Schwartz. Illustrated by Steven Kellogg. New York: Lothrop, Lee & Shepard Books, 1985.

Language Arts

~ One or more copies of the book, preferably one for each writing group (Note: The pages are not numbered; page references in this lesson count the first page of the story, immediately following the copyright page, as page 1. In the Viewing Connection, each student will need to see the picture on page 5, which shows children carrying small goldfish bowls up a ladder that is standing against a giant fish bowl.)

~ **Connection to Viewing Assessment: Writing About a Picture Prompt** (Reproducible Master 1)

~ **Have I...? Checklist** (Reproducible Master 2), a self-monitoring tool for student writers

~ **Rubric for Scoring First Drafts** (Reproducible Master 3)

Mathematics

~ **Thinking About a Million** (Reproducible Master 50)

~ Calculators

~ Rulers or yardsticks to measure heights of children

~ Overhead projector and transparencies of 10 base ten flats (Alternative: 10 base ten flats)

~ 100 copies of **Ten-Thousand Square** (Reproducible Master 51). Make 10 copies each in a variety of colors, ideally 10 different colors.

~ Masking tape

~ Self-stick notes or small pieces of paper

~ Math journals

~ **Psychic Math** (Reproducible Master 52)

~ **Connection to Mathematics Assessment: Check for Understanding** (Reproducible Master 53)

~ **Working with a Million: Problems and Projects I and II** (Reproducible Masters 54–55)

Optional materials for modeling of projects in Extending the Connections:
~ Pennies ~ Scale
~ Rulers ~ Ream of paper
~ Container with mL markings
~ Liter and/or quart containers (several)

VIEWING CONNECTION

INTRODUCING THE LESSON WITH A PICTURE PROMPT AND WRITING

Materials

Copy of the book (fifth page), **Connection to Viewing Assessment: Writing About a Picture Prompt** (Reproducible Master 1), **Have I...? Checklist** (Reproducible Master 2), **Rubric for Scoring First Drafts** (Reproducible Master 3)

Show the class the picture on page 5 of the book. (It shows children climbing up a ladder on the side of a giant fish bowl.) If possible, allow students to continue to look at the picture throughout the writing session. You may distribute a copy of **Connection to Viewing Assessment: Writing About a Picture Prompt** to each student, or they may use notebook paper for their work. Also distribute copies of the **Have I...? Checklist**.

Read these directions to the class:

"You are going to write a composition about this picture. Look at it carefully. Think about what you see and the story it may be telling. It is OK that not everyone will see the same story. If you wish to, you may do prewriting before you start your composition. When you have finished the composition, use the **Have I...? Checklist** as a guide for editing and revising what you have written."

Give the students 20–30 minutes to write their compositions and do initial editing.

Collect and score the students' compositions using the **Rubric for Scoring First Drafts**. Teach students how to compare their scored compositions to the rubric and to make notes about how to improve their compositions. Students also may be taught to use the rubric to score their own work or that of other students.

Reproducible Master 1

Connection to Viewing Assessment 1

Writing About a Picture Prompt

Write a composition about the picture (or pictures). Look at it carefully. Think about what you see and the story it may be telling. Not everyone will see the same story. If you wish to, you may do prewriting before you start your composition. When you have finished the composition, use the **Have I...? Checklist** as a guide for editing and revising what you have written. You may finish your composition on the back of this page or on a separate sheet of paper.

____

____

____

____

____

Mathematics Connection

INTRODUCTION AND ACTIVE READING

Materials

Copies of the book, **Thinking About a Million** (Reproducible Master 50), rulers or yardsticks, calculators

This activity begins with a series of questions to introduce the book and prompt students' thinking about a million. It provides two options for working through the questions after completing the book.

Note: Solutions and methods for solving each of the problems on the **Thinking About a Million** page are described on the last three pages of the book *How Much Is a Million?* in a section called "A Note from the Author."

Introduce the book *How Much Is a Million?* Tell the students that before you read it to them, you want them to think about some situations that are described in the book and to make some guesses about how big a million is.

Distribute copies of **Thinking About a Million** to each student, and have them record their guesses.

Reproducible Master 50 with answers

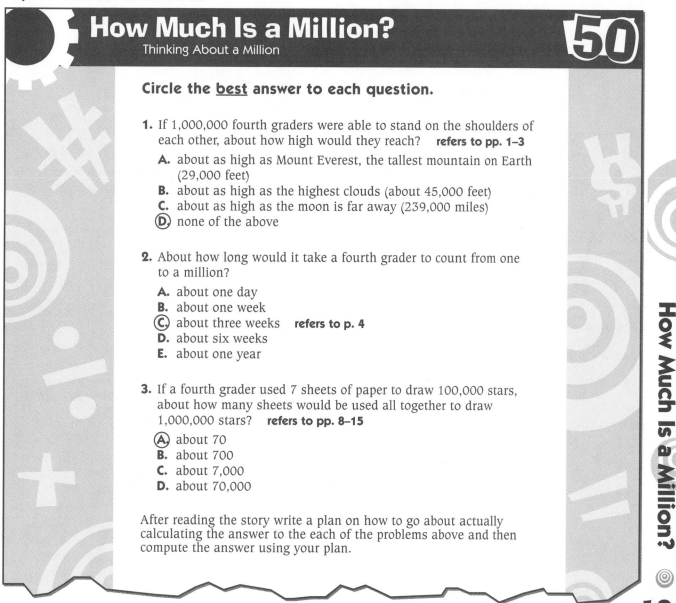

How Much Is a Million? 50

Thinking About a Million

Circle the best answer to each question.

1. If 1,000,000 fourth graders were able to stand on the shoulders of each other, about how high would they reach? **refers to pp. 1–3**
   - A. about as high as Mount Everest, the tallest mountain on Earth (29,000 feet)
   - B. about as high as the highest clouds (about 45,000 feet)
   - C. about as high as the moon is far away (239,000 miles)
   - (D.) none of the above

2. About how long would it take a fourth grader to count from one to a million?
   - A. about one day
   - B. about one week
   - (C.) about three weeks **refers to p. 4**
   - D. about six weeks
   - E. about one year

3. If a fourth grader used 7 sheets of paper to draw 100,000 stars, about how many sheets would be used all together to draw 1,000,000 stars? **refers to pp. 8–15**
   - (A.) about 70
   - B. about 700
   - C. about 7,000
   - D. about 70,000

After reading the story write a plan on how to go about actually calculating the answer to the each of the problems above and then compute the answer using your plan.

Read the book to the class.

OPTION 1

Have pairs or small groups of students write a plan that describes how they would solve each of the problems. Then have them follow their plans to compute the answers. Have calculators available to aid students with solutions.

OPTION 2

Use a think-pair-share technique to establish an answer for the first question about how tall a million fourth graders would be standing on each other's shoulders. You might encourage the use of rulers or yardsticks to measure some children from the floor to their shoulders to arrive at an average height with which to calculate. [Answer: Using an average shoulder height of 4 feet, a million children would stand 4 million feet, or 757.58 miles, high.]

Have pairs of students solve the other two problems on the **Thinking About a Million** sheet. Encourage the use of calculators. Hold a class discussion about the answers and methods for solving the problems.

DEVELOPING UNDERSTANDING: Visualizing a Million Using Ten-Thousand Squares

Materials

Overhead projector, 10 base ten flats or transparencies of 10 base ten flats, 100 copies and a transparency of **Ten-Thousand Square** (Reproducible Master 51). Optional: Use an enlarged copy of the ten-thousand square for the transparency. Also, for the 100 copies of the ten-thousand square, make 10 copies each in 10 different colors or in as many colors are available.

Note about the materials: These activities use an area model of 1,000 rather than the large cube model of 1,000 commonly found in commercial sets of base ten blocks. The area model, which is made with 10 base ten flats, helps students with perceptual problems to see the 1,000 more clearly.

Note about the activities: By the end of this activity, the class will construct a model of a million by taping together copies of a **Ten-Thousand Square** (Reproducible Master xx). The model will measure 6 feet by 6 feet, or more, depending on how the sheets are taped together. Arrange your classroom so that adequate space is available.

Step 1: Visualize 1,000

Have students brainstorm ideas about things they could collect and display in quantities of a thousand. Discuss why one collection of 1,000 objects might not weigh the same or take the same space as another collection of 1,000 objects, yet they are called a thousand.

Use 10 base ten flats or transparencies of them arranged in a 2-x-5 array to model a thousand.

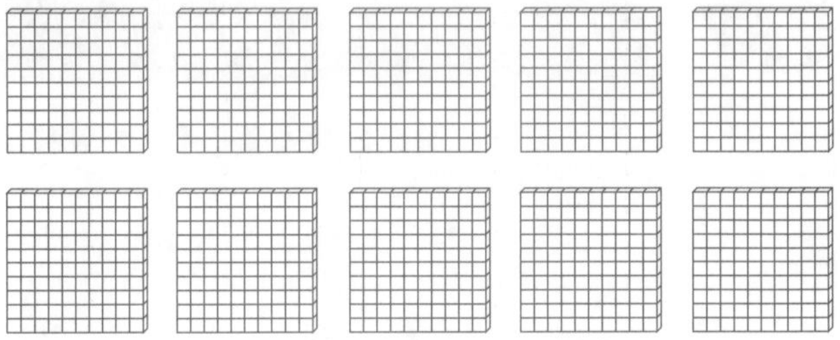

Ensure students understand the model by having them describe how much space various numbers would take up, such as 405, 45, 339, 39, 99, and 999. Have students select several other numbers and use the model to visualize, compare, and order the numbers from smallest to largest.

Note: For more ideas on developing understanding of 1,000, use the lesson on *How Much, How Many, How Far, How Heavy, How Long, How Tall Is a 1000?* The lesson begins on p. 117 of this manual.

Step 2: Construct a Ten-Thousand Square

Rearrange the model of 1,000 to create a single column of 10 base ten flats, which would be a 10-x-1 array.

Show students the Ten-Thousand Square (if possible, a copy that has been enlarged) and ask them to guess how many little squares are on the paper. To help them guess, you may want to first highlight one of the tiny squares and discuss it.

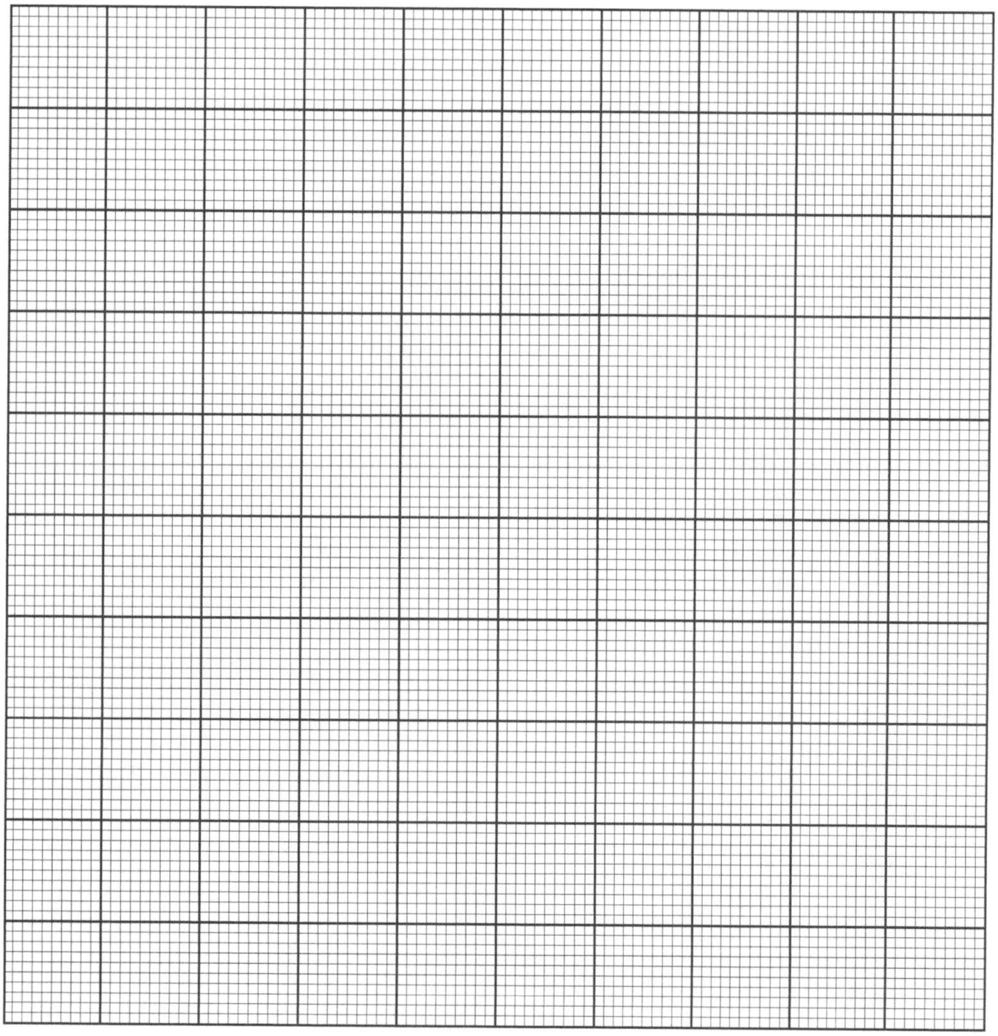

10,000 Model

Discuss how the 1,000 model (the 10-x-1 array of base ten flats) relates to the ten-thousand square and the individual base ten flats. Through discussion, establish that 10 of the 1,000 models they just made will make 10,000.

Note: Some students may have difficulty visualizing the relationship between the 1,000 model and the 10,000 square on the reproducible master because they are not proportional in size. To help them see the 10,000, ask them to imagine that each base ten flat was shrunk so that all 100 of the flats fit on one piece of paper. (You might discuss how you can reduce the size of an image on a photocopy machine or how it's similar to what happened to the children in the movie *Honey, I Shrunk the Kids*. You might even rename the activity, "Honey, I Shrunk the Base Ten Flats.")

Distribute a copy of the **Ten-Thousand Square** reproducible to each student.

How many hundreds make up 10,000? **[Answer: 100]** ***How do you know?*** **[Answer: There are ten hundreds in 1,000 and ten thousands in 10,000 so 10 x 10 = 100.]**

Have students use the model of 10,000 to visualize, compare, and order various numbers between 1 and 10,000.

Step 3: Establishing 100,000

Ask students the following question and have them explain their answers.

What number would be represented by 10 ten-thousand squares? **[Answer: 100,000]**

Tape together 10 copies of the **Ten-Thousand Square** to form a single column in a single color. (Try to tape the sheets in such a way that the grids are as close together as possible.) Show the class this set of 10 ten-thousand squares and verify why it is 100,000.

Have students use the model of 100,000 to visualize, compare, and order various numbers between 1 and 100,000.

Step 4: Establishing a Million

Discuss the concept of a million.

How could you use copies of the Ten-Thousand Square to model 1,000,000?
[Answer: Form 10 columns of 100,000]

Make a model of 1,000,000 by taping together 10 copies of the **Ten-Thousand Square** into columns of 100,000 and then taping 10 columns together. (If possible, use a different color paper for each column so they are easy to distinguish from one another. Also, try to tape the sheets in such a way that the grids are as close together as possible.)

Have students use the model of 1,000,000 to visualize, compare, and order various numbers between 1 and 1,000,000.

JOURNAL ENTRY

Tell students to write journal entries describing:

- The number of 100,000s in a million.
- The number of 10,000s in a million.
- The number of 1,000s in a million.
- The number of 100s in a million.

Responses should make references to the model of 1,000,000 made from the ten-thousand squares and not be algorithmic in nature.

EXAMPLE 1

I know there are one hundred 10,000 squares in a million because there are ten 10,000 squares in each column that stands for 100,000. Since there are ten 100,000 columns in a million, there must be one hundred 10,000 squares (10 x 10 = 100).

EXAMPLE 2

In the 1,000,000 model we made, each column stands for 100,000 and every column has ten 10,000 squares, so 10 x 10 = 100, which means there are one hundred 10,000s in a million.

PRACTICE: PSYCHIC MATH

Materials

Psychic Math (Reproducible Master 52); self-stick notes or small pieces of paper

This activity gives students practice with basic place-value knowledge and number classifications, including multiples and even and odd numbers. In this game, students randomly pick a six-digit number and score points based on how many specific parameters their number meets. Once students know all the parameters, they work individually or in pairs to find six-digit numbers that will score the greatest number of points.

Playing as a Class

Tell the students that you are thinking of rules for making different six-digit numbers. Encourage them to "read your mind" and write a six-digit number on their papers that meets as many rules as possible.

One by one, reveal the rules on the **Psychic Math** reproducible. Students receive points when their numbers meet one of your rules. Have them keep track of and then total their points.

Survey the class to find out who has the greatest number of points. Verify the results by writing this number on the board and checking each of the parameters.

Have students check each other's papers to verify other results.

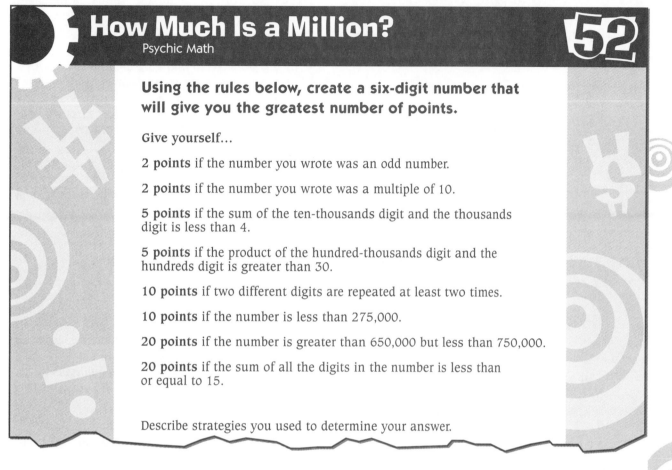

How Much Is a Million?

Psychic Math

52

Using the rules below, create a six-digit number that will give you the greatest number of points.

Give yourself...

2 points if the number you wrote was an odd number.

2 points if the number you wrote was a multiple of 10.

5 points if the sum of the ten-thousands digit and the thousands digit is less than 4.

5 points if the product of the hundred-thousands digit and the hundreds digit is greater than 30.

10 points if two different digits are repeated at least two times.

10 points if the number is less than 275,000.

20 points if the number is greater than 650,000 but less than 750,000.

20 points if the sum of all the digits in the number is less than or equal to 15.

Describe strategies you used to determine your answer.

EXAMPLE

Clark recorded 478,003. He scored a total of 2 points.

Rules	Answer	Possible Points	Points Scored
Is the number an odd number?	yes	2	2
Is the number a multiple of 10?	no	2	0
Is the sum of the ten-thousands digit and the thousands digit less than 4?	no (7 + 8 = 15)	5	0
Is the product of the hundred-thousands digit and the hundreds digit greater than 30?	no (4 x 0 = 0)	5	0
Are two different digits repeated at least two times?	no (only 0 is repeated twice)	10	0
Is the number less than 275,000?	no	10	0
Is the number greater than 650,000 but less than 750,000?	no	20	0
Is the sum of all the digits less than or equal to 15?	no (4 + 7 + 8 + 0 + 0 + 3 = 22)	20	0

Total points: 2

Creating a High-Scoring Number

Distribute Psychic Math and self-stick notes or small pieces of paper to individual students or pairs.

Challenge students to figure out a number that will score the most points. Using self-stick notes or small pieces of paper for each digit makes it easier to experiment with different arrangements of digits to find the one that will generate the highest score. [Answer: 62 points is highest possible score. The numbers that can achieve that score are: 701,610; 710,610; 711,600; 700,611; 701,501; 710,501; 701,510; 700,511; and 711,500.]

Have students check each other's papers to verify results.

EXAMPLE

Once Clark new the parameters, he scored the most points possible. The number Clark recorded was 711,500.

Discuss solutions and methods for finding the highest scoring number. Ask questions such as the following:

- ***Is it possible to find a six-digit number that scores points for every question?*** **[Answer: No. For example, a number cannot be odd and be a multiple of 10, nor can it be less than 275,000 and be between 650,000 and 750,000.]**

- ***Did you focus on the questions in order? Why or why not?*** **[Answer: There are many ways to approach the problem, but some students may focus on the two 20-point questions first.]**

ESTABLISHING A BILLION

Materials

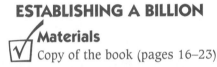

Copy of the book (pages 16–23)

Discuss the concept of a billion. Ask:

- ***How many times larger than a million is a billion?*** **[Answer: 1,000]** ***How do you know?***

Discuss the model of million that the class constructed and how much space it took up. [Answer: about 36 square feet]

- ***How could we use the model of a million to build a model of a billion?*** **[Answer: Attach 1,000 of the models of a million.]**

Rules	Answer	Possible Points	Points Scored
Is the number an odd number?	no	2	0
Is the number a multiple of 10?	yes	2	2
Is the sum of the ten-thousands digit and the thousands digit less than 4?	yes (1 + 1 = 2)	5	5
Is the product of the hundred-thousands digit and the hundreds digit greater than 30?	yes (7 x 5 = 35)	5	5
Are two different digits repeated at least two times?	yes (1 and 0 are repeated twice)	10	10
Is the number less than 275,000?	no	10	0
Is the number greater than 650,000 but less than 750,000?	yes	20	20
Is the sum of all the digits less than or equal to 15?	yes (7 + 1 + 1 + 5 + 0 + 0 = 14)	20	20

Total points: 62

How much space would it take up? [Answer: about 36,000 square feet. A football field is about 43,200 square feet (120 yards by 40 yards), so the billion model would take up about $\frac{4}{5}$ of a football field.]

Re-read pages 16–23 of *How Much Is a Million?* and discuss each of the problems involving a billion that the book introduces and how the author might have arrived at those solutions.

Note: The section called "A Note from the Author" at the end of *How Much Is A Million?* provides detailed methods for solving the problems. Students might easily attain estimates to all but the goldfish problem by multiplying their answers from **Thinking About a Million** (Reproducible Master 50) by 1,000.

MATHEMATICS ASSESSMENT

Materials

Connection to Mathematics Assessment: Check for Understanding (Reproducible Master 53)

Distribute the worksheet with multiple-choice and open-ended questions called **Connection to Mathematics Assessment: Check for Understanding.** Use this activity to check students' understanding of the mathematics concepts covered in this lesson.

Collect and score the students' work using the answers and rubric that follow.

Reproducible Master 53 with answers

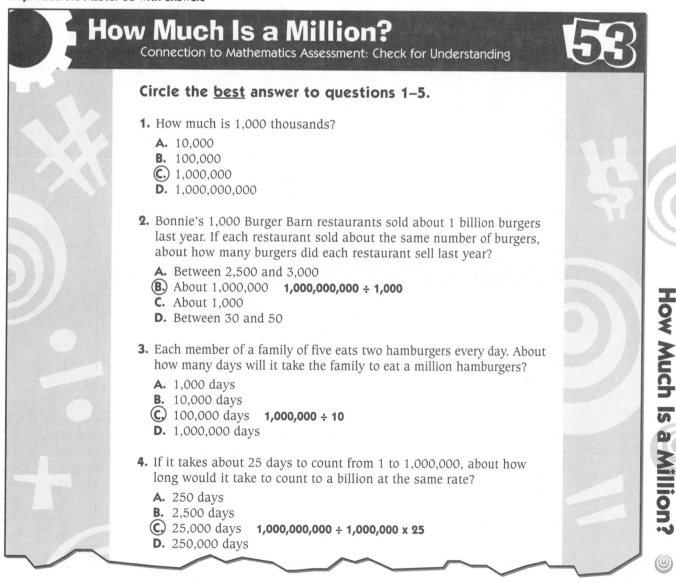

How Much Is a Million?

Connection to Mathematics Assessment: Check for Understanding

53

Circle the best answer to questions 1–5.

1. How much is 1,000 thousands?
   - A. 10,000
   - B. 100,000
   - (C.) 1,000,000
   - D. 1,000,000,000

2. Bonnie's 1,000 Burger Barn restaurants sold about 1 billion burgers last year. If each restaurant sold about the same number of burgers, about how many burgers did each restaurant sell last year?
   - A. Between 2,500 and 3,000
   - (B.) About 1,000,000 **1,000,000,000 ÷ 1,000**
   - C. About 1,000
   - D. Between 30 and 50

3. Each member of a family of five eats two hamburgers every day. About how many days will it take the family to eat a million hamburgers?
   - A. 1,000 days
   - B. 10,000 days
   - (C.) 100,000 days **1,000,000 ÷ 10**
   - D. 1,000,000 days

4. If it takes about 25 days to count from 1 to 1,000,000, about how long would it take to count to a billion at the same rate?
   - A. 250 days
   - B. 2,500 days
   - (C.) 25,000 days **1,000,000,000 ÷ 1,000,000 x 25**
   - D. 250,000 days

Continued...

5. By mistake, Lamar entered 5,600,000 into his calculator instead of 6,500,000. What can he do to the current display to correct his error?

   A. Multiply by 0.1
   B. Divide by 0.1
   C. Subtract 900,000
   (D.) Add 900,000

6. A $100 bill is about 6 inches long. About how many miles long would $1,000,000 be if $100 bills were laid end to end in a single row? Write a plan to solve the problem and then estimate or calculate the answer. (There are 5,280 feet in a mile.) **see rubric that follows for scoring**

RUBRIC FOR SCORING
Problem 6

An effective response will need to:

- calculate the number of bills and their total length.
- indicate an answer that approximates 1 mile.
- give a clear explanation.

POINTS	CRITERIA
3	The student outlines a plan that will give a reasonable answer to the problem (about 1 mile) and accurately makes all calculations or estimations in the plan. Suggested response: *1. Calculate how many $100 bills there are in a $1 million by dividing 1,000,000 by 100, or using another method to estimate 10,000.* *2. Multiply the number of $100 bills in 1,000,000 by 6 because each bill is about 6 inches long. 10,000 x 6 in. = 60,000 in.* *3. Divide 60,000 in. by 12 because there are 12 inches in a foot. 60,000 in. ÷ 12 in./ft = 5,000 ft.* *4. Covert 5,000 feet to miles. Since a mile is 5,280 feet long, the answer is a little bit less than 1 mile or about 1 mile.*
2	The student outlines a plan with minor flaws, but carries out the plan correctly. Or, the student has an accurate plan, but makes minor calculation errors. Or, the student has a correct estimate or calculation, but the plan is not clear or is missing a step. Or, the student has an incorrect estimate or calculation, but the plan would yield a correct estimate if it were implemented correctly.
1	The student outlines a plan with minor flaws and makes calculation/estimation errors when implementing the plan. Or, the student completes correct calculations based on a plan that misses steps or has major errors. Or, the student has an incorrect estimate or calculation, but the work shows evidence of some thinking about a plan. Or, the student has a reasonable estimate or calculation, but provides no explanation.
0	The student provides an incorrect estimate or calculation and no explanation, or leaves the problem blank.

Composition Connection

WRITING A POST-READING COMPOSITION

Materials

Copies of the book (one for each writing group), Rubric for Scoring First Drafts (Reproducible Master 3)

To see how this activity works, review the information on "Implementing Writing As Process," on p. *xviii* of this manual and the lesson *How Much, How Many, How Far, How Heavy, How Long, How Tall Is 1000?* beginning on p. 117.

In this activity, groups of students will work through the entire writing process, from pre-writing to publishing, using the illustrations on pp. 6–7, 8, 16, 22–23, and 30–31 of *How Much Is a Million?* as starting points.

Divide the class into writing groups and have each group select an illustration from *How Much Is a Million?* If possible, arrange it so that no two groups are using the same illustration.

Have each individual write a composition that tells a story about what is happening in the illustration chosen by that group. The story can go well beyond the illustration—describing what might have happened both before and after the moment caught in the picture.

Use this composition to lead the students all the way through a full writing-process cycle from pre-writing to publishing.

As a class, develop a rubric that can be used for evaluating this piece of writing. The students can use the **Rubric for Scoring First Drafts** as a resource, but the expanded rubric for scoring the final essays in this exercise should be more specific. The rubric should be shaped to fit this particular topic.

Have students edit and revise their compositions, based on the rubric the class developed. Members of a writing group should review the work of others in the group.

Each student's final written product should be a polished composition suitable for posting in the classroom or for taking home. As such, it should be as free as possible of errors in Standard English. Use your English grammar textbook or writing handbook as a style sheet for students to follow. They can also look at published texts to see how matters of Standard English are handled in published books. Many pairs of eyes should have studied each student's composition before it is determined to be ready for others outside of the class to read.

It would be appropriate to celebrate the arduous process of producing these polished stories by having a reading celebration for parents or for other students in the school. Select several stories that are representative of what has been produced. Any number of methods can be used to select the stories to be read, but in any case all stories should be bound and on display for the invited guests. Be sure the students who are to read their stories have had many opportunities to practice and polish their oral reading skills. On the day of the presentation, make it special with dress-up day and appropriate refreshments. Certificates can be presented to all of the writers and readers.

If you choose to assign grades on this paper, you can grade effort and understanding of the process. And if you and the class have truly succeeded, every student will earn an A on the finished composition itself. Congratulations!

ALTERNATIVE COMPOSITION ASSIGNMENT

Materials

Copies of the book, **Connection to Viewing Assessment: Writing About a Picture Prompt** (Reproducible Master 1); **Have I...? Checklist** (Reproducible Master 2); **Rubric for Scoring First Drafts** (Reproducible Master 3)

If you wish to provide students with more practice in writing on demand, you may choose to follow the same process used in the Viewing Connection activity. See p. 130 for directions.

You can have the whole class write about an illustration that you choose from *How Much Is a Million?* As an alternative, arrange students into groups and assign each group an illustration. Each student in the group then writes about that illustration.

This activity takes less time than the preceding one, and it will not result in a publishable written product.

Extending the Connections

ESTABLISHING A TRILLION

Materials
Copy of the book (pages 24–33)

Use a question-and-answer technique to establish that 1,000 billions is equal to a trillion (1,000,000,000,000). Refer to the Mathematics Connection activities "Establishing a Million Using Ten-Thousand Squares" on p. 134 and "Establishing a Billion" on p. 136 for ideas.

CLOSURE AND PROJECTS

Materials
Working with a Million: Problems and Projects I and II (Reproducible Masters 54–55), calculators. Optional: scale, pennies, ream of paper, rulers, container with mL markings, several liter and/or quart containers

Use the problems and projects on **Working with a Million: Problems and Projects I and II** to help students establish more of a meaning for the size of a million. Students should not be expected to complete all of the problems or projects. You may want to assign one or more problems or projects to the whole class to solve for a class assignment or homework. Or you can assign different problems to groups of students and have them report their findings to the class.

The problems in **Working with a Million: Problems and Projects I** provide most of the reference information students need to find a solution. Problem 4 may require additional resources to determine the number of days in a school year and a scale and pennies to determine the weight of the coins. Or, students could use the weight information provided in problem 1.

To complete any of the six projects in **Working with a Million: Problems and Projects II**, students will need to use sample materials to establish their own references.

Reproducible Master 54 with answers

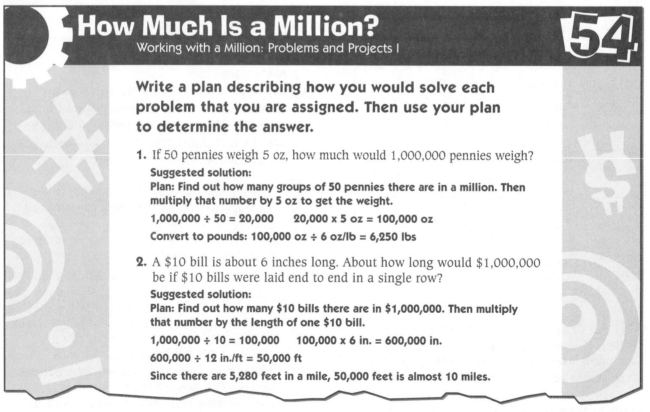

How Much Is a Million?

Working with a Million: Problems and Projects I

54

Write a plan describing how you would solve each problem that you are assigned. Then use your plan to determine the answer.

1. If 50 pennies weigh 5 oz, how much would 1,000,000 pennies weigh?
   Suggested solution:
   Plan: Find out how many groups of 50 pennies there are in a million. Then multiply that number by 5 oz to get the weight.
   1,000,000 ÷ 50 = 20,000 20,000 x 5 oz = 100,000 oz
   Convert to pounds: 100,000 oz ÷ 6 oz/lb = 6,250 lbs

2. A $10 bill is about 6 inches long. About how long would $1,000,000 be if $10 bills were laid end to end in a single row?
   Suggested solution:
   Plan: Find out how many $10 bills there are in $1,000,000. Then multiply that number by the length of one $10 bill.
   1,000,000 ÷ 10 = 100,000 100,000 x 6 in. = 600,000 in.
   600,000 ÷ 12 in./ft = 50,000 ft
   Since there are 5,280 feet in a mile, 50,000 feet is almost 10 miles.

Continued...

Reproducible Master 54 with answers (continued)

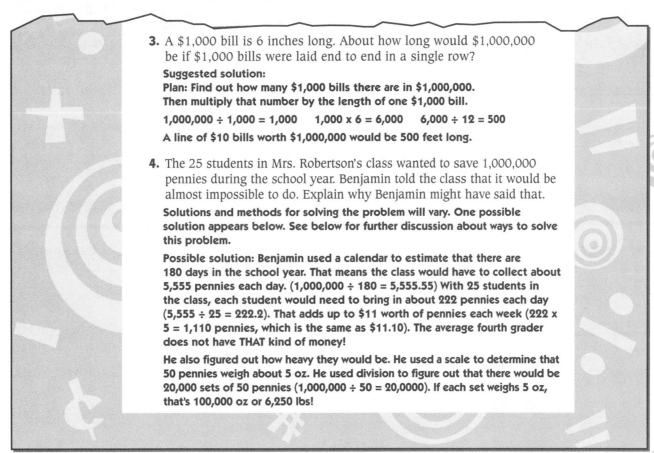

3. A $1,000 bill is 6 inches long. About how long would $1,000,000 be if $1,000 bills were laid end to end in a single row?

   Suggested solution:

   Plan: Find out how many $1,000 bills there are in $1,000,000. Then multiply that number by the length of one $1,000 bill.

   1,000,000 ÷ 1,000 = 1,000 1,000 x 6 = 6,000 6,000 ÷ 12 = 500

   A line of $10 bills worth $1,000,000 would be 500 feet long.

4. The 25 students in Mrs. Robertson's class wanted to save 1,000,000 pennies during the school year. Benjamin told the class that it would be almost impossible to do. Explain why Benjamin might have said that.

   Solutions and methods for solving the problem will vary. One possible solution appears below. See below for further discussion about ways to solve this problem.

   Possible solution: Benjamin used a calendar to estimate that there are 180 days in the school year. That means the class would have to collect about 5,555 pennies each day. (1,000,000 ÷ 180 = 5,555.55) With 25 students in the class, each student would need to bring in about 222 pennies each day (5,555 ÷ 25 = 222.2). That adds up to $11 worth of pennies each week (222 x 5 = 1,110 pennies, which is the same as $11.10). The average fourth grader does not have THAT kind of money!

   He also figured out how heavy they would be. He used a scale to determine that 50 pennies weigh about 5 oz. He used division to figure out that there would be 20,000 sets of 50 pennies (1,000,000 ÷ 50 = 20,0000). If each set weighs 5 oz, that's 100,000 oz or 6,250 lbs!

Students may take a variety of approaches to solving problem 4. Here's just one alternative:

> Benjamin divided 1,000,000 by 25 students to determine that each student would have to collect 40,000 pennies during the school year. He divided by 100 to convert to dollars and realized that each student would have to collect $400. That's way too much money for a fourth grader to collect in one school year!

Depending on the methods students used to solve problem 4, you might prompt them with questions such as the following:

About how many pennies would Mrs. Robertson's class need to collect each day? each week? **[Answer: Based on a 180-day school year, 5,555 daily; 27,775 weekly]**

In the first possible solution suggested, Benjamin calculates the weight of the pennies. On **Working with a Million: Problems and Projects II**, problem 6 involves calculating the weight of 1,000,000 pennies. You might follow up that problem by referring back to problem 4 on **Working with a Million: Problems and Projects I** and asking questions such as the following:

If Mrs. Robertson's students collected the same number of pennies daily toward their goal of 1,000,000, how much would the pennies weigh after a week? after a month? after three months?

[Answer: Based on a 180-day school year, the class would collect 5,555 pennies per day or 27,775 weekly (5,555 x 5). If 50 pennies weigh about 5 oz, 27,775 would weigh about 2,778 oz (27,775 oz ÷ 50 x 5) or 174 lbs weekly (2,778 oz ÷ 16 oz/lb). Using an estimate of 4 weeks in a month, the pennies would weigh 696 lbs after a month (174 x 4), and 2,088 lbs after three months (696 x 3).]

How Much Is a Million?

Working with a Million: Problems and Projects II

55

5. How tall would one million $1 bills be if they were stacked on top of each other?

Possible solution: Plan: Measure a stack of paper instead of $1 bills. A ream of 500 sheets of paper is about 2 inches tall. Find out how many sets of 500 $1 bills it would take to make a million. Multiply by 2 inches.

It would take 2,000 sets of 500 $1 bills to make a million (1,000,000 ÷ 500 = 2,000). If each set is 2 inches tall, the entire group would be 4,000 inches tall (2,000 x 2 in. = 4,000). That's the same as 333 feet 4 inches tall (4,000 ÷ 12 = 333 ft R4).

6. How heavy would a million pennies be?

Suggested solution: 50 pennies weigh approximately 5 oz. Since 1,000,000 ÷ 50 = 20,000, there are 20,000 sets of 50 pennies in a million. Each one of those sets weighs about 5 oz, therefore 1,000,000 pennies would weigh about 100,000 oz. Since 100,000 ÷ 16 = 6,250, a million pennies would weigh about 6,250 lbs.

7. How high would a stack of 1 million pennies be?

Suggested solution: A stack of 100 pennies is about 6 inches high. Since 1,000,000 ÷ 100 = 10,000, there are 10,000 sets of 100 pennies in a million. If each set is 6 inches high, the 10,000 sets would be 60,000 inches or 5,000 feet tall (60,000 ÷ 12 in./ft = 5,000 ft). A stack of pennies would be about 1 mile high because there are 5,280 feet in a mile.

Alternative: If 100 pennies measures 6 inches, 200 pennies would be a foot. 1,000,000 ÷ 200 ft = 5,000 ft.

8. What size container would be needed to hold 1,000,000 drops of water?

Suggested solution: It takes about 20 drops of water to make a milliliter. At that rate, it would take about 20,000 drops to make a liter. (A liter is 1,000 mL, so 1,000 x 20 yields the number of drops in a liter.) Since 1,000,000 ÷ 20,000 = 50, it would take about 50 liter containers to hold 1,000,000 drops. A liter is a little more than a quart, so we would need more than 50, one-quart containers to hold 1,000,000 drops of water. Or, we could convert 50 quarts to about 13 gallons.

9. How long would it take to earn $1,000,000 if you were paid $1 per minute and worked 40 hours per week for 50 weeks per year?

Suggested solution: At $1 per minute, a person would make $60 per hour or $2,400 per week (60 x 40). Since 1,000,000 ÷ 2,400 is 416 R1,600, it would take approximately 417 weeks, which is 8 1/3 years (417 ÷ 52 = 8 R17).

10. Which weighs more, a million dollars in $1 bills or a million dollars in gold?

Possible solution: Twenty $1 bills weigh about 1 oz. Since there are 50,000 sets of 20 in 1,000,000, a million $1 bills must weigh 50,000 oz or 3,125 lbs (50,000 ÷ 16). The value of gold fluctuates each day. If on a particular day, the price of gold is about $300 an ounce, we could purchase about 3,333 oz of gold with a million dollars (1,000,000 ÷ 300). A million dollars in gold weighs about 208 lbs (3,333 ÷ 16), which is a lot less than the 3,125-lb weight of the $1 bills.

A Note of Caution to the Ambitious

After solving some of these problems, students may want to save 1,000,000 of something—but use caution. The students at the Merriam Avenue School in Newton, N.J., saved a million pennies. It took them three years to complete the project! In fact, they went over their goal, saving $12,550. (One million pennies would be worth exactly $10,000.) The 7,530 lbs of pennies they saved were placed in 251 bags weighing 30 lbs each.

Logistics for the collection included having jars in every classroom so students could save pennies on a daily basis. When the jars were full, they were emptied into a 10-gallon jug that held $326 worth of pennies when full. The 10-gallon jug was then emptied into a big wooden box that was kept in the lobby of the school until the day came when the students knew they had over a million pennies. Half the money went to charity; the other half, to materials for the school. An article about their feat appeared in The Newark, N.J., *Star-Ledger* on May 28, 1999.

ADDITIONAL RESOURCES

ESPA^3 Mathematics Daily Activities for Math Success, Books 1 and 2. Iowa City, Iowa: Tutor Tools, Inc., 1998. Call 1-800-776-3454 for information.

Lawrence, Paul. *Computational Competency: Aerobics for the Mind.* LLTeach, 1998. Call 1-800-575-7670 for information.

Ten-thousand square manipulatives for modeling a million. Available from LLTeach. Call 1-800-575-7670 for information.

Windows on Math, Volume 5 Videodisc, Unit 6, Topic 1. "A Penny Saved." Atlanta: Optical Data Corporation, 1996. Call 1-800-524-2481 for information.

Teacher Notes

The King's Commissioners

Written by **Aileen Friedman**
Illustrated by **Susan Guevara**

Overview of the Connections

This story is about a king who has so many commissioners that he decides to count them. His two royal advisors and his daughter, the princess, each count the commissioners in a different way. The different strategies confuse the king until his daughter shows they all counted the same number.

In teaching mathematics, the story shows that when analyzing the same set of objects, counting by twos, fives, or tens will yield the same result. Activities help students develop an understanding of our place-value system by counting and measuring with tens models. Hopefully, students conclude that our place-value system is an efficient way to represent numbers.

Additional activities present alternative methods for adding double-digit numbers. Students use pennies, dimes, and dollars; hundred boards; or color cubes to model problems and then connect them to symbolic representations. Games help build a foundation for understanding, renaming, and regrouping, as students exchange ones, tens, and hundreds models. In addition, students practice mentally adding hundreds, tens, and ones.

Students will also have the opportunity to practice listening skills, making predictions, and writing about their experience and the experiences of others.

MATERIALS FOR THE CONNECTIONS

The King's Commissioners • ISBN 0-590-48989-5
Written by Aileen Friedman. Illustrated by Susan Guevara. New York: Scholastic Inc., 1994.

Language Arts

One to five copies of the book (Note: In the Viewing Connection, each student will need to see the front cover of the book. In Extending the Connection, groups will need to see pages 20–21. You may wish to have several copies available.)

~ **Connection to Viewing Assessment: Writing About a Picture Prompt** (Reproducible Master 1)

~ A self-monitoring tool for student writers called **Have I...? Checklist** (Reproducible Master 2)

~ **Rubric for Scoring First Drafts** (Reproducible Master 3)

~ **Connection to Listening Assessment: Listening to Part of a Story** (Reproducible Master 56)

~ **Connection to Writing Assessment: Post-Reading Composition** (Reproducible Master 59)

~ **Commissioners' Jobs** (Reproducible Master 60)

Mathematics

~ Items to count, such as beans, cubes, macaroni, marbles, or paper clips (110 pieces for each group of 2–3 students)

~ Jar to hold 47 items

~ Self-stick notes or index cards

~ Bags to hold 110 items (1 for each group of 2–3 students)

~ Connecting cubes in assorted colors (about 50 for each group of 2–3 students)

~ Base ten blocks: units, rods, flats

~ Money models: pennies, dimes, \$1 bills, \$10 bills, \$100 bills

~ Random-number generators for 0–9, such as playing cards with jacks as 0, aces as 1, and kings, queens, and 10s removed; or 10-sided die with 0–9; or 0–9 spinners

~ Scoring chips (counters)

~ **Place Value Recording Sheet** (Reproducible Master 57)

~ **Connection to Mathematics Assessment: Check for Understanding**

~ **Hundred Board (0 to 100)** (Reproducible Master 61)

Viewing Connection

INTRODUCING THE LESSON WITH A PICTURE PROMPT AND WRITING

Materials

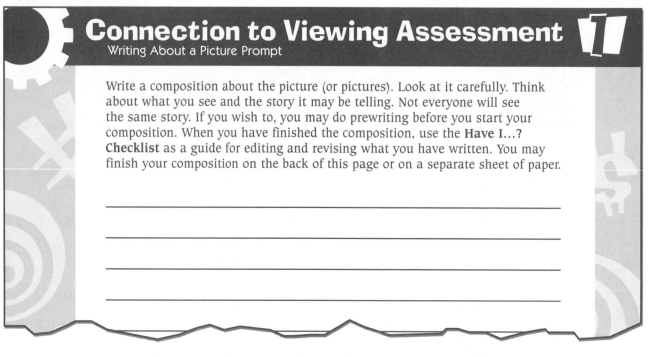

Cover of the book, Connection to Viewing Assessment: Writing About a Picture Prompt (Reproducible Master 1), **Have I...? Checklist** (Reproducible Master 2), **Rubric for Scoring First Drafts** (Reproducible Master 3)

Show the class the picture on the cover of *The King's Commissioners*. If possible, allow students to continue to look at the picture throughout the writing session. You may distribute a copy of **Connection to Assessment: Writing About a Picture Prompt** to each student, or they may use notebook paper for their work. Also distribute copies of the **Have I...? Checklist**.

Read these directions to the class:

"You are going to write a composition about this picture. Look at it carefully. Think about what you see and the story it may be telling. It is OK that not everyone will see the same story. If you wish to, you may do prewriting before you start your composition. When you have finished the composition, use the **Have I...? Checklist** as a guide for editing and revising what you have written."

Give the students 20–30 minutes to write their compositions and do initial editing.

Collect and score the students' compositions using the **Rubric for Scoring First Drafts**. Teach students how to compare their scored compositions to the rubric and to make notes about how to improve their compositions. Students also may be taught to use the rubric to score their own work or that of other students.

Reproducible Master 1

Connection to Viewing Assessment 1

Writing About a Picture Prompt

Write a composition about the picture (or pictures). Look at it carefully. Think about what you see and the story it may be telling. Not everyone will see the same story. If you wish to, you may do prewriting before you start your composition. When you have finished the composition, use the **Have I...? Checklist** as a guide for editing and revising what you have written. You may finish your composition on the back of this page or on a separate sheet of paper.

____

____

____

____

Listening Connection

LISTENING TO PART OF A STORY AND ANSWERING QUESTIONS

Materials

Copy of the book (Listening section: first 9 pages, 313 words), **Connection to Listening Assessment: Listening to Part of a Story** (Reproducible Master 56)

This activity will help students develop effective listening skills. As necessary, teach or review some of the effective listening strategies found on page *xv* of this manual.

Tell the class you are going to read them part of a story. When you are finished, they will answer some questions about what you have read. (The rest of the story will be read in the Mathematics Connection activity.)

Read the first 9 pages aloud to the students. The pages are not numbered, so consider the first page of the text as page 1. The listening section starts with: *The king was confused.* It ends with: *The royal advisors took their places. The king motioned to the Imperial Doorman. "Let in the royal commissioners," he ordered. "One by one."*

Since you are working on listening, don't stop to discuss the story, show the illustrations, or make predictions, as you might do in a reading instructional period.

Distribute the worksheet with multiple-choice and open-ended questions called **Connection to Listening Assessment: Listening to Part of a Story**.

Allow students 15–20 minutes for completing the worksheet.

Collect and score the students' work using the answers and rubric that follow.

Proceed to the Mathematics Connection for instructions on completing the book.

Reproducible Master 56 with answers

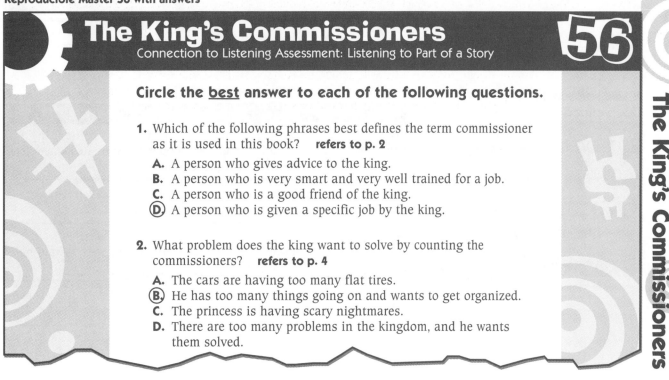

The King's Commissioners 56

Connection to Listening Assessment: Listening to Part of a Story

Circle the best answer to each of the following questions.

1. Which of the following phrases best defines the term commissioner as it is used in this book? **refers to p. 2**
   - **A.** A person who gives advice to the king.
   - **B.** A person who is very smart and very well trained for a job.
   - **C.** A person who is a good friend of the king.
   - **(D)** A person who is given a specific job by the king.

2. What problem does the king want to solve by counting the commissioners? **refers to p. 4**
   - **A.** The cars are having too many flat tires.
   - **(B)** He has too many things going on and wants to get organized.
   - **C.** The princess is having scary nightmares.
   - **D.** There are too many problems in the kingdom, and he wants them solved.

Continued...

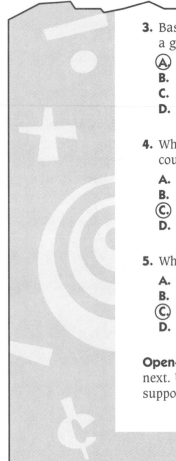

3. Based on the actions of the king and his royal advisors, what is a good first step in completing any difficult task? **refers to p. 7**
   - (A.) Make a plan.
   - B. Immediately start working on the solution.
   - C. Get everyone together to discuss the situation.
   - D. Solve the problem yourself.

4. What is another way of saying that the commissioners will be counted "one by one"? **refers to p. 9**
   - A. They will be counted in the order they come in the door.
   - B. They will be counted by three different people.
   - (C.) They will be counted individually.
   - D. They will be counted all at once.

5. Why are there so many commissioners in the kingdom? **refers to p. 2**
   - A. It is a good way to give a lot of people jobs in the palace.
   - B. The princess has many problems that need to be solved.
   - (C.) Someone is appointed to solve each new problem that arises.
   - D. The king does not want to solve any problems.

Open-ended Listening Task: Explain what you think will happen next. Use details from the story or from your own experience to support your answer. **see rubric that follows for scoring**

RUBRIC FOR SCORING

Open-ended Listening Task

An effective response will need to:

- reflect knowledge of the story.
- justify ideas from the text.
- make logical and reasonable predictions about what might happen.
- be well written with a clear presentation.

POINTS	CRITERIA
4	Writer makes a logical prediction, using evidence from the story. Writer shows insight and understanding. Response is well written with a clear presentation.
3	Response is logical and uses details from the story. It is generally well written but has some errors.
2	Response is logical and is either well written or uses evidence from the story. Or, response may be well written but is lacking in logic or details.
1	Response is sketchy and/or poorly written. It may show that writer does not understand the story.

Mathematics Connection

INTRODUCTION AND ACTIVE READING

Materials

Copy of the book; jar of 47 beans; connecting cubes, or other small items; self-stick notes

Review the section you have already read (pages 1–9) from the Listening Connection, showing students the illustrations and discussing what they have already heard. In some classes, you may find it worthwhile to go back to the beginning and re-read the entire selection. This is a good way to help students confirm the answers they gave in the listening activity. If necessary, explore the rationale behind some of the answers.

Tell students that before you finish the story, you want to discuss some concepts that may help them understand the material more fully.

Place a jar of 47 beans or connecting cubes on a desk where all can see. Ask students to predict how many beans are in the jar and to write their predictions on a self-stick note or index card. Collect the guesses and read the numbers while informally organizing the self-stick notes on the chalkboard. Discuss the range of the guesses, pointing out guesses that are close together or those that stand out by themselves.

Ask students how they think they might be able to tell the number of beans without actually counting them one by one. Discuss their ideas.

ACTING OUT THE STORY

Materials

One or more copies of the book; beans, connecting cubes, or other small items (47 for each group of 2–3 students)

Distribute 47 beans (or cubes) to groups of 2–3 students. Tell them that their bags have the same number of beans that are in the jar. Have the groups count the beans in any manner they like. Discuss the results and the different ways they counted.

Read the rest of the story. As you read, have students use beans to model the counting methods of each royal advisor. Show the pictures of the tally marks and have students use their beans to model the groupings.

- On page 14, the first royal advisor counts "twenty-three 2s and 1 more."
- On page 16, the second royal advisor counts "nine 5s and 2 more."

Ask students if they know how many commissioners there are from the advisors' descriptions and tallies.

Before reading on, ask students to predict what the princess will do. Then have them use the beans to model the princess' method.

- On page 18, the royal organizer makes four rows of 10 commissioners and has 7 left over.

Have students write a journal entry describing the most efficient way to count the commissioners and why.

COUNTING BAGS OF 100

Materials

Bags of 110 cubes, beans, macaroni, or paper clips (1 for each group of 2–3 students)

Distribute bags of 100 items to each team of 2–3 students. Assign each team a counting method, such as counting by twos, threes, fives, or tens.

When you say "Go," teams empty their bags and count the items using the method they were assigned. Team members should raise their hands when they know the total number. Compare the order in which teams finish with the methods they use. Which method was fastest? slowest?

Repeat the race, this time using bags of 110 items. Assign each team a counting method different from the one they used previously. For example, the group that counted by tens might count by twos this time.

Compare the results to what students said in their journal entries. Ask if this activity confirmed what they thought or changed their minds. Discuss how this exercise is similar to the situation the princess and the royal advisors were in.

MEASURING AND COUNTING WITH CUBES

Materials
Connecting cubes, self-stick notes

Distribute one connecting cube and a self-stick note to each student. Explain that they will use connecting-cube towers to measure things. Each "cube" represents a nonstandard unit of measure. Ask them to guess the heights of their desks in "cubes" and write it on a self-stick note. Collect the guesses and read the numbers while informally organizing the self-stick notes on the board. Discuss the range of the guesses, pointing out guesses that are close together or those that stand out by themselves.

Have pairs of students get more cubes and build connecting-cube towers high enough to measure the heights of their desks. Observe how the children build the towers. Some will randomly place different colors together, others will make patterns by alternating colors in groups of two, five, or ten. After students determine heights, ask them to compare the various towers everyone made.

Use a think-pair-share technique to have students test different tower configurations and decide which ones are easiest to measure with. Lead students to see that grouping by tens makes a very efficient measuring device, but don't insist that they count by tens.

Demonstrate the counting and measuring, if necessary, using four different towers. Use a randomly arranged tower to count by ones. Use another tower made with cubes grouped by two to count by twos. A third tower demonstrates cubes grouped by five. Finally, the fourth tower allows you to count by groups of ten. To connect this hands-on model to a recording model, make tally marks on the board as you count the various groups of cubes.

CLOSURE

Use a think-pair-share technique to compare all the counting methods students have experienced in the lesson. Tell them to think about how the king's royal advisors and the princess counted the commissioners. Ask how those methods were similar to or different from the ways they counted the beans or measured the heights of their desks. They should conclude that counting by tens was the most efficient way.

Have students respond to the following prompt in their journals.
Claude wanted to count the number of sugarcoated candies in a 1-pound bag. He decided to count them one by one as he took each candy out of the bag. Is Claude's way of counting the best way to count the candies in the bag? Tell why you agree or disagree. If you disagree, describe a method that would be more efficient.

DEVELOPING PLACE VALUE WITH GAMES: Win a Flat, Lose a Flat

Materials
Base-ten blocks: units, rods, flats; dice (set of materials for each group of players)

The objective of the game is for students to use base-ten models to represent numbers they've randomly generated. Players then add or subtract the numbers, making exchanges between units and rods whenever possible until one of the players reaches or goes over 100 (enough to make a flat).

Distribute a set of materials to each group of 2–3 students.

Play the Win-a-Flat Game. Students take turns rolling dice and build the number that is rolled, using base-ten models. With each subsequent roll, the new number is added to the old and players keep building their models. As play progresses, players must exchange 10 units for 1 rod. The first student to reach 10 rods, or 100, makes a flat and wins the game.

Play the Lose-a-Flat Game. The rules are the same, but players start with 100 (a flat) and remove the base-ten blocks from their sets each time they roll the dice. The first player to get rid of their models wins the game.

DEVELOPING PLACE VALUE WITH MONEY: Modeling Two-Digit Addition

Materials

Money models: pennies, dimes, $1 bills, $10 bills; random-number generators for 0–9 (playing cards with jacks as 0, aces as 1, and kings, queens, and 10s removed; or 10-sided die with 0-9; or 0–9 spinner)

In this activity, students randomly generate two-digit numbers to model and add. Pennies, dimes, and dollars are used to represent the ones, tens, and hundreds, respectively. To add, coins are combined and exchanged so that the fewest number of dollars, dimes, and pennies appears in the answer.

Distribute random-number generators and money models to pairs or small groups. You may provide 10-sided (decahedron) or 20-sided (icosahedron) dice, or spinners as generators. Each pair will generate 2 random two-digit numbers, model them with coins, and add them together.

First, have students randomly generate a two-digit number. The first toss/draw/spin determines the number of tens and the second toss/draw/spin determines the number of ones. Pairs should model the number using the appropriate number of dimes and pennies.

Then, have them create and model another two-digit number in the same way.

Have students add the two numbers. They should combine the money models and make exchanges so that as few pennies and dimes as possible are used to represent the sum. When needed, dollar bills should be exchanged for 10 dimes. Then have them record the two-digit or three-digit sum using symbols.

Simulate this activity on the chalkboard once students become proficient at it. As you write the two-digit numbers and the corresponding sums, have students use coins to model each step of the process. Stress the connection between the symbols and the money models.

Eventually, you may present an addition problem and ask students to explain how they could use dimes and pennies to arrive at an answer.

DEVELOPING PLACE VALUE WITH GAMES: Add the Hundreds, Tens, and Ones

Materials

Random-number generators for 0–9 (playing cards with jacks as 0, aces as 1, and kings, queens, and 10s removed; or 10-sided die with 0–9; or 0–9 spinner); **Place Value Recording Sheets** for each player (Reproducible Master 57)

The objective of the game is for students to add a group of 100s, 10s, and 1s mentally.

Distribute random-number generators and the **Place Value Recording Sheet** to groups of 2–3 students.

Play the game. Each player alternately generates and records sets of 100s, 10s, and 1s by using a random-digit generator and the **Place Value Recording Sheet.**

The first toss/draw/spin represents the first set of 100s, the second toss/draw/spin represents the next set of 100s, the third toss/draw/spin represents the first set of 10s, and so on. After each toss/draw/spin the value of the number is recorded on one row of the **Place Value Recording Sheet.**

After 7 tosses, each player mentally sums the numbers recorded in a row and marks it on the sheet. Players then add all the digits in that sum. The player with the greatest "digit sum" wins the round. The round winner takes a scoring chip. The player with the most chips at the end of play wins the game.

EXAMPLE ROUND

Norma generates the digits 4, 5, 3, 7, 2, 8, and 9 and completes a row in her **Place Value Recording Sheet** as shown below. The "row sum" is 400 + 500 + 30 + 70 + 20 + 8 + 9 = 1,037. The "digit sum" is 1 + 0 + 3 + 7 = 11.

Norton generates the digits 4, 1, 6, 8, 7, 6, and 7. The "row sum" is 400 + 100 + 60 + 80 + 70 + 6 +7 = 723. The "digit sum" is 7 + 2 + 3 = 12. Norton wins the round and takes a chip because 12 > 11.

Name Norma **Date** ______

Round 1

100	100	10	10	10	1	1	Row sum	Digit sum
400	500	30	70	20	8	9	1,037	11

Name Norton **Date** ______

Round 1

100	100	10	10	10	1	1	Row sum	Digit sum
400	100	60	80	70	6	7	723	12

DEVELOPING PLACE VALUE: Chip Trading

Materials

Chips or connecting cubes in four different colors; random-number generators for 0–9, such as playing cards with jacks as 0, aces as 1, and kings, queens, and 10s removed; or 10-sided die with 0–9; or 0–9 spinners

Define different color chips or connecting cubes to represent 1,000s, 100s, 10s, and 1s. Model various two- and three-digit numbers using the colors. Then model randomly generated addition and subtraction problems using the colored chips.

EXAMPLE

The numbers 234 and 789 are randomly generated. The color key is:

Orange cube = 1,000 Blue cube = 100
Yellow cube = 10 Red cube = 1

Students model:

- 2 blue cubes, 3 yellow cubes, and 4 red cubes to represent 234.
- 7 blue cubes, 8 yellow cubes, and 9 red cubes to represent 789.

To add, students:

- exchange 10 red cubes for 1 yellow cube.
- exchange 10 yellow cubes for 1 blue cube.
- exchange 10 blue cubes for 1 orange cube.

The result is 1 orange cube, 0 blue cubes, 2 yellow cubes, and 3 red cubes, which represents the sum 1,023.

MATHEMATICS ASSESSMENT

Materials

Individual copies of **Connection to Mathematics Assessment: Check for Understanding** (Reproducible Master 58)

Distribute the worksheet with multiple-choice and open-ended questions called **Connection to Mathematics Assessment: Check for Understanding.** This activity can be used to check students' understanding of the mathematics concepts covered in this lesson.

Collect and **score** the students' work using the answers and rubric that follow.

Reproducible Master 58 with answers

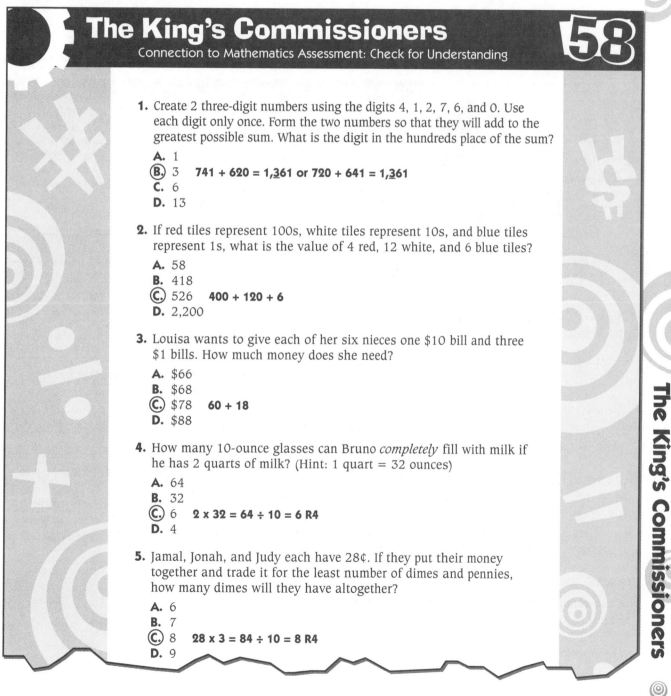

The King's Commissioners

Connection to Mathematics Assessment: Check for Understanding

58

1. Create 2 three-digit numbers using the digits 4, 1, 2, 7, 6, and 0. Use each digit only once. Form the two numbers so that they will add to the greatest possible sum. What is the digit in the hundreds place of the sum?

A. 1
(B.) 3 **741 + 620 = 1,3̲61 or 720 + 641 = 1,3̲61**
C. 6
D. 13

2. If red tiles represent 100s, white tiles represent 10s, and blue tiles represent 1s, what is the value of 4 red, 12 white, and 6 blue tiles?

A. 58
B. 418
(C.) 526 **400 + 120 + 6**
D. 2,200

3. Louisa wants to give each of her six nieces one $10 bill and three $1 bills. How much money does she need?

A. $66
B. $68
(C.) $78 **60 + 18**
D. $88

4. How many 10-ounce glasses can Bruno *completely* fill with milk if he has 2 quarts of milk? (Hint: 1 quart = 32 ounces)

A. 64
B. 32
(C.) 6 **2 x 32 = 64 ÷ 10 = 6 R4**
D. 4

5. Jamal, Jonah, and Judy each have 28¢. If they put their money together and trade it for the least number of dimes and pennies, how many dimes will they have altogether?

A. 6
B. 7
(C.) 8 **28 x 3 = 84 ÷ 10 = 8 R4**
D. 9

6. Latisha, Sue-Ling, and Delbert each bought a 1-pound bag of candy and then counted the candies in their bags. Latisha counted 24 groups of 10. Sue-Ling counted 45 groups of 5. Delbert counted 122 groups of 2. Who had the most candies? Explain how you know. Who probably counted the candies the fastest? Explain why. **see rubric below for scoring**

RUBRIC FOR SCORING

Problem 6

An effective response will need to:

- show that Delbert had the most candies.
- explain good reasoning for whoever is named the fastest counter.
- give a clear explanation.

POINTS	CRITERIA
3	Response indicates and clearly explains why Delbert had the most candies. The student chooses any of the three names as the fastest counter and provides a reasonable explanation for their choice. Possible response: Delbert had the most candies because 122 groups of 2 is equal to 244 candies (2 x 122). Latisha only had 240 candies (24 x 10) and Sue-Ling only had 225 candies (45 x 5). Latisha probably counted the fastest because she grouped her candies by 10s.
2	One or both of the explanations to the two parts of the question are flawed. Or, one of the two parts is correct but the other is unclear or contains minor errors. For example, the student names the wrong person with the most candies because of an error shown in computing the totals.
1	The answer to the first part is correct but provides no explanation, while the answer to the second part has some flaws in the explanation. Or, the answer to the first part is incorrect, and the answer to the second part has a reasonable explanation.
0	The student shows no understanding of either part or leaves the problem blank.

Composition Connection

WRITING A POST-READING COMPOSITION

Materials

One or more copies of the book, Connection to Writing Assessment: Post-Reading Composition (Reproducible Master 59), **Have I...? Checklist** (Reproducible Master 2), **Rubric for Scoring First Drafts** (Reproducible Master 3)

Re-read the story to the class. This time give the students ample opportunities to interact with and discuss the illustrations. Ask them to think about how the illustrations add to their understanding of the story.

Encourage a discussion in which students compare and contrast the experience of reading the book with and without seeing the illustrations. Introduce the idea of using visualization to listen effectively when they cannot see illustrations. Have students compare the illustrations to what they visualized when just listening to the book.

Point out the varying facial expressions of different characters illustrated in the book. The changes in the king's expressions are particularly telling.

Give students the **Connection to Writing Assessment: Post-Reading Composition** along with a copy of the **Have I...? Checklist**. Keep in mind that writing offers students an opportunity to speculate and think on paper. You are not looking for them to give you a single right answer, but rather attempting to help students express their thoughts in writing.

Give students about 20 minutes in which to write the composition and revise/edit it based on the checklist.

Collect and score the students' compositions using the **Rubric for Scoring First Drafts**.

Reproducible Master 59

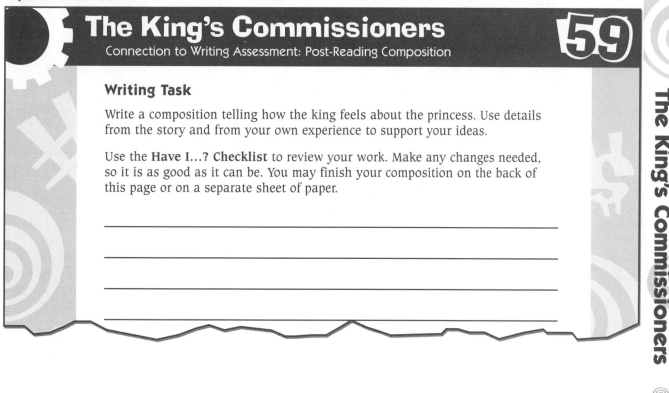

The King's Commissioners

59

Connection to Writing Assessment: Post-Reading Composition

Writing Task

Write a composition telling how the king feels about the princess. Use details from the story and from your own experience to support your ideas.

Use the **Have I...? Checklist** to review your work. Make any changes needed, so it is as good as it can be. You may finish your composition on the back of this page or on a separate sheet of paper.

____

____

____

____

Extending the Connections

MAKING INFERENCES AND PRACTICING SPEAKING

Materials
Copies of book (five, if possible, for analysis of pages 20–21), **Commissioners' Jobs** (Reproducible Master 60)

The purpose of the exercise is to have students look closely at the details in the story, both those that are given and those that are not. Students must decide when information is irrelevant and when they can make inferences. The accuracy of answers is not key, but the thinking process is important.

During the exercise, students will also informally practice speaking skills. The skill of speaking is not limited to the presentation of formal speeches, but often involves the kind of speaking and listening that is necessary to work effectively in pairs or groups.

Present a chart of the commissioners' jobs, by writing the one shown below on the chalkboard. Alternatively, you might distribute the **Commissioners' Jobs** worksheet to students or make it into an overhead transparency. Some of the spaces have been filled in below to demonstrate how the chart works and to spark ideas for discussion. Adjust this information as you feel is appropriate.

Encourage the class to help you complete the chart for the eight commissioners named in the story (see chart below). Students can either infer ideas or they may cite actual information from the book.

Then have the class look at pages 20–21 in the book showing all 47 commissioners in a grid. Challenge students to point out pictures of the eight commissioners listed on the chart below.

Reproducible Master 60 with sample answers

The King's Commissioners 60

Commissioners' Jobs

Commissioner of...	Job	Notes
Flat Tires		
Chicken Pox		
Foul Balls		
Things that go bump in the night	Deal with princess' scary nightmares	
Spilt Milk		Appointed when Princess was a child
Lost Homework		
Wrong Turns		
Late Arri[illegible]		

Divide the class into five small groups. Assign to each group a row of commissioners from the grid on pages 20–21. Each group will be responsible for completing part of the **Commissioners' Jobs** chart, so that all 47 are identified. It may not be possible to locate and name all 47 commissioners. The main point is to do the thinking, not to be accurate. Complete as many as possible.

Groups must name each of their assigned commissioners based on the hats and clothing shown in the illustrations. Note that some of the illustrations may be easier to see elsewhere in the book. Groups should also attempt to infer additional information about each commissioner, including the commissioner's job, and any other notes such as the princess' age when he or she was appointed.

Once each group has finished, have them report to the class, justifying the labels they have given each commissioner. Add this information to the class chart so that all 47 commissioners are named. A similar chart can be created for other characters in the book as well, such as the various royal advisors.

As a conclusion to the activity, have students describe what they did as part of the activity. This informal speaking practice is a good way to build confidence and skills for more formal speaking activities.

USING HUNDRED BOARDS TO MODEL TWO-DIGIT ADDITION AND SUBTRACTION

Materials

Random-number generators for 0–9, such as playing cards with jacks as 0, aces as 1, and kings, queens, and 10s removed; or 10-sided die with 0–9; or 0–9 spinners; **Hundred Board (0 to 100)** (Reproducible Master 61)

Distribute a copy of a **Hundred Board** and a random-number generator to each student.

First, students create and model a two-digit number. Have students randomly generate a two-digit number. Tell them that the first toss/draw/spin determines the number of 10s and the second toss/draw/spin determines the number of 1s. Have them find the number on the **Hundred Board** and mark it.

Next, students create and model another two-digit number in the same way. Have them use the hundred board to add the 10s and 1s for this second number to the first number marked on the hundred board. Have students tell what the final sum is and explain how they found it.

Note: For some classes, it may be necessary to add only multiples of 10 by just using one toss/draw/spin to create the second number. Once this is mastered, students can then progress to using the chart to quickly add 9, 19, and so on, to a given multiple of 10. Eventually they should be able to add 9 to any two-digit number. By adding numbers such as 9 to any two-digit number, students make an important discovery about using the hundred board—moving down one row and then moving back one block is the same as counting forward 9 blocks.

After the class becomes proficient with using the hundred board, complete the same exercises but have the students picture the board in their head to complete the problems. Finalize this addition process by writing a two-digit plus two-digit problem on the board. Have students write about using the hundred-board model to find the answer.

JOURNAL ENTRY

If a penny weighs more than a dime, which do you think is heavier: 72 cents made from the smallest number of dimes and pennies or 68 cents made from smallest number of dimes and pennies? Tell why. [Answer: The 68 cents would be heavier because it has more pennies than the 72 cents and there is only a slight difference between the weights of the dimes.]

PROJECT

Have groups or pairs of students use common household items to create their own models for 1,000s, 100s, 10s and 1s. Different kinds of pasta, different color cubes, different cookies or crackers all work well for this activity. Students then generate random two- or three-digit numbers and use their models to add or subtract the numbers.

ADDITIONAL RESOURCES

Windows on Math, Volume 3, Unit 3 Videodisc, **"Morning Swamp: Nicki's Necklaces."** Atlanta: Optical Data Corporation, 1996. Call 1-800-524-2481.

Windows on Math, Volume 4, Unit 5 Videodisc, **"Beatrice's Big Burger Bun Barn."** Atlanta: Optical Data Corporation, 1996. Call 1-800-524-2481.

One Hundred Hungry Ants

Written by **Elinor J. Pinczes**
Illustrated by **Bonnie MacKain**

Overview of the Connections

This story is about 100 hungry ants who are on their way to a picnic. They begin their march in a single line, but the littlest ant fears that by the time they get there, all the food will be gone. In an attempt to reach the picnic sooner, they re-form into 2 rows, then 3, 4, 5, and, finally, 10 rows. Vivid illustrations, in addition to the written word, express the ants' joys and frustrations.

In mathematics, this book provides an excellent introduction to the concepts of multiplication because of its use of rows and columns. The activities help students to see multiplication as groups of things, arrays, and repeated addition. Multiplication tables are created using the ideas of area and rectangles.

As literature, the story helps students internalize story structure. It also can support instruction in the use of specific details to enhance writing, which will help students improve their own writing.

MATERIALS FOR THE CONNECTIONS

One Hundred Hungry Ants • ISBN 0-395-63116-5

Written by Elinor J. Pinczes. Illustrated by Bonnie MacKain. Boston: Houghton Mifflin Company, 1993.

Language Arts

~ One or more copies of the book (Note: In the Viewing Connection, each student will need to see the picture on page 15 throughout the writing session, but without the written text. You may wish to have several copies available with the text covered.)

~ Optional: **Connection to Viewing Assessment: Writing About a Picture Prompt** (Reproducible Master 1)

~ **Have I…? Checklist** (Reproducible Master 2), a self-monitoring tool for student writers

~ **Rubric for Scoring First Drafts** (Reproducible Master 3)

~ **Connection to Listening Assessment: Listening to a Story** (Reproducible Master 62)

~ **Connection to Writing Assessment: Post-Reading Composition** (Reproducible Master 65)

Mathematics

~ Overhead connecting cubes

~ Overhead projector

~ Connecting cubes (quantities vary by activity)

~ **10 x 10 Grid** (Reproducible Master 63), copies for students and overhead (optional)

~ **Connection to Mathematics Assessment: Check for Understanding** (Reproducible Master 64)

~ Overhead of **Multiplication Table** (Reproducible Master 66)

Viewing Connection

INTRODUCING THE LESSON WITH A PICTURE PROMPT AND WRITING

Materials

Copy of the book (page 15, counting from the first page of text), **Connection to Viewing Assessment: Writing About a Picture Prompt** (Reproducible Master 1), **Have I...? Checklist** (Reproducible Master 2), **Rubric for Scoring First Drafts** (Reproducible Master 3)

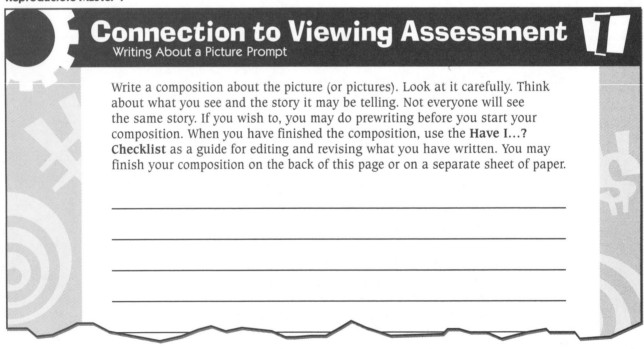

Show the class the picture on page 15 of the book with the text covered. The pages are unnumbered, but counting from the first page of text, the 15th page begins with the sentence: *"Stop!" screamed the littlest ant.* It ends with the sentence: *"... with 5 lines of 20 we'd get there soon, I know."* If possible, allow students to continue to look at the picture throughout the writing session. You may distribute a copy of **Connection to Viewing Assessment: Writing About a Picture Prompt** to each student, or they may use notebook paper for their work. Also distribute copies of the **Have I...? Checklist**.

Read these directions to the class:

"You are going to write a composition about this picture. Look at it carefully. Think about what you see and the story it may be telling. It is OK that not everyone will see the same story. If you wish to, you may do prewriting before you start your composition. When you have finished the composition, use the **Have I...? Checklist** as a guide for editing and revising what you have written."

Give the students 20–30 minutes to write their compositions and do initial editing.

Collect and score the students' compositions using the **Rubric for Scoring First Drafts**. Teach students how to compare their scored compositions to the rubric and to make notes about how to improve their compositions. Students also may be taught to use the rubric to score their own work or that of other students.

Reproducible Master 1

Connection to Viewing Assessment 1

Writing About a Picture Prompt

Write a composition about the picture (or pictures). Look at it carefully. Think about what you see and the story it may be telling. Not everyone will see the same story. If you wish to, you may do prewriting before you start your composition. When you have finished the composition, use the **Have I...? Checklist** as a guide for editing and revising what you have written. You may finish your composition on the back of this page or on a separate sheet of paper.

Listening Connection

LISTENING TO A STORY AND ANSWERING QUESTIONS

Materials

Copy of the book (Listening section: entire story, about 485 words), **Connection to Listening Assessment: Listening to a Story** (Reproducible Master 62)

This activity will help students develop effective listening skills. As necessary, teach or review some of the effective listening strategies found on page *xv* of this manual.

Tell the class you are going to read a story. When you have finished, the students will answer some questions about what you have read to them.

The reading selection for *One Hundred Hungry Ants* is the whole book. Since you are working on listening, don't stop to discuss the story, show the illustrations, or make predictions, as you might do in a reading instructional period.

It is important to read the story with effective oral expression, especially since the class will not be seeing the book's illustrations during the listening section.

Distribute the worksheet with multiple-choice and open-ended questions called **Connection to Listening Assessment: Listening to a Story**.

Allow students 15–20 minutes for completing the worksheet.

Reproducible Master 62 with answers

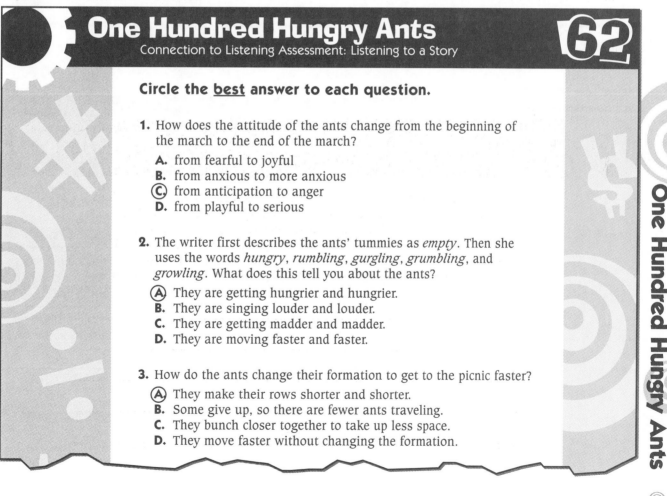

One Hundred Hungry Ants

Connection to Listening Assessment: Listening to a Story

62

Circle the <u>best</u> answer to each question.

1. How does the attitude of the ants change from the beginning of the march to the end of the march?

A. from fearful to joyful
B. from anxious to more anxious
(C) from anticipation to anger
D. from playful to serious

2. The writer first describes the ants' tummies as *empty*. Then she uses the words *hungry*, *rumbling*, *gurgling*, *grumbling*, and *growling*. What does this tell you about the ants?

(A) They are getting hungrier and hungrier.
B. They are singing louder and louder.
C. They are getting madder and madder.
D. They are moving faster and faster.

3. How do the ants change their formation to get to the picnic faster?

(A) They make their rows shorter and shorter.
B. Some give up, so there are fewer ants traveling.
C. They bunch closer together to take up less space.
D. They move faster without changing the formation.

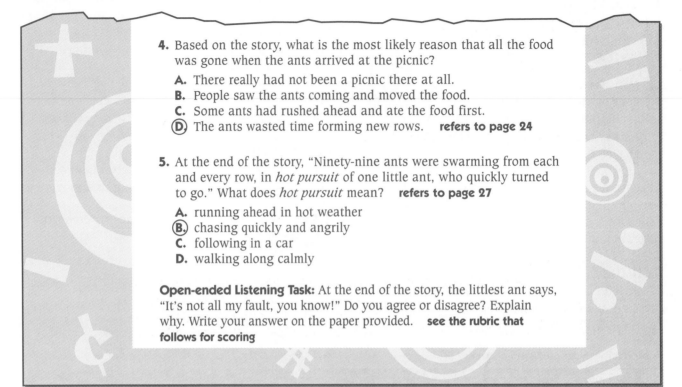

4. Based on the story, what is the most likely reason that all the food was gone when the ants arrived at the picnic?

A. There really had not been a picnic there at all.
B. People saw the ants coming and moved the food.
C. Some ants had rushed ahead and ate the food first.
(D.) The ants wasted time forming new rows. **refers to page 24**

5. At the end of the story, "Ninety-nine ants were swarming from each and every row, in *hot pursuit* of one little ant, who quickly turned to go." What does *hot pursuit* mean? **refers to page 27**

A. running ahead in hot weather
(B.) chasing quickly and angrily
C. following in a car
D. walking along calmly

Open-ended Listening Task: At the end of the story, the littlest ant says, "It's not all my fault, you know!" Do you agree or disagree? Explain why. Write your answer on the paper provided. **see the rubric that follows for scoring**

RUBRIC FOR SCORING

Open-ended Listening Task

An effective response will need to:
- reflect knowledge of the story.
- interpret characters' motivations and actions.
- justify ideas from the text.
- be well written.

POINTS	CRITERIA
4	The student explains a logical conclusion with sufficient supporting details and elaboration to be credible and uses details from the story as appropriate. The student may or may not agree with the little ant.
3	The student may or may not agree with the little ant, but merely states the opinion or provides only a minimal explanation with logic and/or justification.
2	The student doesn't understand the concept of disagreement and provides little or no justification for answer or does not relate the answer to the story.
1	The student restates the question with little elaboration and does not understand that there can be more than one opinion on the topic.
0	The student doesn't respond or doesn't address the task.

Mathematics Connection

INTRODUCTION AND ACTIVE READING: Understanding Rows, Columns, and Arrays

Materials

Copy of the book, overhead projector, overhead connecting cubes

Re-read the story, showing the class the illustrations and discussing how students' interpretations of the story may be different before and after seeing the pictures.

Note: The book *One Hundred Hungry Ants* uses the word *row* to refer to the lines formed by the ants. To be mathematically accurate, the lines are actually *columns*. In mathematics and the activities that follow, it is important to distinguish accurately between rows (horizontal) and columns (vertical).

Use overhead connecting cubes to create and then discuss various arrays of 12 ants. Ensure that students understand the basic vocabulary of rows and columns. Discuss how arrays are named and described.

EXAMPLE

- A 2 x 6 array is described as 2 rows of 6 or 2 groups of 6.
- A 6 x 2 array is described as 6 rows of 2 or 6 groups of 2.

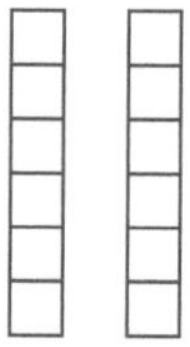

2 groups of 6, or
2 columns of 6

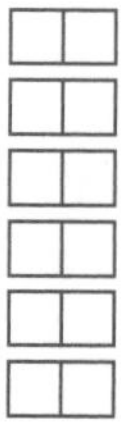

6 groups of 2, or
6 rows of 2

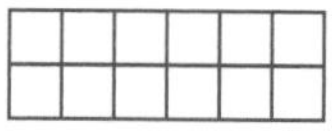

A 2 x 6 array, or
2 rows by 6 columns

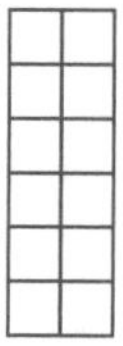

A 6 x 2 array, or
6 rows by 2 columns

ACTING OUT THE STORY: Interpreting Multiplication as Arrays, Area, and Groups

Materials

Connecting cubes (12 for each student). Alternative: 24 connecting cubes for each student. Optional: Transparency of **10 x 10 Grid** (Reproducible Master 63)

One Hundred Hungry Ants provides students with opportunities to develop an understanding of multiplication by experiencing it in many contexts and through various representations. In the following activities, students will model problems similar to those in the book. Instead of 100 ants, however, students will work with 12 ants represented by connecting cubes. Students will move, name, and visualize these 12 ants to represent various interpretations of multiplication.

Tell students that they will be acting out a story similar to *One Hundred Angry Ants*, except this one uses 12 ants instead of 100. They can call it "A Dozen Hungry Ants."

Distribute 12 connecting cubes to each student. Ask them to imagine that the cubes have changed into ants.

Have students create 1 column of 12 ants marching to a picnic at the top of the desk. If possible, act out the story on the overhead as the children do it on their desks.

Tell the class that these ants, like the ants in the story, decide to change to 2 columns. Ask:

How many ants will be in each of the 2 columns?

Have the students form the 2 columns with their cubes. Model the same formation on the overhead.

Emphasize the difference between rows and columns in the following way by first rearranging this formation into 6 rows of 2 and describing it as 6 rows with 2 ants in each row.

The overhead provides an easy way to show students how rows go across and columns go in a vertical direction.

Switch between the two models by reforming the cubes back into 2 columns with 6 ants in each column.

Also refer to the rows and columns as groups of ants. For the formation with 6 rows, indicate there are 6 groups, each with 2 ants. For the formation with 2 columns, indicate that there are 2 groups, each with 6 ants. Confirm the total of 12 by adding the sets of 6 together.

Continue this process to include 4 rows with 3 columns, 3 rows with 4 columns, 2 rows with 6 columns, and 1 row with 12 columns.

Distribute 12 more cubes to each student, or have pairs of students work together, to create as many combinations as possible for 24 ants to march to a picnic. Have students model the arrays, emphasizing the rows and columns in each configuration.

Model each arrangement of 24 ants on the overhead then transfer it to the chalkboard, recording the letter X for each ant. [There are 8 possible arrangements: 24 x 1; 12 x 2; 8 x 3; 6 x 4; 4 x 6; 3 x 8; 2 x 12; and 1 x 24]

Label each of the arrays using the traditional *row x column* notation. An array that is 4 rows by 6 columns should be labeled 4 x 6.

Relate the concept of an array to the idea of a rectangle with area and dimensions. For example, you might use a question-and-answer technique to establish that a 2 x 12 array is the same as a rectangle whose area is 24 square units and whose dimensions are 2 rows by 12 columns or 2 by 12.

Draw a border around one of the arrays on the chalkboard to more clearly demonstrate its rectangular shape.

You also may want to use a transparency of the 10 x 10 grid to draw a rectangle that matches the dimensions of the array.

Continue to model the other arrangements of 24 ants in the same way and relate them to the area and dimensions of a rectangle. Continue to emphasize the vocabulary introduced above.

Act out additional story problems, such as "Eight Hungry Ants," "Six Hungry Ants," etc., until the students are comfortable with the process.

Write a notation on the chalkboard that describes an array, such as 3 x 6. Have students write a description (in rows and columns or groups) by telling a "hungry ant" story.

CREATING A MULTIPLICATION TABLE

Materials

One copy of **10 x 10 Grid** (Reproducible Master 63) for each pair, connecting cubes for each pair

Note about the materials: The number of connecting cubes each pair will need depends on the multiplication family that they will create. For example, they need 30 cubes to create the times table for 3; 60 cubes to create the times table for 6; 80 to create the times table for 8; 100 cubes to create the times table for 100; etc.

Students may have worked with multiplication tables, but this activity helps them gain a deeper understanding of what it is and how it works.

Students work in pairs with connecting cubes and blank 10 x 10 grids to create their own multiplication tables. In each pair, one student uses sets of cubes to create a concrete model of a family of facts by building rectangles, and the other student fills in the grid by recording the area of each rectangle or the total number of cubes in the model.

There are many ways to manage this activity. You could:

- Have each pair of students work on one family of facts and stop there.
- Have each pair of students build and record every family of facts until the entire multiplication table is complete.
- Assign each pair to work on a different family of facts. After everyone has finished, each pair can report on its findings and transfer the numbers to a "master" multiplication table that the whole class can see and discuss.

Building the Table

Choose a multiplication family for students to create, such as the times table for the number 6. Distribute a **10 x 10 Grid** to each pair of students.

Have pairs of students snap together 10 sets of 6 connecting cubes each to create 10 "sticks" (also referred to as *rows* or *groups*) of 6 cubes. One student in each pair will be the builder, and the other will be the recorder.

The builders create one rectangle at a time, first using a single row or "stick" of 6 cubes, then putting together 2 sticks, then 3, etc.

The recorders write the area of each rectangle in the appropriate square on the **10 x 10 Grid**. The appropriate place to record the area is in the square that is defined by the dimensions of the rectangle.

EXAMPLE

The first rectangle is 1 row of 6 cubes. The dimensions are 1 x 6, and the area is 6 cubes or 6 square units. The recorder writes the area of this rectangle in the square on the blank grid that is located in the first row and sixth column.

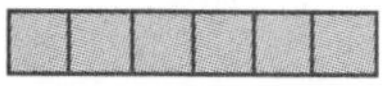

The area of this 1 x 6 rectangle is recorded in the square that is in the first row, sixth column of the grid.

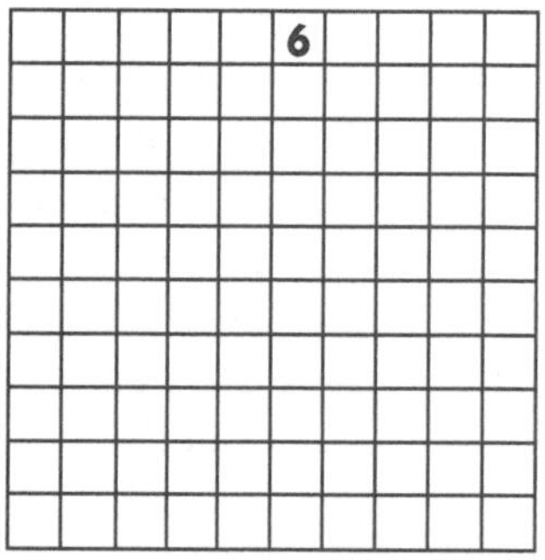

The builder creates a new rectangle by placing another row of 6 cubes under the original. The dimensions of the new rectangle are 2 rows of 6, and its area is 12 cubes or 12 square units.

The recorder writes the number 12 in the second row, sixth column of the grid.

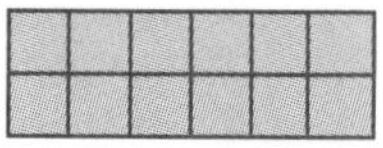

The area of this 2 x 6 rectangle is recorded in the square that is in the second row, sixth column of the grid.

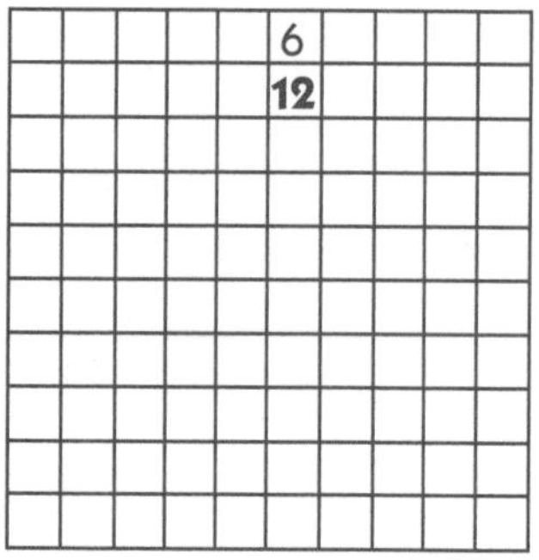

Continue with this procedure, one row at a time, until the sixth column of the table is completely filled in.

Use the same method to create the 6-times table *across* the chart. Have the pairs switch roles, so that the previous builder is now the recorder and vice versa. You may have the pairs of students rebuild 10 sticks of connecting cubes with 6 cubes in each stick or, to save time, rearrange the sticks that were already made so that they form columns instead of rows.

Have the builders create one rectangle at a time, first using a single column or "stick" of 6 cubes that could be described as a 6 x 1 rectangle consisting of 6 rows by 1 column.

The recorders write the area of each rectangle in the appropriate square on the **10 x 10 Grid**. The appropriate place to record the area is in the square that is defined by the dimensions of the rectangle.

EXAMPLE

The first rectangle is 6 rows of cubes by 1 column. The dimensions are 6 x 1, and the area is 6 cubes or 6 square units. The recorder writes the area of this rectangle in the square on the blank grid that is located in the sixth row and first column.

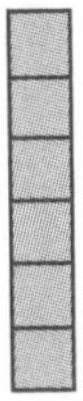

The area of this 6 x 1 rectangle is recorded in the square that is in the sixth row, first column of the grid.

					6				
					12				
					18				
					24				
					30				
6					36				
					42				
					48				
					54				
					60				

The builder creates a new rectangle by placing another column of 6 cubes next to the original. The dimensions of the new rectangle are 6 rows of 2, and its area is 12 cubes or 12 square units.

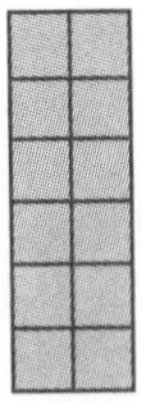

The area of this 6 x 2 rectangle is recorded in the square that is in the sixth row, second column of the grid.

					6				
					12				
					18				
					24				
					30				
6	**12**				36				
					42				
					48				
					54				
					60				

Discuss the times table for 6 that has been created so far. If students don't recognize the chart as a multiplication table, you might have them write the numbers for each row and column outside the border of the grid.

Ask questions such as the following:

What patterns do you notice when you read across the table? down the table?
[Possible answers: The next number in the pattern is 6 more than the one before it; it's like skip-counting by 6.]

Point out that when the table is used to find the product of any two numbers, those numbers can be interpreted as the dimensions of a rectangle. To demonstrate this, write a multiplication problem with 6 as a factor. Have students find the product and outline or lightly shade the rectangle on their grid. Instead of having them draw on the grid, you can have them highlight the rectangle being formed by placing two pieces of paper outside its borders.

EXAMPLE

Use the table to find the product of 3 x 6 and outline or lightly shade the rectangle formed when those factors are used as dimensions. Notice that the product of 3 x 6 is in the bottom right corner of the rectangle.

	1	**2**	**3**	**4**	**5**	**6**	**7**	**8**	**9**	**10**
1						6				
2						12				
3						18				
4						24				
5						30				
6	6	12	18	24	30	36	42	48	54	60
7						42				
8						48				
9						54				
10						60				

You may continue to have students create the times table for other numbers by building models and recording the area or through other methods, such as skip counting or using patterns.

MATHEMATICS ASSESSMENT

Materials

Connection to Mathematics Assessment: Check for Understanding (Reproducible Master 64)

Distribute the worksheet with multiple-choice and open-ended questions called **Connection to Mathematics Assessment: Check for Understanding.**

Collect and score the students' work using the answers and rubric that follow.

Reproducible Master 64 with answers

One Hundred Hungry Ants

Connection to Mathematics Assessment: Check for Understanding

64

Circle the best answer.

1. Which multiplication problem is the same as 4 x 5 + 4 x 3 ?
   (A) 4 x 8 **B.** 4 x 15 **C.** 8 x 8 **D.** 8 x 15

2. Jamal found 6 nickels. How much money did he find?
   A. 11¢ **B.** 25¢ (C) 30¢ **D.** 36¢

3. Which of the following is worth the greatest amount of money?
   A. two quarters (B) six dimes **C.** seven nickels **D.** eight pennies

4. Which sentence best represents the picture below?
   ●●●● ●●●● ●●●● ●●●● ●●●● ●●●●
   A. 2 x 12 = 24
   B. 3 + 3 + 3 + 3 + 3 + 3 + 3 + 3 = 24
   C. 8 x 3 = 24
   (D) 4 + 4 + 4 + 4 + 4 + 4 = 24

5. Juan took a survey at his school about favorite ice-cream flavors. He made the chart below to show his results. Which flavor did 18 people choose as their favorite?

Favorite Ice Cream Flavor at Public School 38

Vanilla	★				
Chocolate	★★				
Strawberry	★★★★				
Vanilla Fudge	★★★				

Each ★ stands for 6 people.

   A. vanilla
   B. chocolate
   C. strawberry
   (D) vanilla fudge

6. Describe how you could find the product of 7 x 6 on a calculator with a broken 7 key. Explain how you know your method is correct.

RUBRIC FOR SCORING
Problem 6

An effective response will need to:

- provide a method that produces a product of 42.
- show a correct interpretation of multiplication.
- provide a clear explanation of why the method works.

POINTS	CRITERIA
3	The student provides an answer that clearly explains how to reach 42 without using the 7 key and shows a correct interpretation of multiplication through the use of repeated addition or the distributive property. Suggested responses: *"I would add 6 + 6 + 6 + 6 + 6 + 6 + 6 because 6 added 7 times is the same as 7 x 6."* OR *"I would enter 6 x 1 + 6 x 6 = in the calculator because 6 x 1 + 6 x 6 is the same as 7 x 6."*
2	The student shows a correct interpretation of multiplication without the 7, but provides an unclear explanation or one with minor flaws.
1	The student shows a correct interpretation of multiplication without using 7, but offers no explanation of why it is correct.
0	The student shows no understanding of multiplication or leaves the question blank.

Composition Connection

INTERPRETING LITERATURE AS A PATTERN AND EXAMPLE FOR WRITING

Materials

Copy of the book

This activity will help students enhance their skills in interpreting text and illustrations.

Re-read the book to the class, this time pausing to show the illustrations and to discuss their relationship to the events in the story.

Ask questions that prompt students to infer what is indicated by changes in the ants' expressions and differences in the drawings as the ants regroup each time. Discuss how the changes in the illustrations (more ants, swirling lines, etc.) are used to reflect speed and frenzy.

Discuss with the class how the changes in descriptive words match the changes in the ants' expressions. Focus on the following progression of descriptions:

"There'll be lots of yummies for our hungry tummies, ..." (on page 8)
to:
"We hope there's yummies for our rumbling tummies, ..." (on page 12)
to:
"There might be a yummy for a gurgling tummy, ..." (on page 16)
to:
"There better be yummies for our grumbling tummies, ..." (on page 20)

You may want to have students copy these words and phrases into their writing folders or notebooks to use as a resource when they are attempting to write about how something increases or decreases.

Using examples from authentic texts in this way helps students to understand how language works and how to make their own compositions more vivid, specific, elaborate, and interesting.

WRITING A POST-READING COMPOSITION

Materials

Connection to Writing Assessment: Post-Reading Composition (Reproducible Master 65), **Have I...? Checklist** (Reproducible Master 2), **Rubric for Scoring First Drafts** (Reproducible Master 3)

Distribute a copy of **Connection to Writing Assessment: Post-Reading Composition** to each student along with the **Have I...? Checklist**.

Allow students 25 minutes for writing and reviewing their compositions.

Collect and score the compositions using the **Rubric for Scoring First Drafts**.

Reproducible Master 65

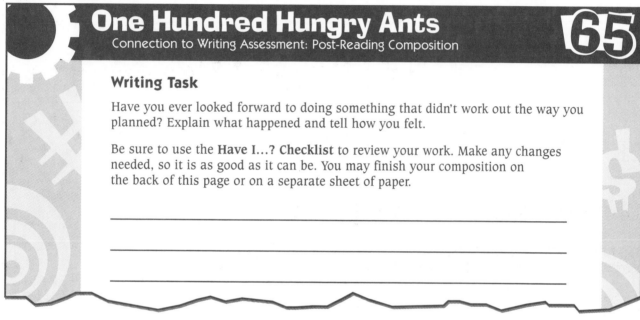

One Hundred Hungry Ants 65

Connection to Writing Assessment: Post-Reading Composition

Writing Task

Have you ever looked forward to doing something that didn't work out the way you planned? Explain what happened and tell how you felt.

Be sure to use the **Have I...? Checklist** to review your work. Make any changes needed, so it is as good as it can be. You may finish your composition on the back of this page or on a separate sheet of paper.

____

____

____

Extending the Connection

INTERPRETING THE MULTIPLICATION TABLE AS DIMENSIONS, AREA, ARRAYS, AND GROUPS

Materials

Overhead projector, overhead of **Multiplication Table** (Reproducible Master 66), 2 sheets of paper

Place a completed multiplication table on the overhead. Demonstrate how to find a fact such as 8 x 7 by placing 2 sheets of paper on the outside of the rectangle that is formed when one finds 8 x 7 on the grid.

Ask students to close their eyes and visualize 8 rows of 7 ants in that rectangle or 8 rows of 7 cubes. This transfer helps student to connect the concrete model to the more abstract model of multiplication as area, arrays, and groups of things.

DEVELOPING ALTERNATIVE STRATEGIES FOR MULTIPLICATION FACTS

Materials

Overhead projector, overhead connecting cubes

Use cubes to demonstrate strategies that will help students remember multiplication facts. Show the commutative property by rotating the arrays so that rows become columns and vice versa. For example, 3 x 4 = 4 x 3. Break arrays in parts such as 8 x 7 = 8 x 5 + 8 x 2. Adding together 40 + 16 is another way to remember that 8 x 7 = 56.

EXAMPLE

8 x 7 = 8 x 5 + 8 x 2

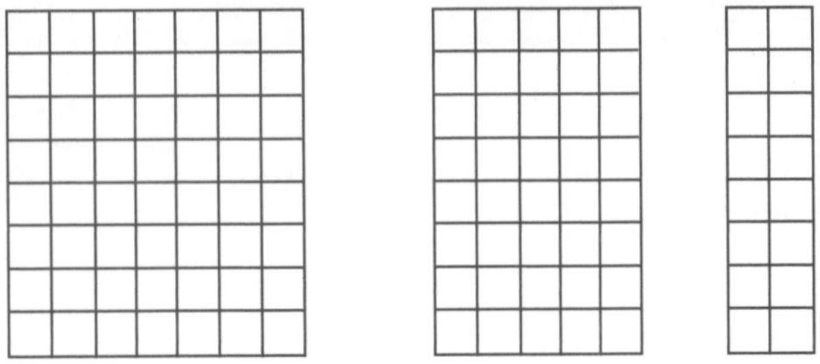

PROJECTS

Have students create and illustrate stories about a dozen hungry animals or objects. Examples: "A Dozen Hungry Cats," "A Dozen Hungry Dogs," "A Dozen Hungry Dinosaurs."

ADDITIONAL RESOURCES

Windows on Math, Volume 3 Videodisc, Unit 1, "Spider Pie" and "Marissa's Marvelous Multiplication Machine." Volume 4 Videodisc, Unit 6, "Fleas in Formation." Atlanta: Optical Data Corporation, 1996. Call 1-800-524-2481.

ESPA³ Book III: Tile Month. Iowa City, Iowa: Tutor Tools, Inc., 1998. Call 1-800-776-3454.

Pigs Will Be Pigs

Written by **Amy Axelrod**
Illustrated by **Sharon McGinley-Nally**

Overview of the Connections

This story is about a family of four pigs who love to eat. One day, they find that the refrigerator is empty, and they don't have enough money to dine out. Together, they frantically hunt through their house searching for money. Eventually, they find enough money to pay for dinner at their favorite restaurant, the "Enchanted Enchilada."

In mathematics instruction, this story provides opportunities for students to practice decimal algorithms by using money models to act out the story. Students will add and subtract decimals, make change, and create various denomination equivalencies for given amounts of money. Students also will apply chart-reading skills, estimation, and decision-making skills to playing games and solving non-routine problems involving menu choices and given amounts of money.

In language arts, students will practice viewing and then writing, as well as listening to elements of a story to explore meaning as it is conveyed by oral expression, such as tone and inflection.

MATERIALS FOR THE CONNECTION

Pigs Will Be Pigs • ISBN 0-02-765415-X • ISBN 0-689-81219-1 (pbk) • Written by Amy Axelrod. Illustrated by Sharon McGinley-Nally. New York: Simon and Schuster Children's Publishing, 1994.

Language Arts

One or more copies of the book (Note: In the Viewing Connection, each student will need to see pages 4–5, preferably with the text covered up. Pages are not numbered, so consider the title page as page 1. You may wish to have several copies available.)

~ **Connection to Viewing Assessment: Writing About a Picture Prompt** (Reproducible Master 1)

~ A self-monitoring checklist for student writers called **Have I...? Checklist** (Reproducible Master 2)

~ **Rubric for Scoring First Drafts** (Reproducible Master 3)

~ **Connection to Listening Assessment: Listening to a Story** (Reproducible Master 67)

~ **Connection to Writing Assessment: Post-Reading Composition** (Reproducible Master 77)

Mathematics

~ Calculators (1 for each group of 2–3 students)

~ Index cards

~ Play money (bills: $20, $5, $2, $1; coins: 1¢, 5¢, 10¢, 25¢, 50¢)

~ Shoebox (or other container) to hold the $34.67 from story

~ **Paying the Bill** (Reproducible Master 68)

~ **Finding Money Game Organizer** (Reproducible Master 69)

~ Icosahedron dice (1 for each group of 3–4 students). Alternative: number cards or spinners marked 0–9

~ **Tasty Triangle Menu** (Reproducible Master 70)

~ **Problem Solving I and II** (Reproducible Masters 71–72)

~ **Estimation I and II** (Reproducible Masters 73–74)

Optional: copies of book (for each group of 3–4 students)

~ Number cubes or dice (for each group of 4 students)

~ **Connection to Mathematics Assessment: Check for Understanding I and II** (Reproducible Masters 75–76)

The Viewing Connection

INTRODUCING THE LESSON WITH A PICTURE PROMPT AND WRITING

Materials

Copy of the book (pages 3–4), Connection to Viewing Assessment: Writing About a Picture Prompt (Reproducible Master 1), **Have I...? Checklist** (Reproducible Master 2), **Rubric for Scoring First Drafts** (Reproducible Master 3)

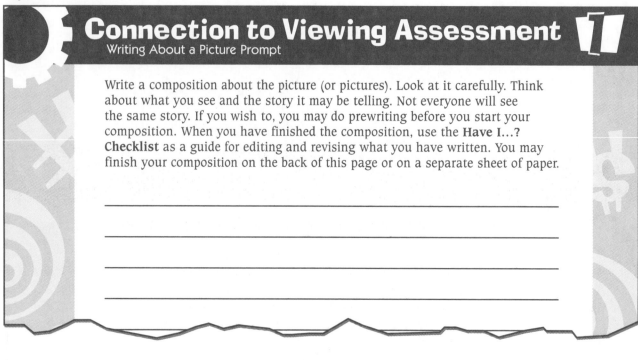

Show the class the picture on pages 3–4 where the pigs are looking into the open refrigerator. (Note that the pages are not numbered.) The words on the page should be covered up so students will concentrate on the illustrations.

If possible, allow students to continue to look at the picture throughout the writing session. You may distribute a copy of Connection to Assessment: Writing About a Picture Prompt to each student, or they may use notebook paper for their work. Also provide copies of the **Have I...? Checklist**.

Read these directions to the class:

"You are going to write a composition about this picture. Look at it carefully. Think about what you see and the story it may be telling. It is OK that not everyone will see the same story. If you wish to, you may do prewriting before you start your composition. When you have finished the composition, use the **Have I...? Checklist** as a guide for editing and revising what you have written."

Give the students 20–30 minutes to write their compositions and do initial editing.

Collect the students' compositions and score **them** using the **Rubric for Scoring First Drafts**. Teach students how to compare their scored compositions to the rubric and to make notes about how to improve their compositions. Students also may be taught to use the rubric to score their own work or that of other students.

Reproducible Master 1

Connection to Viewing Assessment 1

Writing About a Picture Prompt

Write a composition about the picture (or pictures). Look at it carefully. Think about what you see and the story it may be telling. Not everyone will see the same story. If you wish to, you may do prewriting before you start your composition. When you have finished the composition, use the **Have I...? Checklist** as a guide for editing and revising what you have written. You may finish your composition on the back of this page or on a separate sheet of paper.

____

____

____

____

The Listening Connection

LISTENING TO A STORY AND ANSWERING QUESTIONS

Materials

Copy of the book (Listening section: pages 1–23, 26–31; 582 words), **Connection to Listening Assessment: Listening to a Story** (Reproducible Master 67)

This activity will help students develop effective listening skills. As necessary, teach or review some of the effective listening strategies found on page *xv* of this manual.

Tell the class you are going to read them a story. When you are finished, they will answer some questions about what you have read. (It is not necessary to read the menu on pages 24–25 during the listening activity, although it will be very important later in the Mathematics Connection activity.)

Tell students they also will be asked to speculate about what may happen to the characters after the story ends. It is important for students to understand that predictions are simply ideas about what may logically happen, but not necessarily what does happen.

Pigs Will Be Pigs gives you an opportunity to show how variations in tone and inflection can enable a storyteller to communicate character changes to his or her audience. You may want to practice using different "voices" for each character by reading aloud to yourself beforehand. Tell students to listen for your vocal changes as you read so they can identify who is speaking in the story. The narrative may also identify the character speaking, thus helping the listeners "hear" these shifts.

Read the entire story to the class. Since you are working on listening, don't stop to discuss the story, show the illustrations, or make predictions as you might do in a ready instructional period.

Distribute the multiple-choice and open-ended questions called **Connection to Listening Assessment: Listening to a Story**.

Allow students 15–20 minutes for completing the worksheet.

Collect and score the students' work using the answers and rubric that follow.

Proceed to the Mathematics Connection, which provides an opportunity for students to review their listening skills.

Reproducible Master 67 with answers

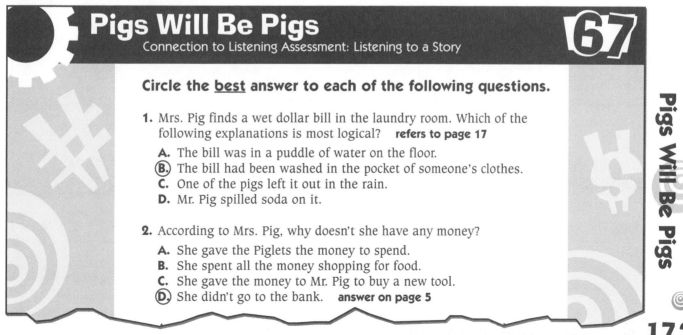

Pigs Will Be Pigs

Connection to Listening Assessment: Listening to a Story

67

Circle the best answer to each of the following questions.

1. Mrs. Pig finds a wet dollar bill in the laundry room. Which of the following explanations is most logical? **refers to page 17**
   - A. The bill was in a puddle of water on the floor.
   - (B.) The bill had been washed in the pocket of someone's clothes.
   - C. One of the pigs left it out in the rain.
   - D. Mr. Pig spilled soda on it.

2. According to Mrs. Pig, why doesn't she have any money?
   - A. She gave the Piglets the money to spend.
   - B. She spent all the money shopping for food.
   - C. She gave the money to Mr. Pig to buy a new tool.
   - (D.) She didn't go to the bank. **answer on page 5**

Continued...

3. At what point in the story do the pigs know they have enough money to go out to eat?

   (A.) Mr. Pig finds money in the basement. **refers to page 18**
   B. Mrs. Pig finds money in the bedroom.
   C. Mr. Pig finds his lucky two-dollar bill.
   D. The Piglets find money in their toy chest, bookshelf, and penny collection.

4. What is a reasonable explanation as to why Mrs. Pig counts the money "several times" on the way to the restaurant? **refers to page 20**

   A. She wants to know which coins and bills she has.
   B. She wants to divide the money equally among the family members.
   C. She wants to know if there is exact change for a parking meter.
   (D.) She wants to be sure of the amount they have to spend.

5. When they arrive at the restaurant, the Pigs say to the waitress: "We're the Pigs and we're very hungry." What should the waitress think after hearing this? **refers to page 23**

   A. She should expect them to be very messy.
   B. She should leave them alone to let them eat.
   (C.) She should expect them to eat a lot.
   D. She should expect to earn a good tip.

Open-ended Listening Task: During the hunt for money, the Pigs search everywhere in their house. When they find enough money, they rush out to the restaurant because they're so hungry. After stuffing themselves, they go home to relax. What do you think they find when they get home? Use details from the story and your own experience to support your answer.
see rubric that follows for scoring

RUBRIC FOR SCORING
Open-ended Listening Task

Score the Open-ended Listening Task using the following rubric. Students should be encouraged to think creatively. It is not essential that they conclude the house was messy, as illustrated in the book. It is more important that students have developed logical responses and have supported their conclusions with good reasoning.

An effective response will need to:

- reflect knowledge of the story.
- justify ideas using specific details from the story.
- make logical and reasonable predictions.
- be well written with a clear presentation.

POINTS	CRITERIA
4	Response is logical and includes clear references to the activities of the Pigs prior to going to the restaurant. The writer refers to the figurative language of the title *Pigs Will Be Pigs*. Answer is well written and complete.
3	Response is generally well written and logical, citing most major points from the events prior to the Pigs leaving for the restaurant. The writer may or may not recognize the significance of the figurative title, but if it is recognized, details from the search of the house are insufficient.
2	Response is organized and touches on the main points, but the rationale may be weak. Or, the logic and rationale are strong, but the writing is poorly organized. The writer probably ignores the meaning of the title *Pigs Will Be Pigs*.
1	Response is poorly written and/or illogical. If the logic is reasonable, it is poorly supported and unconvincing.
0	Student does not write a response, or response is off-topic.

The Mathematics Connection

DETERMINING THE TOTAL AMOUNT OF MONEY THE PIGS FOUND

Materials
Copy of the book, calculators (1 for each group of 2–3 students), index cards

Read the story to the class again. Before starting, tell students to listen closely and take notes so they can tell you how much money the pigs found when you're finished with the story. As you read, show the illustrations and allow students to discuss them. (The illustrations may help confirm some of the predictions students made during the Listening Connection.)

After reading the story, distribute calculators and index cards to groups of 2–3 students. Without referring to the book, have each group use their notes to calculate the amount of money the Pigs found and record the amount on an index card. Collect the completed index cards and read the totals aloud.

It is likely some groups will not agree. Discuss the answers and some different ways to find out which answer is correct. To determine the correct answer, the class can act out the story in the activity that follows.

ACTING OUT THE STORY: Modeling a Solution

Materials
Play money (1 twenty-dollar bill, 1 five-dollar bill, 1 two-dollar bill, 2 one-dollar bills, 222 pennies, 2 nickels, 16 dimes, 5 quarters, 1 fifty-cent piece), shoebox (or other container) to hold the $34.67, copy of the book, calculators (optional)

Set up a shoebox or other container at the front of the classroom to hold the money from the story. The total should be $34.67 in the bill and coin denominations described on page 32 of *Pigs Will Be Pigs*. Tell students that to determine the total amount of money the Pigs found, they are going to use play money to act out the story. You may wish to assign character roles for students to play Mr. Pig, Mrs. Pig, and the two piglets. Other students can be recorders at the chalkboard.

Read the story again while students act it out. As you read, "characters" or volunteers should come up to the shoebox and find the exact amount of money described in the story. A recorder then writes the value of the amount on the chalkboard. Each time an amount is "discovered" its value is figured and recorded. The "found" money should be put aside so that the shoebox is gradually emptied.

Discuss with students the operations of decimals (multiplication, addition, and subtraction) used to determine the values for each amount of money found in the story.

At the end of the story, total the money. The total amount should be $34.67. You may wish to have students add the amounts using a calculator to check the results. To check individual values, refer to the last page of the story, page 32, for a list of the monies each Pig found.

COMPUTING THE AMOUNT OF THE CHECK

Have students determine how much money the Pigs spent and how much was left over. Remind students of the amount of money in the shoebox ($34.67). You may wish to have students refer to the menu on pages 24–25 of the book to find out how much the Pigs spent. They bought four "specials" at $7.99 each.

[Answer: The Pigs spent $31.96 (4 x 7.99 = 31.96). They have $2.71 left over after paying the bill (34.67 – 31.96 = 2.71).]

Compare answers and discuss ways to solve the problems. Show students alternate methods for calculating such as:

- 4 x 7.99 is the same as 4 x (8 – .01) = (4 x 8) – (4 x .01) = 32 – .04 = 31.96
- 34.67 – 31.96 is the same as 34.67 – 32 + .04 = 2.67 + .04 = 2.71

The answer to how much was spent is also hidden somewhere in the book. You might challenge students to find it. [On page 29, Mrs. Pig's purse contains a receipt for $31.96.]

PAYING THE CHECK

Materials

Individual copies of **Paying the Bill** (Reproducible Master 68)

This activity will provide practice in dealing with money and determining change.

Distribute a copy of the **Paying the Bills** chart to each student. Explain that the chart shows the numbers and values of each bill and coin in Mrs. Pig's shoebox. It also has blank spaces that can be used to show various payment methods the Pigs could have used to settle the $31.96 bill at the Enchanted Enchilada.

Have students complete the chart by finding three different payment methods. For each method, they should list the numbers and values of coins used. Then they should find the total and check that it equals $31.96.

Extend thinking by asking questions, such as:

- ***What is the greatest number of coins and bills that could be used to pay the bill?*** **[Answer: See Payment Method 1 below.]**
- ***What is the least number of bills and coins that could be used to pay the bill?*** **[Answer: See Payment Method 3 on the next page.]**
- ***Which method would you prefer—paying with the greatest number or the least number of coins or bills? Explain why.***

Pigs Will Be Pigs

Paying the Bill

68

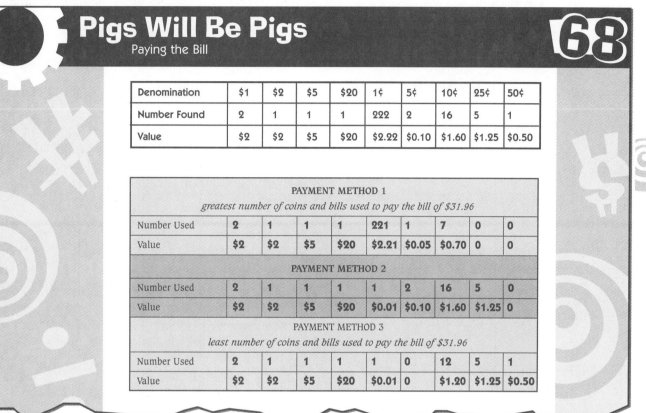

Denomination	$1	$2	$5	$20	1¢	5¢	10¢	25¢	50¢
Number Found	2	1	1	1	222	2	16	5	1
Value	$2	$2	$5	$20	$2.22	$0.10	$1.60	$1.25	$0.50

PAYMENT METHOD 1 *greatest number of coins and bills used to pay the bill of $31.96*									
Number Used	2	1	1	1	221	1	7	0	0
Value	$2	$2	$5	$20	$2.21	$0.05	$0.70	0	0
PAYMENT METHOD 2									
Number Used	2	1	1	1	1	2	16	5	0
Value	$2	$2	$5	$20	$0.01	$0.10	$1.60	$1.25	0
PAYMENT METHOD 3 *least number of coins and bills used to pay the bill of $31.96*									
Number Used	2	1	1	1	1	0	12	5	1
Value	$2	$2	$5	$20	$0.01	0	$1.20	$1.25	$0.50

PRACTICE ADDING MONEY: Finding Money Game

Materials

Individual copies of Finding Money Game Organizer (Reproducible Master 69); index cards (16 for each group of 3–4 students); icosahedron die, number cards, or spinners marked 0–9 (for each group)

For more practice in working with money and adding decimals, have students play the Finding Money Game. This game simulates the Pigs' hunt for money by having players randomly generate varying amounts of money in different denominations. Students take turns calculating the values of "found" money and then totaling each round. The player with the most money in a round gets a point. The player with the most points at the end of the game wins.

Distribute the **Finding Money Game Organizer** to each student and 16 index cards to each group. Have students make "money cards" by marking two index cards each as follows: 1¢, 5¢, 10¢, 25¢, 50¢, $1, $10, and $20. Give each group a random-number generator such as an icosohedron die, number cards 0–9, or a spinner marked 0–9.

Play the game. First, shuffle the cards and place them face down. Have players take turns choosing a "money card" and then randomly generating a number from 0–9. The "money card" indicates the denomination of the found money. The randomly generated number indicates how many of the "money cards" have been found.

After each turn, players record their information on the **Finding Money Game Organizer.** After each player has taken four turns, individual totals are calculated and the round is ended. The player with the greatest total for the round gets one point. All money cards are replaced at the end of a round and reshuffled. Play continues for additional rounds. At the end of the allotted time for play, the player with the most points wins the game.

Pigs Will Be Pigs

Finding Money Game Organizer

69

Circle the round and total if you've won that round.

Round		Turn 1	Turn 2	Turn 3	Turn 4	Totals
1	Value of "money card"					Round 1 Total
	Number					
	Total value					
2	Value of "money card"					Round 2 Total
	Number					
	Total value					
3	Value of "money card"					Round 3 Total
	Number					
	Total value					
4	Value of "money card"					Round 4 Total
	Number					
	Total value					
5	Value of "money card"					Round 5 Total
	Number					
	Total value					

PROBLEM SOLVING: The Tasty Triangle Restaurant

Materials

Individual copies of Tasty Triangle Menu (Reproducible Master 70) and **Problem Solving I and II** (Reproducible Masters 71–72)

This activity provides problem-solving situations based on a fictitious menu from "The Tasty Triangle" restaurant.

Distribute copies of the **Tasty Triangle Menu** and **Problem Solving I and II** to each student. Have students use the menu to complete the problem-solving worksheets shown with answers that follow.

Reproducible Master 70

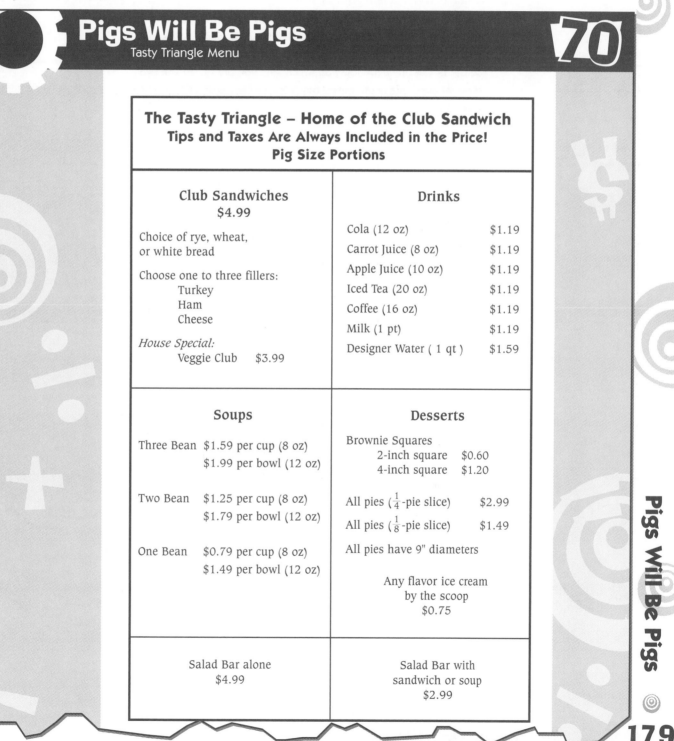

Pigs Will Be Pigs

Tasty Triangle Menu

70

The Tasty Triangle – Home of the Club Sandwich
Tips and Taxes Are Always Included in the Price!
Pig Size Portions

Club Sandwiches
$4.99

Choice of rye, wheat, or white bread

Choose one to three fillers:
- Turkey
- Ham
- Cheese

House Special: Veggie Club $3.99

Drinks

Cola (12 oz)	$1.19
Carrot Juice (8 oz)	$1.19
Apple Juice (10 oz)	$1.19
Iced Tea (20 oz)	$1.19
Coffee (16 oz)	$1.19
Milk (1 pt)	$1.19
Designer Water (1 qt)	$1.59

Soups

Three Bean	$1.59 per cup (8 oz)
	$1.99 per bowl (12 oz)
Two Bean	$1.25 per cup (8 oz)
	$1.79 per bowl (12 oz)
One Bean	$0.79 per cup (8 oz)
	$1.49 per bowl (12 oz)

Desserts

Brownie Squares

2-inch square	$0.60
4-inch square	$1.20
All pies ($\frac{1}{4}$-pie slice)	$2.99
All pies ($\frac{1}{8}$-pie slice)	$1.49

All pies have 9" diameters

Any flavor ice cream by the scoop $0.75

Salad Bar alone $4.99

Salad Bar with sandwich or soup $2.99

Pigs Will Be Pigs

Problem Solving I

71

Use the menu from the Tasty Triangle restaurant to solve these problems.

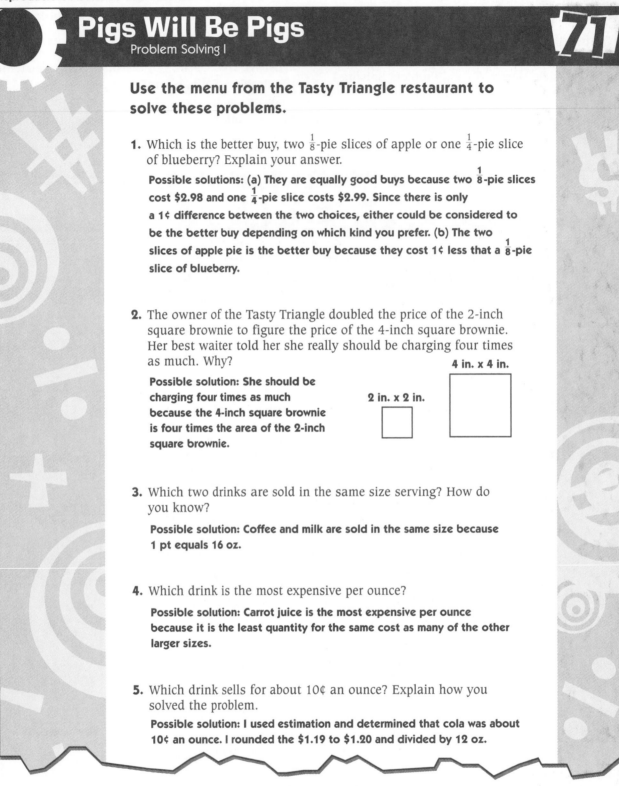

1. Which is the better buy, two $\frac{1}{8}$-pie slices of apple or one $\frac{1}{4}$-pie slice of blueberry? Explain your answer.

   Possible solutions: (a) They are equally good buys because two $\frac{1}{8}$-pie slices cost $2.98 and one $\frac{1}{4}$-pie slice costs $2.99. Since there is only a 1¢ difference between the two choices, either could be considered to be the better buy depending on which kind you prefer. (b) The two slices of apple pie is the better buy because they cost 1¢ less that a $\frac{1}{8}$-pie slice of blueberry.

2. The owner of the Tasty Triangle doubled the price of the 2-inch square brownie to figure the price of the 4-inch square brownie. Her best waiter told her she really should be charging four times as much. Why?

   Possible solution: She should be charging four times as much because the 4-inch square brownie is four times the area of the 2-inch square brownie.

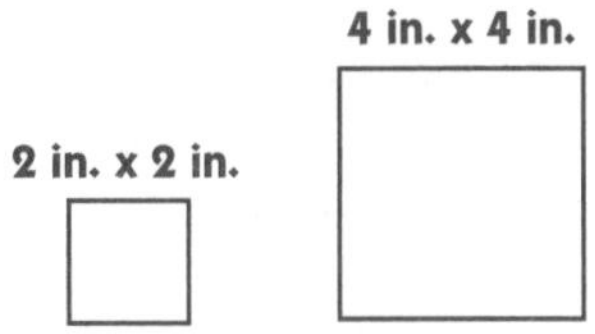

3. Which two drinks are sold in the same size serving? How do you know?

   Possible solution: Coffee and milk are sold in the same size because 1 pt equals 16 oz.

4. Which drink is the most expensive per ounce?

   Possible solution: Carrot juice is the most expensive per ounce because it is the least quantity for the same cost as many of the other larger sizes.

5. Which drink sells for about 10¢ an ounce? Explain how you solved the problem.

   Possible solution: I used estimation and determined that cola was about 10¢ an ounce. I rounded the $1.19 to $1.20 and divided by 12 oz.

Pigs Will Be Pigs

Problem Solving II

72

Use the menu from the Tasty Triangle restaurant to solve these problems.

6. Mitch figured that designer water was about a dime an ounce. Explain why you agree or disagree with Mitch.
Possible solution: I disagree. First I rounded $1.59 to $1.60 and figured how much it would cost for 16 oz ($1.60 ÷ 16 oz = $0.10 per oz). I took half of that because there are 32 oz. in a quart ($0.10 ÷ 2 = $0.05).

7. Which drink is the best buy per ounce? How do you know?
Possible solution: I used estimation and determined that designer water is the cheapest because it is about 5¢ per ounce. I rounded so I could estimate the costs as follows: water about 5¢ per ounce (1.60 ÷ 32); cola about 10¢ per ounce (1.20 ÷ 12); carrot juice about 15¢ per ounce (1.20 ÷ 8); apple juice about 12¢ per ounce (1.20 ÷ 10); iced tea about 6¢ per ounce (1.20 ÷ 20); and milk or coffee about 8¢ per ounce (1.20 ÷ 16).

8. Which kind of bean soup is the better buy in the 12-oz size compared to the 8-oz size? Why?
Possible solutions: (a) The soup with the smallest difference between serving-size price is the best deal. The difference between the prices of the three-bean soup is 40¢ ($1.99 – $1.59). The difference between the prices of the two-bean soup is 54¢ ($1.79 – $1.25). The difference between the prices of the one-bean soup is 70¢ ($1.49 – $.79). Therefore the best buy is the three-bean soup. (b) Since the bowl size is $1\frac{1}{2}$ times as big as the cup size, any bowl price that is less than $1\frac{1}{2}$ times the cup price is a good deal. I figured what the cost would be for the 12-oz bowl if it were $1\frac{1}{2}$ times the 8-oz cup. Three-bean soup should cost about $1.88 but costs $1.79, which saves $0.09. One-bean soup should cost about $1.19 but sells for $1.49, which is $0.30 more. Three-bean soup is the best deal for the customer.

9. When Tara orders a club sandwich she chooses one filler: turkey, ham, or cheese. Then she chooses one kind of bread: rye, wheat, or white. List all of the possible combinations of bread and filler Tara can choose. What is the probability of Tara ordering a ham-on-rye club sandwich?

Answer:

BREAD	FILLER
Rye	Turkey
Rye	Ham
Rye	Cheese
Wheat	Turkey
Wheat	Ham
Wheat	Cheese
White	Turkey
White	Ham
White	Cheese

The probability of her ordering a ham-on rye is $\frac{1}{9}$.

ESTIMATING MENU ORDERS

Materials

Copies of the book (pages 24–25), calculators (optional)

Provide multiple copies of *Pigs Will Be Pigs*, if possible, so students can view the menu on pages 24–25. Challenge individual students or small groups to order other selections from the menu without going over $34.67. Have them estimate the costs of their orders and then check the actual amounts using a calculator.

PLAY THE FEAST OR FAMINE GAME

Materials

Index cards with menu selections (35 for each group of 4 students), dice or number cubes, calculator

In preparation, make food cards from the menu on pages 24–25 by recording each selection and price on an index card. There are 35 selections in the menu. Make enough copies so each group of four students can have a set of the 35 food cards. Provide a die or a number cube and a calculator to each group, as well.

Play the game. Shuffle the cards and place them face down. One of the players becomes the dealer. The dealer chooses four cards. He or she then reads each card aloud and shows it to the other players. To vary the game, someone may toss a die to indicate how many of that selection has been ordered.

After the four cards are read, each player records an estimated total for the bill. The dealer uses a calculator to total the bill exactly. The player that is closest to the actual total gets one point (in a tie both players get a point). Play continues for an allotted amount of time, with players taking turns being the dealer. The player with the most points at the end wins the game.

MORE ESTIMATION

Materials

Individual copies of **Tasty Triangle Menu** (Reproducible Master 70) and **Estimation I and II** (Reproducible Masters 73–74)

This activity provides practice with estimation based on a fictitious menu from "The Tasty Triangle" restaurant.

Distribute copies of the **Tasty Triangle Menu** and **Estimation I and II** to each student. Have students use the menu to complete the estimation worksheets shown with answers on the next page.

Pigs Will Be Pigs

Estimation I

73

Use the menu from the Tasty Triangle restaurant to solve these problems.

1. Each of the people shown below has exactly $10. Which one of them will not have enough to pay for their order?

Prudence ordered	
bowl of three-bean soup	1.99
a 4-inch brownie square	1.20
apple juice	1.19
turkey club	4.99
TOTAL	**9.37**

José ordered	
bowl of one-bean soup	1.49
$\frac{1}{4}$-pie slice of blueberry with one scoop of vanilla ice cream	3.74
carrot juice	1.19
veggie club	3.99
TOTAL	**10.41**

Julio ordered	
cup of one-bean soup	.79
milk	1.19
salad bar	2.99
ham club	4.99
TOTAL	**9.96**

Nancy ordered	
bowl of two-bean soup	1.79
two scoops of vanilla ice cream	1.50
coffee	1.19
salad bar	2.99
TOTAL	**7.47**

Possible solution: I used estimation to determine that José would not have enough money. The one-bean soup and pie combined cost over $5. The carrot juice and veggie club combined cost over $5. Since these two amounts are each over $5, their sum will be over $10.

2. Can Hannah buy a club sandwich, soup, a drink, and a dessert for under $5.00? Tell why or why not.

Possible solution: No, because the cheapest club sandwich is $3.99, and the cheapest drink is $1.19. Those two items together without the dessert is over $5.

Pigs Will Be Pigs

Estimation II

74

Use the menu from the Tasty Triangle restaurant to solve these problems.

3. Without making exact calculations, tell whether or not someone with \$10 can buy one of each type of drink. Explain how you estimated.

Possible solution: Yes. There are 7 drinks. Since each is over \$1, I know there is a total of at least \$7. I also know that 6 of the drinks are \$1.19, so there is an additional \$1.20 (rounded 19 cents to 20 and multiplied by 6). Now I have a total of \$8.20 plus \$1.59 for the water. Altogether, everything is \$9.79, which is less than \$10.

4. Each member in a family of four orders a 4-inch brownie with 3 scoops of ice cream. Will there be enough money to pay in cash if Mom only has a \$10 bill and a \$5 bill in her pocket? Explain how you found your answer.

Possible solution: Yes, because 4 brownies would cost about \$5 (4 x \$1.20 = \$4.80). Each person's 3 scoops of ice cream would cost \$2.25 (3 x \$0.75) for a total of \$9 (4 x \$2.25). Since \$5 + \$9 = \$14, which is less than \$15, Mom will have enough money to pay in cash.

5. John told the waitress he wanted to eat two bowlfuls of one-bean soup. But to save money, he asked that the soup be served in 8-oz cup servings. How much money did John save buying the soup this way? Explain.

Possible solution: Two bowls of one-bean soup cost \$2.98 (2 x \$1.49) and amounts to 24 oz of soup (2 x 12 oz = 24 oz). To get the same amount of soup in 8-oz cup servings, he needed three cups of soup (24 oz ÷ 8), which cost 2.37 (3 x \$0.79). He saved 67¢ (\$2.98 – \$2.37 = \$0.67).

MATHEMATICS ASSESSMENT

Materials

Individual copies of **Connection to Mathematics Assessment: Check for Understanding I and II** (Reproducible Masters 75–76)

Distribute the multiple-choice and open-ended **questions** called **Connection to Mathematics Assessment: Check for Understanding I and II**. This activity can be used to check students' understanding of the mathematics concepts covered in this lesson.

Collect and score the students' work using the answers and rubric that follow.

Reproducible Master 75 with answers

Pigs Will Be Pigs

Connection to Mathematics Assessment: Check for Understanding I

75

1. Waldo found 2 quarters, 4 dimes, 7 nickels, and 2 pennies. How much money did he find?
   - (A.) $1.27
   - B. $0.99
   - C. $4.42
   - D. $1.50

2. Each child has the number of coins shown in the chart. If they put all their money together and then share it equally, how much money will each person get?

Name	Coins
April	4 quarters
Bruno	8 dimes
Carlos	12 nickels
Dena	16 pennies

   - A. $10
   - B. $2.56
   - C. $0.54
   - (D.) $0.64

Pigs Will Be Pigs

Connection to Mathematics Assessment: Check for Understanding II

76

Use the chart below to answer questions 3–6.

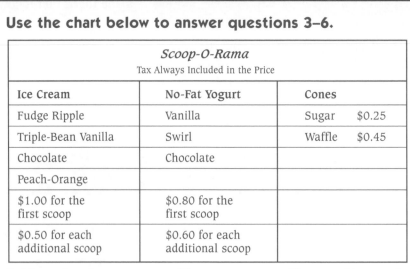

Scoop-O-Rama Tax Always Included in the Price		
Ice Cream	**No-Fat Yogurt**	**Cones**
Fudge Ripple	Vanilla	Sugar $0.25
Triple-Bean Vanilla	Swirl	Waffle $0.45
Chocolate	Chocolate	
Peach-Orange		
$1.00 for the first scoop	$0.80 for the first scoop	
$0.50 for each additional scoop	$0.60 for each additional scoop	

3. Lamar bought two scoops of ice cream on a waffle cone. How much change did Lamar get back from $5.00?
- **A.** $1.55
- **B.** $1.95
- **C.** $3.15
- **(D.)** $3.05

4. Alexander has exactly 7 quarters in his pocket. Which of the following could he buy at the Scoop-O-Rama for the exact amount he has in his pocket?
- **A.** two scoops of no-fat yogurt on a waffle cone
- **(B.)** two scoops of ice cream on a sugar cone
- **C.** three scoops of ice cream on a sugar cone
- **D.** three scoops of no-fat yogurt on a waffle cone

5. Sibilia saw Reggie leaving the Scoop-O-Rama with a cone that had one scoop of no-fat yogurt on it. What is the probability that he was eating a scoop of peach-orange on a waffle cone?
- **(A.)** 0
- **B.** $\frac{1}{6}$
- **C.** $\frac{1}{8}$
- **D.** $\frac{1}{4}$

6. Priscilla found out that Lemma spent 10¢ more than Willie at the Scoop-O-Rama and that each of them had the same kind of cone. After hearing this, she knew without even seeing the treats exactly how many scoops and what kinds of treats each person had. Tell the type of treat and number of scoops that each person had and explain how Priscilla knew. **see rubric that follows for scoring**

RUBRIC FOR SCORING
Question 6

An effective response will need to:

- show that Lemma had 2 scoops of ice cream while Willie had 2 scoops of no-fat yogurt.
- give a clear explanation.

POINTS	CRITERIA
3	The student states that Lemma had 2 scoops of ice cream and Willie had 2 scoops of no-fat yogurt. The student gives a clear explanation of how the answer was determined. Possible response: Lemma had 2 scoops of ice cream for \$1.50. Willie had 2 scoops of no-fat yogurt for \$1.40. There is a difference of 10¢ between the two. Since the cones were the same, I only had to test prices for different amounts of ice cream and yogurt. I knew it couldn't be 3 scoops of each because then they would have been the same price, \$2. I knew it couldn't be one scoop of each because there would have been a difference of 20¢.
2	Student provides a correct answer but explanation is flawed or is unclear. Answer shows some evidence of why various combinations were eliminated.
1	Student shows attempts at logic and solves part of the problem, but never indicates the correct answer.
0	Leaves blank, or answer makes no sense.

Composition Connection

WRITING A POST-READING COMPOSITION

Materials

Connection to Writing Assessment: Post-Reading Composition (Reproducible Master 77), **Have I...? Checklist** (Reproducible Master 2), **Rubric for Scoring First Drafts** (Reproducible Master 3)

Distribute the **Connection to Writing Assessment: Post-Reading Composition** along with a copy of the **Have I...? Checklist** to each student.

Give students about 30 minutes in which to plan and write the composition, and then revise/edit it based on the checklist.

Collect the students' compositions and score them using the **Rubric for Scoring First Drafts**. This draft of the composition may be revised and edited as described on pp. *xix–xx* of this manual to prepare it for sharing with a larger audience. Or, the draft may go into a "Works in Progress" folder so that the student may use it as a resource for additional ideas or revise at a later date.

Pigs Will Be Pigs

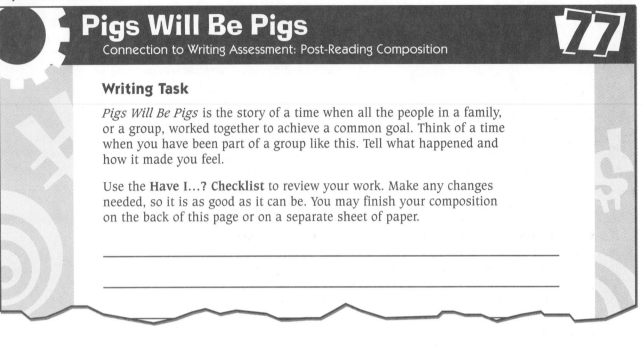

Connection to Writing Assessment: Post-Reading Composition

77

Writing Task

Pigs Will Be Pigs is the story of a time when all the people in a family, or a group, worked together to achieve a common goal. Think of a time when you have been part of a group like this. Tell what happened and how it made you feel.

Use the **Have I...? Checklist** to review your work. Make any changes needed, so it is as good as it can be. You may finish your composition on the back of this page or on a separate sheet of paper.

____

____

Extending the Connection

WRITING WITH FIGURATIVE LANGUAGE

Materials

One or more copies of the book

Discuss with the class the concept of figurative language. Teach or review the following terms:

- simile — a comparison using the words *like* or *as*.
- metaphor — an implied comparison that does not use one of those words.

Use the following prompt to initiate a class discussion:

> "Part of the delight in reading *Pigs Will Be Pigs* is in the meaning that we get from the extended metaphor that grows from the title. What does it mean to "act like a pig"? Find as many instances as you can from the text and the illustrations when you think that members of the Pigs' family are acting like pigs. Find instances when the Pigs are not acting true to form."

Assign the following composition topic as either a timed writing or an extended writing that is carried through the writing process to the point of publication. See p. *xviii* of this manual for a discussion of that process.

> "Explain what the title of the book means. Use details from the story to support your conclusion."

ADDITIONAL RESOURCES

Windows on Math, Volume 5, Unit 5 Videodisc, "Skeeter's Skate Shop." Atlanta: Optical Data Corporation, 1996. Call 1-800-524-2481.

A Remainder of One

Written by **Elinor J. Pinczes**
Illustrated by **Bonnie MacKain**

Overview of the Connections

This story is about a squadron of 25 bugs planning to march in a parade past the queen. The queen insists on having an "even" number of bugs in each line with no remainders. Private Joe, however, is always left out as the squadron first forms 2 lines, then 3 lines, and then 4 lines. Finally, when 5 lines are formed, Private Joe is no longer a remainder of one!

In teaching mathematics, this book provides the foundation for understanding basic division facts and remainders. First students use models for bugs to build an understanding of forming arrays. As they act out the story, they experience what happens as 25 is divided by different numbers. The models are then transferred to symbols to connect the symbols and situations together. Students then have a chance to model new problems with symbols.

Students also will have the opportunity to practice listening skills, making predictions, and writing about their experience and the experiences of others.

MATERIALS FOR THE CONNECTIONS

A Remainder of One • ISBN 0-395-69455-8
Written by Elinor J. Pinczes. Illustrated by Bonnie MacKain. Boston: Houghton Mifflin Company, 1995.

Language Arts

~ One or more copies of the book (Note: In the Viewing Connection, each student will need to see pages 4–5, which are not numbered. You may wish to have several copies of the book available.)

~ Optional: **Connection to Viewing Assessment: Writing About a Picture Prompt** (Reproducible Master 1)

~ **Have I...? Checklist** (Reproducible Master 2) a self-monitoring tool for student writers

~ **Rubric for Scoring First Drafts** (Reproducible Master 3)

~ **Connection to Listening Assessment: Listening to Part of a Story** (Reproducible Master 78)

~ **Connection to Writing Assessment: Post-Reading Composition** (Reproducible Master 80)

Mathematics

~ Counters, such as cubes, beans, or tiles (36 for each student)

~ Overhead projector to demonstrate acting out the story

~ **Connection to Mathematics Assessment: Check for Understanding** (Reproducible Master 79)

~ Math journals

~ **One Bug** (Reproducible Master 81)

~ Scissors

~ **Bug Grid** (Reproducible Master 82)

~ Cubes (24 of one color, 1 of another)

~ Large container

~ Colored cubes (6 red, 6 white, and 6 blue for groups of 2–3 students)

~ Map of local city streets from telephone book, atlases, road maps, etc.

Viewing Connection

INTRODUCING THE LESSON WITH A PICTURE PROMPT AND WRITING

Materials

Copy of the book (pages 4–5), **Connection to Viewing Assessment: Writing About a Picture Prompt** (Reproducible Master 1), **Have I...? Checklist** (Reproducible Master 2), **Rubric for Scoring First Drafts** (Reproducible Master 3)

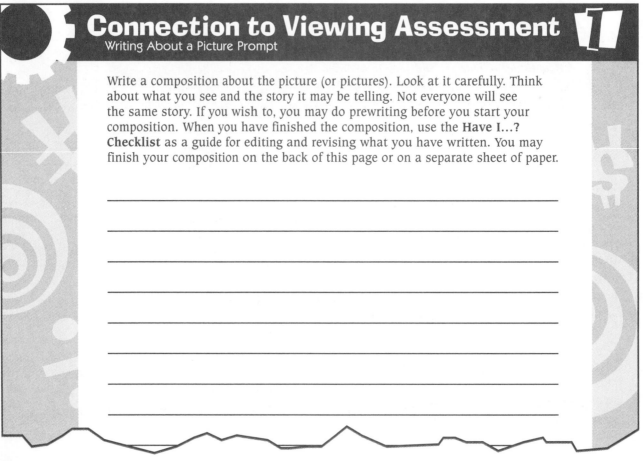

Show the class the picture on pages 4–5 of the book. This is the second double-page spread, which has a bug on the right-hand page holding a pink flower umbrella. If possible, allow students to continue to look at the picture throughout the writing session. You may distribute a copy of **Connection to Viewing Assessment: Writing About a Picture Prompt** to each student, or they may use notebook paper for their work. Also distribute copies of the **Have I...? Checklist**.

Read these directions to the class:

"You are going to write a composition about this picture. Look at it carefully. Think about what you see and the story it may be telling. It is ok that not everyone will see the same story. If you wish to, you may do prewriting before you start your compostition. When you have finished the composition, use the **Have I...? Checklist** as a guide for editing and revising what you have written."

Give the students 20–30 minutes to write their compositions and do initial editing.

Collect and score the students' compositions using the **Rubric for Scoring First Drafts**. Teach students how to compare their scored compositions to the rubric and to make notes about how to improve their compositions. Students also may be taught to use the rubric to score their own work or that of other students.

Reproducible Master 1

Connection to Viewing Assessment 1

Writing About a Picture Prompt

Write a composition about the picture (or pictures). Look at it carefully. Think about what you see and the story it may be telling. Not everyone will see the same story. If you wish to, you may do prewriting before you start your composition. When you have finished the composition, use the **Have I...? Checklist** as a guide for editing and revising what you have written. You may finish your composition on the back of this page or on a separate sheet of paper.

____

____

____

____

____

____

____

____

Listening Connection

LISTENING TO PART OF A STORY AND ANSWERING QUESTIONS

Materials

Copy of the book (Listening section: first 11 pages, 220 words), **Connection to Listening Assessment: Listening to Part of a Story** (Reproducible Master 78)

This activity will help students develop effective listening skills. As necessary, teach or review some of the effective listening strategies found on page *xv* of this manual.

Tell the class you are going to read them part of a story. When you are finished, they will answer some questions about what you have read. (The rest of the story will be read in the Mathematics Connection activity.)

Read the first 11 pages aloud to the students. The listening section starts with: *The story of Joe might just well explain…* . It ends where the bugs are marching in twos with: *Lone soldier Joe learned it wasn't much fun to find himself labeled "remainder of one"! The brainy bug-soldier stayed up the whole night. Perhaps one more line would make everything right?*

Since you are working on listening, don't stop to discuss the story, show the illustrations, or make predictions as you might do in a reading instructional period.

Distribute the multiple-choice and open-ended questions called **Connection to Listening Assessment: Listening to Part of a Story.**

Allow 15-20 minutes for completing the worksheet.

Collect and score the students' work using the answers and rubric that follow.

Proceed to the Mathematics Connection for instructions on completing the book.

Reproducible Master 78 with answers

A Remainder of One 78

Connection to Listening Assessment: Listening to Part of a Story

Circle the best answer to each question.

1. According to the story, why were the insects hurrying to find shade where they could watch the parade?
   - (A) It was hot out, and they were looking for a cool place to sit. **answer on p. 2**
   - B. They wanted to hide from the queen when she was mad.
   - C. They wanted a place where they could clearly see what was happening.
   - D. They wanted to hide so they didn't have to march.

2. Which of the following statements best describes why the queen didn't like to see a remainder?
   - A. She wanted more soldiers in the infantry.
   - B. She didn't like for Joe to be lonely.
   - C. She wanted the parade to be over because it was hot out.
   - (D) She didn't think it seemed tidy. **answer on p. 9**

A Remainder of One

Continued...

3. According to the selection, what were the bugs determined to do as they marched?
   - **A.** They wanted to walk quickly.
   - **B.** The wanted to keep the rows even.
   - **(C.)** They wanted the queen to be proud of them. **answer on p. 4**
   - **D.** They wanted the crowd to like the parade.

4. When the honeybee tells Joe why the queen didn't like what she saw, he speaks "sternly." What does the word *sternly* mean? **refers to p. 9**
   - **A.** loud and threateningly
   - **B.** joking and happily
   - **(C)** serious and firmly
   - **D.** soft and sweetly

5. The story describes Joe as "brainy." What does *brainy* mean? **refers to p. 11**
   - **A.** Lonesome
   - **B.** Hard-working
   - **(C.)** Smart
   - **D.** Well-liked

Open-ended Listening Task: Describe how you think Joe felt when the other soldiers left him behind. How do you think he will manage to get back into the troop? **see rubric that follows for scoring**

RUBRIC FOR SCORING

Open-ended Listening Task

An effective response will need to:
- reflect knowledge of the story.
- justify ideas from the text.
- identify appropriate character motivations and actions.
- be well written with a clear presentation.

POINTS	CRITERIA
4	Identifies appropriate emotions and makes a logical prediction of what might happen. Recognizes the importance of Joe's "brainy" approach to the problem and provides sufficient explanation and/or details to fully support response.
3	Identifies appropriate emotions and makes a logical prediction of what might happen next in the story. May or may not take Joe's "brainy" approach into account, but does provide reasoning to support response.
2	Identifies appropriate emotions and/or makes a logical prediction of what might happen next. The response addresses both the emotion and a prediction, but the reasoning is shallow. Or, only one element is included, but the reasoning is somewhat more fully developed.
1	Identifies an emotion and/or makes a prediction, but reasoning is shallow and poorly developed.
0	Fails to address question or to respond.

Mathematics Connection

INTRODUCTION AND ACTIVE READING

Review the section you have already read from the Listening Connection (pages 1–11), showing students the illustrations and discussing what they already have heard. In some classes, you may find it worthwhile to go back to the beginning and re-read the entire selection. This is a good way to help students confirm the answers they gave in the listening activity. If necessary, explore the rationale behind some of the answers.

ACTING OUT THE STORY

Materials

Copy of the book; counters, such as cubes, beans, or tiles (25 for each individual student); overhead projector. Alternative: **Bug Grid** (Reproducible Master 82)

Hold a class discussion about parades. Ask students if they have ever been to a parade. Encourage students to share their experiences. Have them describe the way bands and other large groups of people march in a parade. Discuss the purpose of a reviewing stand and who might watch a parade from there.

Read the story. Before starting, explain that this story is about a squadron of bugs that must march in certain formations in order to please the queen. Tell students to listen carefully as you read and to think about the following:

- What does the queen require?
- What might happen after Joe goes to bed and thinks about being a remainder of one?
- Can you explain the story in your own words?

When the story is complete, use a think-pair-share activity or group technique to have students discuss the queen's requirement. Have pairs/groups discuss the story and prepare a statement explaining what the queen required and why. Then ask them to give an accurate summary of the story without retelling the whole thing. [Possible reponse: The queen required that all 25 bugs march in rows and columns, forming a rectangle.]

Read the story again, and have students act it out by using counters to model the squadron formations. Give each student 25 counters or bugs. Tell them that you are going to re-read the story, but this time they will act out the story as you read it. As you read the story, demonstrate the formations on an overhead so that students can check their work. Discuss the number of rows and columns in each of the formations. (Rows are horizontal; columns are vertical.) Ask why there is a remainder of one in each of the first three formations.

EXAMPLE

This formation has 8 rows and 3 columns. There is a remainder of one.

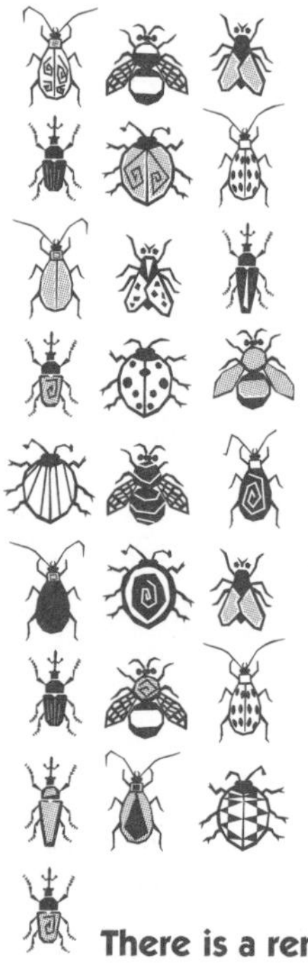

There is a remainder of 1.

TRANSFER TO SYMBOLS

When the story is finished, transfer each array to symbols by writing each problem in both formats:

$25 \div 2$ or $2\overline{)25}$

$25 \div 3$ or $3\overline{)25}$

$25 \div 4$ or $4\overline{)25}$

$25 \div 5$ or $5\overline{)25}$

Have students connect the symbolic representations to each situation in the book and to the models they've created.

Transfer this learning by asking students to model other problems, such as $21 \div 4$, $6\overline{)31}$ or $46 \div 9$. Also have them make up stories using the parade model as a guide.

INTERPRETING DIVISION AS ARRAYS

Materials

Counters, such as cubes, beans, or tiles (25 for each student)

Have students form different arrays using cubes, beans, or tiles. Connect each problem to standard division notation as you provide examples similar to the following.

EXAMPLE 1

Tell students to take 24 cubes and form 6 rows with equal numbers of cubes.

How many cubes should be in each column? **[4]**

Write the division notation on the chalkboard.

$24 \div 6$ or $6\overline{)24}$

What is the answer to the division problem? **[4]**

Continue with several problems similar to the one above. Then give the students an example that will have a remainder, such as:

EXAMPLE 2

Tell students to take 18 cubes and form 4 rows with equal numbers of cubes.

How many cubes should be in each column? **[Answer: 4 with 2 left over]**

Write the division notation on the chalkboard.

$18 \div 4$ or $4\overline{)18}$

What is the answer to the division problem? **[4 R2]**

CLOSURE

Materials

Math journals; counters, such as cubes, beans, or tiles (36 for each student)

Present the following problems for the students to solve. Have them write their responses in their math journals. You may wish to provide counters for students to model the problems.

The All-American Scout Troop plans to march in a parade. Its 36 members want to make a formation of even rows, so they decide on 5 members across in each row. Using this model, Cadet Jean will not be able to march within the formation. What other formation could you make with even rows that will allow all of the cadets to march? Explain why you chose this formation. **[Possible answers: 6 rows of 6; or 1 row of 36; or 36 rows of 1]**

- ***The Loud-and-Good Marching Band from Oak Swamp, Ohio, is planning to march in a parade. There are 30 members in the band. How many different formations (arrays) can they make if no members are to be left out? Explain your answer.*** **[Answer: Eight formations—1 row of 30; 2 rows of 15; 3 rows of 10; 5 rows of 6; 6 rows of 5; 10 rows of 3; 15 rows of 2; 30 rows of 1]**

MATHEMATICS ASSESSMENT

Materials

Connection to Mathematics Assessment: Check for Understanding (Reproducible Master 79)

Distribute the multiple-choice and open-ended questions called **Connection to Mathematics Assessment: Check for Understanding**. This activity can be used to check students' understanding of
the mathematics concepts covered in this lesson.

Collect and score the students' work using the answers and rubric that follow.

A Remainder of One

79

Connection to Mathematics Assessment: Check for Understanding

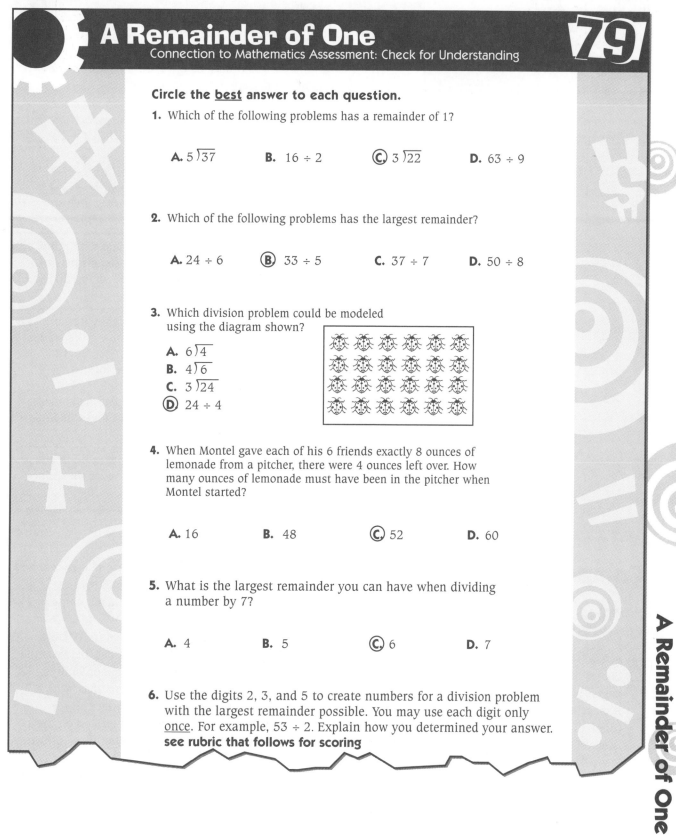

Circle the best answer to each question.

1. Which of the following problems has a remainder of 1?

   A. $5\overline{)37}$ B. $16 \div 2$ (C.) $3\overline{)22}$ D. $63 \div 9$

2. Which of the following problems has the largest remainder?

   A. $24 \div 6$ (B.) $33 \div 5$ C. $37 \div 7$ D. $50 \div 8$

3. Which division problem could be modeled using the diagram shown?

   A. $6\overline{)4}$
   B. $4\overline{)6}$
   C. $3\overline{)24}$
   (D.) $24 \div 4$

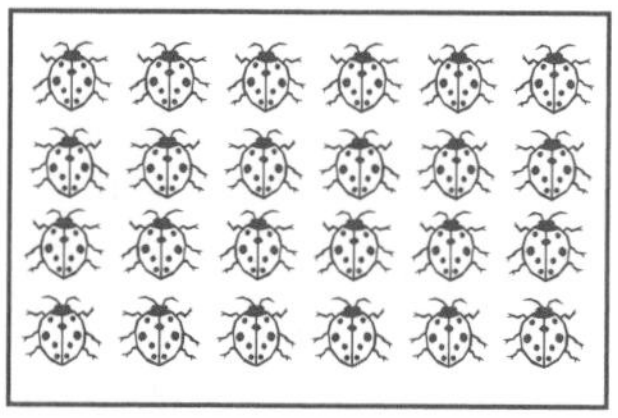

4. When Montel gave each of his 6 friends exactly 8 ounces of lemonade from a pitcher, there were 4 ounces left over. How many ounces of lemonade must have been in the pitcher when Montel started?

   A. 16 B. 48 (C.) 52 D. 60

5. What is the largest remainder you can have when dividing a number by 7?

   A. 4 B. 5 (C.) 6 D. 7

6. Use the digits 2, 3, and 5 to create numbers for a division problem with the largest remainder possible. You may use each digit only once. For example, $53 \div 2$. Explain how you determined your answer.
   see rubric that follows for scoring

RUBRIC FOR SCORING
Problem 6

An effective response will need to:

- have a correct answer of $23 \div 5$.
- give a clear explanation.

POINTS	CRITERIA
3	The student gives the correct answer of $23 \div 5$ with a clear explanation. Possible explanations include: • *I tried different combinations of divisors until I found the one that had the greatest remainder.* • *I made 6 different division problems from the numbers and worked each one out so I knew which one had the largest remainder.* $23 \div 5$, $32 \div 5$, $52 \div 3$, $25 \div 3$, $35 \div 2$, $53 \div 2$ • *I knew the divisor had to be 5 because the largest possible remainders with either 2 or 3 would be 1 or 2. I worked out the two possible problems with a divisor of 5 and found that* $23 \div 5$ *had the larger remainder.*
2	The student gives the correct division problem with minor flaws or errors in the explanation. Or, the student lists or refers to all of the possibilities but gives the wrong division problem as the answer.
1	The student gives the correct division problem with no explanation or a very confusing explanation. Or, the student gives the wrong division problem and lists or refers to some of the possible problems that could be formed. Or, the student shows evidence of problem solving but misunderstands the terminology. For example, the student gives the problem with the greatest quotient and explains why it is the greatest quotient.
0	The student gives the wrong answer and makes no reference to listing the possibilities. Or, the student leaves the question blank.

Composition Connection

WRITING A POST-READING COMPOSITION

Materials

Copies of the book (focus on illustrations on pages 16–17 and 22–23), **Connection to Writing Assessment: Post-Reading Composition** (Reproducible Master 80), **Have I...? Checklist** (Reproducible Master 2), **Rubric for Scoring First Drafts** (Reproducible Master 3)

Re-read or review the story with the class, this time showing and discussing the illustrations. Call students' attention to the facial expressions of the queen each time she is shown. Have the class discuss what her expression might indicate and how it changes each time the bugs march by.

Also note the expressions of the marching bugs. Pay particular attention to pages 12 and 13. Notice how the bugs have their fists raised in the air to indicate their determination. Contrast this with the bugs' faces on pages 4–5. They are not smiling like they were earlier. Point out that the lines, which indicate their movements, are stronger.

Also notice the changes of expression on Joe's face. Talk about what students think these drawings indicate about what Joe is saying and feeling. His emotions seem particularly poignant in the illustration on page 24.

When you are ready to have the students complete the writing task, go back and show the students the illustrations of the queen's messengers on pages 16–17 (mosquito) and 22–23 (dragonfly) without comment. If the students call out responses, there is no need to respond in any way that shows that they are correct or incorrect. After you have shown the illustrations and are sure that students have had a sufficient opportunity to study them, give the class the writing prompt below. If students have individual copies of the book, they may continue to look at the illustrations throughout the writing session, or you may leave the book at a location where students may refer to it as needed during writing.

Give students the **Connection to Writing Assessment: Post-Reading Composition** along with a copy of the **Have I...? Checklist**.

Give students about 20 minutes in which to write the composition and revise/edit it based on the checklist.

Collect and score the students' compositions using the **Rubric for Scoring First Drafts**.

Reproducible Master 80

A Remainder of One

80

Connection to Writing Assessment: Post-Reading Composition

Writing Task

You have studied pictures of two "bugs" who took messages from the queen to Joe. Think about from which of the two bugs you would rather get a message, the mosquito or the dragonfly. Write a composition in which you decide which bug is the better messenger and explain why this is so.

Be sure to use the **Have I . . . ? Checklist** to review your work. Make any changes needed, so it is as good as it can be. You may finish your composition on the back of this page or on a separate sheet of paper.

____

____

____

____

Extending the Connections

PROBABILITY

Materials

One Bug (Reproducible Master 81), Alternative: **Bug Grid** (Reproducible Master 82), colored pencils, scissors, large container for the bugs, 24 cubes of one color and 1 of another

Have the class make a collection of 25 bugs from copies of the **One Bug** reproducible master. They can decorate, name, and display the bugs on a 5 x 5 grid. Make a list of the bug names on the chalkboard for reference. As an alternative, you may use **Bug Grid**, which has 25 unique bugs that can be colored and cut out. See examples below.

Bug Jane	Bug Bill	Bug Alice
Bug Tyrone	Bug Jim	Bug Paul
Bug Ann	Bug Mary	Bug Latisha
Bug Joe	Bug Jeff	Bug Sue-Lee
Bug Bob	Bug Eric	Bug Lionel
Bug Kim	Bug Fran	Bug Lucy
Bug Karen	Bug Dennis	Bug Naja
Bug Nina	Bug Barry	Bug Wanda
Bug Lee		

Fold and place all the bugs in a container and then pose probability questions, such as:

What is the probability of choosing the bug named Karen? **[$\frac{1}{25}$]**

- ***What is the probability of choosing a bug whose name starts with the letter J?*** **Answer: $\frac{4}{25}$ (Jane, Jeff, Jim, and Joe)**
- ***What is the probability of choosing a bug whose name has three letters?*** **[Answer: $\frac{6}{25}$ (Kim, Ann, Bob, Jim, Joe, or Lee)]**

To model the idea another way, place 24 of one color cube in a container and 1 of another color to represent "Private Joe."

What is the probability of choosing Joe from the container? **[Answer: $\frac{1}{25}$]**

COMBINATIONS AND ARRANGEMENTS

Materials

Colored cubes (6 red, 6 white, and 6 blue for groups of 2–3 students)

Present the following problem for the students to solve.

The Loud-and-Good Marching Band from Oak Swamp, Ohio, has 24 members. The band has only red, white, or blue uniforms, which have been fairly distributed among its members. When the band forms to march, each row is supposed to have three members, each wearing a different color uniform. How many different ways could the colors of the uniforms in the front line be arranged?

You may wish to have students work in small groups to help them find all of the possible combinations. Provide each group of 2–3 students with 6 red, 6 white, and 6 blue cubes. Have them model the answer before recording the combinations.

[Answer: Possible combinations include:

RWB	RBW	WRB
WBR	BRW	BWR]

COORDINATES

Materials

One Bug (Reproducible Master 81);
Alternative: **Bug Grid** (Reproducible Master 82)

Have the class make models of the 25 bugs from the story, using **One Bug**. They can decorate and name the bugs. Have students organize the 25 bugs in 5 rows and 5 columns, using coordinates to locate and identify each bug's position.

You may wish to write the resulting coordinates on the chalkboard. As an alternative, you may use **Bug Grid**, which has 25 unique bugs that are already arranged into a coordinate grid. See example grid shown below.

5	Bug Jane	Bug Bill	Bug Alice	Bug Tyrone	Bug Jim
4	Bug Paul	Bug Ann	Bug Mary	Bug Latisha	Bug Joe
3	Bug Jeff	Bug Sue-Lee	Bug Bob	Bug Eric	Bug Lionel
2	Bug Kim	Bug Fran	Bug Lucy	Bug Karen	Bug Dennis
1	Bug Naja	Bug Nina	Bug Barry	Bug Wanda	Bug Lee
	1	**2**	**3**	**4**	**5**

Challenge students to locate bugs using the coordinate codes. You can name a bug and have students give the coordinates or give the coordinates and have them find the name. Always give the number of the column first and the row second. (Rows are horizontal. Columns are vertical.)

Where is Bug Lucy? **[Answer: column 3, row 2 indicated by (3,2)]**

- ***Where is Bug Sue-Lee ?*** **[Answer: column 2, row 3 indicated by (2,3)]**
- ***Who has the coordinates (4,5)?*** **[Answer: Bug Tyrone]**
- ***What are the coordinates of Bug Dennis?*** **[Answer: (5,2)]**

If possible, arrange students in 5 rows and 5 columns with their bugs. Then call on them by their coordinates to answer questions.

PATHS AND MAPS

Materials

Map of local city streets from telephone book, atlases, road maps, etc.

Using a map of city streets, have students describe the shortest route that the Good-and-Loud Marching Band could take for a parade that will be between a starting and ending point established by the teacher and/or the class.

CLOSURE

Materials

Math journals

Ask students to respond to the following in their math journals.

José's teacher asked him to use tiles to show what 12 ÷ 6 means. José drew the following sketch. Tell why you agree or disagree with José's sketch. **[Answer: José's sketch is wrong because it shows 6 groups of 3 rather than 6 groups of 2.]**

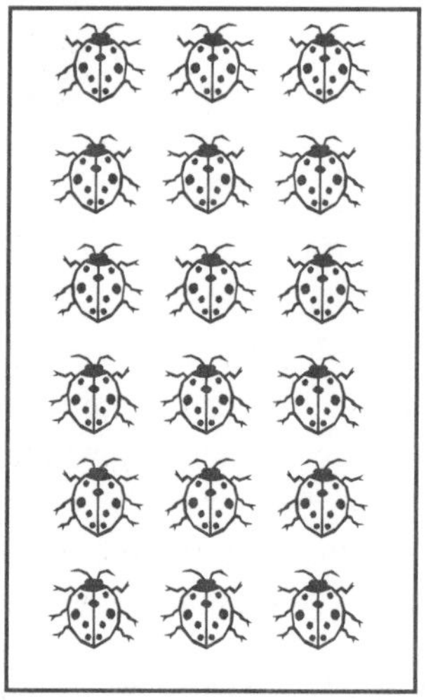

ADDITIONAL RESOURCES

Windows on Math, Volume 4, Unit 1 Videodisc, "Lemma's Dilemma" and "Manny Makes Muffins." Atlanta: Optical Data Corporation, 1996. Call 1-800-524-2481.

ESPA^3 Mathematics, Daily Activities for Math Success, Book 5, Base-Ten Block Month. Iowa City, Iowa: Tutor Tools, Inc. Contact 800-776-3454.

Teacher Notes

Spaghetti and Meatballs for All! A Mathematical Story

Written by **Marilyn Burns**
Illustrated by **Debbie Tilley**

Overview of the Connections

In this book, Mr. and Mrs. Comfort love gardening, cooking, and entertaining their family and friends, so they invite everyone over for spaghetti and meatballs. Mrs. Comfort organizes the seating arrangement while Mr. Comfort cooks. Each time new people arrive, they rearrange the tables and chairs. During the mayhem, Mr. Comfort continues to serve salad, garlic bread, and spaghetti and meatballs. In the end, they have enough tables, chairs, and food for all.

In teaching mathematics, this book provides the foundation for understanding how 12 unique pentomino shapes are formed. First students use models for tables and chairs to build an understanding of perimeter and area. As they act out the story, they experience what happens to perimeters when sides of figures are joined together. This concept of arranging the tables is extended as the students use connecting cubes or tiles to build unique triominoes, tetrominoes, and pentominoes. Through this building, students informally develop an understanding of flips, turns, and slides. Basic arithmetic skills are also addressed in problems based on the story.

Students will also have the opportunity to practice listening skills, making predictions, and writing about their experience and the experiences of others.

MATERIALS FOR THE CONNECTIONS

Spaghetti and Meatballs for All! A Mathematical Story • ISBN 0-590-94459-2
Written by Marilyn Burns. Illustrated by Debbie Tilley. New York: Scholastic Press, 1997.

Language Arts

~ One or more copies of the book (Note: In the Viewing Connection, each student will need to see the front cover of the book. You may wish to have several copies available.)

~ Optional: **Connection to Viewing Assessment: Writing About a Picture Prompt** (Reproducible Master 1)

~ **Have I...? Checklist** (Reproducible Master 2) a self-monitoring tool for student writers

~ **Rubric for Scoring First Drafts** (Reproducible Master 3)

~ **Connection to Listening Assessment: Listening to Part of a Story** (Reproducible Master 83)

~ **Connection to Writing Assessment: Post-Reading Composition** (Reproducible Master 86)

Mathematics

~ Connecting cubes or tiles to create the 12 unique pentomino shapes (60 for each group of 3–4 students; 8 for each group of 2–3 students)

~ Toothpicks, or straws cut to match the sides of the tiles, to model chair and table arrangements from the story (32 for each group of 2–3 students). Alternative: 32 centimeter cubes could also be used as the chairs.

~ **Optional:** overhead projector to demonstrate acting out the story

~ Math journals

~ **Connection to Mathematics Assessment: Check for Understanding I and II** (Reproducible Masters 84 – 85)

~ **Optional:** Grid paper to act out the "extending the pattern" problem

~ **Thinking About the Story** (Reproducible Master 87)

Viewing Connection

INTRODUCING THE LESSON WITH A PICTURE PROMPT AND WRITING

Materials

Cover of the book, **Connection to Viewing Assessment: Writing About a Picture Prompt** (Reproducible Master 1), **Have I...? Checklist** (Reproducible Master 2), **Rubric for Scoring First Drafts** (Reproducible Master 3)

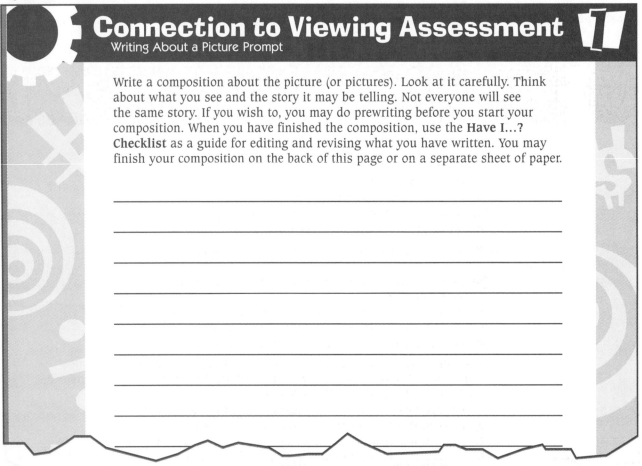

Show the class the picture on the cover of *Spaghetti and Meatballs for All!* If possible, allow students to continue to look at the picture throughout the writing session. You may distribute a copy of **Connection to Viewing Assessment: Writing About a Picture Prompt** to each student, or they may use notebook paper for their work. Also distribute copies of the **Have I...? Checklist.**

Read these directions to the class:

"You are going to write a composition about this picture. Look at it carefully. Think about what you see and the story it may be telling. It is OK that not everyone will see the same story. If you wish to, you may do prewriting before you start your composition. When you have finished the composition, use the **Have I... Checklist** as a guide for editing and revising what you have written."

Give the students 20–30 minutes to write their compositions and do initial editing.

Collect and score the students' compositions using the **Rubric for Scoring First Drafts**. Teach students how to compare their scored compositions to the rubric and to make notes about how to improve their compositions. Students also may be taught to use the rubric to score their own work or that of other students.

Reproducible Master 1

Connection to Viewing Assessment 1

Writing About a Picture Prompt

Write a composition about the picture (or pictures). Look at it carefully. Think about what you see and the story it may be telling. Not everyone will see the same story. If you wish to, you may do prewriting before you start your composition. When you have finished the composition, use the **Have I...? Checklist** as a guide for editing and revising what you have written. You may finish your composition on the back of this page or on a separate sheet of paper.

Listening Connection

LISTENING TO PART OF A STORY AND ANSWERING QUESTIONS

Materials

Copy of the book (Listening section: first 8 pages, 370 words), **Connection to Listening Assessment: Listening to Part of a Story** (Reproducible Master 83)

This activity will help students develop effective listening skills. As necessary, teach or review some of the effective listening strategies found on page *xv* of this manual.

Tell the class you are going to read them part of a story. When you are finished, they will answer some questions about what you have read. (The rest of the story will be read in the Mathematics Connection activity.)

Read the first 8 pages aloud to the students. The pages are not numbered so consider the first page of the story as page 1.

The listening section starts with the phrase: *One fine day,...* and ends with: *"But there is," said Mr. Comfort. "There's plenty of room and plenty of garlic bread."*

Since you are working on listening, don't stop to discuss the story, show the illustrations, or make predictions, as you might do in a reading instructional period. In this particular selection, two characters are talking to one another. It will be essential for you to practice two different voices, since students will have to hear the character changes in your voice.

Distribute the worksheet with multiple-choice and open-ended questions called **Connection to Listening Assessment: Listening to Part of a Story.**

Allow students 15–20 minutes for completing the worksheet.

Collect and score the students' work using the answers and rubric that follow.

Proceed to the Mathematics Connection for instructions on completing the book.

Reproducible Master 83 with answers

Spaghetti and Meatballs for All! 83

Connection to Listening Assessment: Listening to Part of a Story

Circle the <u>best</u> answer to each question.

1. What does Mr. Comfort like to do best in a vegetable garden?
   - **A.** He likes to tend the plants.
   - **B.** He likes to munch on the vegetables.
   - **(C)** He likes to read cookbooks. **answer on p. 1**
   - **D.** He likes to talk to his wife while she gardens.
2. What major problem does Mr. Comfort overcome by making spaghetti and meatballs?
   - **(A)** He doesn't have to worry about the oven being too small. **answer on p. 4**
   - **B.** He doesn't have to worry that people will not like the food.
   - **C.** He doesn't have to worry about having enough food to serve everyone.
   - **D.** He doesn't have to worry about having enough dishes for everyone.
3. When the rental company arrives, they were one chair short. Mr. Comfort tells his wife, "Don't worry. You'll think of something." Which is the most likely reason he says this? **refers to p. 6**
   - **A.** He knew that Mrs. Comfort had ordered more chairs than would be needed.
   - **(B)** He knew that Mrs. Comfort had solved other problems in the past.
   - **C.** He knew that some of the people they had invited wouldn't show up.
   - **D.** He knew that he would be working in the kitchen and wouldn't need a chair.

Spaghetti and Meatballs for All!

Continued...

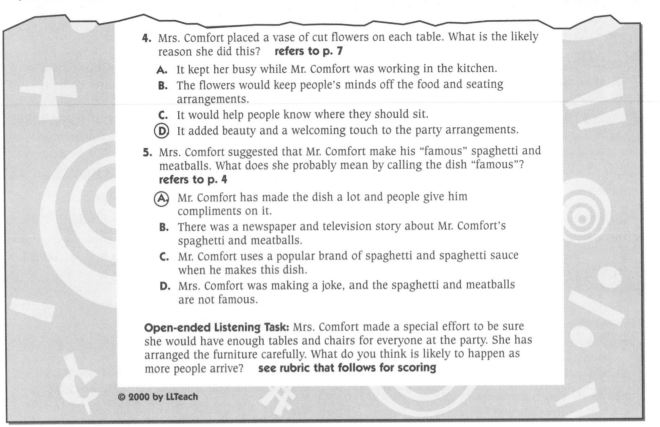

4. Mrs. Comfort placed a vase of cut flowers on each table. What is the likely reason she did this? **refers to p. 7**
   - **A.** It kept her busy while Mr. Comfort was working in the kitchen.
   - **B.** The flowers would keep people's minds off the food and seating arrangements.
   - **C.** It would help people know where they should sit.
   - **(D)** It added beauty and a welcoming touch to the party arrangements.

5. Mrs. Comfort suggested that Mr. Comfort make his "famous" spaghetti and meatballs. What does she probably mean by calling the dish "famous"? **refers to p. 4**
   - **(A)** Mr. Comfort has made the dish a lot and people give him compliments on it.
   - **B.** There was a newspaper and television story about Mr. Comfort's spaghetti and meatballs.
   - **C.** Mr. Comfort uses a popular brand of spaghetti and spaghetti sauce when he makes this dish.
   - **D.** Mrs. Comfort was making a joke, and the spaghetti and meatballs are not famous.

Open-ended Listening Task: Mrs. Comfort made a special effort to be sure she would have enough tables and chairs for everyone at the party. She has arranged the furniture carefully. What do you think is likely to happen as more people arrive? **see rubric that follows for scoring**

RUBRIC FOR SCORING

Open-ended Listening Task

An effective response will need to:

- reflect knowledge of the story.
- justify ideas from the text.
- make logical and reasonable predictions about what might happen.
- be well written with a clear presentation.

POINTS	CRITERIA
4	Makes a logical prediction, which may be that people will push chairs together. Answer is well written with good supporting details reflecting knowledge of the story.
3	Answer is logical and/or well written, but shows some weaknesses in one or the other element. The logic may not be well supported by the story, even though it is a reasonable conclusion. Or, the answer may be logical and supported, but the writing is poor and lacking in an appropriate level of sophistication.
2	Answer is either logical or well written, but shows major weaknesses in one or the other areas. The student appears to have a general understanding of the story, but lacks the sophistication to tie it into a logical prediction.
1	Answer is sketchy with an illogical conclusion. The student may merely retell the story or restate the question. Answer shows a lack of understanding.
0	Student doesn't respond or doesn't attend to the task.

Mathematics Connection

INTRODUCTION AND ACTIVE READING

Review the section you have already read from the Listening Connection (pages 1–8), showing students the illustrations and discussing what they have already heard. In some classes, you may find it worthwhile to go back to the beginning and re-read the entire selection. This is a good way to help students confirm the answers they gave in the listening activity. If necessary, explore the rationale behind some of the answers.

ACTING OUT THE STORY

Materials
Connecting cubes or tiles (8 for each group of 2–3 students), toothpicks or straws cut to match the sides of the tiles (32 for each group of 2–3 students), overhead projector (optional)

Tell students that before you finish the story, you want to discuss some other concepts that will help them understand the material more fully.

Hold a class discussion about situations where large groups of people get together. Discuss the fact that the family reunion in *Spaghetti and Meatballs for All!* is one kind of large gathering. Encourage students to share their own experiences at large celebrations.

Use a think-pair-share activity to generate a list of things you would have to do to hold a celebration for 32 people. Have pairs make a "to do" list.

Read the story. Before starting, tell students you want them to think about the following questions as you read:

- ***How do their "to do" lists compare with the things that Mr. and Mrs. Comfort did to prepare for their celebration?***

- ***What did Mrs. Comfort know about rearranging the tables that nobody else seemed to know?*** **[Answer: Each time that sides of the tables are joined, they lose places for people to sit. Originally, there are 32 seats at 8 separate tables, but when 2 tables are put together, there are only 30 places to sit.]**

After reading the story, ask students what they noticed about their "to do" lists that was similar to and different from Mr. and Mrs. Comfort's plans.

Read the story again, and have students act it out by using tiles and toothpicks to model seating arrangements. Give each group of 3–4 children 8 tiles and 32 toothpicks.

You may want to model a seating arrangement on an overhead. Use tiles or connecting cubes to represent the tables. Use centimeter cubes to represent the chairs in order to more clearly show how seats are lost as tables are pushed together. (Toothpicks or straws cut into appropriate lengths can also be used to represent the chairs.)

When you get to the page that pictures Mrs. Comfort's seating plan (page 6), have students build a model of it. Students should start with 8 "tables" and 32 "chairs" placed appropriately around the "tables." Ask them to find the total length of all the perimeters of all 8 tables when the tables are arranged individually. [Answer: Each table has a perimeter of 4 units. Since there are 8 tables, the total of the perimeters is 32 units. If each guest takes one unit on the perimeter, there would be enough room for all 32 guests to sit.]

Each time new guests arrive, students should note how many people are now at the party and then model the new seating arrangement. They may want to place any extra "chairs" in a separate area. As you continue through the story, ask questions about the perimeter and area of the rectangles that are formed by moving the tables together. Ask why the total perimeter changes. [Answer: Every time sides are lost, the perimeter gets smaller.]

Below is a sampling of drawings and questions for each arrival described in the book. Be sure to have the children act out each of the changes in table arrangements before showing them the answers.

EXAMPLE 1

Arrangements after the arrival of the Comfort's daughter and her husband with their two children.
[Total number of people: 2 + 4 = 6]

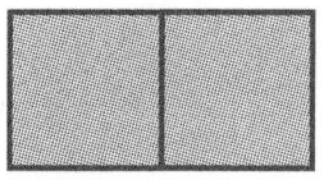

What is the perimeter of this figure? [6] ***How do you know?***

EXAMPLE 2

Arrangements after the arrival of Mrs. Comfort's brother and his wife, their daughter, her husband, and their twin sons.

[Total number of people: 6 + 6 = 12]

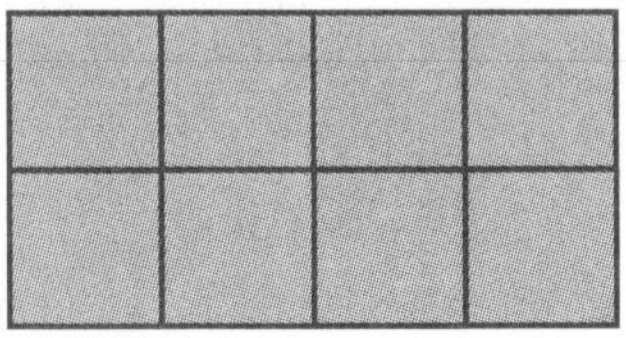

At first they added only two tables. Why didn't this arrangement work? **[Answer: Not enough room for all the chairs on the perimeter.]**

- ***What is the perimeter of the 8 tables put together as shown above?*** **[12]** ***How do you know?***

EXAMPLE 3

Arrangements after the arrival of the next-door neighbors with their daughter and son.

[Total number of people: 12 + 4 = 16]

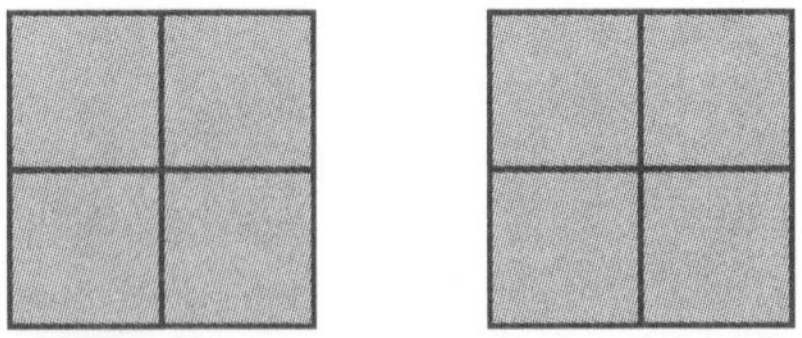

Why did they have to separate the tables into 2 sets of 4 tables? **[Answer: To gain 4 more sides for the 4 additional people]**

EXAMPLE 4

Arrangements after the arrival of Mr. Comfort's mother and father.

[Total number of people: 16 + 2 = 18]

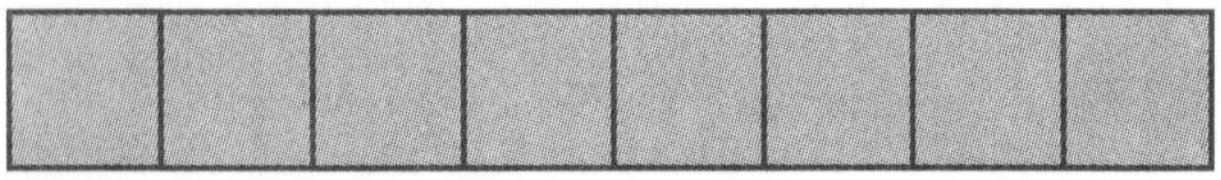

What is the perimeter of the tables after this arrangement? **[18]** ***Why?***

EXAMPLE 5

Arrangements after the arrival of Mrs. Comfort's mother and father.

[Total number of people: 18 + 2 = 20]

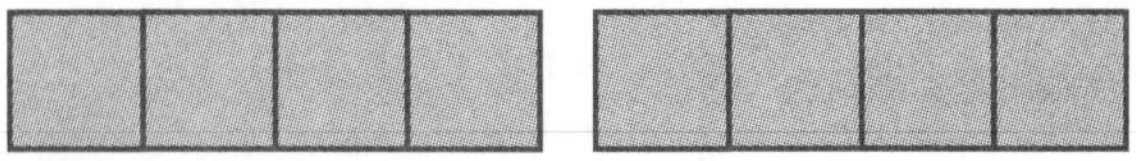

Why did separating the 8 tables into 2 groups of 4 increase the perimeter by 2 units? **[Answer: Two more sides were gained.]**

EXAMPLE 6

Arrangements after the arrival of the Comforts' son and his wife and their twin daughters.

[Total number of people: 20 + 4 = 24]

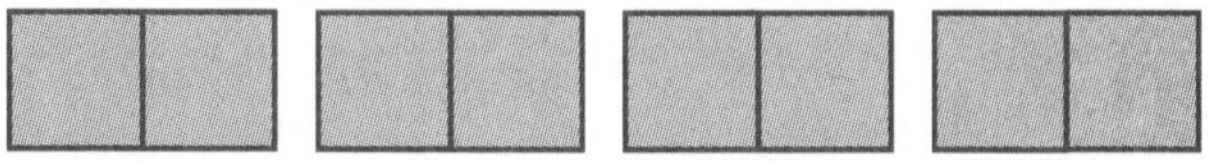

Why did separating the 2 groups of 4 tables into 4 groups of 2 tables make enough room? **[Answer: Four more sides were gained.]**

EXAMPLE 7

Arrangements after the arrival of Mrs. Comfort's sister and her husband with their triplets and triplet boyfriends.

[Total number of people: 24 + 8 = 32]

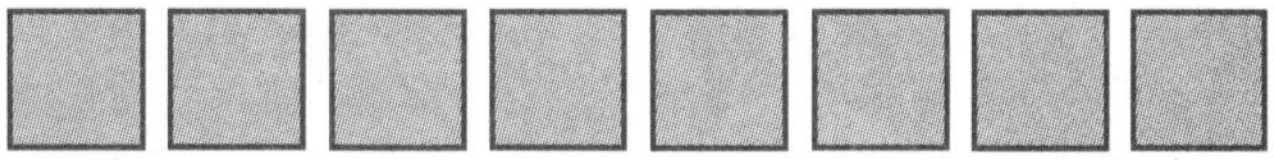

Why did separating the 4 groups of 2 tables into 8 separate tables work when 8 more people arrived? **[Answer: Eight sides were gained.]**

FLIPS, TURNS, AND SLIDES

Materials

Connecting cubes or tiles (60 for each group of 3–4 students)

Distribute 60 connecting cubes to each group of 3–4 students. Explain that the class will be building triominoes (sets of three connecting cubes), tetrominoes (sets of four connecting cubes), and pentominoes (sets of five connecting cubes). Then students will find the number of unique figures for each of the different classifications. The only requirements are that all the cubes in each group must be connected and that they must sit flat on the table.

Model the two possible triominoes. Point out that the position of the triomino doesn't matter. There are only two unique triominoes. Even though four are shown below, only two of them are unique shapes.

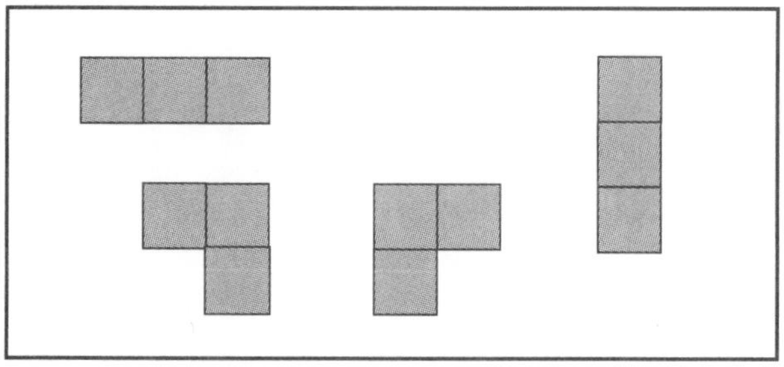

Show one tetromino. Have students construct the other four. Circulate about the class to help students use flips, turns, and slides to model the five unique shapes that can be made from sets of four cubes.

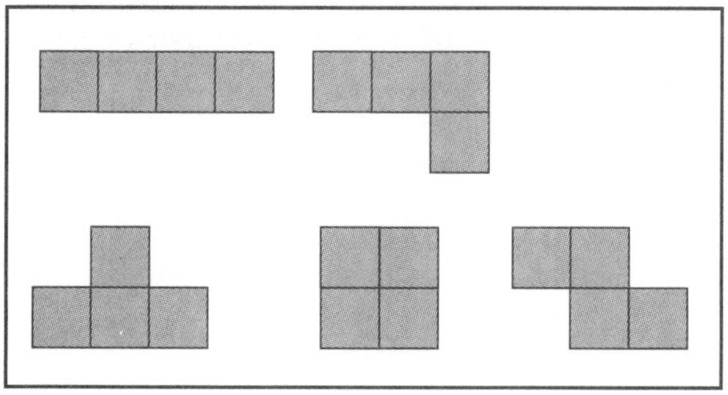

Have groups of students make pentominoes by arranging sets of five cubes. There are 12 unique shapes. Then have them find the perimeters of each. Ask: What makes the perimeters change? [Answer: Sides are lost or gained.]

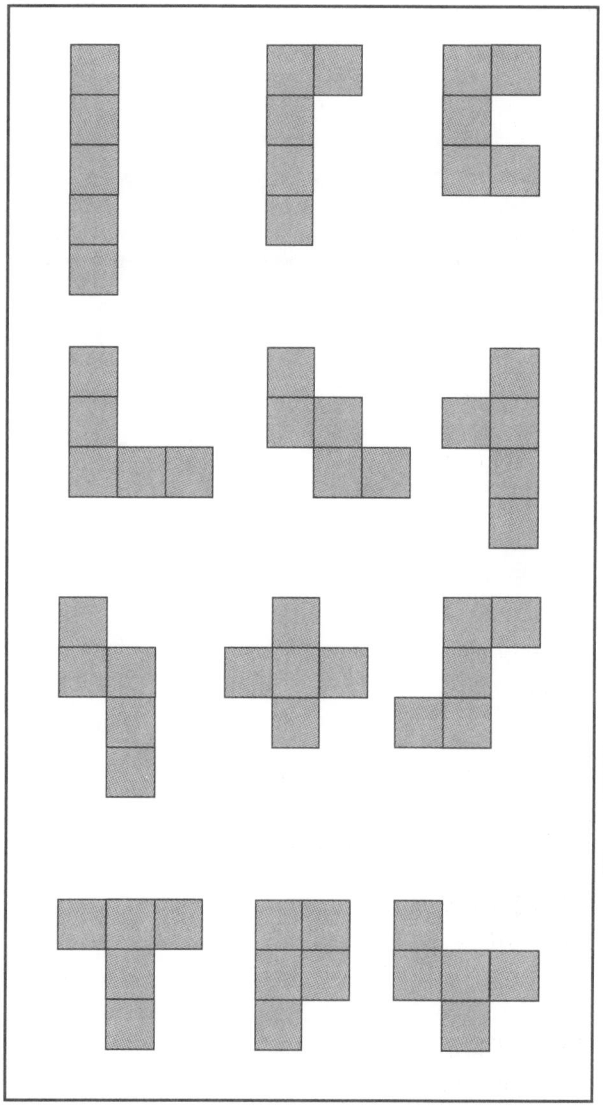

CLOSURE

Have students make a journal entry describing what Mrs. Comfort seemed to know that nobody else knew until they rearranged and solved the problems by moving furniture. [Answer: Mrs. Comfort knew that every time tables were placed so they had a common edge they would lose two sides. She also knew that the total sides for 8 separate tables was 32.]

Alternative: Ask students to describe why it might be important to plan ahead like Mrs. Comfort did. Have them describe a time when they didn't plan and something took longer than it should have.

MATHEMATICS ASSESSMENT

Materials

Connection to Mathematics Assessment: Check for Understanding I and II (Reproducible Masters 84–85), tiles or connecting cubes

Distribute the worksheets with multiple-choice and open-ended questions called **Connection to Mathematics Assessment: Check for Understanding I and II**. This activity can be used to check students' understanding of the mathematics concepts covered in this lesson.

Collect and score the students' work using the answers and rubric that follow.

Reproducible Master 84 with answers

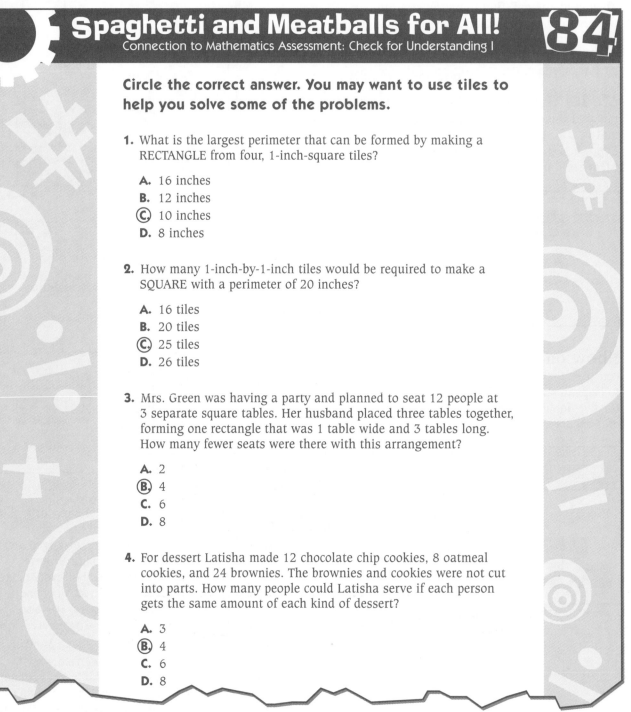

Spaghetti and Meatballs for All!

Connection to Mathematics Assessment: Check for Understanding I

84

Circle the correct answer. You may want to use tiles to help you solve some of the problems.

1. What is the largest perimeter that can be formed by making a RECTANGLE from four, 1-inch-square tiles?

   A. 16 inches
   B. 12 inches
   (C.) 10 inches
   D. 8 inches

2. How many 1-inch-by-1-inch tiles would be required to make a SQUARE with a perimeter of 20 inches?

   A. 16 tiles
   B. 20 tiles
   (C.) 25 tiles
   D. 26 tiles

3. Mrs. Green was having a party and planned to seat 12 people at 3 separate square tables. Her husband placed three tables together, forming one rectangle that was 1 table wide and 3 tables long. How many fewer seats were there with this arrangement?

   A. 2
   (B.) 4
   C. 6
   D. 8

4. For dessert Latisha made 12 chocolate chip cookies, 8 oatmeal cookies, and 24 brownies. The brownies and cookies were not cut into parts. How many people could Latisha serve if each person gets the same amount of each kind of dessert?

   A. 3
   (B.) 4
   C. 6
   D. 8

Spaghetti and Meatballs for All!

Connection to Mathematics Assessment: Check for Understanding II

85

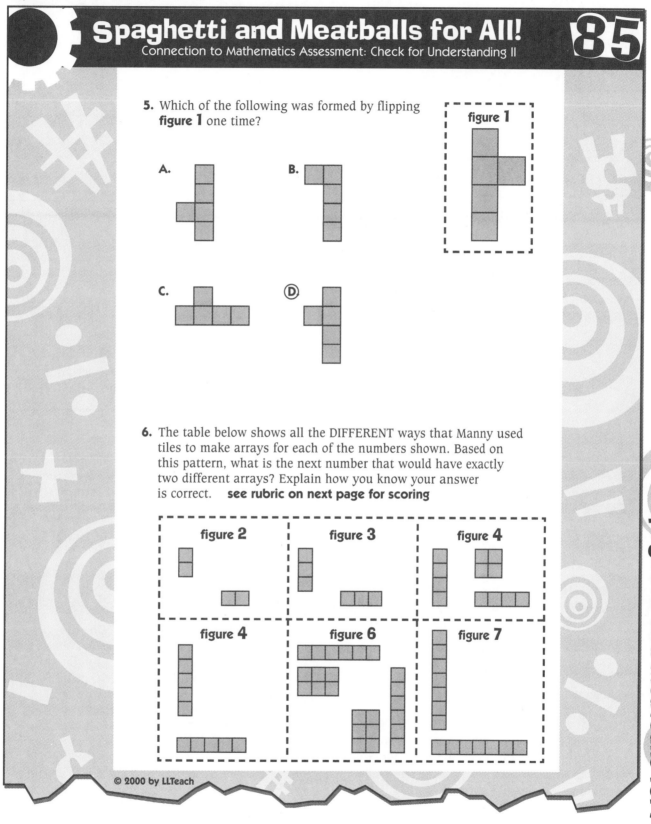

5. Which of the following was formed by flipping **figure 1** one time?

figure 1

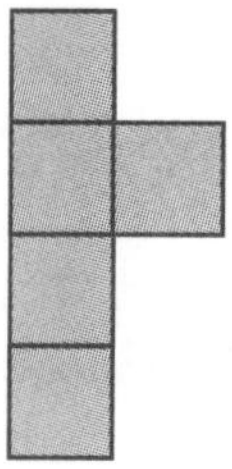

A.

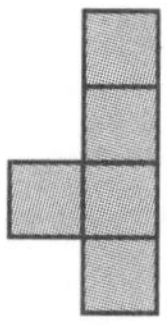

B.

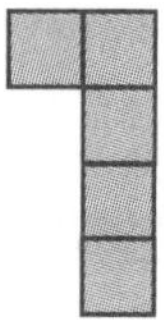

C.

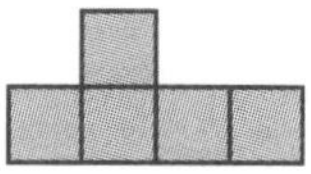

(D)

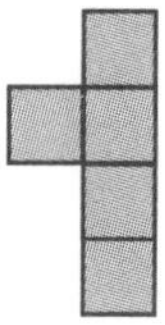

6. The table below shows all the DIFFERENT ways that Manny used tiles to make arrays for each of the numbers shown. Based on this pattern, what is the next number that would have exactly two different arrays? Explain how you know your answer is correct. **see rubric on next page for scoring**

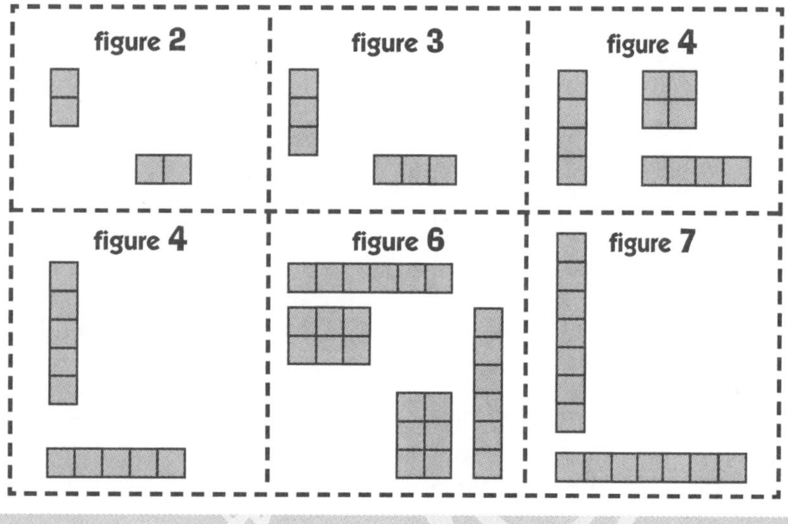

RUBRIC FOR SCORING
Problem 6

An effective response will need to:
- show that 11 is the next number.
- give a clear explanation.

POINTS	CRITERIA
3	The student explains or shows that 11 is the next number that would have exactly two different arrays. Possible explanation may include: *"I kept drawing arrays for each number after 7 until I got to two arrays. Eight had four arrays, 9 had three arrays, 10 had four arrays, and 11 had two arrays."* OR *"The only numbers that have exactly two arrays are prime numbers. The next prime number after 7 is 11, so 11 is the answer."*
2	The student indicates that 11 is the answer but provides an unclear explanation or an explanation with minor errors. OR The student provides a correct explanation but draws or shows the wrong number.
1	The student indicates that 11 is the answer but provides no explanation or an incorrect explanation.
0	The student gives the wrong answer with an unclear or no explanation OR leaves the question blank.

Composition Connection

WRITING A POST-READING COMPOSITION

Materials

Copy of the book (focus on illustrations on pages 29–30), **Connection to Writing Assessment: Post-Reading Composition** (Reproducible Master 86), **Have I...? Checklist** (Reproducible Master 2), **Rubric for Scoring First Drafts** (Reproducible Master 3)

Review the book's illustrations in order by showing and discussing them with the class. Do not read the story this time, but discuss it by focusing on what the pictures suggest. You might point out the cat throughout the story. It adds humor, but it doesn't seem to advance the story. Be sure students notice and comment on Mrs. Comfort and her seating chart throughout the story. Encourage students to talk about what the illustrations suggest about each of the groups of guests as they arrive. Your goal is to help them interpret ideas presented visually and recognize the importance of details as well as why some details may be irrelevant.

Ask students to compare the different ways they've experienced the story—first by listening to the story without seeing the illustrations, then by reading and acting out the changes in table arrangements, and finally by talking about it while studying the pictures.

Give students the **Connection to Writing Assessment: Post-Reading Composition** along with a copy of the **Have I...? Checklist**.

Give students about 20 minutes in which to write the composition and revise/edit it based on the checklist.

Collect and score the students' compositions using the **Rubric for Scoring First Drafts**.

Reproducible Master 86

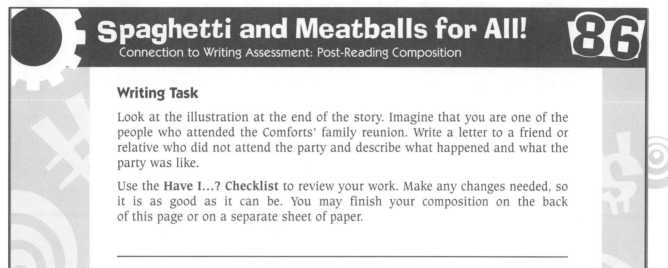

Spaghetti and Meatballs for All! 86

Connection to Writing Assessment: Post-Reading Composition

Writing Task

Look at the illustration at the end of the story. Imagine that you are one of the people who attended the Comforts' family reunion. Write a letter to a friend or relative who did not attend the party and describe what happened and what the party was like.

Use the **Have I...? Checklist** to review your work. Make any changes needed, so it is as good as it can be. You may finish your composition on the back of this page or on a separate sheet of paper.

Extending the Connections

PERIMETER AND AREA

To extend the concepts of perimeter and area, have students answer questions similar to the following:

Pretend you are putting "reunion" edging around each of the 8 tables. How many feet of edging would be needed if each table measured 2 feet on each side? **[Answer: 64 feet]**

- ***How would you arrange 6 square tiles with 1-inch sides so that the distance around the single shape you form is 10 inches?*** **[Answer: Make two rows with three tiles in each row—a 2 x 3 array.]**
- ***How would you arrange them so there is a perimeter of 14 inches?*** **[Answer: Make 1 row of 6 tiles—a 1 x 6 array.]**

EXTENDING THE PATTERN

Tell the students to listen as you describe the following pattern:

"Four toothpicks are used to make a square. Then 3 more are added to the model to make two squares with one side in common. Then another 3 toothpicks are added to the model to make three squares, each of which has one side in common."

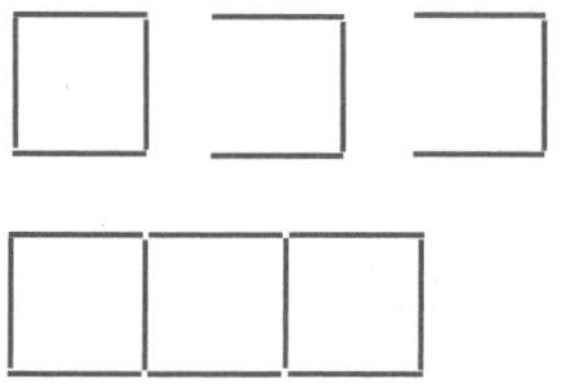

How many toothpicks would be needed to model eight such squares? Explain how you found your answer. You may want to sketch your answer using grid paper or use toothpicks to act it out. **[Answer: There would be a total of 25 toothpicks needed to model eight squares.]**

BASIC OPERATIONS

Materials

Thinking About the Story (Reproducible Master 87)

Use **Thinking About the Story** to extend thinking about the story and to review word problems that involve basic arithmetic operations.

Spaghetti and Meatballs for All! 87

Thinking About the Story

1. Why do you think Mr. Comfort made 96 meatballs, 16 loaves of bread, and 8 pounds of fresh pasta? **Answer: They are amounts that can be easily shared among 32 people.**

2. What quantity of meatballs, bread, and pasta was Mr. Comfort planning for each person to eat? **Answer: 96 ÷ 32 = 3 meatballs, 16 ÷ 32 = half a loaf of bread, 8 ÷ 32 = a quarter of a pound of pasta.**

3. If Mr. Comfort continued his same amounts per person, how many loaves of bread, how many meatballs, and how many pounds of fresh pasta would he need if he invited 8 more people? Explain how you determined your answer. **Answer: He would need 24 more meatballs, 4 more loaves of bread, and 2 more pounds of pasta.**

___

___

4. One place setting contained a fork, knife, spoon, glass, dinner plate, bread plate, salad bowl, dessert dish, napkin, and napkin holder. If each item in a place setting costs 5 cents to rent, how much would the rental of 32 place settings cost? Explain how you determined your answer. **Answer: Each place setting would cost 50 cents to rent (10 x 5¢) for a total of 32 x 0.50 = $16.00. Or, 32 of each item in the place setting would cost $1.60. For example, 32 forks would cost $1.60 because 32 x 0.05 = $1.60. Since there are 10 items, the total would be 10 x $1.60 or $16.00.**

PROJECTS

Have groups of students plan their own reunion or party. Have them calculate all of the costs, including the cost of food and the rental of tables, chairs, and place settings. Tell students to add any extras they may want, such as renting a tent, buying soda, or making a cake.

To complete the project in less time, you may want to have the entire class create a list of items needed. Groups could then be assigned to calculate costs for particular items. The total cost for the party could be calculated as a class after each group has presented the costs for its assigned items.

ADDITIONAL RESOURCES

Windows on Math, Volume 4, Unit 2 Videodisc, "Polly Mino's Designer Cookies." Atlanta: Optical Data Corporation, 1996. Call 1-800-524-2481.

A Three Hat Day

Written by **Laura Geringer**
Illustrated by **Arnold Lobel**

Overview of the Connections

This story is about R.R. Pottle the Third and his love of hats. He collected all sorts of hats. His father had collected canes, and his mother had collected umbrellas. R.R. Pottle loved hats so much that he would wear several at one time. When walking one day with three hats on his head, R.R. Pottle got caught in the rain and went into a hat store where he met the future Mrs. Pottle. Their child, R.R. Pottle the Fourth, loved neither hats nor canes nor umbrellas. She loved shoes.

A Three Hat Day assists the teacher in leading children to understand the mathematical concepts of patterns, combinations, and probability. In language arts, students will focus on making predictions and listening for details, as well as learning to use them in writing.

MATERIALS FOR THE CONNECTIONS

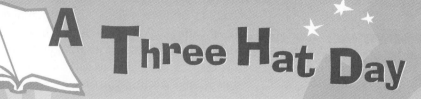

A Three Hat Day • ISBN 0-06-443157-6
Written by Laura Geringer. Illustrated by Arnold Lobel. New York: Harper Collins Publishers, 1987.

Language Arts

~ One or more copies of the book (Note: In the Viewing Connection, each student will need to see the very first page in the book. You may wish to have several copies available.)

~ **Connection to Viewing Assessment: Writing About a Picture Prompt** (Reproducible Master 1)

~ A self-monitoring tool for student writers called **Have I...? Checklist** (Reproducible Master 2)

~ **Rubric for Scoring First Drafts** (Reproducible Master 3)

~ **Connection to Listening Assessment: Listening to Part of a Story** (Reproducible Master 88)

~ **Connection to Writing Assessment: Post-Reading Composition** (Reproducible Master 94)

~ Reference resources (e.g., dictionaries and encyclopedia)

~ Journals

Mathematics

~ Connecting cubes or tiles in 4 different colors (6 of each color for each pair or small group)

~ Hats (as many as possible)

~ **Guided Practice and Discoveries: Looking for Patterns I and II** (Reproducible Masters 89–90)

~ Various styles of hats (12 hats in total) or 12 index cards for drawing hats

~ Box or paper bag to hold hats or index cards

~ **Guided Practice and Discoveries: Probability I and II** (Reproducible Masters 91–92)

~ **Connection to Mathematics Assessment: Check for Understanding** (Reproducible Master 93)

~ **More Discoveries I, II, and III** (Reproducible Masters 95–97)

~ Several copies of **Large Grid Paper** (Reproducible Master 98) for each pair or small group. Alternative: cubes, tiles, or counters

~ Scissors

~ **Dresser Drawers** (Reproducible Master 99) for each pair or small group

~ **Applying Discoveries I, II, and III** (Reproducible Masters 100–102)

Viewing Connection

INTRODUCING THE LESSON WITH A PICTURE PROMPT AND WRITING

Materials

Copy of the book (first page), **Connection to Viewing Assessment: Writing About a Picture Prompt** (Reproducible Master 1), **Have I...? Checklist** (Reproducible Master 2), **Rubric for Scoring First Drafts** (Reproducible Master 3)

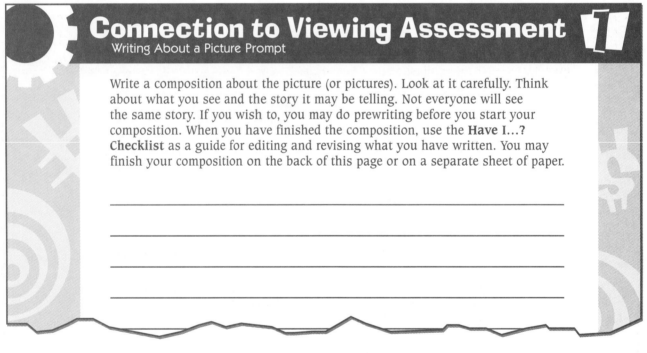

Show the class the picture on the very first page. (The unnumbered page is opposite the title page and shows a man entering what appears to be a hat store.) If possible, allow students to continue to look at the picture throughout the writing session. You may distribute a copy of **Connection to Viewing Assessment: Writing About a Picture Prompt** to each student, or they may use notebook paper for their work. Also distribute copies of the **Have I...? Checklist**.

Read these directions to the class:

"You are going to write a composition about this picture. Look at it carefully. Think about what you see and the story it may be telling. It is OK that not everyone will see the same story. If you wish to, you may do prewriting before you start your composition. When you have finished the composition, use the **Have I...? Checklist** as a guide for editing and revising what you have written."

Give the students 20–30 minutes to write their compositions and do initial editing.

Collect the students' compositions and score them using the **Rubric for Scoring First Drafts**. Teach students how to compare their scored compositions to the rubric and to make notes about how to improve their compositions. Students also may be taught to use the rubric to score their own work or that of other students.

Reproducible Master 1

Connection to Viewing Assessment 1

Writing About a Picture Prompt

Write a composition about the picture (or pictures). Look at it carefully. Think about what you see and the story it may be telling. Not everyone will see the same story. If you wish to, you may do prewriting before you start your composition. When you have finished the composition, use the **Have I...? Checklist** as a guide for editing and revising what you have written. You may finish your composition on the back of this page or on a separate sheet of paper.

____

____

____

____

Listening Connection

LISTENING TO PART OF A STORY AND ANSWERING QUESTIONS

Materials

Copy of the book (Listening section: pages 7–17, 280 words), **Connection to Listening Assessment: Listening to Part of a Story** (Reproducible Master 88)

This activity will help students develop effective listening skills. As necessary, teach or review some of the effective listening strategies found on page *xv* of this manual.

Tell the class you are going to read them part of a story. When finished, they will answer some questions about what you have read. (The rest of the story will be read in the Mathematics Connection activity.)

Read pages 7–17 aloud to the students. The listening section begins on page 7 with the sentence: *R. R. Pottle the Third loved hats*. It concludes on page 17 with the sentence: *With a sigh of relief, he glided through the revolving doors of the largest hat store in town.*

Since you are working on listening, don't stop to discuss the story, show the illustrations, or make predictions as you might do in a reading instructional period.

Distribute the multiple-choice and open-ended questions called **Connection to Listening Assessment: Listening to Part of a Story**.

Allow students 15–20 minutes to complete the worksheet.

Collect and score the students' work using the answers and rubric that follow.

Proceed to the Mathematics Connection for instructions on completing this book.

Reproducible Master 88 with answers

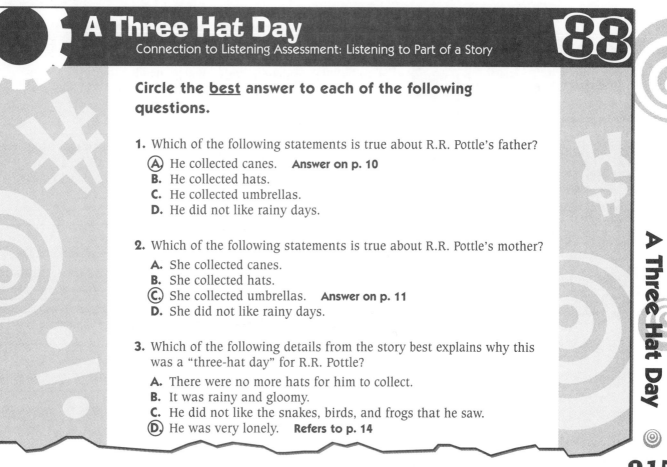

A Three Hat Day

Connection to Listening Assessment: Listening to Part of a Story

88

Circle the <u>best</u> answer to each of the following questions.

1. Which of the following statements is true about R.R. Pottle's father?

- (**A**) He collected canes. **Answer on p. 10**
- **B.** He collected hats.
- **C.** He collected umbrellas.
- **D.** He did not like rainy days.

2. Which of the following statements is true about R.R. Pottle's mother?

- **A.** She collected canes.
- **B.** She collected hats.
- (**C**) She collected umbrellas. **Answer on p. 11**
- **D.** She did not like rainy days.

3. Which of the following details from the story best explains why this was a "three-hat day" for R.R. Pottle?

- **A.** There were no more hats for him to collect.
- **B.** It was rainy and gloomy.
- **C.** He did not like the snakes, birds, and frogs that he saw.
- (**D**) He was very lonely. **Refers to p. 14**

Continued...

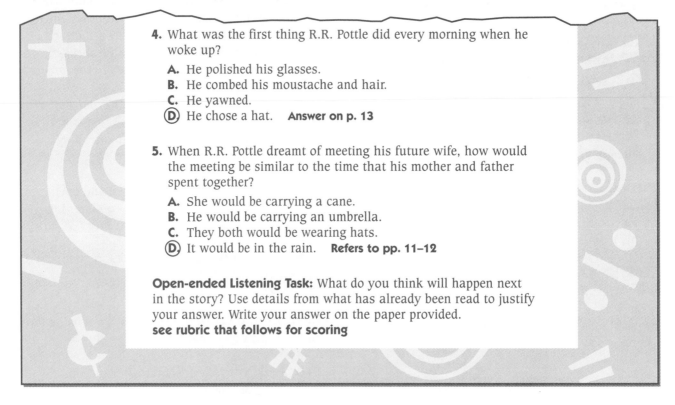

4. What was the first thing R.R. Pottle did every morning when he woke up?

A. He polished his glasses.
B. He combed his moustache and hair.
C. He yawned.
(D) He chose a hat. **Answer on p. 13**

5. When R.R. Pottle dreamt of meeting his future wife, how would the meeting be similar to the time that his mother and father spent together?

A. She would be carrying a cane.
B. He would be carrying an umbrella.
C. They both would be wearing hats.
(D) It would be in the rain. **Refers to pp. 11–12**

Open-ended Listening Task: What do you think will happen next in the story? Use details from what has already been read to justify your answer. Write your answer on the paper provided.
see rubric that follows for scoring

RUBRIC FOR SCORING
Open-ended Listening Task

An effective response will need to:
- reflect knowledge of the story.
- justify ideas from the text, especially about meeting his wife in the rain, that she likes hats, or other details of similar weight.
- make logical and reasonable predictions about what might happen.
- be well written with a clear presentation.

POINTS	CRITERIA
4	Answer is logical and well developed, based on the story. Significant details could include the idea that his parents liked the rain and that they collected things. The idea that his wife will like hats is important. Answer is well organized and executed.
3	Answer is close to, but not exactly on the mark. It may include important details, but miss significance of them. Or, it may include all the significant ideas, but require the reader to make the connections between details and predictions, or it may be bumpy in some of the writing.
2	Answer has most of the significant details or is well written, but not both. Or, it may have some details well explained, but miss some, or explain them poorly or not at all. Writing may be inconsistent.
1	Misses the main points, but attempts an answer. Writing is generally poor and shows little control of the language.
0	Student does not respond.

Mathematics Connection

INTRODUCTION AND ACTIVE READING

Review the section you already have read from the Listening Connection, showing students the illustrations and discussing what they already have heard. In some classes, you may find it worthwhile to go back to the beginning and re-read the entire selection (pages 7–17). This is a good way to help students confirm the answers they gave in the listening activity. If necessary, explore the rationale behind some of the answers.

As you re-read pages 8 and 9, discuss the names of various hats and how each is different. In doing this, you will help students understand why specific words are more descriptive than general ones and the importance of using details.

Read the rest of the story with the class. Continue to point out the illustrations, make predictions and discuss the events as you read. In this way, you model active reading and help students to internalize the practices that effective readers use to make meaning from the words on the page.

MAKING LISTS

Materials
Three or more different hats, color cubes in three colors (e.g., red, white, and blue)

Show students the picture on page 13 of the book and ask them to guess how many ways R.R. Pottle could have worn the three hats. (The picture shows R.R. Pottle in bed with the fishing pole and three hats on a hat rack.)

Model the problem by putting on three different hats in various combinations. Tell the class that since you don't have enough hats for every student, they will use sets of cubes in 3 different colors to determine how many ways R.R. Pottle could have worn his hats. Model how the red, white, and blue cubes could represent the three hats you just tried on. Use the cubes to model the hat sequences you showed the children.

EXAMPLE

Bring in a red baseball cap, a white sailor's hat, and a blue bonnet. If you put the red baseball cap on your head with the white sailor's hat on top of that and the blue bonnet on top of that, you would show the class a stack that could be represented in cubes as RWB (first red, then white, then blue). Record the combination on the board. When you put on the blue bonnet first, the red baseball cap next, and the white sailor hat on top, show them BRW cubes.

DEVELOPING UNDERSTANDING

Materials
Color cubes in four colors (6 of each color for each pair or group; e.g., 6 red, 6 white, 6 blue, and 6 green for each group)

Once students understand the process of modeling the various arrangements of hats, distribute cubes in three colors (6 red, 6 white, 6 blue) to pairs or groups of students. Have them try to form all the various combinations of three hats that can be made with 1 red, 1 white, and 1 blue cube. (Having 6 cubes in each color allows students to display a model for each combination of three colors.)

RWB	WRB	BRW
RBW	WBR	BWR

Have students write about how they solved the problem. As a class, discuss the answer and how students went about finding all the different combinations.

Ask students how many combinations would have been possible if R.R. Pottle had 4 different hats on the rack instead of 3. Give them 6 more cubes of a different color and let them find all of the possibilities.

RWBG	WRBG	BGRW	GBRW
RWGB	WRGB	BGWR	GBWR
RBGW	WGBR	BWGR	GWRB
RBWG	WGRB	BWRG	GWBR
RGBW	WBGR	BRGW	GRWB
RGWB	WBRG	BRWG	GRBW

MAKING DISCOVERIES: LOOKING FOR PATTERNS

Materials
Tiles or cubes in 4 different colors (6 of every color for each pair or group of students), **Guided Practice and Discoveries: Looking for Patterns I and II** (Reproducible Masters 89–90)

Students will work through a set of problems to discover patterns in the number of combinations possible for a given number of choices.

Depending on time and the ability of your class, you may want to choose all or only some of the problems. The questions on **Guided Practice and Discoveries: Looking for Patterns II** is a continuation of the first page. It asks students to reflect on and extend the problems on **Guided Practice and Discoveries: Looking for Patterns I**, as well as the "hat" problems from the Developing Understanding activity on the previous page.

Distribute 24 cubes or tiles (6 each of 4 colors) and copies of **Guided Practice and Discoveries: Looking for Patterns I and II** to each group or pair of students. Have them solve some or all of the problems on each page.

Reproducible Master 89 with answers

A Three Hat Day

Guided Practice and Discoveries: Looking for Patterns I

89

It may be helpful to use tiles or cubes to help solve the problems below.

1. Suppose R.R. Pottle's father had a wooden cane, a plastic cane, and a gold cane. He placed all three canes on his arm at one time. How many different ways could his father arrange the three canes? List all the ways.

Answer:

6 ways. W = wooden, P = plastic, and G = gold

WPG	**PWG**	**GPW**
WGP	**PGW**	**GWP**

2. Suppose R.R. Pottle's mother had a polka-dotted umbrella, a plaid umbrella, a plain umbrella, and a striped umbrella. How many different ways could his mother arrange all four umbrellas in a row? List all the ways.

Answer:

24 ways. D = polka-dotted, P = plaid, L = plain, and S = striped

DPLS	**PDLS**	**LSPD**	**SLPD**
DPSL	**PDSL**	**LSDP**	**SLDP**
DLSP	**PSLD**	**LDPS**	**SDPL**
DLPS	**PSDL**	**LDSP**	**SDLP**
DSPL	**PLSD**	**LPDS**	**SPDL**
DSLP	**PLDS**	**LPSD**	**SPLD**

3. Suppose R.R. Pottle the Fourth had a pair of sneakers, a pair of sandals, and a pair of slippers. How many different ways could the pairs of shoes be placed on a shelf in the closet? List all the ways.

Answer:

6 ways. S = pair of sneakers, A = pair of sandals, and L = pair of slippers

SAL	**ALS**	**LAS**
SLA	**ASL**	**LSA**

4. Suppose R.R. Pottle the Fourth had a red pair of sneakers, a green pair, an orange pair, and a blue pair. How many different ways could the pairs of sneakers be placed on a shelf in the closet? List all the ways.

Answer:

24 ways. R = red, G = green, O = orange, and B = blue

Possible combinations are listed below:

RGOB	**GROB**	**ORBG**	**BGOR**
RGBO	**GRBO**	**ORGB**	**BGRO**
ROGB	**GOBR**	**OGBR**	**BRGO**
ROBG	**GORB**	**OGRB**	**BROG**
RBOG	**GBOR**	**OBRG**	**BORG**
RBGO	**GBRO**	**OBGR**	**BOGR**

A Three Hat Day

90

Guided Practice and Discoveries: Looking for Patterns II

To answer the following questions, think about the "hat" problems you solved in class and the other questions on Guided Practice and Discoveries: Looking for Patterns I.

5. How are problems 1 and 3 like the problem about R.R. Pottle's three hats?

Answer: Instead of three hats to be arranged, there are three different canes and three pairs of shoes to be arranged.

6. How are problems 2 and 4 like the problem about R.R. Pottle's four hats?

Answer: Both involve finding arrangements of four different items.

7. Study the solutions to problems 1–4 and think about how you found the answers. Describe any pattern you see that would help you solve similar problems in the future.

Answer: If you are using each item in every arrangement, you can figure out the number of possible arrangements by multiplying all the numbers by 1 less until you get to one. The answer to problem 4, for example, could be figured out this way: $4 \times 3 \times 2 \times 1 = 24$.

8. Latisha had to arrange a social studies book, a math book, an English book, and a science book on her shelf at home. How many different ways could she arrange the books on the shelf? Which of the problems that you have solved is this like? Explain why.

Answer: 24 ways. This is like problems 2 and 4 because there are four items to arrange.

9. Make up a problem like the ones above and find the solution.

____

MAKING DISCOVERIES: PROBABILITY

Materials

Various styles of hats (12 hats in total) or 12 index cards for drawing hats, a box or paper bag to hold hats or index cards, **Guided Practice and Discoveries: Probability I and II** (Reproducible Masters 91–92)

This activity provides opportunities for students to work with probability. Begin by modeling several problems like those in **Guided Practice and Discoveries: Probability I**.

Place 12 hats in a box or paper bag and take them from the bag at random. If hats are not available, draw pictures of each of the 12 hats on page 9 of *A Three Hat Day* on index cards and select cards at random.

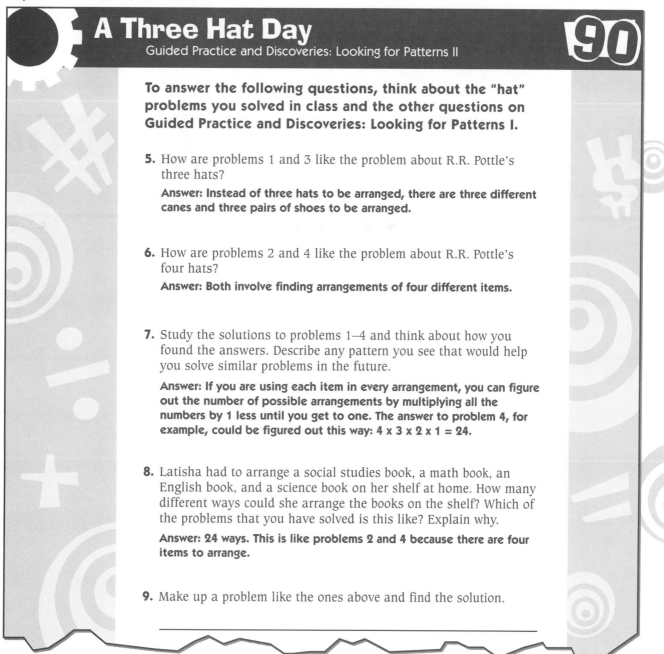

Make several trials and compare the results to the predicted outcomes.

Discuss the concept that mathematical probability is what will happen over a long period of time, although actual events may vary from the mathematical predictions. Encourage students to express their answers as fractions.

Reproducible Master 91 with answers

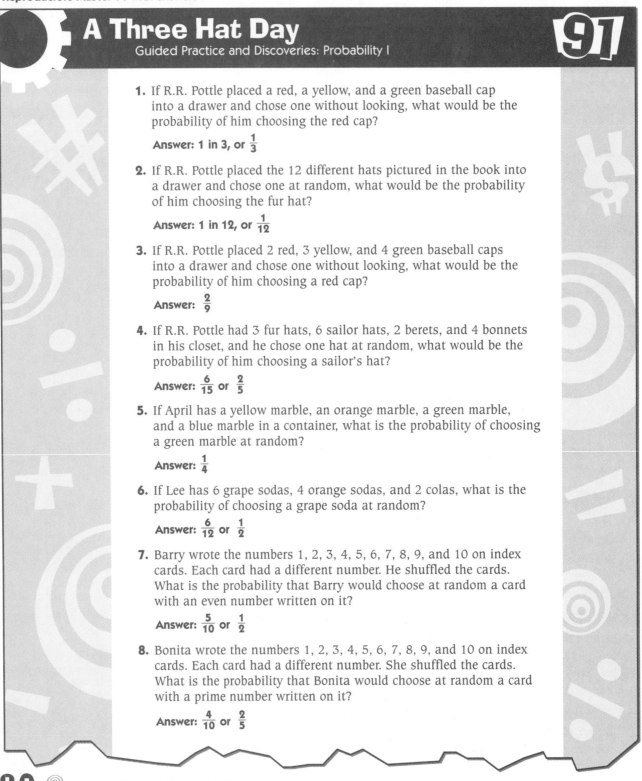

A Three Hat Day

Guided Practice and Discoveries: Probability I

91

1. If R.R. Pottle placed a red, a yellow, and a green baseball cap into a drawer and chose one without looking, what would be the probability of him choosing the red cap?

   Answer: 1 in 3, or $\frac{1}{3}$

2. If R.R. Pottle placed the 12 different hats pictured in the book into a drawer and chose one at random, what would be the probability of him choosing the fur hat?

   Answer: 1 in 12, or $\frac{1}{12}$

3. If R.R. Pottle placed 2 red, 3 yellow, and 4 green baseball caps into a drawer and chose one without looking, what would be the probability of him choosing a red cap?

   Answer: $\frac{2}{9}$

4. If R.R. Pottle had 3 fur hats, 6 sailor hats, 2 berets, and 4 bonnets in his closet, and he chose one hat at random, what would be the probability of him choosing a sailor's hat?

   Answer: $\frac{6}{15}$ or $\frac{2}{5}$

5. If April has a yellow marble, an orange marble, a green marble, and a blue marble in a container, what is the probability of choosing a green marble at random?

   Answer: $\frac{1}{4}$

6. If Lee has 6 grape sodas, 4 orange sodas, and 2 colas, what is the probability of choosing a grape soda at random?

   Answer: $\frac{6}{12}$ or $\frac{1}{2}$

7. Barry wrote the numbers 1, 2, 3, 4, 5, 6, 7, 8, 9, and 10 on index cards. Each card had a different number. He shuffled the cards. What is the probability that Barry would choose at random a card with an even number written on it?

   Answer: $\frac{5}{10}$ or $\frac{1}{2}$

8. Bonita wrote the numbers 1, 2, 3, 4, 5, 6, 7, 8, 9, and 10 on index cards. Each card had a different number. She shuffled the cards. What is the probability that Bonita would choose at random a card with a prime number written on it?

   Answer: $\frac{4}{10}$ or $\frac{2}{5}$

Have students complete the Challenge Problems on **Guided Practice and Discoveries: Probability II**.

As a class, study problems 1–4, 5–6, 7–8 and 9–10 from **Guided Practice and Discoveries: Probability I and II** before having students proceed to questions 11–14. These questions ask students to draw conclusions and look for patterns.

Reproducible Master 92 with answers

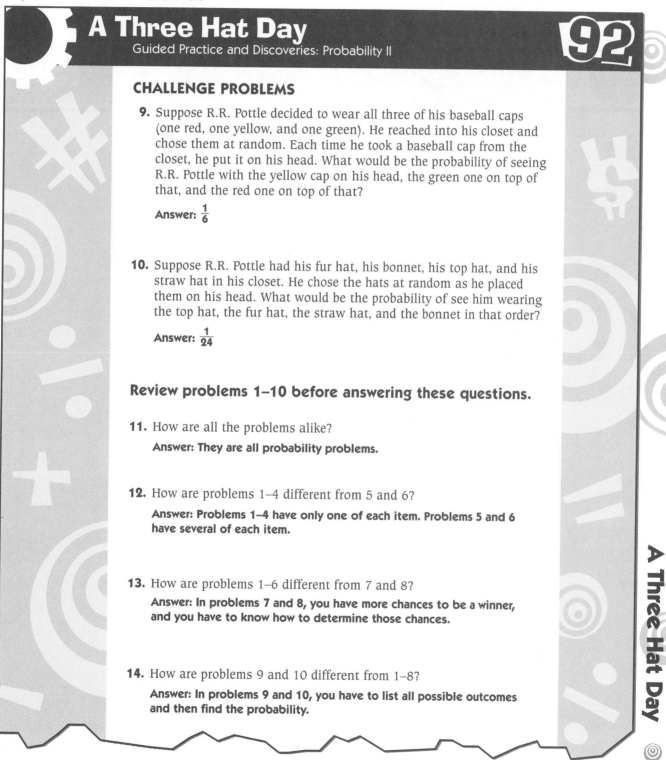

A Three Hat Day

92

Guided Practice and Discoveries: Probability II

CHALLENGE PROBLEMS

9. Suppose R.R. Pottle decided to wear all three of his baseball caps (one red, one yellow, and one green). He reached into his closet and chose them at random. Each time he took a baseball cap from the closet, he put it on his head. What would be the probability of seeing R.R. Pottle with the yellow cap on his head, the green one on top of that, and the red one on top of that?

Answer: $\frac{1}{6}$

10. Suppose R.R. Pottle had his fur hat, his bonnet, his top hat, and his straw hat in his closet. He chose the hats at random as he placed them on his head. What would be the probability of see him wearing the top hat, the fur hat, the straw hat, and the bonnet in that order?

Answer: $\frac{1}{24}$

Review problems 1–10 before answering these questions.

11. How are all the problems alike?

Answer: They are all probability problems.

12. How are problems 1–4 different from 5 and 6?

Answer: Problems 1–4 have only one of each item. Problems 5 and 6 have several of each item.

13. How are problems 1–6 different from 7 and 8?

Answer: In problems 7 and 8, you have more chances to be a winner, and you have to know how to determine those chances.

14. How are problems 9 and 10 different from 1–8?

Answer: In problems 9 and 10, you have to list all possible outcomes and then find the probability.

MATHEMATICS ASSESSMENT

Materials

Connection to Mathematics Assessment: Check for Understanding (Reproducible Master 93)

Distribute the multiple-choice and open-ended questions called **Connection to Mathematics Assessment: Check for Understanding.** Use this activity to check students' understanding of the mathematics concepts covered in this lesson.

Collect and **score** the students' work using the answers and rubric that follow.

Reproducible Master 93 with answers

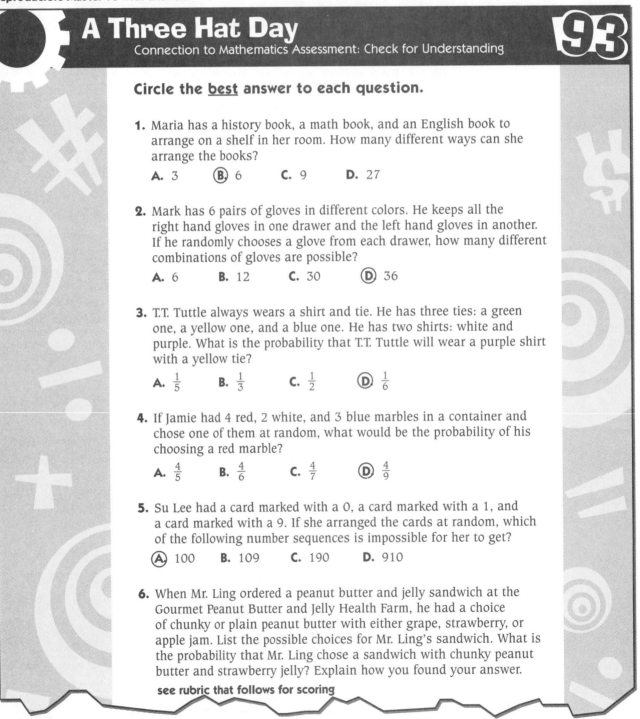

A Three Hat Day

Connection to Mathematics Assessment: Check for Understanding

93

Circle the best answer to each question.

1. Maria has a history book, a math book, and an English book to arrange on a shelf in her room. How many different ways can she arrange the books?

   A. 3 **(B.)** 6 **C.** 9 **D.** 27

2. Mark has 6 pairs of gloves in different colors. He keeps all the right hand gloves in one drawer and the left hand gloves in another. If he randomly chooses a glove from each drawer, how many different combinations of gloves are possible?

   A. 6 **B.** 12 **C.** 30 **(D.)** 36

3. T.T. Tuttle always wears a shirt and tie. He has three ties: a green one, a yellow one, and a blue one. He has two shirts: white and purple. What is the probability that T.T. Tuttle will wear a purple shirt with a yellow tie?

   A. $\frac{1}{5}$ **B.** $\frac{1}{3}$ **C.** $\frac{1}{2}$ **(D.)** $\frac{1}{6}$

4. If Jamie had 4 red, 2 white, and 3 blue marbles in a container and chose one of them at random, what would be the probability of his choosing a red marble?

   A. $\frac{4}{5}$ **B.** $\frac{4}{6}$ **C.** $\frac{4}{7}$ **(D.)** $\frac{4}{9}$

5. Su Lee had a card marked with a 0, a card marked with a 1, and a card marked with a 9. If she arranged the cards at random, which of the following number sequences is impossible for her to get?

   (A.) 100 **B.** 109 **C.** 190 **D.** 910

6. When Mr. Ling ordered a peanut butter and jelly sandwich at the Gourmet Peanut Butter and Jelly Health Farm, he had a choice of chunky or plain peanut butter with either grape, strawberry, or apple jam. List the possible choices for Mr. Ling's sandwich. What is the probability that Mr. Ling chose a sandwich with chunky peanut butter and strawberry jelly? Explain how you found your answer.

   see rubric that follows for scoring

RUBRIC FOR SCORING
Problem 6

An effective response will need to:
- list all possible combinations.
- indicate that $\frac{1}{6}$ is the correct answer.
- give a clear explanation.

POINTS	CRITERIA
3	The student correctly lists all the possible combinations of sandwiches, correctly indicates the probability that Mr. Ling will have a sandwich with chunky peanut butter and strawberry jelly, and clearly explains why the answer is correct. Suggested response: *If C = chunky peanut butter, P = plain peanut butter, G = grape jelly, S = strawberry jelly, and A = apple jam, there would be 6 combinations of peanut butter and jelly sandwiches:* *CG PG* *CS PS* *CA PA* *The probability of seeing Mr. Ling eating a sandwich with chunky peanut butter and strawberry jelly would be* $\frac{1}{6}$ *because there are six possible combinations and only one of them is chunky peanut butter with strawberry jelly.*
2	The student lists all the possibilities and the correct probability, but offers no explanation. Or, the student lists all the possibilities, gives the wrong probability, but provides an explanation that shows understanding. Or, the student explains why there are six possibilities but does not list the combinations and indicates the correct probability with an appropriate explanation.
1	The student indicates there are six possibilities with the correct probability, but the explanation is unclear or has some flaws. Or, the student lists the six possibilities incorrectly or has some, but not all, of the possible combinations yet provides the correct probability.
0	The student indicates the wrong number of combinations with little or no explanation and presents the wrong probability as well. Or, the student offers no response.

Composition Connection

WRITING A POST-READING COMPOSITION

Materials

Connection to Writing Assessment: Post-Reading Composition (Reproducible Master 94), **Have I...? Checklist** (Reproducible Master 2), **Rubric for Scoring First Drafts** (Reproducible Master 3)

Have the class complete the following composition as an "on demand" timed writing.

Allow 30 minutes for planning, drafting, and reviewing/editing.

Give students individual copies of **Connection to Writing Assessment: Post-Reading Composition** along with a copy of the **Have I...? Checklist**.

Reproducible Master 94

A Three Hat Day

Connection to Writing Assessment: Post-Reading Composition

94

Writing Task

Think about how R.R. Pottle the Third and his wife, Isabel, are similar to and different from R.R.'s parents. Then think about how R.R. Pottle the Fourth is similar to and different from her parents. Write a story or composition in which you describe the man that R.R. Pottle the Fourth will marry.

Use the **Have I...? Checklist** to review your work. Make any changes needed, so it is as good as it can be. You may finish your composition on the back of this page or on a separate sheet of paper.

Collect the students' compositions and score them using the **Rubric for Scoring First Drafts**. This composition also may be revised and edited as described on page *xxi* of this manual to be prepared for sharing with a larger audience.

JOURNAL WRITING

Materials

One or more copies of *A Three Hat Day*, journals

Have students write in their journals on one or more of the following topics at any time during your instruction with *A Three Hat Day*. Where necessary, have extra copies of the book available for students to study closely.

1. Look at the picture of the Pottle Mansion on p. 12. Explain how it accurately reflects Mr. and Mrs. R.R. Pottle the Third.
2. Count the number of different words that are used in the story to name different kinds of hats. What are the different qualities or characteristics that make some hats different from others? Make a list of these different qualities or characteristics.
3. Think of other objects that have many different names to describe them. Make a list of the objects and list as many objects of each type as you can.
4. The author's use of details in *A Three Hat Day* makes the story interesting and successful. Study the book to find three interesting details. Write those details in your journal and explain why you like them or what makes them interesting.

Extending the Connections

MORE MATHEMATICAL DISCOVERIES

Materials

More Discoveries I, II, and III (Reproducible Masters 95–97); **Large Grid Paper** (Reproducible Master 98), scissors, **Dresser Drawers** (Reproducible Master 99). Alternative: cubes, tiles, or counters.

The exercises for More Discoveries and Applying Discoveries (in the following section) help to extend student thinking. Students will begin to see that the number of combinations that can occur depends on events and the number of choices in each event. In these discovery-based extensions, students solve and analyze sets of problems. Through appropriate question-and-answer techniques, students will discover a pattern to help them solve problems involving combinations.

Provide students with models to help them work out solutions to the problems. They can use cubes, tiles, or counters in different colors, but to ensure that they have enough to model all of the combinations, you might have each pair or small group of students cut squares from several sheets of **Large Grid Paper**. For each problem, they can label the squares to represent the items.

Distribute individual copies of **More Discoveries I, II, and III** to students.

Model the first problem as a class. Have the students label squares as 5 different hats. They might label them as 5 different colors or 5 different types of hats (e.g., cowboy hat, sailor hat, construction hat, firefighter helmet, baseball cap). Have them place 3 "hats" in the top drawer of the **Dresser Drawers** page and 2 hats in the second drawer. Have them record the possible combinations of 2 hats that R.R. Pottle could wear if he always picked a hat from the top drawer to put on his head and a hat from the second drawer to put on top of the first hat.

A Three Hat Day

More Discoveries I

95

You may want to label squares cut from grid paper and act out the problems to help you find the answers. Write on the back of the page if you need more space.

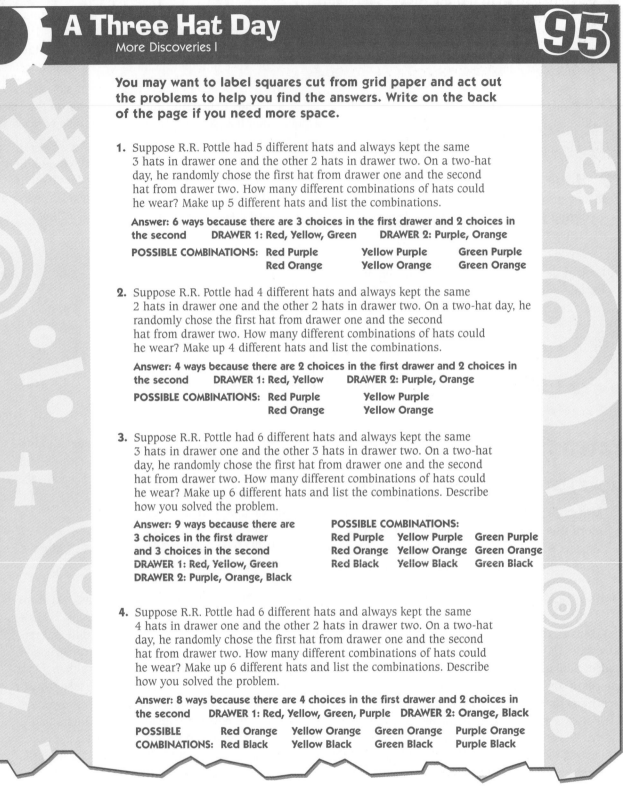

1. Suppose R.R. Pottle had 5 different hats and always kept the same 3 hats in drawer one and the other 2 hats in drawer two. On a two-hat day, he randomly chose the first hat from drawer one and the second hat from drawer two. How many different combinations of hats could he wear? Make up 5 different hats and list the combinations.

   Answer: 6 ways because there are 3 choices in the first drawer and 2 choices in the second DRAWER 1: Red, Yellow, Green DRAWER 2: Purple, Orange

   POSSIBLE COMBINATIONS: Red Purple, Red Orange, Yellow Purple, Yellow Orange, Green Purple, Green Orange

2. Suppose R.R. Pottle had 4 different hats and always kept the same 2 hats in drawer one and the other 2 hats in drawer two. On a two-hat day, he randomly chose the first hat from drawer one and the second hat from drawer two. How many different combinations of hats could he wear? Make up 4 different hats and list the combinations.

   Answer: 4 ways because there are 2 choices in the first drawer and 2 choices in the second DRAWER 1: Red, Yellow DRAWER 2: Purple, Orange

   POSSIBLE COMBINATIONS: Red Purple, Red Orange, Yellow Purple, Yellow Orange

3. Suppose R.R. Pottle had 6 different hats and always kept the same 3 hats in drawer one and the other 3 hats in drawer two. On a two-hat day, he randomly chose the first hat from drawer one and the second hat from drawer two. How many different combinations of hats could he wear? Make up 6 different hats and list the combinations. Describe how you solved the problem.

   Answer: 9 ways because there are 3 choices in the first drawer and 3 choices in the second DRAWER 1: Red, Yellow, Green DRAWER 2: Purple, Orange, Black

   POSSIBLE COMBINATIONS: Red Purple, Red Orange, Red Black, Yellow Purple, Yellow Orange, Yellow Black, Green Purple, Green Orange, Green Black

4. Suppose R.R. Pottle had 6 different hats and always kept the same 4 hats in drawer one and the other 2 hats in drawer two. On a two-hat day, he randomly chose the first hat from drawer one and the second hat from drawer two. How many different combinations of hats could he wear? Make up 6 different hats and list the combinations. Describe how you solved the problem.

   Answer: 8 ways because there are 4 choices in the first drawer and 2 choices in the second DRAWER 1: Red, Yellow, Green, Purple DRAWER 2: Orange, Black

   POSSIBLE COMBINATIONS: Red Orange, Red Black, Yellow Orange, Yellow Black, Green Orange, Green Black, Purple Orange, Purple Black

A Three Hat Day

More Discoveries II

96

5. Suppose R.R. Pottle had 8 different hats and always kept the same 4 hats in drawer one and the other 4 hats in drawer two. On a two-hat day, he randomly chose the first hat from drawer one and the second hat from drawer two. How many different combinations of hats could he wear? Make up 8 different hats and list the combinations. Describe how you solved the problem.

Answer: 16 ways because there are 4 choices in the first drawer and 4 choices for the second
DRAWER 1: Red, Yellow, Green, Purple DRAWER 2: Orange, Black, Tan, White

POSSIBLE COMBINATIONS:				
	Red Orange	Yellow Orange	Green Orange	Purple Orange
	Red Black	Yellow Black	Green Black	Purple Black
	Red Tan	Yellow Tan	Green Tan	Purple Tan
	Red White	Yellow White	Green White	Purple White

6. Suppose R.R. Pottle had 8 different hats and always kept the same 6 hats in drawer one and the other 2 hats in drawer two. On a two-hat day, he randomly chose the first hat from drawer one and the second hat from drawer two. How many different combinations of hats could he wear? Make up 8 different hats and list the combinations. Describe how you went about solving the problem.

Answer: 12 ways because there are 6 choices in the first drawer and 2 choices for the second
DRAWER 1: Red, Yellow, Green, Purple, Orange, Black DRAWER 2: Tan, White

POSSIBLE COMBINATIONS:

Red Tan	Yellow Tan	Green Tan	Purple Tan	Orange Tan	Black Tan
Red White	Yellow White	Green White	Purple White	Orange White	Black White

7. Suppose R.R. Pottle had 8 different hats and always kept the same 3 hats in drawer one and the other 5 hats in drawer two. On a two-hat day, he randomly chose the first hat from drawer one and the second hat from drawer two. How many different combinations of hats could he wear? Make up 8 different hats and list the combinations. Describe how you went about solving the problem.

Answer: 15 ways because there are 3 choices in the first drawer and 5 choices for the second

DRAWER 1: Red, Yellow, Green
DRAWER 2: Purple, Orange, Black, Tan, White

POSSIBLE COMBINATIONS:

Red Purple	Yellow Purple	Green Purple
Red Orange	Yellow Orange	Green Orange
Red Black	Yellow Black	Green Black
Red Tan	Yellow Tan	Green Tan
Red White	Yellow White	Green White

8. Suppose R.R. Pottle had 12 different hats and always kept the same 6 hats in drawer one and the other 6 hats in drawer two. On a two-hat day, he randomly chose the first hat from drawer one and the second hat from drawer two. How many different combinations of hats could he wear? Make up 12 different hats and list the combinations. Describe how you went about solving the problem.

Answer: 36 ways because there are 6 choices in the first drawer and 6 choices for the second

DRAWER 1: Red, Yellow, Green, Purple, Orange, Black
DRAWER 2: Tan, White, Cream, Maroon, Lilac, Salmon

POSSIBLE COMBINATIONS:

RT	YT	GT	PT	OT	BT
RW	YW	GW	PW	OW	BW
RC	YC	GC	PC	OC	BC
RM	YM	GM	PM	OM	BM
RL	YL	GL	PL	OL	BL
RS	YS	GS	PS	OS	BS

9. Suppose R.R. Pottle the Fourth had 6 pairs of shoes, and she placed the left shoe of each pair in drawer one and the right shoe of each pair in drawer two. If she randomly chose a shoe from drawer one and then one from drawer two, how many different combinations of shoes could R.R. Pottle the Fourth wear? Make up 6 different pairs of shoes and list the combinations.

Answer: 36 ways because there are 6 choices in the first drawer and 6 choices for the second

DRAWER 1: Red, Yellow, Green, Purple, Orange, Black
DRAWER 2: Red, Yellow, Green, Purple, Orange, Black

POSSIBLE COMBINATIONS:

RR	YR	GR	PR	OR	BR
RY	YY	GY	PY	OY	BY
RG	YG	GG	PG	OG	BG
RP	YP	GP	PP	OP	BP
RO	YO	GO	PO	OO	BO
RB	YB	GB	PB	OB	BB

A Three Hat Day

97

More Discoveries III

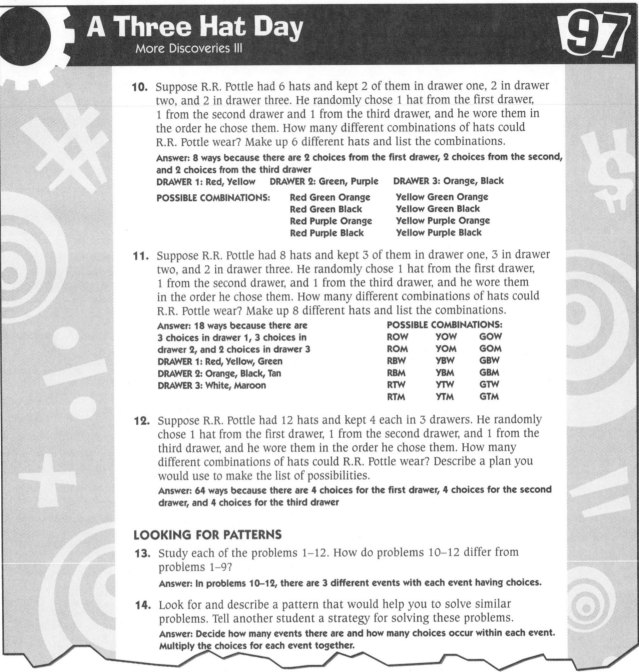

10. Suppose R.R. Pottle had 6 hats and kept 2 of them in drawer one, 2 in drawer two, and 2 in drawer three. He randomly chose 1 hat from the first drawer, 1 from the second drawer and 1 from the third drawer, and he wore them in the order he chose them. How many different combinations of hats could R.R. Pottle wear? Make up 6 different hats and list the combinations.

Answer: 8 ways because there are 2 choices from the first drawer, 2 choices from the second, and 2 choices from the third drawer

DRAWER 1: Red, Yellow DRAWER 2: Green, Purple DRAWER 3: Orange, Black

POSSIBLE COMBINATIONS:		
	Red Green Orange	Yellow Green Orange
	Red Green Black	Yellow Green Black
	Red Purple Orange	Yellow Purple Orange
	Red Purple Black	Yellow Purple Black

11. Suppose R.R. Pottle had 8 hats and kept 3 of them in drawer one, 3 in drawer two, and 2 in drawer three. He randomly chose 1 hat from the first drawer, 1 from the second drawer, and 1 from the third drawer, and he wore them in the order he chose them. How many different combinations of hats could R.R. Pottle wear? Make up 8 different hats and list the combinations.

Answer: 18 ways because there are 3 choices in drawer 1, 3 choices in drawer 2, and 2 choices in drawer 3
DRAWER 1: Red, Yellow, Green
DRAWER 2: Orange, Black, Tan
DRAWER 3: White, Maroon

POSSIBLE COMBINATIONS:

ROW	YOW	GOW
ROM	YOM	GOM
RBW	YBW	GBW
RBM	YBM	GBM
RTW	YTW	GTW
RTM	YTM	GTM

12. Suppose R.R. Pottle had 12 hats and kept 4 each in 3 drawers. He randomly chose 1 hat from the first drawer, 1 from the second drawer, and 1 from the third drawer, and he wore them in the order he chose them. How many different combinations of hats could R.R. Pottle wear? Describe a plan you would use to make the list of possibilities.

Answer: 64 ways because there are 4 choices for the first drawer, 4 choices for the second drawer, and 4 choices for the third drawer

LOOKING FOR PATTERNS

13. Study each of the problems 1–12. How do problems 10–12 differ from problems 1–9?

Answer: In problems 10–12, there are 3 different events with each event having choices.

14. Look for and describe a pattern that would help you to solve similar problems. Tell another student a strategy for solving these problems.

Answer: Decide how many events there are and how many choices occur within each event. Multiply the choices for each event together.

APPLYING MATHEMATICAL DISCOVERIES

Materials

Applying Discoveries I, II, and III (Reproducible Masters 100–102), several copies of **Large Grid Paper** (Reproducible Master 98), scissors (to cut grid paper). Alternative: cubes, tiles, or counters.

The following problems provide an additional way for students to develop and practice their understanding of probability and combinations.

Provide students with models to help them work out solutions to the problems. They can use cubes, tiles, or counters in different colors, but to ensure that they have enough to model all of the combinations, you might have them cut squares from several sheets of **Large Grid Paper**. For each problem, they can label the squares to represent the items.

Distribute individual copies of **Applying Discoveries I, II, and III** to students.

A Three Hat Day

Applying Discoveries I

100

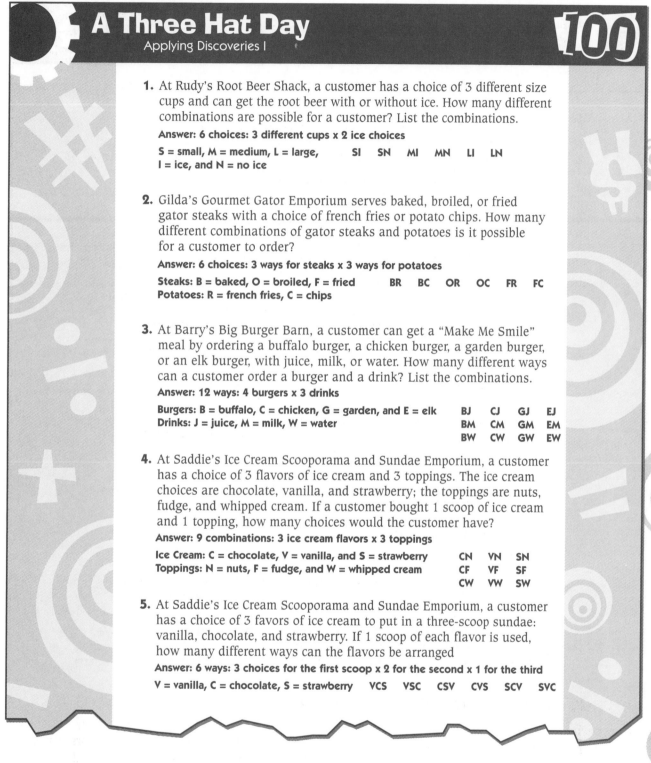

1. At Rudy's Root Beer Shack, a customer has a choice of 3 different size cups and can get the root beer with or without ice. How many different combinations are possible for a customer? List the combinations.

   Answer: 6 choices: 3 different cups x 2 ice choices

   S = small, M = medium, L = large, I = ice, and N = no ice

   SI SN MI MN LI LN

2. Gilda's Gourmet Gator Emporium serves baked, broiled, or fried gator steaks with a choice of french fries or potato chips. How many different combinations of gator steaks and potatoes is it possible for a customer to order?

   Answer: 6 choices: 3 ways for steaks x 3 ways for potatoes

   Steaks: B = baked, O = broiled, F = fried
   Potatoes: R = french fries, C = chips

   BR BC OR OC FR FC

3. At Barry's Big Burger Barn, a customer can get a "Make Me Smile" meal by ordering a buffalo burger, a chicken burger, a garden burger, or an elk burger, with juice, milk, or water. How many different ways can a customer order a burger and a drink? List the combinations.

   Answer: 12 ways: 4 burgers x 3 drinks

   Burgers: B = buffalo, C = chicken, G = garden, and E = elk
   Drinks: J = juice, M = milk, W = water

BJ	**CJ**	**GJ**	**EJ**
BM	**CM**	**GM**	**EM**
BW	**CW**	**GW**	**EW**

4. At Saddie's Ice Cream Scooporama and Sundae Emporium, a customer has a choice of 3 flavors of ice cream and 3 toppings. The ice cream choices are chocolate, vanilla, and strawberry; the toppings are nuts, fudge, and whipped cream. If a customer bought 1 scoop of ice cream and 1 topping, how many choices would the customer have?

   Answer: 9 combinations: 3 ice cream flavors x 3 toppings

   Ice Cream: C = chocolate, V = vanilla, and S = strawberry
   Toppings: N = nuts, F = fudge, and W = whipped cream

CN	**VN**	**SN**
CF	**VF**	**SF**
CW	**VW**	**SW**

5. At Saddie's Ice Cream Scooporama and Sundae Emporium, a customer has a choice of 3 favors of ice cream to put in a three-scoop sundae: vanilla, chocolate, and strawberry. If 1 scoop of each flavor is used, how many different ways can the flavors be arranged

   Answer: 6 ways: 3 choices for the first scoop x 2 for the second x 1 for the third

   V = vanilla, C = chocolate, S = strawberry

   VCS VSC CSV CVS SCV SVC

A Three Hat Day

Applying Discoveries II

101

6. At Paul's Pizza Palace, a customer has a choice of 4 different size pizzas, 4 different crusts, and 4 different toppings. How many pizza choices does a customer have?

Answer: 64 choices: 4 x 4 x 4

7. The three best-selling flavors of juice at Oresta's Organic Juice Bar are apple, banana, and cranberry. How many different ways can Oresta arrange 1 each of the 3 flavors on a shelf? List the combinations.

Answer: 6 ways: 3 choices x 2 choices x 1 choice

A = apple, B = banana, C = cranberry ABC ACB BCA BAC CAB CBA

8. Barry is going to toss 3 pennies all at the same time. How many different ways could the pennies land? List the combinations.

Answer: 8 ways: 2 choices for each penny x 3 pennies

H = heads T = tails

HHH HHT HTH HTT THH THT TTH TTT

9. John has a red, a white, and a blue shirt. He also has green pants and orange pants. How many different ways can John wear the shirt and pants? List the combinations.

Answer: 6 ways: 3 shirts x 2 pants

Shirts: R = red, W = white, and B = blue
Pants: G = green and O = orange

RG WG BG
RO WO BO

10. If 2 dice are tossed at once, how many different ways could the faces of the dice appear? List the combinations and explain how you found your answer.

Answer: 36 ways: 6 choices for the first die x 6 for the second

1,1	2,1	3,1	4,1	5,1	6,1
1,2	2,2	3,2	4,2	5,2	6,2
1,3	2,3	3,3	4,3	5,3	6,3
1,4	2,4	3,4	4,4	5,4	6,4
1,5	2,5	3,5	4,5	5,5	6,5
1,6	2,6	3,6	4,6	5,6	6,6

Ask students the following question before proceeding to the Challenge and Probability problems in **Applying Discoveries III.**

How did solving problems 1–12 in the "More Discoveries" activity help you solve problems 1–10 in the "Applying Discoveries" activity?

Reproducible Master 102 with answers

A Three Hat Day

Applying Discoveries III

102

CHALLENGE PROBLEMS

11. R.R. Pottle had all 12 hats in a drawer and chose to wear 2 of them. How many ways could he wear them? Explain how you found the answer.

Answer: 132 ways: 12 choices for the first hat x 11 choices for the second.

12. R.R. Pottle had all 12 hats in a drawer and chose to wear 3 of them. How many ways could he wear them? Explain how you found the answer.

Answer: 1,320 ways: 12 choices for the first, 11 for the second, and 10 for the third. 12 x 11 x 10 = 1,320

13. R.R. Pottle had all 12 hats in a drawer and chose to wear 4 of them. How many ways could he wear them? Explain how you found the answer.

Answer: 11,880 ways: 12 choices for the first, 11 for the second, 10 for the third, and 9 for the fourth. 12 x 11 x 10 x 9 = 11,880

PROBABILITY PROBLEMS

14. R.R. Pottle had a red, yellow, and green baseball cap in each of 2 drawers. If he chose a hat to wear from each drawer, what would be the probability of seeing him with 2 yellow baseball caps on? **Answer:** $\frac{1}{9}$
What would be the probability of seeing him wearing 2 baseball caps of the same color?

Answer: $\frac{3}{9}$ **or** $\frac{1}{3}$

RR	YR	GR
RY	YY	GY
RG	YG	GG

15. R.R. Pottle had 1 red and 1 white baseball cap in each of his 3 drawers. If he decided to choose a hat at random from each of the drawers, what would be the probability of him wearing 3 red hats?

Answer: $\frac{1}{8}$

RRR	WRR
RRW	WWR
RWR	WRW
RWW	WWW

More Writing and Thinking Connections

Have students work on some or all of these problems individually, in pairs, or in groups. Then have them share their solutions with the class, which will develop and strengthen speaking skills.

If you assign different problems to different groups, students will need to be able to explain their problem thoroughly to the rest of the class before they can explain their solution. Note that in problem 3, the students will need to understand the first two problems to be able to answer the question. If possible, have students prepare posters to illustrate their solutions.

1. At the Rip-You-Off Game and Marble Arcade, a man has a container with three compartments. Each compartment has a red, a white, and a blue marble. He shakes the container to mix up the marbles. How many different ways can the marbles appear if a marble is chosen at random from each compartment? [Answer: 27 ways: 3 choices for the first compartment, 3 for the second compartment, 3 for the third compartment.]
2. At the House-Is-Happy Game and Marble Arcade, a man has a container with only one compartment that contains a red marble, a white marble, and a blue marble. He shakes the container to mix up the marbles. When he opens the door, the marbles appear one at a time. How many different ways can the marbles appear? [Answer: 6 ways: 3 choices for the first marble, 2 choices for the second, and 1 for the third.]
3. At which arcade does a person have a greater chance of seeing a red, a white, and a blue marble in that order? Explain how you found your answer. [Answer: At the House-Is-Happy Game and Marble Arcade. With six different ways for the marbles to appear, the probability of seeing red, white, and blue in that order is $\frac{1}{6}$. At the Rip-You-Off Game and Marble Arcade, the probability is $\frac{1}{27}$. $\frac{1}{6}$ is greater than $\frac{1}{27}$.]
4. Billy Baker's Back-Country Bicycle Tours has 4 different helmets, 4 different jerseys, and 4 different pants to choose from. The advertising claims that customers have 64 combinations to choose from for their helmet, jersey, and pants. Billy Baker's competitor claims Billy offers only 12 choices for the helmet, jersey, and pants. Who do you agree with? Explain your answer. [Answer: 64 combinations is correct because there are 4 choices for each item and 4 x 4 x 4 = 64.]

SPECIAL PROJECTS

Materials

Reference resources (e.g., dictionaries and encyclopedia)

This special writing project develops revision skills.

In the journal entries from the Composition Connection, students have developed two major concepts relating to the use of details. The first one is moving from general to specific. There are many different names for specific types of hats. The second concept relates to descriptive details. Specific details —such as size, material, purpose, decoration, fit, etc.—make the hats different from one another.

Review this concept with students. Then have them select a composition from their "works in progress" folder to revise by adding details. You might have students get into groups after they have selected the composition they want to work on. Then have students read their compositions to their writing group. The group can then make suggestions about where additional details are needed and brainstorm appropriate details that the writer might use.

You might have students work from the book and do additional research on the hats shown so they can provide richer detail. A good dictionary or encyclopedia will have illustrations as well as descriptions of various hats. The library can provide additional resources.

You might have students develop a chart similar to the one below to help them think of and organize details and qualities. This chart identifies some qualities, but it would be best to have the groups of students develop their own lists.

Details About Hats

Type of Hat	Qualities				
	Purpose	Size	Material	Decoration	Culture
Panama	sun shade	large	palm leaves		Central American
fez	head cover	small	red felt	black tassel	Morocco/ Turkey
beret					
bowler					

When students have finished their chart, they can discuss the different qualities they see in the details. For example, each of the materials has specific characteristics that make it appropriate or inappropriate for certain purposes. The goal here is to get students to look at details and to really understand what details are and why they add strength to writing and communication.

VOCABULARY DEVELOPMENT

Materials

Class or individual vocabulary lists

The use of ongoing vocabulary lists will make students' writing stronger. Consistently remind students to use their vocabulary lists when they are revising compositions. Reviewing their lists in this way will help students move words into their long-term memory.

Add the words from the story that appear in the chart below to the class vocabulary list, or have students add them to their own personal lists. Students may need to look up some of the words in the dictionary. If there is more than one definition provided, they will need to decide which one fits the context in the book.

See page *xxiii* of this manual for general information about vocabulary instruction.

As a class, discuss the vocabulary words. Ask the questions provided in the chart and discuss the answers.

Word	Page #	Question or Comment
hovering	14	Describe what a hovering cloud is doing and means.
tender	16	How is tender duet similar to or different from tender food?
drooped	16	Stand like R.R. was standing when his shoulders drooped. What does that action mean?
glum	17	The day is glum. R.R. is glum. Find other details in the book that mean the same or similar things to glum.
glided	17	Why might R.R. want to glide through the door? What other things might we be doing when we glide? What does gliding look like?
devil-may-care	20	What does this phrase mean? What else might be done in a devil-may-care way?
pose	20	What does pose mean in this sentence? How is that similar to or different from posing for a photograph or a model striking a pose? Can someone pose as someone else? What does the word mean then?
sharp	21	The woman speaks with a sharp voice. Imitate what that sounds like. How is a sharp voice similar to or different from a sharp knife? What do we mean if we say an individual is "really sharp"? Does a "really sharp" person have a "really sharp" voice? Do you know what a sharp note is in music?
pirouette	21	What action is this? What does it indicate? When is one likely to see a pirouette? How does this action show that R.R.'s mood has changed? How is pirouetting different from or similar to gliding or hovering or drooping? All of these are specific kinds of actions that reveal meaning by what they describe.
blinked	22	What is a blink? What does it indicate in this instance? What other words can you think of to describe eye actions? Can something other than an eye blink? What about the eye of a camera?
lopsided	22	Draw a picture of something that is lopsided.
plume	24	What is a plume? List some other things that can make plumes or appear as a plume.

Anno's Hat Tricks

Written by **Akihiro Nozaki**
Illustrated by **Mitsumasa Anno**

Overview of the Connections

A*nno's Hat Tricks* invites readers to play the role of Shadowchild, one of the book's central figures, and to solve logic puzzles involving hats. It is a book of active thinking.

In mathematics, this book provides opportunities for students to use logic, reasoning, and other problem-solving skills to identify and explain solutions to puzzle-type problems. Extensions include working with probability and listing possible combinations and choices.

In language arts, the book offers opportunities for writing as well as a unique opportunity to explore the benefits and limitations of point of view. The book does not lend itself to an appropriate listening activity, so this lesson does not include one.

MATERIALS FOR THE CONNECTIONS

Anno's Hat Tricks • ISBN 0-15-300349-9 (Harcourt)
Written by Akihiro Nozaki. Illustrated by Mitsumasa Anno. New York: Philomel Books, 1985; reprint, Orlando: Harcourt Brace & Company, [1993].

Language Arts

~ One or more copies of the book (Note: In the Viewing Connection, each student will need to see p. 23. You may wish to have several copies available.)

~ Optional: **Connection to Viewing Assessment: Writing About a Picture Prompt** (Reproducible Master 1)

~ **Have I...? Checklist** (Reproducible Master 2), a self-monitoring tool for student writers

~ **Rubric for Scoring First Drafts** (Reproducible Master 3)

~ **Connection to Writing Assessment: Post-Reading Composition** (Reproducible Master 105)

Mathematics

~ Hats (3 red, 2 white, or others labeled as red and white). Alternative: 5 hat signs (3 showing a red hat, 2 showing a white hat)

~ Opaque bag large enough to hold 5 hats

~ Box large enough to hold 1 hat

For each group of 3 students:

~ 3 red cubes, 2 white cubes (or 3 x 5 cards made from tag board)

~ 5 lengths of string for necklaces

~ Paper bag (for each group of 3 students)

~ **Connection to Mathematics Assessment: Check for Understanding I and II** (Reproducible Masters 103–104)

Viewing Connection

INTRODUCING THE LESSON WITH A PICTURE PROMPT AND WRITING

Materials

One or more copies of the book (page 23), **Connection to Viewing Assessment: Writing About a Picture Prompt** (Reproducible Master 1), **Have I...? Checklist** (Reproducible Master 2), **Rubric for Scoring First Drafts** (Reproducible Master 3)

Show the class the picture on page 23 of the book with the text covered so the students can focus on the illustration. The illustration shows a boy and a girl reacting to a shadow that is waving to them. If possible, allow students to continue to look at the picture throughout the writing session. You may distribute a copy of the **Connection to Viewing Assessment: Writing About a Picture Prompt** to each student, or they may use notebook paper for their work. Also distribute copies of the **Have I...? Checklist**.

Read these directions to the class:

"You are going to write a composition about this picture. Look at it carefully. Think about what you see and the story it may be telling. It is OK that not everyone will see the same story. If you wish to, you may do prewriting before you start your composition. When you have finished the composition, use the **Have I...? Checklist** as a guide for editing and revising what you have written."

Give the students 20–30 minutes to write their compositions and do initial editing.

Collect and score the students' compositions using the **Rubric for Scoring First Drafts**. Teach students how to compare their scored compositions to the rubric and to make notes about how to improve their compositions. Students also may be taught to use the rubric to score their own work or that of other students.

To extend this activity, see "Interpreting Illustrations," in the Extending the Connections section of this lesson.

Reproducible Master 1

Connection to Viewing Assessment 1

Writing About a Picture Prompt

Write a composition about the picture (or pictures). Look at it carefully. Think about what you see and the story it may be telling. Not everyone will see the same story. If you wish to, you may do prewriting before you start your composition. When you have finished the composition, use the **Have I...? Checklist** as a guide for editing and revising what you have written. You may finish your composition on the back of this page or on a separate sheet of paper.

____

____

____

____

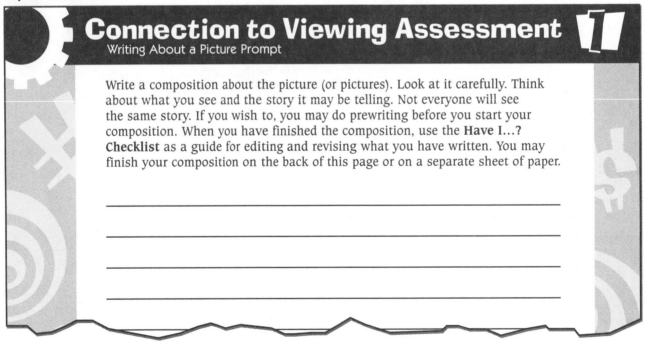

Mathematics Connection

INTRODUCTION AND ACTIVE READING

Materials

A copy of the book, 5 hats (3 red and 2 white, or others labeled as red and white), bag large enough to hold 5 hats, box large enough to hold 1 hat. For each group of 3 students: a paper lunch bag, 3 red cubes and 2 white cubes, five pieces of string to make necklaces.

Alternative materials: Instead of using 5 hats, you might create 5 signs: 3 with a picture of a red hat or the word *red* and 2 with a picture of a white hat or the word *white*. Instead of cubes and string, you might give each group 5 pieces of tag board about the size of index cards.

In *Anno's Hat Tricks*, the hatter tells the characters how many hats he has of different colors. He places one hat atop each character's head and asks each in turn to determine the color. To figure out which color hat they are wearing, the characters consider information about the number of hats in each color, the hats that they see others wearing, and the answers provided by other characters. Sometimes a character determines that there isn't enough information to figure out what color hat he or she is wearing. The inability of one character to figure out the color is sometimes a clue that helps other characters determine their hat color.

In these activities, students model the situations in the book. For the purposes of this lesson, the book has been divided into nine groups of activities, or "hat tricks." Each activity references the page number where the problem is introduced in the book.

You can choose to complete any or all of the hat trick activities. Each activity works independently, although they do become increasingly complex.

For each activity, present the situation described in the book, have students think about, model, and solve the problem. Then read the pages from the story to verify solutions.

As you read selections, tell the students to think about the questions that are being asked. Ensure that they understand that as part of the practice of effective reading they should ask themselves questions such as these while they read.

GENERAL HAT TRICK INSTRUCTIONS

The situations in this book involve four characters: the hatter, who introduces the problem; two children, Tom and Hannah; and Shadowchild. The hatter explains that Shadowchild is the reader. By writing in this second-person point of view, the author invites readers to actively participate in the story.

Some activities are done as a class, and others are conducted in small groups. Some hat trick activities for the whole class have extensions designed for small groups.

For the whole-class activities: Assign students to play the roles of Tom and, when appropriate, Hannah. (The first few hat tricks include only the hatter, Tom, and Shadowchild; the others include Hannah, too.) The rest of the class will play Shadowchild. You will play the role of the hatter.

Place a box on its side so Tom and Hannah can see in it but the rest of the class cannot. This will represent Shadowchild.

For each activity, place in a bag the number of red and white hats detailed by the hatter. Stand behind the child playing Tom and place a hat on his head, making sure that he does not see the color. If Hannah is included in the hat trick, do the same for her.

If you use baseball caps, have the students wear them backward so they cannot see the color of the hat on the underside of the bill. If you are using signs to represent hats, have the students playing Tom and Hannah stand in front of the board and tape the appropriate signs on the board above their heads.

Place a hat in the box in front of Tom and Hannah so that they can see the color but the rest of the class cannot. The hat in the box represents the hat on Shadowchild's head.

For the group activities: Students work in groups of 3 or 4 students, depending on the number of characters in the hat trick they are modeling. One student in the group is the leader, or the "hatter."

The hatter puts a given number of red cube necklaces and white cube necklaces in a bag. As the other students close their eyes, the hatter places a cube necklace around the neck of each one so the cube is at each student's back. With the cubes at their backs, the students can see what colors the other students have, but they cannot see their own.

Read pages 2–5 to the class as an introduction.

Hat Trick #1 (pages 6–7)

Choose one student to be Tom, and have him stand in front of the class. Tell the students that you are the hatter and the rest of the class will play the part of Shadowchild.

Tell the students that you have placed 2 red hats and 2 white hats in the bag and that you want them to close their eyes as you place a hat on Tom's head and another on Shadowchild.

Stand behind Tom and place a red hat on his head, ensuring that he does not see the color. Place another hat in the box without allowing the class to see what color it is. Position the box on a desk in front of Tom so that only he can see it. Tell the children to imagine that they are wearing the hat in the box as Shadowchild.

Tell the students to open their eyes. Make sure they do not reveal to Tom what color his hat is.

Use a pair-share-discussion technique to establish whether or not it is possible for Tom to determine his hat color and for Shadowchild to determine its hat color based on the information they have. [Answer: They cannot figure out the color because there are no clues.]

Verify the answer by reading pages 6–7 to the class, and discuss what the hatter says.

EXTENSION

Ask probability questions similar to the ones that follow. Ensure that students understand that picking a hat "without looking" is the same as picking a hat "at random."

Suppose that after I put the red hat on Tom, there are 2 red and 2 white hats left in the bag. What is the probability of picking a red hat at random for Shadowchild?

[Answer: $\frac{2}{4}$ or $\frac{1}{2}$]

What is the probability of picking a white hat without looking?

[Answer: $\frac{2}{4}$ or $\frac{1}{2}$]

Suppose that after putting a red hat on Tom, there are 2 red hats and 1 white hat left in the bag. What is the probability of pulling out a white hat without looking? [Answer: $\frac{1}{3}$]

What is the probability of pulling out a red hat at random? [Answer: $\frac{2}{3}$]

Hat Trick #2 (pages 8–9)

Tell the class that you are placing exactly 1 red hat and 1 white hat in the bag.

Select a student to be Tom, and use the box for Shadowchild's hat.

Tell students to close their eyes as you place a red hat on Tom and a white hat in the box for Shadowchild. Position the box so that only Tom can see the color of the hat inside.

Tell students that when they open their eyes, Tom and Shadowchild will try to figure out the colors of their hats without being able to see them.

Ask Tom if he knows the color of his hat. Ask the class the color of Shadowchild's hat.

Ask Tom to explain how he knew his hat was red. Then ask the rest of the students to explain how they knew Shadowchild's hat was white. [Answer: If there is only 1 red hat and 1 white hat to start, and Tom sees that Shadowchild has the white hat, then he knows he must have the red hat. The class knows that if Tom is wearing the red hat, Shadowchild must have the white hat.]

Discuss the answers, then read pages 8–9 to verify their solutions and explanations.

EXTENSION

Arrange students in groups of 3, and give each group a paper lunch bag, 1 red cube and 1 white cube, and two lengths of string. Have them thread the strings through the cubes to make a red-cube necklace and a white-cube necklace. Have them put the cube necklaces in the bag.

As an alternative to cubes, give each group two pieces of tag board, each about the size of an index card. Have them position the cards vertically and write the word *red* on the top half of one card, and *white* on the top half of the other. Have them fold the cards in half and put them in the bag.

Have each group select one person to be the "hatter." (For purposes of explanation, one student will be referred to as Tom and the other as Shadowchild.)

If you will be using cards instead of cube necklaces, the two other students should sit facing directly across from one another at a desk or table.

Tell the students who are not hatters to close their eyes. Direct each hatter to randomly choose one necklace or card from the bag for Tom. Have the hatter place the necklace around Tom's neck with the cube against his back so he cannot see the color. The hatter should do the same for Shadowchild with the remaining cube necklace.

When the students open their eyes, allow them to see the color of the other person's cube necklace, but not their own.

If you use cards instead of cubes, the hatter should set the first card in front of Tom so that Shadowchild can read the color, but Tom cannot. (With the bottom half of the folded card resting on the desk and facing away from Tom, the top half will display the word for Shadowchild.) Then have the hatter display the other card in front of Shadowchild so that Tom can read the color but Shadowchild cannot.

Have each hatter call on the others in the group to tell the color of their cube or their card and how they know. [Answer: If only two colors are used, and you can see one color, you know you must have the other one.]

Hat Trick #3 (pages 10–17)

Arrange students into groups of 3. Give each group 2 red cubes, 1 white cube, 3 lengths of string, and a paper bag. Have them thread a length of string through each cube to create three necklaces (2 with a red cube, 1 with a white cube).

If you wish to use cards instead of cube necklaces, see the instructions described in the Extension for Hat Trick #2 for preparing and positioning the cards. In this case, the group will need to write the word *red* on 2 cards and the word *white* on 1 card.

Have each group select one student to be the hatter.

Tell the students who are not hatters to close their eyes. Direct each hatter to randomly choose one necklace from the bag for Tom. Have the hatter place the necklace around Tom's neck with the cube against his back so he cannot see the color. The hatter should do the same for Shadowchild with another cube necklace.

When the students open their eyes, allow them to see the color of the other person's cube necklace, but not their own. Have them try to determine what color they have.

The students will discover that sometimes they can determine the color, and other times they cannot. Discuss the circumstances under which they can and cannot tell the color.

Answer:
If the person wearing the white cube (Tom) must answer first, he cannot determine the color of his own cube. He sees that Shadowchild has a red cube, but he knows that one red cube and one white cube were left in the bag. He can't know which one of those he has.

But if the person wearing the white cube answers second, he can always tell what color he has. How? First he listens to the answer given by Shadowchild, who answers first. Shadowchild sees that Tom has a white cube. Shadowchild knows the only other cubes are red, so its cube must be red. Therefore, Shadowchild answers "red." Tom now knows for sure that he must have a white cube. Why? Because if he had a red cube, Shadowchild could not have determined its color first.

Read pages 10–13 and discuss the similarities between the story and what they did during this last experiment.

EXTENSION

List all the possible combinations that could occur in the problem above. Make sure to include the cube that would be left in the bag.

Answer: There are three possible combinations of cubes.

Tom	Shadow	Bag
Red	Red	White
Red	White	Red
White	Red	Red

Hat Trick #4 (pages 18–21)

Choose a student to be Tom, and use the box turned on its side to be the Shadowchild. Tell the class that you are placing 2 red hats and 1 white hat in a bag.

Have all the students close their eyes as you place a red hat on Tom and a red one in the box for Shadowchild.

Ask Tom what color hat he has on. Then ask the class what color Shadowchild's hat is.

Answer:
Tom should say he cannot tell what color his hat is. He sees the Shadowchild's hat is red. That means his hat could be red or white. He can't know which.

Once the rest of the class hears that Tom can't determine the color, the students should be able to tell you that Shadowchild's hat is red. They can see that Tom is wearing a red hat. If Tom saw that the Shadowchild's hat was white, he would have known his hat was red. That means that the Shadowchild's hat must not be white. So it must be red.

Discuss the solution, then read pages 18–21 and have students compare the problem they just solved with models to the story in the book.

Hat Trick #5 (pages 22–25)

Choose students to be Tom and Hannah. Use a box turned on its side to be Shadowchild. Tell the class that you are placing 2 red hats and 1 white hat in the bag.

Ask students to close their eyes as you place a red hat on Tom , a white hat on Hannah, and a red hat in the box for Shadowchild. Position the box so that only Tom and Hannah can see the color of the hat inside.

When they open their eyes, ask them if they can tell the color of the hat they are wearing by looking at the other two hats. Ask if any other characters can tell which color they have on and why. [Answer: All people can tell what color hat they have on because they see the other two hats. They know they must be wearing the remaining color.]

EXTENSION

List all the combinations of hats that could occur when randomly placing two red hats and a white hat on the three children.

Answer: There are three possible combinations of hats.

Tom	Hannah	Shadow
Red	Red	White
Red	White	Red
White	Red	Red

Hat Trick #6 (pages 26–29)

Choose students to be Tom and Hannah. Use a box turned on its side to be Shadowchild. Position the box so that only Tom and Hannah would be able to see the color of the hat inside.

Tell the class that you are placing 3 red hats and 2 white hats in the bag. Tell them that you will be choosing one hat at a time to place it on each character's head. Before picking hats, ask:

Could Tom, Hannah, and Shadowchild all wear white hats? Why or why not?
[Answer: No, because there are only two white hats available.]

Place a red hat on Tom and a white hat on Hannah. Ask:

If I put the next hat drawn from the bag on Shadowchild, would Shadowchild know what color it is? **[Answer: Shadowchild would not know because there is still at least one red hat and one white hat in the bag.]**

Return Tom and Hannah's hats to the bag. Then place a white hat on Tom and a white hat on Hannah. Ask:

If I put the next hat drawn from the bag on Shadowchild, would Shadowchild know what color it is? **[Answer: Yes. Shadowchild's hat must be red because there were only 2 white hats in the bag, and they were used for Tom and Hannah. That left only red for Shadowchild.]**

Read pages 26–29 and have the class discuss how the story is similar to what they just acted out.

Hat Trick #7 (pages 30–33)

Choose students to be Tom and Hannah. Use a box turned on its side to be Shadowchild. Position the box so that only Tom and Hannah would be able to see the color of the hat inside.

Tell the class that you are placing 3 red hats and 2 white hats in the bag. Tell them that you will be choosing one hat at a time to place it on each character's head, making sure that a least one of the hats is red.

Have the students close their eyes. Place a white hat on Tom, a red hat on Hannah, and a white hat in the box for Shadowchild. Then tell them to open their eyes.

Ask Hannah if she can tell what color hat she has by looking at the other two. [Answer: Yes. She should know her hat is red for one of two reasons. First, the teacher/hatter said one of the hats would be red. Since Hannah sees 2 white hats, she knows she must have red. Second, hers must be red because there were only 2 white hats in the bag and she sees that Tom and Shadowchild have them.]

Ask the class if Shadowchild knows what color its hat is. [Answer: Based on Hannah's response, the class can conclude that Shawdowchild has a white hat. Why? Because the only way that Hannah could know she has red is if she sees 2 white hats on Tom and Shadowchild.]

Read pages 30–33 to the class and discuss similarities and differences between the story and the modeling done previously.

EXTENSION

Arrange students into groups of 4. Give each group 3 red cubes, 2 white cubes, 4 lengths of string, and a paper bag. Have them thread a length of string through each cube to create four necklaces (3 with a red cube, 2 with a white cube).

If you wish to use cards instead of cube necklaces, see the instructions described in the Extension for Hat Trick #2.

Have each group select one person to be the "hatter." Tell the students who are not hatters to close their eyes.

Direct each hatter to randomly choose one necklace from the bag for each of the others in the group. The hatter should place the necklaces around the students' necks with the cube against their backs so they cannot see their own colors. When the students open their eyes, allow them to see the color of the other students' cube necklaces, but not their own.

Have the hatters call on others in their group to tell what color cube necklace they are wearing and how they know they are correct.

Hat Trick #8 (pages 34–39)

Choose students to be Tom and Hannah. Use a box turned on its side to be Shadowchild. Position the box so that only Tom and Hannah would be able to see the color of the hat inside.

Tell the class you've placed 3 red hats and 2 white hats in the bag. Ask:

How do you know that one of the characters will be wearing a red hat? **[Answer: There are only 2 white hats, so if 3 people are wearing hats, at least 1 must wear red.]**

Have the students close their eyes. Place a red hat on Tom, a red hat on Hannah, and a red hat in the box for Shadowchild.

Tell students to listen for hints as you ask a series of questions to Tom, Hannah, and Shadowchild (the class).

Question 1: Ask Tom if he knows what color hat he is wearing. [Tom should say "no." He sees 2 red hats, but that means his could be the third red hat or one of the 2 white ones.]

Question 2: Ask Hannah if she knows what color hat she is wearing. [Hannah also should say "no." She sees 2 red hats, which means that she could have a red or a white. The fact that Tom didn't know the color of his hat doesn't help her determine her color.]

Question 3: Ask the class how Tom and Hannah's answers can help Shadowchild determine the color of its hat.

> **Answer:**
> Shadowchild can tell it is wearing a red hat because Tom and Hannah could not tell what hats they were wearing. Here's how:
>
> The only way Tom could know he had a red hat was if he saw 2 white hats. Shadowchild and Hannah now know that Tom saw at least 1 red hat.
>
> Because Shadowchild is wearing red, Hannah does not know if her hat is white or red.
>
> Shadowchild knows that if Hannah had seen a white hat on its head, she would have known her hat was red. Since Hannah did not know her hat color, she must not have seen white. That means Shadowchild knows it must be wearing red.

Read pages 34–39 to the class and discuss similarities and differences between the story and the modeling done previously.

EXTENSION

List all possible combinations that could occur and discuss them.

Tom	Hannah	Shadowchild
Red	Red	Red
Red	Red	White
Red	White	Red
Red	White	White
White	Red	Red
White	Red	White
White	White	Red

Hat Trick #9 (pages 40–41)

Read pages 40–41 to the class. Challenge them to work in small groups to solve the problem. Or, you may wish to act it out as a class.

> **Answer:**
> Shadowchild is wearing a white hat. It knows this because Tom said "no." That means Tom saw at least one red hat. Hannah said "yes," so she must have seen a white hat on Shadowchild to know she's wearing the red hat that Tom saw. Shadowchild knows it must be wearing the white hat for Hannah to have known her hat. Shadowchild therefore knows its hat is white.

MATHEMATICS ASSESSMENT

Materials

- **Connection to Mathematics Assessment: Check for Understanding I and II** (Reproducible Masters 103–104)

Distribute the worksheets with multiple-choice and open-ended questions called **Connection to Mathematics Assessment: Check for Understanding I and II.**

Collect and score the students' work using the answers and rubric that follow.

Reproducible Master 103 with answers

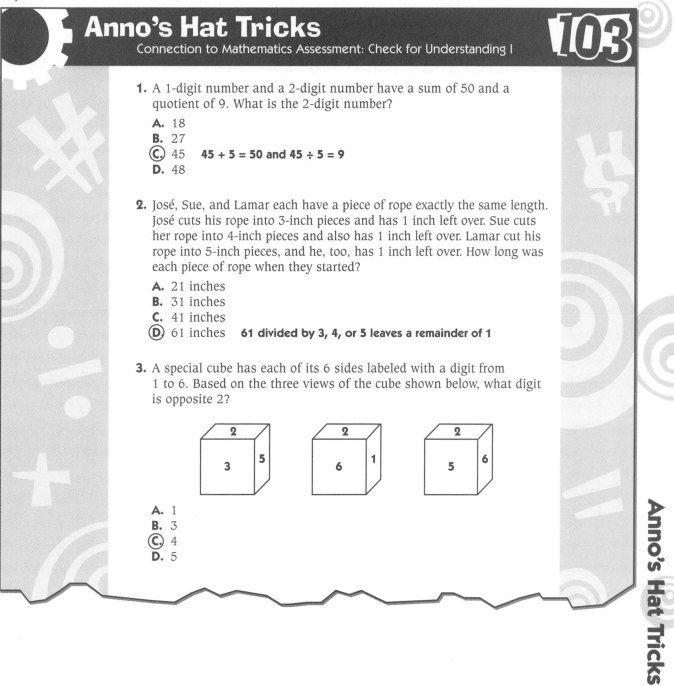

Anno's Hat Tricks

Connection to Mathematics Assessment: Check for Understanding I

103

1. A 1-digit number and a 2-digit number have a sum of 50 and a quotient of 9. What is the 2-digit number?

   A. 18
   B. 27
   (C.) 45 **45 + 5 = 50 and 45 ÷ 5 = 9**
   D. 48

2. José, Sue, and Lamar each have a piece of rope exactly the same length. José cuts his rope into 3-inch pieces and has 1 inch left over. Sue cuts her rope into 4-inch pieces and also has 1 inch left over. Lamar cut his rope into 5-inch pieces, and he, too, has 1 inch left over. How long was each piece of rope when they started?

   A. 21 inches
   B. 31 inches
   C. 41 inches
   (D.) 61 inches **61 divided by 3, 4, or 5 leaves a remainder of 1**

3. A special cube has each of its 6 sides labeled with a digit from 1 to 6. Based on the three views of the cube shown below, what digit is opposite 2?

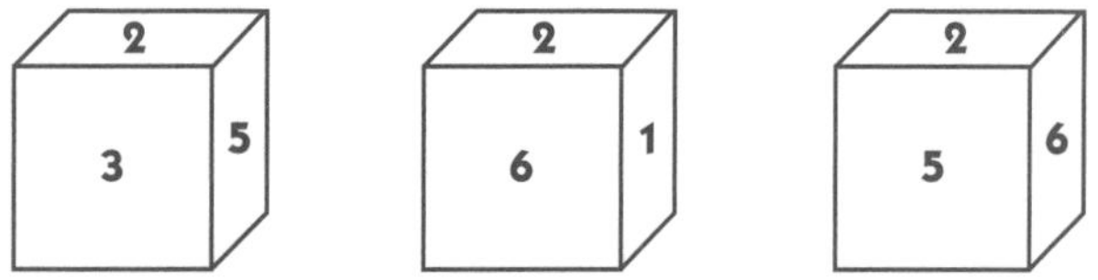

   A. 1
   B. 3
   (C.) 4
   D. 5

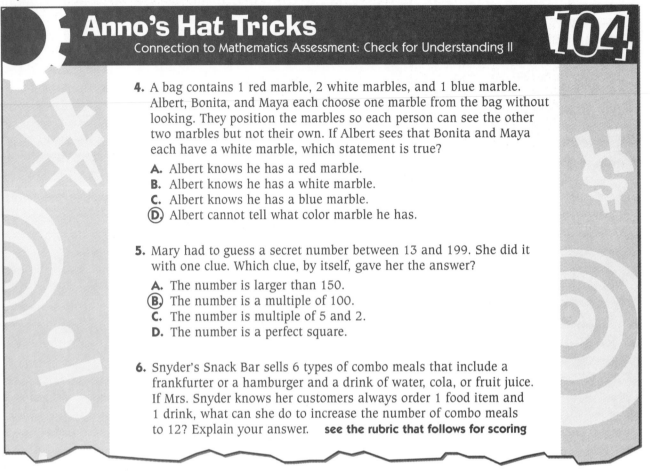

Anno's Hat Tricks

Connection to Mathematics Assessment: Check for Understanding II

104

4. A bag contains 1 red marble, 2 white marbles, and 1 blue marble. Albert, Bonita, and Maya each choose one marble from the bag without looking. They position the marbles so each person can see the other two marbles but not their own. If Albert sees that Bonita and Maya each have a white marble, which statement is true?
   - A. Albert knows he has a red marble.
   - B. Albert knows he has a white marble.
   - C. Albert knows he has a blue marble.
   - (D) Albert cannot tell what color marble he has.

5. Mary had to guess a secret number between 13 and 199. She did it with one clue. Which clue, by itself, gave her the answer?
   - A. The number is larger than 150.
   - (B) The number is a multiple of 100.
   - C. The number is multiple of 5 and 2.
   - D. The number is a perfect square.

6. Snyder's Snack Bar sells 6 types of combo meals that include a frankfurter or a hamburger and a drink of water, cola, or fruit juice. If Mrs. Snyder knows her customers always order 1 food item and 1 drink, what can she do to increase the number of combo meals to 12? Explain your answer. **see the rubric that follows for scoring**

RUBRIC FOR SCORING
Problem 6

An effective response will need to:

- introduce a choice that makes the product of the numbers of food and drink choices equal 12.
- explains why the answer is correct through narrative or listing all combinations.

POINTS	CRITERIA
3	The student introduces a choice that makes the product of the choices for food and drinks equal 12. The student explains why the solution is correct or provides a list of all the combinations. Possible responses: Example 1 *I know that if I multiply the number of choices for each part of the problem, that this product will give me the total number of choices, so I added two more food choices. 4 x 3 = 12.* Example 2 *I added pizza to give one more choice of something to eat and tea to give one more choice of something to drink. My choices are listed below.* *F = frankfurter, H = hamburger, P = pizza* *W = water, C = cola, J = juice, T = tea* *FW HW PW* *FJ HC PC* *FC HJ PJ* *FT HT PT* Example 3 *I added 3 new drinks to the menu.* *Frank with water — Burger with water* *Frank with cola — Burger with cola* *Frank with juice — Burger with juice* *Frank with tea — Burger with tea* *Frank with punch — Burger with punch* *Frank with milk — Burger with milk*
2	The student provides correct additional choices, but the explanation is unclear or not all the choices are listed. Or, the student does not mention what is being added, but lists most of the 12 combinations with new choices. Or, the student lists 12 combinations with some new choices, but some are repeated or are incorrect.
1	The student provides the correct number of additional choices, but the explanation has gaps or flaws or is missing completely; or, some of the combinations are missing or are incorrect. OR The student does not mention what is being added, but lists only some of the 12 combinations with new choices; or, some of the 12 are repeated or incorrect.
0	The student shows no understanding of the problem or leaves it blank.

Composition Connection

WRITING A POST-READING COMPOSITION

Materials

Connection to Writing Assessment: Post-Reading Composition (Reproducible Master 105), **Have I...? Checklist** (Reproducible Master 2), **Rubric for Scoring First Drafts** (Reproducible Master 3)

Distribute a copy of **Connection to Writing Assessment: Post-Reading Composition** to each student along with the **Have I...? Checklist**.

Allow students 25 minutes for writing and reviewing their compositions.

Collect and score the compositions using the **Rubric for Scoring First Drafts**. You may wish to encourage students to put their scored drafts into a folder of "works in progress" and to edit and revise it further to be shared with an audience at some later date.

Reproducible Master 105

Anno's Hat Tricks

Connection to Writing Assessment: Post-Reading Composition

105

Writing Task

In *Anno's Hat Tricks*, Shadowchild is asked to think carefully to solve problems. Think about a time when you have had to solve a problem by thinking very carefully. Explain what the problem was, how you solved it, what you learned from the experience, and how you felt about it.

Be sure to use the **Have I. . . ? Checklist** to review your work. Make any changes needed so it as good as it can be. You may finish your composition on the back of this page or on a separate sheet of paper.

___

___

___

___

Extending the Connections

INTERPRETING AND WRITING ABOUT CHARACTERS

Materials

One or more copies of the book. Optional: **Rubric for Scoring First Drafts** (Reproducible Master 3)

Discuss the illustration on the book cover with the class. Focus attention on the person pictured in the center and how he is dressed like the character Sherlock Holmes. Tell students that Sherlock Holmes is one of the most famous fictional detectives ever created. He used his thinking abilities to solve difficult mysteries.

Read these directions to the class:

> "The speaker in this book calls himself a 'hatter.' In what ways is the speaker like Sherlock Holmes (or other detectives who use their minds to solve problems)? As I review the story, make a list of the characteristics that the hatter shares with Sherlock Holmes (or other detectives). If you know more about Sherlock Holmes from stories, movies, or TV shows, add some other characteristics that you can think of to the list. Work with your partners in your writing group to develop as complete a list as you can."

Re-read the story slowly so students can take notes as you read.

Once students have a complete list, finish the directions:

> "Use the information on your list to write a composition that describes a detective or write a story in which your detective is the main character and solves a problem using her/his mental powers.

If this writing product is scored as a draft, use the **Rubric for Scoring First Drafts** to assess it. Instead, you might provide students the opportunity to work on it over an extended period of time and edit and revise it so that it becomes a "publishable" product. In that case, score it using the criteria generally used in your class for grading compositions that are polished to the point to being ready to share with a larger audience. See page *xxi* of this manual for a discussion of assessing students' writing skills and evaluating or grading written products.

INTERPRETING AND WRITING ABOUT ILLUSTRATIONS

Materials

One or more copies of the book

The illustration on page 23, which was the subject of the Viewing Connection activity, is quite similar to other pictures in the book. You can help students develop skills in "reading" material presented visually by looking at some of the other pictures and discussing what they show. Contrast pages 9 and 11, for example, or examine the facial expression on page 15.

Transfer these visual skills into writing and speaking skills by offering students the opportunity to write descriptions about what they see on the page and to share those descriptions with each other. Also, the teacher who writes with the class will be able to share a model of good description and will help to demonstrate that writing is an adult activity as well as a "school" one.

EXPLORING POINT OF VIEW

Materials

One or more copies of the book

Some students may be ready to think about the concept of point of view in literature by identifying who is telling the story or through whose eyes we see the story.

Discuss the point of view the author chose for *Anno's Hat Tricks*. Ask:

How would the book be different if it were told from Hannah's or Tom's point of view?

Select a fictional book that the class has already studied and have students talk about how the story would be different if it were told from the point of view of other characters in the story.

Follow up with a group or individual writing activity in which a story is retold through the eyes of another character.

Anno's Math Games

Written and illustrated by
Mitsumasa Anno

Overview of the Connections

The book *Anno's Math Games* consists of four distinct chapters, each of which is explored in a separate lesson. Each chapter of *Anno's Math Games* includes a sequenced set of vivid pictures and activities. The book presents opportunities for students to conceptually investigate and explore various mathematical topics, which are embedded in the national standards. Because the individual chapters are each equal in size to a typical trade book, they are treated as separate lessons with unique activities and assessments.

The four chapters can be used independently or in various combinations. Each chapter addresses specific mathematical concepts.

Chapter	*Anno's Math Games* Pages	Lesson pages	Math Concepts
CHAPTER 1 What Is Different?	2 – 21	251 – 258	Classifying, sorting, looking for patterns, using logic
CHAPTER 2 Putting Together and Taking Apart	22 – 44	259 – 272	Coordinates, graphs, tables, charts; mathematical partitioning
CHAPTER 3 Numbers in Order	44 – 67	273 – 282	Ordinal numbers, patterns, coordinates
CHAPTER 4 Who's the Tallest?	68 – 93	283 – 298	Measurement; organizing, representing, and analyzing data

Although *Anno's Math Games* is not a traditional storybook, for language arts instruction this book offers many opportunities for writing both longer and shorter compositions, as well as implementing a writing workshop in your class. There are no Listening Connections in these lessons, but a variety of other language arts activities are presented throughout. *Anno's Math Games* is an especially good resource for sparking students' own ideas for writing. To read more about helping students find their own writing topics, see the "Writer's Workshop" discussion on page *xxii* of this manual.

MATERIALS FOR THE CONNECTIONS

Anno's Math Games • ISBN 0-698-11671-2
Written and illustrated by Mitsumasa Anno. New York: Putnam & Grosset Group, 1997.
Note: Additional materials are listed under the individual lessons for each chapter.

Anno's Math Games

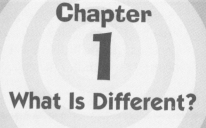

Overview of the Connections

Chapter 1: What Is Different? (pages 2–21) provides many opportunities for students to make conjectures, look for patterns, and find attributes, which can help them classify and sort familiar objects. At first, clues are given to help students classify objects. Later they are left to draw their own conclusions. Students build a mathematical foundation for the meaning of one, using their skills of observation.

These observation skills also assist students in becoming better writers as they apply the concept of "using details" to their own compositions. This chapter builds foundational skills for future lessons, and therefore it does not provide a Mathematics Assessment.

Chapter 1
What Is Different?

MATERIALS FOR THE CONNECTIONS

Anno's Math Games • ISBN 0-698-11671-2
Written and illustrated by Mitsumasa Anno. New York: Putnam & Grosset Group, 1997.

Language Arts

~ Copies of the book (1 for each group of 2–4 students)

~ Optional: **Connection to Viewing Assessment: Writing About a Picture Prompt** (Reproducible Master 1)

~ **Have I...? Checklist** (Reproducible Master 2), a self-monitoring tool for student writers

~ **Rubric for Scoring First Drafts** (Reproducible Master 3)

~ **Connection to Writing Assessment: Post-Reading Composition** (Reproducible Master 108)

Mathematics

~**Various Vehicles** (Reproducible Master 106)

~**Tell What Is Different** (Reproducible Master 107)

Viewing Connection

INTRODUCING THE LESSON WITH A PICTURE PROMPT AND WRITING

Materials

Copy of the book (pages 6–7), **Connection to Viewing Assessment: Writing About a Picture Prompt** (Reproducible Master 1), **Have I...? Checklist** (Reproducible Master 2), **Rubric for Scoring First Drafts** (Reproducible Master 3)

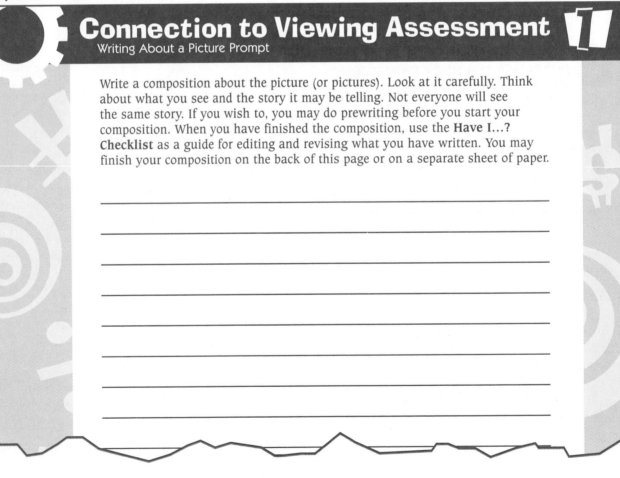

Show the class the pictures on pages 6 and 7 with the text covered. This page shows a group of ducks and others living things. If possible, allow students to continue to look at the picture throughout the writing session. You may distribute a copy of **Connection to Viewing Assessment: Writing About a Picture Prompt** to each student, or they may use notebook paper for their work. Also distribute copies of the **Have I...? Checklist**.

Read these directions to the class:

"You are going to write a composition about this picture. Look at it carefully. Think about what you see and the story it may be telling. It is OK that not everyone will see the same story. If you wish to, you may do prewriting before you start your composition. When you have finished the composition, use the **Have I...? Checklist** as a guide for editing and revising what you have written."

Give the students 20-30 minutes to write their compositions and do initial editing.

Collect and score the students' compositions using the **Rubric for Scoring First Drafts**. Teach students how to compare their scored compositions to the rubric and to make notes about how to improve their compositions. Students also may be taught to use the rubric to score their own work or that of other students.

Reproducible Master 1

Connection to Viewing Assessment 1

Writing About a Picture Prompt

Write a composition about the picture (or pictures). Look at it carefully. Think about what you see and the story it may be telling. Not everyone will see the same story. If you wish to, you may do prewriting before you start your composition. When you have finished the composition, use the **Have I...? Checklist** as a guide for editing and revising what you have written. You may finish your composition on the back of this page or on a separate sheet of paper.

Mathematics Connection

INTRODUCTION AND ACTIVE READING

Materials

Several copies of the book (ideally, 1 for each group of 2–4 students), Various Vehicles (Reproducible Master 106)

As you read *Chapter 1: What Is Different?* pose questions and conduct activities as described in the book and in the guide below. Encourage students to practice active reading skills, such as asking questions, thinking to themselves, and discussing their ideas. Ensure that they understand that practicing effective reading means asking themselves questions while they read. You might choose to do some or all of the activities provided here.

PAGE 4

How is a circle different from a square? **[Answer: A square has straight sides, a circle does not; it is curved.]**

- ***Which figures are congruent to each other in this picture?*** **[Answer: All the squares shown are congruent because they have the same size and shape.]**
- ***Which has the larger area: the circle or the square? Explain how you know.*** **[Answer: The square has the larger area because the circle will fit inside the square.]**
- ***How do the diameter of the circle and the length of a side compare?*** **[Answer: They are equal in length.]**

PAGE 5

How is the ladybug that stands out different from the others? **[Answer: The spots are bigger, and it is darker.]**

- ***Even though the rest of the ladybugs look the same, how are they different from each other?*** **[Answer: They are in different positions.]**
- ***How many legs are there altogether on these ladybugs?*** **[Answer: 12 x 6 = 72]**
- ***The bugs appear to be in an array. Name the column and row of the bug that seems to be turned the most to the left.*** **[Answer: The bug in the column on the extreme right and in the bottom row.]**
- ***Name the column and row of the bug that seems to be turned the most to the right.*** **[Answer: The bug in the column on the extreme left, in the middle row.]**

Introduce or extend the concept of coordinates by naming the column first and the row second. Using this method, label the bottom row as 1 and the left column as 1. For example, the bug turned to the left is (4,1), and the bug turned to the right is (1,2).

Row 4	bug (1,4)	bug (2,4)	bug (3,4)	bug (4,4)
Row 3	bug (1,3)	bug (2,3)	bug (3,3)	bug (4,3)
Row 2	bug (1,2)	bug (2,2)	bug (3,2)	bug (4,2)
Row 1	bug (1,1)	bug (2,1)	bug (3,1)	bug (4,1)
	Column 1	**Column 2**	**Column 3**	**Column 4**

PAGES 6–7

Show the pictures on pages 6 and 7 to the students. Do not read the text. If groups have their own copies of the book, have them cover the text.

Ask students to explain what they think is different on page 6 and why. Ask students to describe how the flower is different from all the other pictures on page 7.

List students' responses and hold a class discussion about the differences. Read the description at the bottom of each page and discuss how the students' observations compare to those of the author.

PAGES 8–9

Materials

Various Vehicles (Reproducible Master 106)

Tell students to study the pictures on pages 8–9. Have them write down which vehicle they think is different from the others and tell why it is different. Possible responses:

- **Bus:** the only one that is designed to carry many passengers
- **Oil truck:** the only one designed to carry liquid; has a bar and a valve on the top
- **Sports car:** the only one with a number on it; the only motor vehicle that is a convertible
- **Sedan:** the only one designed to carry about 4–5 people; the only purple vehicle
- **Dump truck:** only one whose body lifts up and is designed to dump things
- **Bicycle:** the only one that is not motorized; designed for one person; has two wheels
- **Fire truck:** the only one with a ladder that extends; the only motor vehicle without doors; has jacks for balance; has three wheels showing; has a siren
- **Crane:** the only one with a crane; designed to lift things; has a hook
- **Cement truck:** the only one that has a body that turns; carries cement

For additional practice, have students complete the **Various Vehicles** reproducible. In this worksheet, students read statements and compare them with the illustrations on pages 8–9 of *Anno's Math Games* to determine if they are true or false. This exercise helps them to think more critically when looking for unique attributes of each object. It also can provide an opportunity to test students' abilities to apply the concepts of sorting and classifying after they've tried it themselves.

Reproducible Master 106 with answers

Anno's Math Games: Chapter 1 — 106

Various Vehicles

Look at the pictures on pages 8 – 9. Tell whether each statement is *True* or *False* and explain why.

1. False ______ There is only one orange vehicle in the picture.
   The dump truck, crane, and sports car are orange.

2. True ______ There is only one orange car in the picture.

3. False ______ There is only one vehicle that has a ladder.
   The oil truck and the fire truck each have ladders.

4. True ______ There is only one vehicle that has handlebars.
   The bicycle.

5. False ______ There is only one vehicle that moves heavy materials.
   The dump truck, cement truck, and crane all move heavy materials.

Continued...

Reproducible Master 106 with answers (continued)

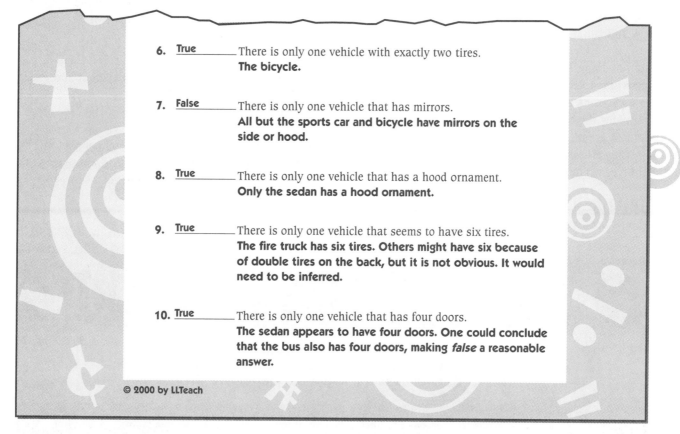

6. True ________ There is only one vehicle with exactly two tires.
The bicycle.

7. False ________ There is only one vehicle that has mirrors.
All but the sports car and bicycle have mirrors on the side or hood.

8. True ________ There is only one vehicle that has a hood ornament.
Only the sedan has a hood ornament.

9. True ________ There is only one vehicle that seems to have six tires.
The fire truck has six tires. Others might have six because of double tires on the back, but it is not obvious. It would need to be inferred.

10. True ________ There is only one vehicle that has four doors.
The sedan appears to have four doors. One could conclude that the bus also has four doors, making *false* a reasonable answer.

PAGES 10–19

These pages can be treated in the same manner as the previous pages by asking students to identify one object that is different from the rest and tell why it is different.

There are many connections to science in this section, especially for classification of living things. Focus on those pages that relate to science topics your class is studying.

EXAMPLES

- **pages 10–11:** land animals
  [Possible answer: one bird]
- **pages 12–13:** sea animals
  [Possible answer: one mushroom]
- **page 14:** flowers
  [Possible answer: one leaf]
- **page 15:** fruits
  [Possible answer: two cherries]
- **page 16:** insects
  [Possible answer: butterfly has no legs showing]
- **page 17:** kitchen utensils
  [Possible answer: one lock]
- **pages 18–19:** variety of creatures
  [Possible answer: one snail with no legs]

PAGES 20–21

These pages show the following pairs of mothers and babies:

Page 20	Page 21
chick	hen
frog	tadpole
grasshopper	nymph
praying mantis	nymph
nymph	locust
dragonfly	(missing)

Which one is different? **[Answers will vary depending on the attributes students point out.]**

- ***Which one does not have a baby and an adult shown?*** **[Answer: The dragonfly has no nymph.]**

APPLYING LOGIC SKILLS TO MATH

Materials

☑ **Tell What Is Different** (Reproducible Master 107)

Before doing this activity, complete several previous activities to ensure students are comfortable making comparisons and finding differences. This activity provides the opportunity to encourage risk taking and to use alternative thinking approaches to solving problems. (See Additional Resources for sources of more math examples like these.)

Tell the students that they are going to apply their classification skills to sets of math problems.

Distribute Tell What Is Different to individual students or small groups. Review the directions, explaining that each question has a set of four math problems. Three of the four problems fit a rule or pattern and one doesn't. Tell them it is their job to find the one that is different and to tell why.

You may want to first try some of the problems as a whole class. Any choice can be correct, as long as there is a logical answer to support it. The answers provided below give possible reasons that students might suggest for the various choices.

Reproducible Master 107 with answers

Anno's Math Games: Chapter 1 — 107

Tell What Is Different

For each set, circle the item that does not fit the rule or pattern. Explain why your choice is different from the others. [Accept any answer that makes sense. Suggested reasons are given below.]

1. **A.** $\frac{1}{4}$ **B.** $\frac{3}{5}$ **C.** $\frac{5}{4}$ **D.** $\frac{2}{8}$

Suggested reason: (A) The only unit fraction (has 1 as the numerator). For more suggestions see p. 257.

2. **A.** $6\overline{)4{,}786}$ **B.** $4\overline{)7{,}684}$ **C.** $5\overline{)6{,}874}$ **D.** $2\overline{)2{,}531}$

Suggested reason: (B) The only quotient without a remainder. For more suggestions see p. 257.

3.

A.	B.	C.	D.
3	4	3	4
4	4	5	8
2	6	3	2
+ 6	+ 4	+ 1	+ 6
15	**18**	**12**	**20**

Suggested reason: (C) The only one with all odd numbers as addends; or the only one without a pair of addends that add to 10. For more suggestions see p. 257.

4.

A.	B.	C.	D.
3,562	4,172	1,234	5,346
+ 2,653	+ 2,714	+ 2,143	+ 6,275
6,215	**6,886**	**3,377**	**11,621**

Suggested reason: (D) The only one that does not use the same digits in the top addend and the bottom addend; or the only one whose sum is greater than 10,000; the only one whose sum has five digits. For more suggestions see p. 257.

Continued...

Reproducible Master 107 with answers (continued)

5. **A.** **B.** **C.** **D.**

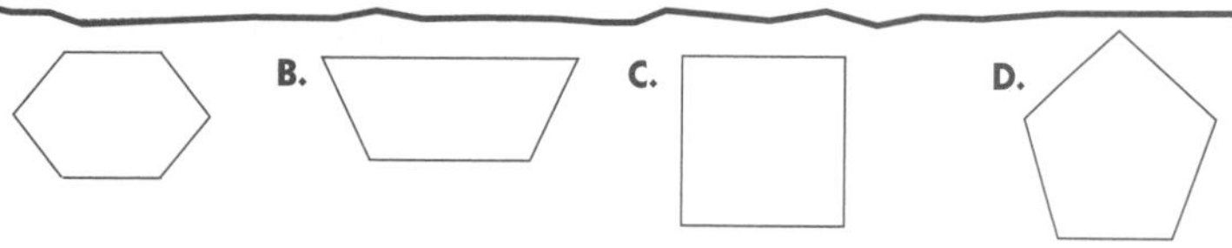

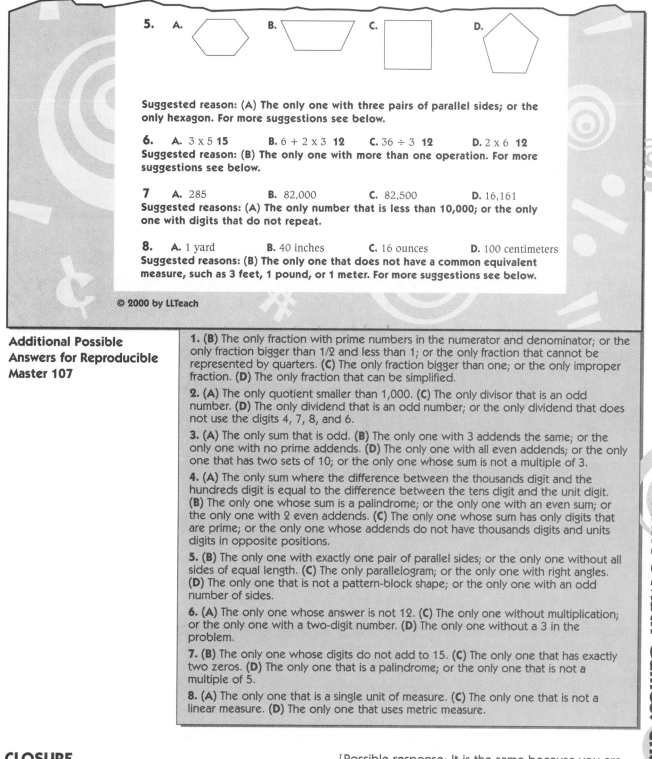

Suggested reason: (A) The only one with three pairs of parallel sides; or the only hexagon. For more suggestions see below.

6. **A.** 3 x 5 **15** **B.** 6 + 2 x 3 **12** **C.** 36 ÷ 3 **12** **D.** 2 x 6 **12**
Suggested reason: (B) The only one with more than one operation. For more suggestions see below.

7 **A.** 285 **B.** 82,000 **C.** 82,500 **D.** 16,161
Suggested reasons: (A) The only number that is less than 10,000; or the only one with digits that do not repeat.

8. **A.** 1 yard **B.** 40 inches **C.** 16 ounces **D.** 100 centimeters
Suggested reasons: (B) The only one that does not have a common equivalent measure, such as 3 feet, 1 pound, or 1 meter. For more suggestions see below.

Additional Possible Answers for Reproducible Master 107

1. (B) The only fraction with prime numbers in the numerator and denominator; or the only fraction bigger than 1/2 and less than 1; or the only fraction that cannot be represented by quarters. **(C)** The only fraction bigger than one; or the only improper fraction. **(D)** The only fraction that can be simplified.

2. (A) The only quotient smaller than 1,000. **(C)** The only divisor that is an odd number. **(D)** The only dividend that is an odd number; or the only dividend that does not use the digits 4, 7, 8, and 6.

3. (A) The only sum that is odd. **(B)** The only one with 3 addends the same; or the only one with no prime addends. **(D)** The only one with all even addends; or the only one that has two sets of 10; or the only one whose sum is not a multiple of 3.

4. (A) The only sum where the difference between the thousands digit and the hundreds digit is equal to the difference between the tens digit and the unit digit. **(B)** The only one whose sum is a palindrome; or the only one with an even sum; or the only one with 2 even addends. **(C)** The only one whose sum has only digits that are prime; or the only one whose addends do not have thousands digits and units digits in opposite positions.

5. (B) The only one with exactly one pair of parallel sides; or the only one without all sides of equal length. **(C)** The only parallelogram; or the only one with right angles. **(D)** The only one that is not a pattern-block shape; or the only one with an odd number of sides.

6. (A) The only one whose answer is not 12. **(C)** The only one without multiplication; or the only one with a two-digit number. **(D)** The only one without a 3 in the problem.

7. (B) The only one whose digits do not add to 15. **(C)** The only one that has exactly two zeros. **(D)** The only one that is a palindrome; or the only one that is not a multiple of 5.

8. (A) The only one that is a single unit of measure. **(C)** The only one that is not a linear measure. **(D)** The only one that uses metric measure.

CLOSURE

Have students respond to the following prompt in their math journals.

"Explain how playing **Tell What Is Different?** is similar to finding similarities and differences between the various objects shown in *Anno's Math Games.*"

[Possible response: It is the same because you are trying to find things in common but also trying to find things that make each situation special. They are also the same because, in both cases, we had to give reasons to support the answer.]

Composition Connection

WRITING A POST-READING COMPOSITION

Materials

Copy of the book (focus on illustrations on pages 20–21), **Connection to Writing Assessment: Post-Reading Composition** (Reproducible Master 108), **Have I...? Checklist** (Reproducible Master 2), **Rubric for Scoring First Drafts** (Reproducible Master 3)

Have students complete the following activity after finishing Chapter 1 of *Anno's Math Games*.

Give students the **Connection to Writing Assessment: Post-Reading Composition** along with a copy of the **Have I . . .? Checklist**.

Give students about 20 minutes in which to write the composition and edit/revise it based on the checklist.

Collect and score the students' compositions using the **Rubric for Scoring First Drafts**. Students may also be encouraged to put their scored drafts into a folder of "works in progress," which can be further edited and revised for sharing with an audience at some later date.

Reproducible Master 108

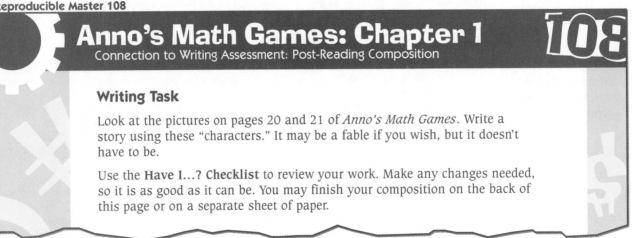

Anno's Math Games: Chapter 1

108

Connection to Writing Assessment: Post-Reading Composition

Writing Task

Look at the pictures on pages 20 and 21 of *Anno's Math Games*. Write a story using these "characters." It may be a fable if you wish, but it doesn't have to be.

Use the **Have I...? Checklist** to review your work. Make any changes needed, so it is as good as it can be. You may finish your composition on the back of this page or on a separate sheet of paper.

Extending the Connections

WRITING ACTIVITY: DEVELOPING SKILLS IN DESCRIPTIONS

Materials

Copies of the book (1 for each group of 2–4 students)

Have the students select a picture from any page in Chapter 1 of the book (pages 2–21). Ask them to write a vivid description of that picture. There are many rich options since the pictures are generally clear and direct.

Have students read their descriptions to one another and then store them in their "works in progress" folder. (See page *xxii* of this book for a description of this device.)

Students may choose to develop this description into a full story or composition; use it to remind themselves about how they used descriptive techniques; or incorporate the description into another writing piece that they develop later.

ADDITIONAL RESOURCES

Glatzer, Joyce and David J. *Math Connections: Activities for Grades 4–6*. Available from Cuisenaire. Call 1-800-237-0338.

Anno's Math Games

Overview of the Connections

Chapter 2: Putting Together and Taking Apart (pages 22–43) provides many opportunities for discussion and application of logic skills and making connections. Students gain an appreciation for divergent thinking and see that there are alternate ways to interpret the same things. The mathematics activities also will help students understand coordinates, graphs, tables, and charts, as well as partitioning in mathematics. They will apply these skills, along with those learned in Chapter 1, in a three-page Mathematics Assessment.

Language arts activities will develop students' skills in using details in writing.

Chapter 2
Putting Together and Taking Apart

MATERIALS FOR THE CONNECTIONS

Anno's Math Games • ISBN 0-698-11671-2
Written and illustrated by Mitsumasa Anno. New York: Putnam & Grosset Group, 1997.

Language Arts

~ Copies of the book (1 for each group of 2–4 students). (Note: In the Viewing Connection, each student will need to see page 31. You may wish to have several copies available.)

~ Optional: **Connection to Viewing Assessment: Writing About a Picture Prompt** (Reproducible Master 1)

~ **Have I...? Checklist** (Reproducible Master 2), a self-monitoring tool for student writers

~ **Rubric for Scoring First Drafts** (Reproducible Master 3)

~ **Connection to Writing Assessment: Post-Reading Composition** (Reproducible Master 117)

Mathematics

~ **Clothing Grid** (Reproducible Master 109)

~ Colored cubes or slips of colored paper (yellow, black, red, blue, green)

~ **Coordinates Table** (Reproducible Master 110)

~ **Thinking About the Coordinates Table** (Reproducible Master 111)

~ **6-by-6 Grid** (Reproducible Master 112)

~ **Shape Puzzle** (Reproducible Master 113)

~ **Connection to Mathematics Assessment: Check for Understanding I, II, and III** (Reproducible Master 114–116)

Viewing Connection

INTRODUCING THE LESSON WITH A PICTURE PROMPT AND WRITING

Materials

Copy of the book (page 31), **Connection to Viewing Assessment: Writing About a Picture Prompt** (Reproducible Master 1), **Have I...? Checklist** (Reproducible Master 2), **Rubric for Scoring First Drafts** (Reproducible Master 3)

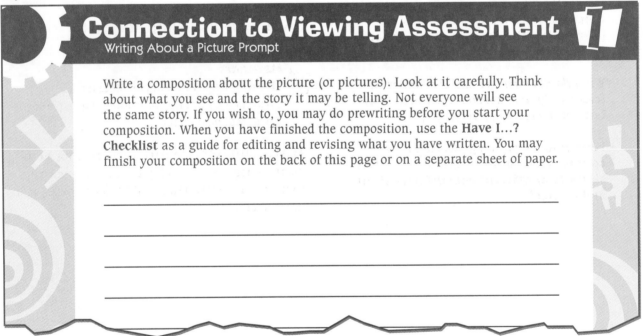

Show the class the pictures on page 31 with the text covered up. This page shows the characters, Kriss and Kross, with red suits. If possible, allow students to continue to look at the picture throughout the writing session. You may distribute a copy of **Connection to Viewing Assessment: Writing About a Picture Prompt** to each student, or they may use notebook paper for their work. Also distribute copies of the **Have I...? Checklist.**

Read these directions to the class:

"You are going to write a composition about this picture. Look at it carefully. Think about what you see and the story it may be telling. It is OK that not everyone will see the same story. If you wish to, you may do prewriting before you start your composition. When you have finished the composition, use the **Have I...? Checklist** as a guide for editing and revising what you have written."

Give the students 20–30 minutes to write their compositions and do initial editing.

Collect and score the students' compositions using the **Rubric for Scoring First Drafts**. Teach students how to compare their scored compositions to the rubric and to make notes about how to improve their compositions. Students also may be taught to use the rubric to score their own work or that of other students.

Reproducible Master 1

Connection to Viewing Assessment 1

Writing About a Picture Prompt

Write a composition about the picture (or pictures). Look at it carefully. Think about what you see and the story it may be telling. Not everyone will see the same story. If you wish to, you may do prewriting before you start your composition. When you have finished the composition, use the **Have I...? Checklist** as a guide for editing and revising what you have written. You may finish your composition on the back of this page or on a separate sheet of paper.

____

____

____

____

Mathematics Connection

INTRODUCTION AND ACTIVE READING

Materials

Several copies of the book (ideally, 1 for each group of 2–4 students),

As you read Chapter 2, pose questions and conduct activities as described in the book and in the guide below. Encourage students to practice active reading skills, such as asking questions, thinking to themselves, and discussing their ideas. Ensure that they understand that practicing effective reading means asking themselves questions while they read. You might choose to do some or all of the activities provided here.

PAGES 24–27

Why does the cat look so distressed in the picture on page 25? **[Possible answer: Cats and mice do not go together.]**

- *How is the "flying horse" different from the other combinations on pages 26–27?* **[Answer: It is the only one that is not at least part human.]**
- *What do the mermaid and the horseman (centaur) have in common?* **[Answer: They both play musical instruments.]**
- *What other mythical figures made from combinations can you name? How are they similar to or different from the ones shown in the book?*

PAGES 28–31

What two things were put together to make each object shown? **[Answer: (p. 29) umbrella and cane, jacket and pocketbook, pencil and eraser, knife and utensils; (p. 30) pen and ink, clock and bell, shoes and a shoehorn, hammer and claw.]**

- *What things did Kriss and Kross combine to make the red suits?* **[Answer: hat, gloves, shirt, pants, socks]**

PAGES 32–33

Wheels were placed on all the objects on page 32. Which ones don't make sense? Tell why. **[Possible answers: pencil, doghouse, wheel, and snail]**

- *Handles were placed on all the objects on page 33. Which objects do not need handles?* **[Answer: crocodile]**

PAGES 34–35: Using Words to Locate Objects on a Grid

Materials

Clothing Grid (Reproducible Master 109), colored cubes or slips of colored paper (yellow, black, red, blue, green)

Have children identify various items in the chart on page 34 by naming the column and the row, such as yellow hat, red shirt, black socks, and green shoes.

Distribute Clothing Grid sheets and colored cubes or slips of paper to students. Have them place cubes or paper on the **Clothing Grid** to represent each of the character's outfits on page 35.

EXAMPLE

The outfit of the top right child can be represented by:

- black cube in hat row in the black column
- yellow cube in shirt row in the yellow column
- black cube in skirt/pants row in the black column
- blue cube in sock row in the blue column
- green cube in shoe row in the green column

Ask:

Which people will have cubes in the same column? Why? **[Answer: All four will have cubes in the yellow, black, and blue columns because they all are wearing those colors; the first and third children will have cubes in the red column; the first, second, and fourth children will have cubes in the green column.]**

Have students also practice naming coordinates, using the **Clothing Grid** and colored cubes.

EXAMPLE

"Place a cube in the grid that that would show the yellow hat."

"Place a cube in the grid that would show the blue shoes."

PAGES 34–35: Using Numbers to Locate Objects on a Grid

Materials

Coordinates Table (Reproducible Master 110), **Clothing Grid** (Reproducible Master 109), copies of the book (enough for each group of 2–4 students)

To extend the use of grids, change the notation from words and visual descriptions to numbers. Use the numbers 1–5 for the columns, starting with 1 on the left and ending with 5 on the right. Use the numbers 1–5 for the rows, starting with 1 on the bottom and 5 on the top. Each square then gets a coordinate, by naming the column first and the row second. Thus, the red shirt is located at (3,4). It's in the third column and the fourth row.

Distribute a copy of **Coordinates Table** and **Thinking About the Coordinates Table** to each student or small group. You might also provide copies of the **Clothing Grid** worksheet, on which students can number the rows and columns. If possible, provide copies of the book to individuals or small groups of students.

Check student understanding by asking:

What object has the coordinates (4,5)? **[Answer: blue hat]**

- ***What object has the coordinates (1,3)?*** **[Answer: yellow skirt/pants]**

Have students look at the children on page 35 of the book. Ask them to give the coordinates in the grid for each article of clothing that the children and Kross (the character on the bottom left) are wearing. Tell students to use the **Coordinates Table** to help them organize their responses to the questions on **Thinking About the Coordinates Table**, which appears on page 264.

Anno's Math Games: Chapter 2

110

Coordinates Table

Name the coordinates for each article of clothing the children and Kross are wearing on page 35. Start with the child on the top left.

Object	Coordinates
Blue hat	(4,5)
Green shirt	(5,4)
Red shirt	(3,3)
Yellow socks	(1,2)
Black shoes	(2,1)
Yellow hat	(1,5)
Blue shirt	(4,4)
Black pants	(2,3)
Green socks	(5,2)
Blue shoes	(4,1)
Red hat	(3,5)
Red shirt	(3,4)
Blue skirt	(4,3)
Black socks	(2,2)
Yellow shoes	(1,1)
Black hat	(2,5)
Yellow shirt	(1,4)
Black pants	(2,3)
Blue socks	(4,2)
Green shoes	(5,1)
Yellow hat	(1,5)
Black shirt	(2,4)
Red skirt	(3,3)
Blue socks	(4,2)
Yellow shoes	(1,1)

Anno's Math Games: Chapter 2

111

Thinking About the Coordinates Table

Use the Coordinates Table you completed for the articles of clothing the children and Kross are wearing. Study the number pairs in the table by looking at sets of five. Each set of five represents a complete outfit: hat, shirt, skirt or pants, socks, and shoes. Answer the questions below.

1. What pattern do you see in the second numbers in each set of five coordinate pairs? Why do you think that pattern occurs?
   Answers: Each number appears in the same order from 5 to 1. The second number in each pair identifies a different article of clothing, and the order of clothing given in each set is the same.

2. What does it mean if two coordinate pairs within a set of five have the same first number?
   Answer: The person must be wearing at least two articles of clothing that are the same color.

3. Why can't the second numbers of the coordinate pairs in a set of five be the same?
   Answer: Because no one is wearing two of any article of clothing.

4. What outfit would you be wearing if your clothing had the coordinates: (3,5), (1,4), (5,3), (4,2), and (2,1)?
   Answer: red hat, yellow shirt, green pants or skirt, blue socks, and black shoes

5. José read the clothing coordinates (3,5), (3,4), (3,3), (3,2), and (3,1). He knew immediately that the entire outfit is all one color. How did José arrive at that conclusion?
   Answer: He saw that the first numbers in the coordinate pairs are all the same, and he knows the first number identifies color.

PAGES 36–37

Materials

Copies of the book, **6-by-6 Grid** (Reproducible Master 112), connecting cubes

Distribute two copies of the **6-by-6 Grid** and connecting cubes to each student. As a class or in small groups, have students complete the outer rows and columns with the words and objects from the grids on pages 36 and 37.

As you read pages 36 and 37, have students place connecting cubes in the squares that represent the descriptions. Provide additional descriptions for students to locate on the grids.

EXAMPLES (PAGE 36)

"a chimney placed on a dog house"
"a bell placed on an elephant"
"a donkey with a rearview mirror"

EXAMPLES (PAGE 37)

"black whale"
"very tasty carrot"
"lost lollipop"

PAGES 38–43: Making and Using Shape Puzzles

Materials

Copies of the book (1 for each small group if possible), construction paper cut into 5-cm squares, scissors (optional). Alternative: **Shape Puzzle** (Reproducible Master 113), scissors

These pages provide exercises using manipulatives similar to tangrams, but with fewer pieces. Tell students they are going to reconstruct the puzzle square shown on page 38.

Provide each student with a 5-cm square of construction paper. Follow the directions below to make a square similar in size to the one in the book. (As an alternative, you may wish to simply provide copies of the reproducible **Shape Puzzle** for students to cut out and use in the activity.)

DIRECTIONS

1. Fold the square in half to make two rectangles. Weaken the crease by folding back and forth along it. Tear or cut the pieces apart.
2. Take one of the rectangles formed and fold it in half to make two squares. Weaken the crease and tear or cut the pieces apart.
3. Take one of the squares and fold it on an angle to form two triangles. Weaken the crease and tear or cut the pieces apart.
4. Take the remaining large rectangle and fold it in half, but this time just crimp the midpoint. Fold one corner over to meet the midpoint (crimp) on the opposite side. This forms a triangle and a trapezoid. Weaken the crease and tear or cut the pieces apart.
5. Put the shapes together to form the original larger square.

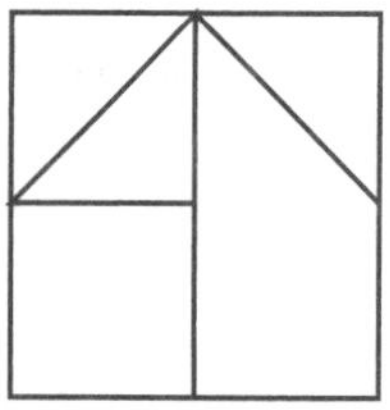

As you read pages 38–43 have children try to make each of the shapes shown. [The solutions to these constructions are found on page 95 of *Anno's Math Games.*]

PAGES 38-43: Practice with Fractions

Materials

Shape Puzzle (Reproducible Master 113)

Establish the "shape puzzle" as a model for fractions by discussing and extending the questions on the **Shape Puzzle** reproducible:

If the entire square is one unit, what is the fractional area of each of the pieces?

[Answer: The triangles are each $\frac{1}{8}$, the trapezoid is $\frac{3}{8}$, and the square is $\frac{1}{4}$ or $\frac{2}{8}$.]

Develop the idea of using models to add fractions by giving problems similar to the following:

Combine one triangle with the square to form a trapezoid. What is the fractional area of this trapezoid? Explain how you know. **[Answer: This right trapezoid has an area equal to $\frac{3}{8}$.]**

- ***How could you show this same problem using fractional notation?*** **[Answer: $\frac{1}{4} + \frac{1}{8} = \frac{3}{8}$]**

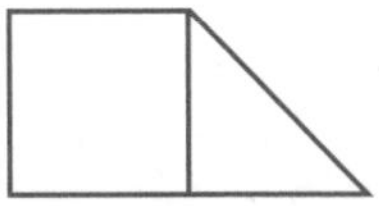

- ***What is the sum of the fractional areas of the trapezoid and the square?*** **[$\frac{5}{8}$]**

- ***How could you show this same problem using fractional notation?*** **[Answer: $\frac{3}{8} + \frac{1}{4} = \frac{5}{8}$]**

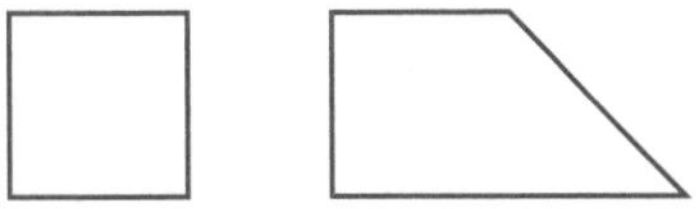

- ***What is the sum of the trapezoid and the triangle?*** **[$\frac{1}{2}$]**

- ***How could you show this same problem using fractional notation?*** **[Answer: $\frac{3}{8} + \frac{1}{8} = \frac{4}{8}$ or $\frac{1}{2}$]**

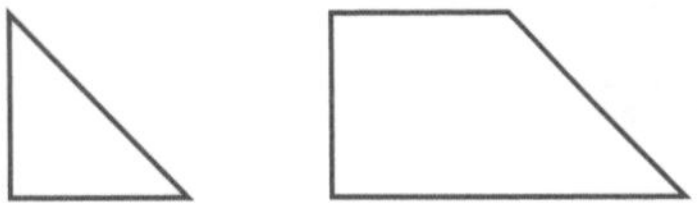

- ***How can you make a trapezoid whose sum is $\frac{1}{2}$?*** **[Answer: Use two triangles and the square to make an isosceles trapezoid.]**

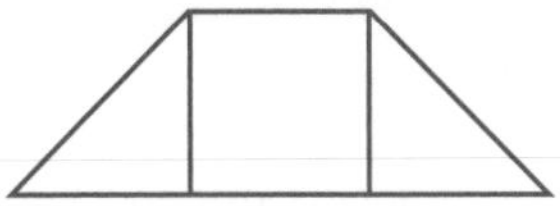

- ***How can you make a triangle whose area is equal to $\frac{1}{4}$?*** **[Answer: Combine the two small triangles to make one large triangle.]**

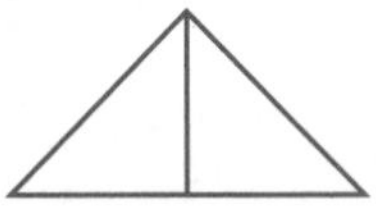

- ***How can you make a triangle whose area is equal to $\frac{1}{2}$?*** **[Answer: Combine the square and two small triangles.]**

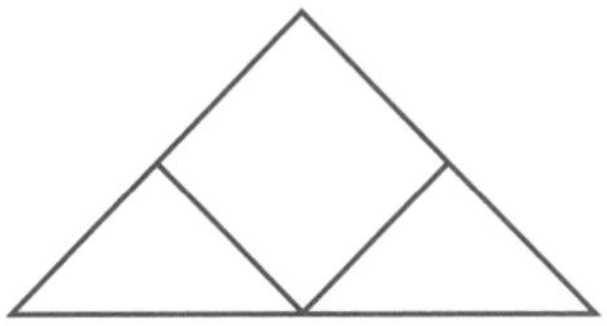

MATHEMATICS ASSESSMENT

Materials

Connection to Mathematics Assessment: Check for Understanding I, II, and III (Reproducible Masters 114–116), rulers

Distribute the worksheets with multiple-choice and open-ended questions called **Connection to Mathematics Assessment: Check for Understanding I, II, and III**. This activity can be used to check students' understanding of the mathematics concepts covered in this lesson.

Collect and score the students' work using the answers and rubric on the following pages.

Reproducible Master 114 with answers

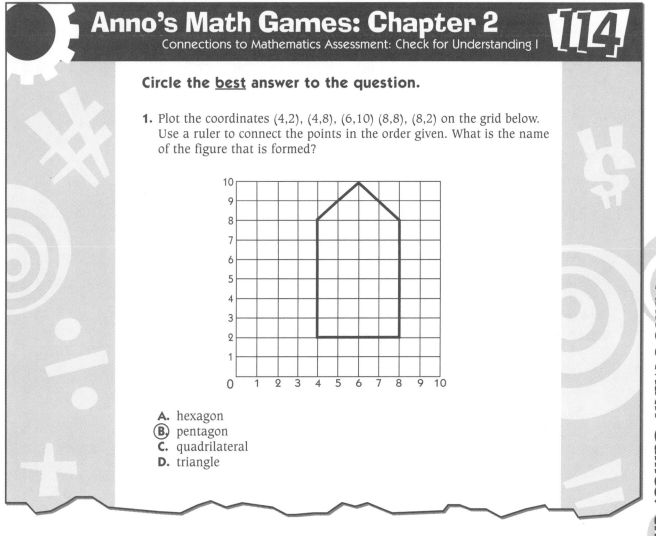

Anno's Math Games: Chapter 2

114

Connections to Mathematics Assessment: Check for Understanding I

Circle the best answer to the question.

1. Plot the coordinates (4,2), (4,8), (6,10) (8,8), (8,2) on the grid below. Use a ruler to connect the points in the order given. What is the name of the figure that is formed?

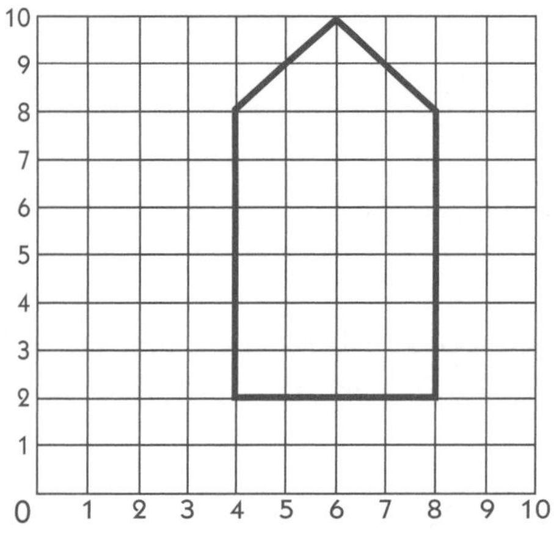

A. hexagon
(B.) pentagon
C. quadrilateral
D. triangle

Anno's Math Games: Chapter 2

Connection to Mathematics Assessment: Check for Understanding II

115

Circle the best answer to each question. Use the diagram below to answer questions 2–4.

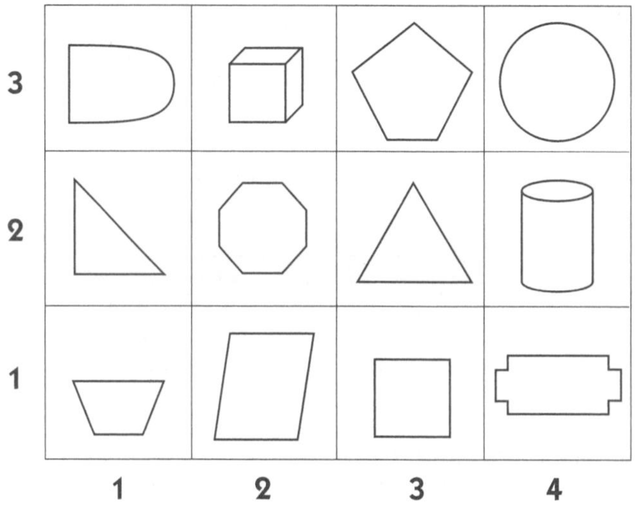

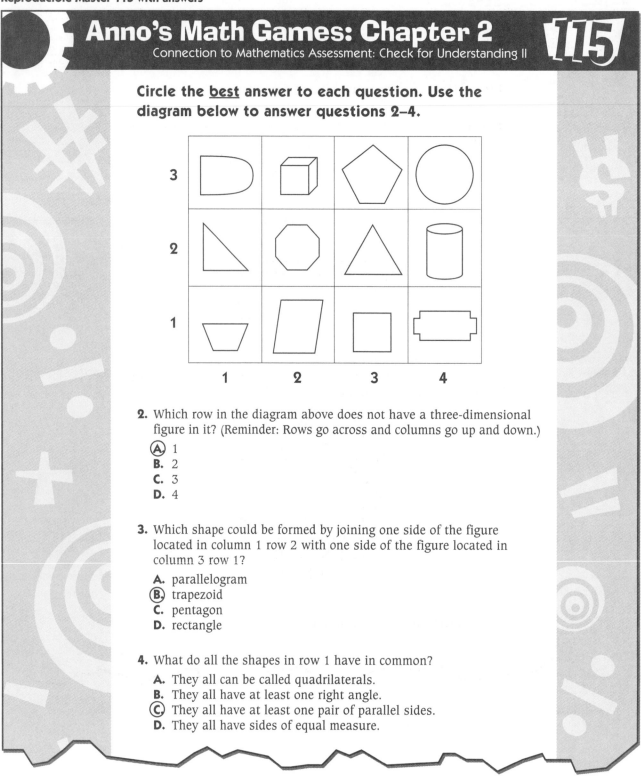

2. Which row in the diagram above does not have a three-dimensional figure in it? (Reminder: Rows go across and columns go up and down.)
   A. 1
   B. 2
   C. 3
   D. 4

3. Which shape could be formed by joining one side of the figure located in column 1 row 2 with one side of the figure located in column 3 row 1?
   A. parallelogram
   B. trapezoid
   C. pentagon
   D. rectangle

4. What do all the shapes in row 1 have in common?
   A. They all can be called quadrilaterals.
   B. They all have at least one right angle.
   C. They all have at least one pair of parallel sides.
   D. They all have sides of equal measure.

Anno's Math Games: Chapter 2

Connection to Mathematics Assessment: Check for Understanding III

116

Circle the best answer to each question.

5. What is the sum of the numbers located in column 3 row 4 plus column 1 row 5?

5	3	6	9	12	15
4	2	4	6	8	10
3	5	10	15	20	25
2	2	3	5	7	11
1	4	8	16	32	64
	1	**2**	**3**	**4**	**5**

(A.) 9
B. 70
C. 84
D. 23

6. Plot the coordinates (4,0), (8,4), (4,8), (0,4) on the grid below. Use a ruler to connect the points in the order given. What is the area of the square you have drawn? Explain how you know.

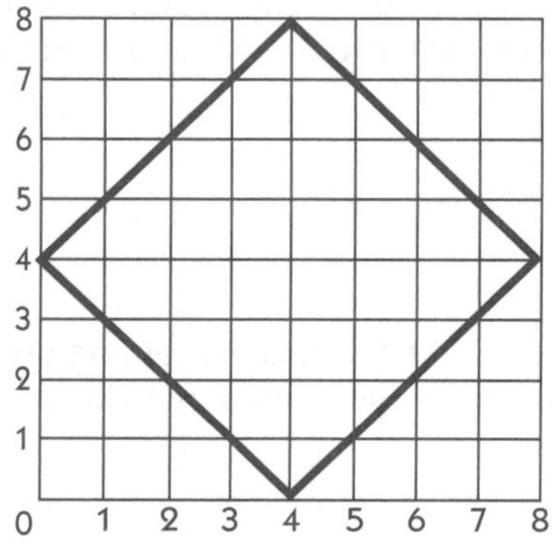

see rubric that follows for scoring

RUBRIC FOR SCORING

Question 6

An effective response will need to:

- show that the area is 32 square units.
- give a clear explanation.

POINTS	CRITERIA
3	Student indicates the area of the rectangle to be 32 square units and provides a clear explanation of how the solution was determined. Possible responses: Example 1 *The area of the square equals 32 square units. I know this because I counted all the full squares inside the square I drew and found there were 24 squares. I then counted the half squares and got a total of 16 halves or 8 squares. I added the two amounts for a total of 32 squares.* Example 2 *I drew four triangles inside the square. The lines broke the grid into four squares (quadrants) each having an area of 16 square units. The area of each triangle is half of each of the squares formed, so 16 square units divided by 2 is 8 square units. Since there were four triangles, I found a total of 32 square units (8 x 4).* Example 3 *I counted the squares and half-squares in each of the outside triangles and found the area of each one to be 8 square units. Since there were four of them I knew they totaled 32 square units. The whole grid is 8 x 8 or 64, so 64 – 32 = 32.*
2	The student indicates the area to be 32 square units, but provides an explanation that is somewhat unclear. OR The student does not have the correct answer, but the explanation indicates a clear understanding of the underlying concept of area and the process that was needed to solve the problem.
1	The student indicates the area to be 32 square units, but provides no explanation or provides an explanation that has flaws or has major gaps. OR The student does not have the correct answer, but the explanation indicates some understanding of the concepts and process needed to determine the answer.
0	The student shows no understanding of the problem or leaves it blank.

Composition Connection

WRITING A POST-READING COMPOSITION

Materials

Copy of the book (focus on illustration on page 23), **Connection to Writing Assessment: Post-Reading Composition** (Reproducible Master 117), **Have I...? Checklist** (Reproducible Master 2), **Rubric for Scoring First Drafts** (Reproducible Master 3)

To practice skills in "using writing to interpret text," have students complete the following activity.

Give students the **Connection to Writing Assessment: Post-Reading Composition** along with a copy of the **Have I...? Checklist**.

Give students about 25 minutes in which to write the composition and edit/revise it based on the checklist.

Collect and score the students' compositions using the **Rubric for Scoring First Drafts**. Students may also be encouraged to put their scored drafts into a folder of "works in progress," which can be further edited and revised for sharing with an audience at some later date.

Reproducible Master 117

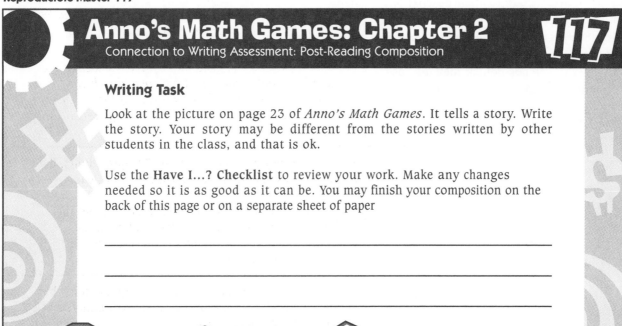

Anno's Math Games: Chapter 2

Connection to Writing Assessment: Post-Reading Composition

117

Writing Task

Look at the picture on page 23 of *Anno's Math Games*. It tells a story. Write the story. Your story may be different from the stories written by other students in the class, and that is ok.

Use the **Have I...? Checklist** to review your work. Make any changes needed so it is as good as it can be. You may finish your composition on the back of this page or on a separate sheet of paper

____

____

____

Extending the Connections

WRITING ACTIVITY: Developing Skill in Descriptions

Materials
Copies of the book

Have the students select a picture from any page in Chapter 2 of *Anno's Math Games*. Have them write a vivid description of that picture.

Before they write their own descriptions, you may want to use a class writing activity to model writing a vivid description. There are many rich options since the pictures are generally clear and direct.

Have students read their descriptions to one another and keep them in their "works in progress" folder. (See page *xxii* for a description of this device.) They may choose to develop this description into a full story or composition, or they may use it to remind themselves about using descriptive techniques. Finally, they may choose to incorporate the description into another writing piece that they develop later.

Anno's Math Games

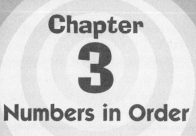

Overview of the Connections

Chapter 3: *Numbers in Order* (pages 44–67) asks students to look for patterns in numbers, colors, and shapes. Students are encouraged to use ordinal numbers and the directional descriptions *left* and *right* to identify locations in various coordinate grids. Card games provide engaging practice opportunities for students to apply the skills of sorting, ordering, and using coordinates. This chapter builds foundational skills in mathematics and therefore no Mathematics Assessment is provided.

Both the Viewing and Composition Connections provide timed writing activities that require observation skills. Through observation, students become better writers as they apply the concept of "interpreting text and illustrations" to writing their own compositions.

Chapter 3

Numbers in Order

MATERIALS FOR THE CONNECTIONS

Anno's Math Games • ISBN 0-698-11671-2

Written and illustrated by Mitsumasa Anno. New York: Putnam & Grosset Group, 1997.

Language Arts

~ Copies of the book (preferably 1 for each group of 2–4 students)

~ Optional: **Connection to Viewing Assessment: Writing About a Picture Prompt** (Reproducible Master 1)

~ **Have I...? Checklist** (Reproducible Master 2), a self-monitoring tool for student writers

~ **Rubric for Scoring First Drafts** (Reproducible Master 3)

~ **Connection to Writing Assessment: Post-Reading Composition** (Reproducible Master 121)

Mathematics

~ Playing cards (1 deck for each group of 2–3 students)

~ **Theater Seats** (Reproducible Master 118)

~ **Game Rules** (Reproducible Master 119)

~ **Suits-and-Numbers Grid** (Reproducible Master 120)

~ Graph paper

Viewing Connection

INTRODUCING THE LESSON WITH A PICTURE PROMPT AND WRITING

Materials

Copy of the book (pages 54–55), **Connection to Viewing Assessment: Writing About a Picture Prompt** (Reproducible Master 1), **Have I...? Checklist** (Reproducible Master 2), **Rubric for Scoring First Drafts** (Reproducible Master 3)

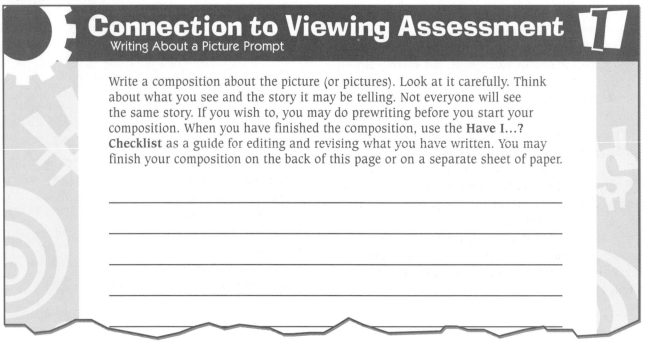

Show the class the pictures on pages 54–55 with the text covered. This two-page spread shows a scene of an apartment building and playground. If possible, allow students to continue to look at the picture throughout the writing session. You may distribute a copy of **Connection to Viewing Assessment: Writing About a Picture Prompt** to each student, or they may use notebook paper for their work. Also distribute copies of the **Have I...? Checklist**.

Read these directions to the class:

"You are going to write a composition about this picture. Look at it carefully. Think about what you see and the story it may be telling. It is OK that not everyone will see the same story. If you wish to, you may do prewriting before you start your composition. When you have finished the composition, use the **Have I...? Checklist** as a guide for editing and revising what you have written."

Give the students 20–30 minutes to write their compositions and do initial editing.

Collect and score the students' compositions using the **Rubric for Scoring First Drafts**. Teach students how to compare their scored compositions to the rubric and to make notes about how to improve their compositions. Students also may be taught to use the rubric to score their own work or that of other students.

Reproducible Master 1

Connection to Viewing Assessment 1

Writing About a Picture Prompt

Write a composition about the picture (or pictures). Look at it carefully. Think about what you see and the story it may be telling. Not everyone will see the same story. If you wish to, you may do prewriting before you start your composition. When you have finished the composition, use the **Have I...? Checklist** as a guide for editing and revising what you have written. You may finish your composition on the back of this page or on a separate sheet of paper.

Mathematics Connection

INTRODUCTION AND ACTIVE READING

Materials

Several copies of the book (ideally, 1 for each pair or group of 2–4 students)

As you read Chapter 3, pose questions and conduct activities as described in the book and in the guide below. Encourage them to practice active reading skills, such as asking questions, thinking to themselves, and discussing their ideas. Ensure they understand that practicing effective reading means asking themselves questions while they read. You might choose to do some or all of the activities provided here.

PAGES 46–49

Materials

Deck of cards for each group

If needed, discuss the structure of a deck of standard playing cards. Discuss the four suits in a deck by showing the cards being created on pages 46–47. Be sure students can clearly identify the symbols for each suit and name them as *hearts*, *clubs*, *spades*, or *diamonds*. Point out which suits are red and which are black.

Be sure that students also understand the numbering system of playing cards. Each suit has 13 cards. There are four suits, thus making a deck of 52 cards. If you count *jokers*, there are 54 cards. The *ace* stands for 1. The numbers 2–10 have a corresponding number of symbols and a numeral on them. The *jack* stands for 11. The *queen* stands for 12. The *king* stands for 13.

You might distribute cards from a deck for students to examine. Have small groups sort the decks by suit and then order the cards in each suit from 1–13.

Tell the children to study the cards on pages 48 and 49. Ask them to describe the cards that are incorrect.

Cards may be incorrect because the number of symbols does not match the numeral; because colors are incorrect; or because a numeral is missing. Note that the card Kriss is holding does not exist in a regular deck of cards.

Ask students to make up number sentences that could show how to correct the number of symbols on the card when they do not equal the number indicated.

EXAMPLE

The five of clubs is missing 1 club. A number sentence for the correction is 4 + ■ = 5. [1]

The cards on pages 48–49 (from left to right) are listed below. Any errors and suggested corrections also are given.

- The five of clubs is missing 1 club.
  4 + ■ = 5 [1]
- The four of diamonds is OK.
- Both spades on the two of spades should be black.
- The eight of clubs is OK.
- The three of spades is OK.
- The seven of hearts is missing 1 heart.
  6 + ■ = 7 [1]
- The ten of hearts is missing 1 heart.
  9 + ■ = 10 [1]
- The nine of spades is OK.
- The 15 of diamonds is not real a card. Card numerals stop at 10. The diamond is black and it should be red. Kross is not a character found in a regular deck of cards.
- The five of diamonds is OK.
- The six of spades is OK.
- The eight of diamonds is OK.
- The numeral 6 is missing on the six of hearts.

PAGES 50–51: Using Coordinates to Locate Cards with Errors

Tell the students to look at pages 50–51 and find the errors. Have them use coordinates to identify the locations of the cards with mistakes. They should name the column first and the row second. Tell them that column 1 is on the far left and row 1 is at the bottom.

As an alternative, you may want to give the coordinates below and ask the students to find that card and describe what is wrong. The incorrect cards are given row by row, from left to right.

ROW 1

(3,1) The five of spades has one red spade, which should be black.
(4,1) The five of clubs is missing 1 club.

ROW 2

(1,2) The eight of diamonds is missing 6 diamonds.
(6,2) The seven of spades is missing 2 spades.

ROW 3

(1,3) The nine of clubs is missing 1 club.
(2,3) The six of diamonds has 4 black diamonds that should be red.
(4,3) The seven of spades has 6 red spades that should be black.

ROW 4

(6,4) The seven of clubs is missing 1 club.

PAGES 52–53

Ask students to locate some of the cards on the two-page display. Use coordinate locators formed by combining ordinals and directions, such as *fourth from the left* or *third from the right in the bottom row.*

What card is third from the left in the top row? **[Answer: seven of spades]**

- ***What card is fourth from the right in the bottom row?*** **[Answer: seven of hearts]**
- ***What is the location of the five of hearts?*** **[Answer: sixth from the left or fifth from the right in the bottom row]**
- ***What is the location of the queen of spades?*** **[Answer: first from the right or tenth from the left in the top row]**

Transfer this concept to using coordinate numbers. Label the top row 1 and the bottom row 0. Number the columns 1 to 10 starting from the left.

What card has the coordinates of (9,0)? **[Answer: ten of clubs]**

- ***What card has the coordinates of (7,1)?*** **[Answer: ten of spades]**
- ***What are the coordinates of the two of spades?*** **[Answer: (6,1)]**
- ***What are the coordinates of the six of clubs?*** **[Answer: (5,0)]**

PAGES 54–55

Using descriptors similar to those presented in the story, ask questions such as:

What is the location of the parrot? **[Answer: seventh from the left or second from the right on the sixth floor]**

- ***What is the location of the birdhouse?*** **[Answer: second from the left or seventh from the right on the fourth floor]**
- ***What is in the window of the apartment that is third from the left on the first floor?*** **[Answer: clock]**

PAGES 56–58

These pages provide more practice naming locations of objects using coordinates. They differ from previous pages in that the objects in building number 3 can only be seen when the page is turned. Thus, the coordinates are reversed on the back of the page. In other words, what was to the right on page 57 will be to the left on page 58 and vice versa.

Give students locations in each building using methods similar to those given previously.

PAGES 59–61

Materials

Theater Seats (Reproducible Master 118)

Before reading and showing pages 59–61, point out to students that so far they have been using only two descriptors or numbers to identify locations. Explain that there are situations where two descriptors or numbers are insufficient. For example, at stadiums or large theaters you need three descriptors, or numbers, to identify a seating location, such as "row 5, seat 12, in red section."

Encourage students to share their experiences going to events at stadiums or auditoriums. Ask if they had tickets with section numbers, as well as row and seat numbers. Point out the seat descriptors shown on the tickets on page 59 of *Anno's Math Games*.

Distribute copies of **Theater Seats** to each student. This chart is a replica of the one shown on pages 60–61 of the book. Have students refer to this sheet as you read pages 59–61 aloud. (Sections are from left to right: Hearts, Spades, Diamonds, and Clubs. Rows are numbered from front to back, so row 1 is closest to the stage and row 10 is farthest away. Seats are numbered from left to right, with 1 at the start of each row in each section.)

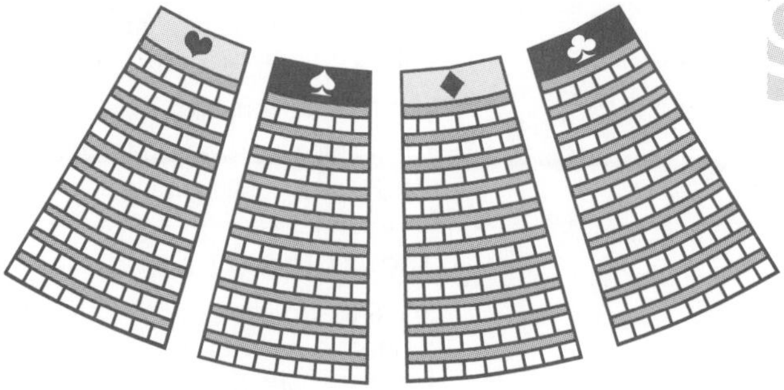

PAGES 59–61: Playing the Theater Seating Game

Materials

Playing cards (1 deck for each group of 2–3 students), **Theater Seats** (Reproducible Master 118), **Game Rules** (Reproducible Master 119)

This game provides practice using a three-level coordinate system. You may want to have the class practice locating a few seats before playing the game in small groups. Use the examples below to assess understanding of the coordinate system.

(♣,3,6)
(♦,10,2)
(♥,4,8)
(♣,9,1)

Anno's Math Games: Chapter 3

Game Rules

119

Materials: Deck of playing cards, **Theater Seats** game board, **Game Rules**

PREPARATION

- Separate the people cards (jacks, queens, and kings) from the deck into one pile.
- Sort the rest of the deck into suits, making four sets of ten number cards each.
- Shuffle each suit of number cards separately.
- Place the number cards face up in four stacks (one for each suit).
- Shuffle the people cards.
- Place the people cards face down in one stack.
- Decide on an allotted time for playing the game.

ABOUT THE GAME BOARD

Sections are from left to right: Hearts, Spades, Diamonds, and Clubs. Rows are numbered from front to back, so row 1 is closest to the stage and row 10 is farthest away. Seats are numbered from left to right, with 1 at the start of each row in each section.

PLAY THE GAME

To play, 2–3 players take turns doing the following steps.

Step 1 Choose a people card from the face-down stack. The suit of this card tells the section of the theater your seat is in—Hearts, Spades, Diamonds, or Clubs.

Step 2 Go to the stack of number cards that is the same suit as the card from Step 1. Choose the top two number cards from that stack.*

Step 3 Look at the first number card you choose. This tells you the row of your seat. The second number card gives the seat number in that row.

Step 4 Find your seat on the game board and write your initials on the seat. If that seat location does not exist or is taken, you lose your turn.

Step 5 The next player does Steps 1 to 4. Play continues for the allotted time.

*Note: If there are no more cards in a stack, reshuffle and use them over again.

HOW TO SCORE POINTS

When a player has three seats in one section he or she wins points. To figure your points, add all the coordinate numbers of the three seats together. Check off those seats so you don't score them twice. The person with the most points at the end of the game wins.

EXAMPLE PLAY

Sue chooses the queen of hearts. Then she draws two cards from the Hearts number stack. She draws a five of hearts and then a three of hearts. She writes her initials on the seat in row 5, seat 2 of the Hearts section. After three turns Sue has initials on three seats in Hearts section. She adds together (5 + 2) + (10 + 3) + (4 + 1) to score 25 points.

PAGES 62–63

Materials

Optional: **Suits-and-Numbers Grid** (Reproducible Master 120); crayons or color pencils (green, pink, blue, yellow)

These pages present a variation on using three-level coordinates. You may wish to provide copies of the **Suits-and-Numbers Grid** for students to color and use as you read pages 62–63.

Read pages 62–63 aloud. Have student pairs work together to create a system for naming and locating the squares on the grid.

EXAMPLE

Say that P = pink, B = blue, Y = yellow, and G = green. The number 3, on top of the Clubs, in pink square is located at (P,♣,3).

Ask:

Why do you need a combination of three identifiers to locate each square?
[Answer: Because the numbers and suits are repeated over and over. If you name just a suit and/or number, it does not describe the exact location.]

PAGES 64–65

Materials

Optional: **Suits-and-Numbers Grid** (Reproducible Master 120)

Have students study the town that is drawn on pages 64–65. Tell them to compare this map to the grid on page 63 or to the **Suits-and-Numbers Grid**.

Ask:

How is the map similar to or different from the Suits-and-Numbers Grid?
[Possible answers: The colors of the roads correspond to the colors of the sections on the Suits-and-Numbers Grid. There are no gaps between the squares on the grid, but the roads create gaps on the map. Not all of the houses are numbered, but you can figure out the numbers by looking at the Suits-and-Numbers Grid.]

- ***What is the property like at (Y,♠,4)?***
  [Answer: It's an empty lot where people are playing baseball.]

EXTENDING PAGES 64–65: Develop a New Coordinate System

Tell students that the town has grown tired of using three symbols for property addresses. They've decided to use two numbers instead. They divided the town into columns and rows. Column numbers start with 1 on the left and go to 8 on the right. The row numbers start on the bottom with 1 and go to 8 at the top. In an address, the first number tells the column and the second tells the row.

Ask:

Using this new system, describe the property with the address (7,6). What was the old address for this property?
[Answers: A house with a purple roof and a picnic set in the yard. The old address was (B,♣,1).]

- ***What is the house like at address (2,4)? What was the old address for this property?***
  [Answers: A house with a red roof and a slide in the yard. The old address was (P,♠,2).]
- ***What are the new addresses of the four empty lots?*** **[Answer: (2,2), (3,5), (5,3) and (5,5)]**
- ***What is the new address for (B,♠,2)?***
  [Answer: (6,8)]
- ***What is the new address for (P,♥,1)?***
  [Answer: (3,4)]
- ***What is the new address for (Y,♦, 2)?***
  [Answer: (6,2)]
- ***What is the old address for (8,6)?***
  [Answer: (B,♣,2)]
- ***What is the old address for (4,8)?***
  [Answer: G,♥,2)]
- ***What is the old address for (2,5)?***
  [Answer: G,♦,3)]

PAGES 66–67

Give the locations of the cards that are missing on pages 66–67 by naming the column number first and the row second. Use the numbers 1 to 13 for the column numbers beginning with the 1 on the left. Use the suits to name the rows.

Ask:

- ***What card should be below (10,♣)?***
  [Answer: The ten of diamonds.]

- ***What card should be below (3,♠)?***
  [Answer: The three of hearts.]

- ***What are the coordinates for each of the missing cards?***
  [Answer: (4,♦), (10,♦), (6,♣), (9,♣), (1,♥), (3,♥), (12,♥)]

CLOSURE

Materials
Graph paper

Discuss the different ways students have explored locating places using coordinates. Point out that in *Anno's Math Games: Chapter 3*, they used letters, symbols, and numbers.

Use graph paper to present a 10-by-10 coordinate plane to the class. Explain that sometimes the lines will be numbered instead of the squares, so points where the lines cross can be located.

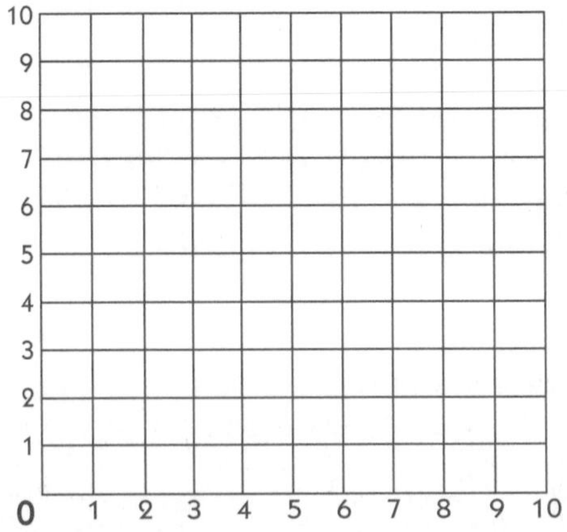

Ask question such as:

- ***How can you plot the point (4,6)?*** **[Answer: draw a dot on the fourth line over and the sixth line up]**

- ***How is this system similar to the systems we have been using?***
  [Answer: It uses two numbers to find a location.]

- ***How is this system different from the systems we have been using?***
  [Answer: It locates points instead of squares.]

Composition Connection

WRITING A POST-READING COMPOSITION

Materials

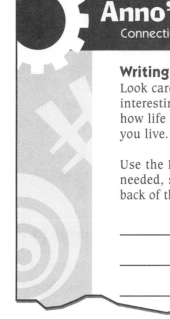

Copy of the book (focus on illustrations on pages 64-65), **Connection to Writing Assessment: Post-Reading Composition** (Reproducible Master 1), **Have I...? Checklist** (Reproducible Master 2), **Rubric for Scoring First Drafts** (Reproducible Master 3)

Give students the **Connection to Writing Assessment: Post-Reading Composition** along with a copy of the **Have I...? checklist**.

Give students about 30 minutes in which to write the composition and edit/revise it based on the checklist.

Collect and score the students' compositions using the **Rubric for Scoring First Drafts**.

Reproducible Master 121

Anno's Math Games: Chapter 3

Connection to Writing Assessment: Post-Reading Composition

121

Writing Task

Look carefully at the picture on pages 64–65 of *Anno's Math Games*. Many interesting things are happening in this town. Write a composition explaining how life in this town is similar to or different from life in the town where you live.

Use the **Have I...? Checklist** to review your work. Make any changes needed, so it is as good as it can be. You may finish your composition on the back of this page or on a separate sheet of paper.

____

____

____

Teacher Notes

Anno's Math Games

Overview of the Connections

Chapter 4: Who's the Tallest (pages 68–93) will help students develop an understanding of bar graphs and averages. In a logical progression, students are exposed to methods for comparing and displaying data about various amounts, lengths, weights, and even volume. Data collection and analysis are extended to proportions as students compare concentrations of sugar in differing volumes of water to determine level of "sweetness." Students apply their data analysis skills in a four-page Mathematics Assessment.

Writing activities and assessments provide opportunities for students to interpret illustrations and apply details in creative ways.

Chapter 4
Who's the Tallest?

MATERIALS FOR THE CONNECTIONS

Anno's Math Games • ISBN 0-698-11671-2
Written and illustrated by Mitsumasa Anno. New York: Putnam & Grosset Group, 1997.

Language Arts

~ Copies of the book (preferably 1 for each group of 2–4 students)

~ Optional: **Connection to Viewing Assessment: Writing About a Picture Prompt** (Reproducible Master 1)

~ **Have I...? Checklist** (Reproducible Master 2), a self-monitoring checklist for student writers

~ **Rubric for Scoring First Drafts** (Reproducible Master 3)

~ **Connection to Writing Assessment: Post-Reading Composition** (Reproducible Master 128)

Mathematics

~ Connecting cubes

~ **Comparing Tomato Plants** (Reproducible Master 122)

~ **Comparing Bags of Sugar-Coated Candies** (Reproducible Master 123)

~ Assorted containers for holding liquids (eight cans, jars, bottles, cartons, etc. that can hold 2 oz, 4 oz, 6 oz, 8 oz, 10 oz, 12 oz, 16 oz, and 24 oz)

~ Clear containers of uniform size (for example eight 32- or 24-oz measuring cups or beakers, nine 16-oz measuring cups or beakers, or 13 one-cup measures)

~ Water

~ **Connection to Mathematics Assessment: Check for Understanding I, II, III, and IV** (Reproducible Masters 124–127)

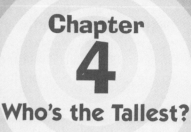

~ Grid paper

Viewing Connection

INTRODUCING THE LESSON WITH A PICTURE PROMPT AND WRITING

Materials

Copies of the book (page 85), **Connection to Viewing Assessment: Writing About a Picture Prompt** (Reproducible Master 1), **Have I...? Checklist** (Reproducible Master 2), **Rubric for Scoring First Drafts** (Reproducible Master 3)

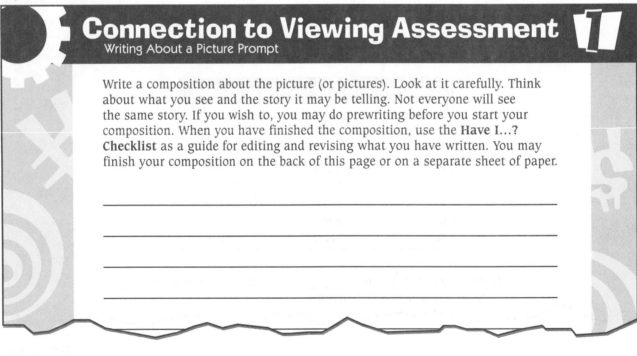

Show the class the pictures on pages 85 with the text covered. This page shows six different frames illustrating various emotions. Students may write about one, some, or all of the frames. If possible, allow students to continue to look at the pictures throughout the writing session. You may distribute a copy of **Connection to Viewing Assessment: Writing About a Picture Prompt** to each student, or they may use notebook paper for their work. Also distribute copies of the **Have I...? Checklist**.

Read these directions to the class:

"You are going to write a composition about one or more of these pictures. Look at them carefully. Think about what you see and the story they may be telling. It is OK that not everyone will see the same story. If you wish to, you may do prewriting before you start your composition. When you have finished the composition, use the **Have I...? Checklist** as a guide for editing and revising what you have written."

Give the students 20–30 minutes to write their compositions and do initial editing.

Collect and score the students' compositions using the **Rubric for Scoring First Drafts**. Teach students how to compare their scored compositions to the rubric and to make notes about how to improve their compositions. Students also may be taught to use the rubric to score their own work or that of other students.

Reproducible Master 1

Connection to Viewing Assessment 1

Writing About a Picture Prompt

Write a composition about the picture (or pictures). Look at it carefully. Think about what you see and the story it may be telling. Not everyone will see the same story. If you wish to, you may do prewriting before you start your composition. When you have finished the composition, use the **Have I...? Checklist** as a guide for editing and revising what you have written. You may finish your composition on the back of this page or on a separate sheet of paper.

____

____

____

____

Mathematics Connection

DEVELOPING UNDERSTANDING

Materials

Connecting cubes (90 in each of 2 colors per group), **Comparing Tomato Plants** (Reproducible Master 122)

This activity lets students explore ways that data can be presented more effectively. It also will help them discover conceptual methods for finding averages as alternatives to using algorithms. To provide a readiness experience for the concepts presented in the Chapter 4, complete the following activity before reading the chapter.

Provide connecting cubes and a copy of **Comparing Tomato Plants** to each group of 3–4 students. Have groups work together to make a connecting-cube graph and answer the questions on the worksheet.

Reproducible Master 122 with answers

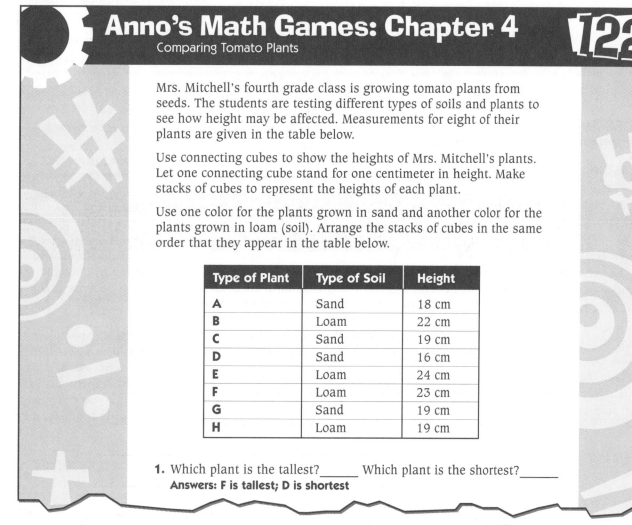

Anno's Math Games: Chapter 4

Comparing Tomato Plants

122

Mrs. Mitchell's fourth grade class is growing tomato plants from seeds. The students are testing different types of soils and plants to see how height may be affected. Measurements for eight of their plants are given in the table below.

Use connecting cubes to show the heights of Mrs. Mitchell's plants. Let one connecting cube stand for one centimeter in height. Make stacks of cubes to represent the heights of each plant.

Use one color for the plants grown in sand and another color for the plants grown in loam (soil). Arrange the stacks of cubes in the same order that they appear in the table below.

Type of Plant	Type of Soil	Height
A	Sand	18 cm
B	Loam	22 cm
C	Sand	19 cm
D	Sand	16 cm
E	Loam	24 cm
F	Loam	23 cm
G	Sand	19 cm
H	Loam	19 cm

1. Which plant is the tallest?_____ Which plant is the shortest?_____
   Answers: F is tallest; D is shortest

Continued...

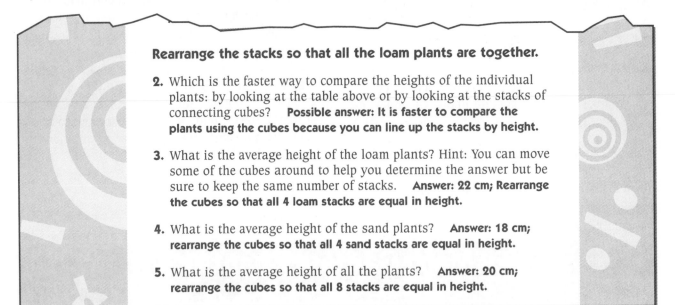

Rearrange the stacks so that all the loam plants are together.

2. Which is the faster way to compare the heights of the individual plants: by looking at the table above or by looking at the stacks of connecting cubes? **Possible answer: It is faster to compare the plants using the cubes because you can line up the stacks by height.**

3. What is the average height of the loam plants? Hint: You can move some of the cubes around to help you determine the answer but be sure to keep the same number of stacks. **Answer: 22 cm; Rearrange the cubes so that all 4 loam stacks are equal in height.**

4. What is the average height of the sand plants? **Answer: 18 cm; rearrange the cubes so that all 4 sand stacks are equal in height.**

5. What is the average height of all the plants? **Answer: 20 cm; rearrange the cubes so that all 8 stacks are equal in height.**

PAGES 69–75: Introduction and Active Reading

Materials

Several copies of the book (ideally, 1 for each pair or group of 4–6 students), connecting cubes (about 300 for each group)

As you read Chapter 4, pose questions and conduct activities as described in the book and in the guide below. Encourage students to practice active reading skills, such as asking questions, thinking to themselves, and discussing their ideas. Ensure that they understand that practicing effective reading means asking themselves questions while they read. You might choose to do some or all of the activities provided here. Read pages 69–74 to the class, stopping to discuss the illustrations.

Show students the graph on page 75. Ask:

What can be concluded about the heights of Kriss and Kross as compared to the heights of the six children? **[Answer: They are both much shorter than the children.]**

- ***Why are some of the bars blue and some orange?*** **[Answer: Blue represents boys, and orange represents girls. This way, the heights of the boys and the girls can be more easily studied and compared.]**

- ***How is this graph like the plant experiments from the Comparing Tomato Plants activity?*** **[Answer: There are two different sets of data being compared. In the plant activity, the loam and sandy soil were shown by different colors just as the boys and girls are in *Anno's Math Games.*]**

The table below provides an estimation of each child's height on page 75 in order from tallest to shortest.

Child	A	B	C	D	E	F
Height	54 inches	51 inches	50 inches	50 inches	48 inches	47 inches

Present the data from the table on page 286 to the class. Have small groups of 4–6 students use connecting cubes to represent the data visually. Then have students manipulate the cubes to find the average (or *mean*) height. To do this, they can move cubes from one stack to another to make all the stacks have equal numbers of cubes. Tell students they must keep the same number of stacks.

Pose the following problems:

Barry looked at the data in the table and knew without making any calculations that the average height of the six children was 50 inches. How was he able to figure out the answer so quickly? Explain your thinking. **[Possible response: The 54 and 51 represent a total of 5 units above 50. The 48 and 47 represent 5 units below 50, which balance to be an average of 50.]**

- ***Based on the data, Barry concluded that Kriss (black hat) was a little less than 47 inches tall. Do you agree or disagree? Tell why.*** **[Possible response: I agree because Kriss's bar is a little shorter than child F's height.]**

- ***Would the average height of all eight people be the same, taller, or shorter if both Kriss's height and Kross's heights were included in the calculations when finding the mean? Explain.*** **[Answer: It would be shorter because their heights are less than the average child's height of 50 inches, so it would bring the average down.]**

PAGES 76–77: Comparing Scores

Read pages 76–77. Use pair-share technique to discuss whether it would be easier to determine each team's score by leaving the beanbags in the basket or by using the "sticks." Tell why.

PAGES 78–79: Comparing Weights

Read pages 78–79. Show students the graph on page 79. Ask:

Who is the heaviest? **[Answer: The girl with the long, orange hair.]**

- ***How do you know?*** **[Answer: The bar above her head is the longest.]**

- ***What do you notice about the weights of Kriss and Kross as compared to the children? Explain.*** **[Answer: Kross (red hat) weighs more than the lightest boy and girl because his bar is longer than theirs. Kriss (black hat) is lighter than all the children because his bar is shorter than theirs.]**

PAGES 80–81: Comparing Attendance

Read pages 80–81, and discuss the illustrations. Ask:

Which child attended school most? How do you know? **[Answer: The child on the far right attended most often; her row of stickers is tallest.]**

- ***From which set of data is it easier to tell who attended school the most during the month? Explain your answer.*** **[Answer: The graph on page 81 is easier to understand because it compares the total days as lengths of bars or sticks. It's harder to compare on the calendar pages.]**

REPRESENTING DATA EFFECTIVELY

✓ **Materials**
Comparing Bags of Sugar-Coated Candies
(Reproducible Master 123)

Provide copies of Comparing Bags of Sugar-Coated Candies to each student.

After reading pages 69–81 of *Anno's Math Games*, have students complete the worksheet.

Reproducible Master 123 with answers

Anno's Math Games: Chapter 4
Comparing Bags of Sugar-Coated Candies

123

Look at Chart A and Graph B shown below. They both present the same set of data but in different ways.

CHART A: Number of sugar-coated candies in sample bags of Rut Gut Super Sugar Minnies

Bag #	1	2	3	4	5	6	7	8
Number of Candies	21	23	17	17	21	26	14	15

GRAPH B: Number of sugar-coated candies in sample bags of Rut Gut Super Sugar Minnies

Bag #1	OOOOOOOOOOOOOOOOOOOOO
Bag #2	OOOOOOOOOOOOOOOOOOOOOOO
Bag #3	OOOOOOOOOOOOOOOOO
Bag #4	OOOOOOOOOOOOOOOOO
Bag #5	OOOOOOOOOOOOOOOOOOOOO
Bag #6	OOOOOOOOOOOOOOOOOOOOOOOOOO
Bag #7	OOOOOOOOOOOOOO
Bag #8	OOOOOOOOOOOOOOO

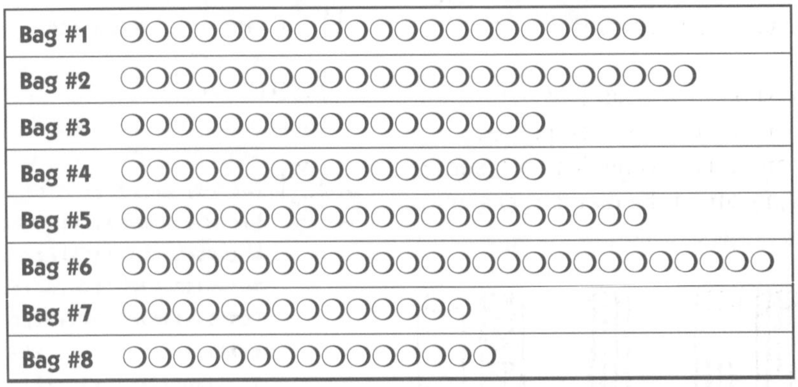

Key O = 1 sugar-coated candy

1. Which bag has the most candies? **Answer: Bag #6 has the most**

   Which has the least candies? **Answer: Bag #7 has the least**

2. Which is the faster way to compare the quantities of candies in the bags: by looking at Chart A or by looking at Graph B? Tell why.
Possible answer: It is faster to look at Graph B because it is easier to compare the lengths of the rows than to compare the numbers.

3. How is the story in the *Anno's Math Games* like the chart and graph that shows Rut Gut Super Sugar Minnies? **Possible answer: In the book, they lined up sticks or rows of things to compare measurements and amounts. To compare the numbers of Rut Gut Super Sugar Minnies, we lined up the candies. In both cases, the sticks or rows were faster to use for comparisons than just numbers.**

PAGES 82–83: Comparing Liquid Measures

Materials

Assorted containers for holding liquids (eight cans, jars, bottles, cartons, etc. that can hold 2 oz, 4 oz, 6 oz, 8 oz, 10 oz, 12 oz, 16 oz, and 24 oz), clear containers of uniform size (for example eight 32- or 24-oz measuring cups or beakers, nine 16-oz measuring cups or beakers, or 13 one-cup measures), water.

In preparation, measure the following amounts of water into the appropriate containers: 2 oz, 4 oz, 6 oz, 8 oz, 10 oz, 12 oz, 16 oz, and 24 oz. Display them out of sequence. Without telling the class the amounts of water in each container, challenge them guess which container has the most water.

Have the class observe as you empty the water from each container into the uniform cups or beakers. As you complete the experiment, discuss how much liquid each container held, how you can compare the amounts visually, and why having a uniform unit of measure is important.

The diagram below shows the results of the demonstration: each amount has been poured from the original container into uniform measuring cups. Each measuring cup in the diagram has an 8-ounce capacity.

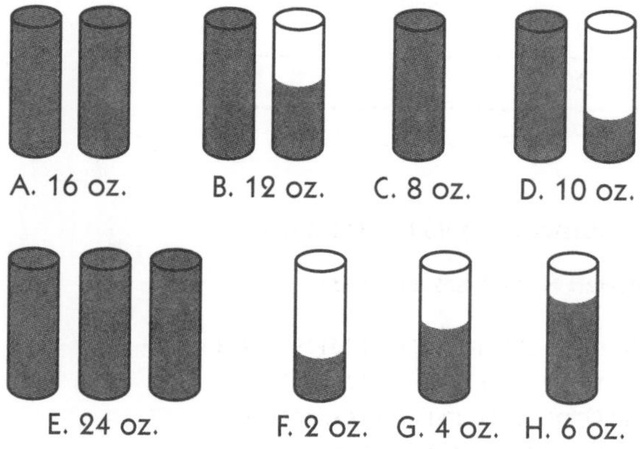

PAGES 84–85: Standard Measures

Read pages 84–85. Discuss with students the fact that unit measurements such as ounces, miles, hours, kilograms, degrees, etc., are called standard measurements. Ask:

Why can't we measure fear, sadness, happiness? **[Answer: There are no standard units of measure for emotions. They are *intangible* or untouchable. The measure of emotion is individual and unique from person to person.]**

To review the uses of standard units of measure, use a pair-share-discussion technique to brainstorm applications of different units of measure. Tell students to:

- Name three things we measure with ounces.
- Name three things we measure with inches.
- Name three things we measure in degrees.
- Name three things we measure in pounds.

PAGES 86–89: Comparing Sweetness

Materials

Connecting cubes; small self-stick notes

Read pages 86–87 and ask questions similar to:

Do you agree or disagree with Kriss's and Kross's statements about the sweetness of the water? Why? **[Possible answer: Yes because the containers on page 86 have the same amount of water so the one with the most sugar is the sweetest. The containers on page 87 have different amounts of water and sugar so it is harder to tell.]**

Read pages 88–89 and discuss the illustrations. Ask:

Which container do you think has the sweetest water? Why? **[Possible response: I think the milk carton has the sweetest water because it has the most sugar but less water than the big bottle.]**

Explain to students how to use connecting cubes to model containers of sugar and water. Have them use two different colors: one color for sugar cubes and the other for the water above the sugar. Tell students that one connecting cube equals 1 sugar cube or 1 ounce of water above the sugar.

EXAMPLES

- For a container with 2 ounces of water and 1 sugar cube, use 1 white cube for the sugar and 1 blue for the water that can be seen above the sugar. The ratio of sugar to water is 1 out of 2, or $\frac{1}{2}$.
- For a container with 4 ounces of water and 2 cubes of sugar, use 2 white cubes and 2 blue cubes. The ratio of sugar to water is 2 out of 4, or $\frac{2}{4}$.
- For a container with 6 ounces of water and 4 sugar cubes, use 4 white cubes and 2 blue cubes. The ratio of sugar to water is 4 out of 6, or $\frac{4}{6}$, or $\frac{2}{3}$.

Use small self-stick notes to label the containers on pages 88–89 with the letters "A" through "H," from left to right. On each label, also note the amount of liquid in each container as follows: A = 3 oz; B = 6 oz; C = 9 oz; D = 10 oz; E = 11 oz; F = 12 oz; G = 22 oz; H = 26 oz. Have students use connecting cubes in two colors to create models representing the amount of sugar and the amount of water above the sugar in each of the various containers.

The results are shown in the pictograph below.

Ensure students understand that the total number of cubes together represents the total amount of water. Container A, for example, has 1 part sugar to 3 parts water.

Have the students describe the ratio of sugar to the total amount of water. In container C, for example, the ratio of sugar to water is 4 out of 9 or $\frac{4}{9}$.

Ask:

Which of the models represents the liquid that is the sweetest? Why? **[Answer: G has the most sugar because $\frac{13}{22}$ is sugar, which is more than half. In all the other containers sugar represents half or less than half of the whole.]**

PAGES 90–91: Extending Sweetness Comparison

Read and discuss pages 90–91. The device used to compare the data is explained on pages 101–102 of *Anno's Math Games*. You may wish to skip this page, which is fairly sophisticated for this grade level.

PAGES 92–93: Mountains and Rivers

Read and discuss the diagram shown. Ask:

Why does using sticks or bars make the data easier to compare than using lists of numbers? **[Answer: Because it is easier to compare the lengths of the bars; the longest and shortest bars can be chosen quickly. Analyzing a list of numbers takes longer because you need to compare each of the numbers.]**

Key ❑ = sugar ■ = water above level of sugar cubes

Container A (small bottle)	❑ ■■
Container B (small jar)	❑❑ ■■■■
Container C (milk bottle)	❑❑❑❑ ■■■■■
Container D (soda bottle)	❑❑❑❑❑ ■■■■■
Container E (tall can)	❑❑❑❑ ■■■■■■■
Container F (bottle)	❑❑❑❑❑ ■■■■■■■
Container G (milk carton)	❑❑❑❑❑❑❑❑❑❑❑❑❑ ■■■■■■■■■
Container H (large bottle)	❑❑❑❑❑❑❑❑❑❑❑❑❑ ■■■■■■■■■■■■■

MATHEMATICS ASSESSMENT

Materials

Connection to Mathematics Assessment: Check for Understanding I, II, III, and IV (Reproducible Masters 124–127), grid paper

Distribute the worksheets with multiple-choice and open-ended questions called **Connection to Mathematics Assessment: Check for Understanding I, II, III, and IV**. This activity can be used to check students' understanding of the mathematics concepts covered in this lesson.

Collect and score the students' work using the answers and rubric that follow.

Reproducible Master 124 with answers

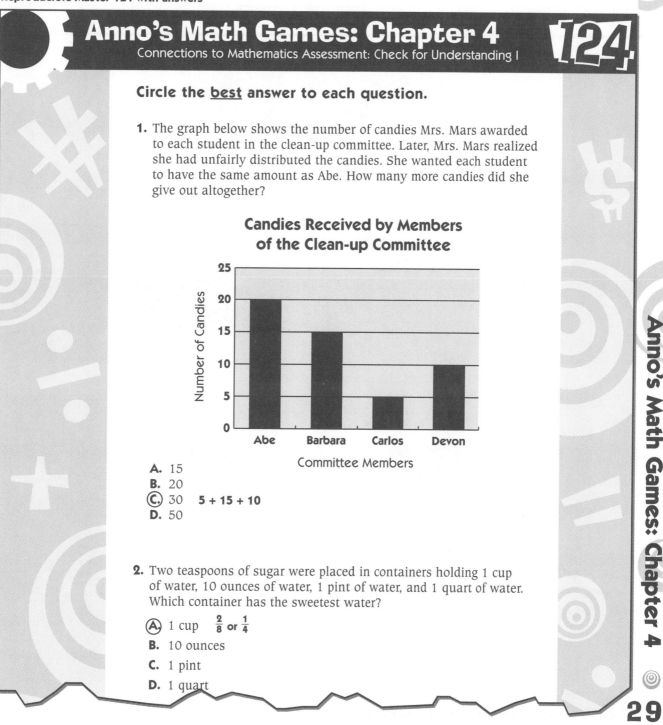

Anno's Math Games: Chapter 4 124

Connections to Mathematics Assessment: Check for Understanding I

Circle the best answer to each question.

1. The graph below shows the number of candies Mrs. Mars awarded to each student in the clean-up committee. Later, Mrs. Mars realized she had unfairly distributed the candies. She wanted each student to have the same amount as Abe. How many more candies did she give out altogether?

Candies Received by Members of the Clean-up Committee

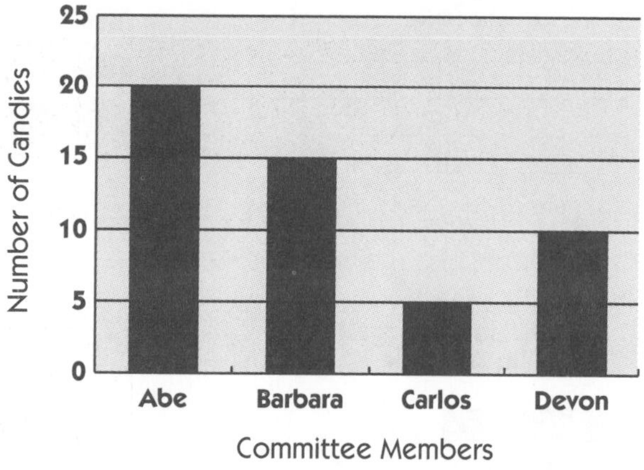

A. 15
B. 20
(C.) 30 **5 + 15 + 10**
D. 50

2. Two teaspoons of sugar were placed in containers holding 1 cup of water, 10 ounces of water, 1 pint of water, and 1 quart of water. Which container has the sweetest water?

(A.) 1 cup $\frac{2}{8}$ **or** $\frac{1}{4}$
B. 10 ounces
C. 1 pint
D. 1 quart

Anno's Math Games: Chapter 4

Connections to Mathematics Assessment: Check for Understanding II

125

Circle the best answer to the question.

3. Which of the graphs below show the same data as this graph?

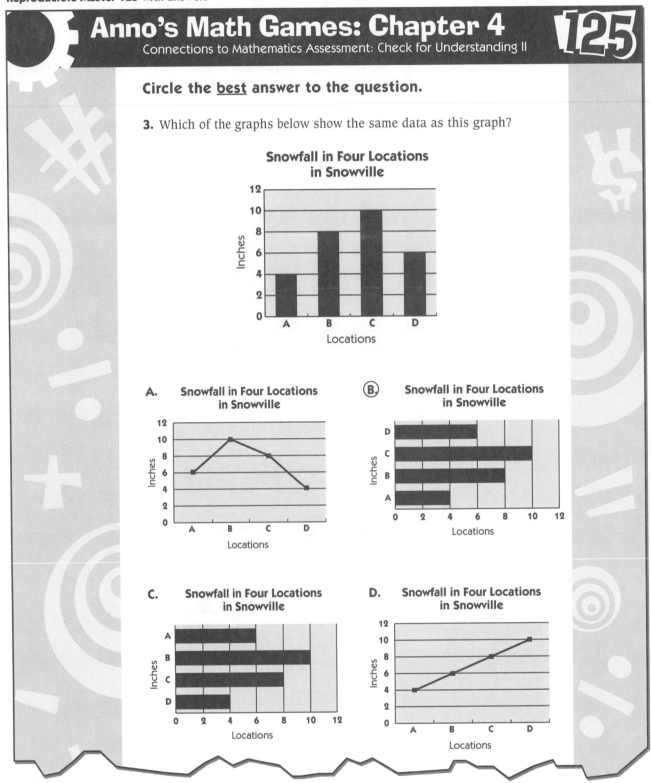

Snowfall in Four Locations in Snowville

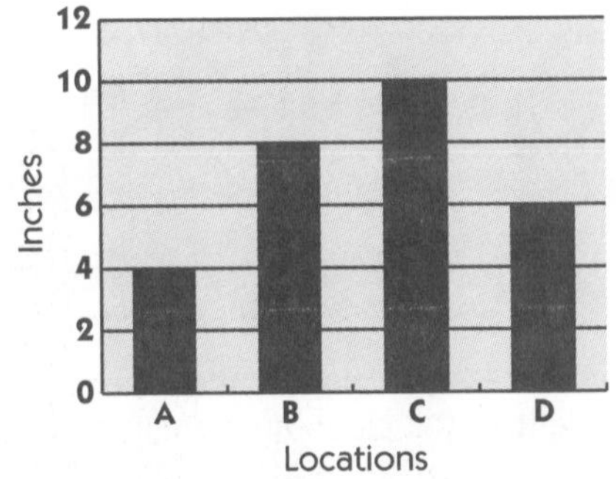

A. **Snowfall in Four Locations in Snowville**

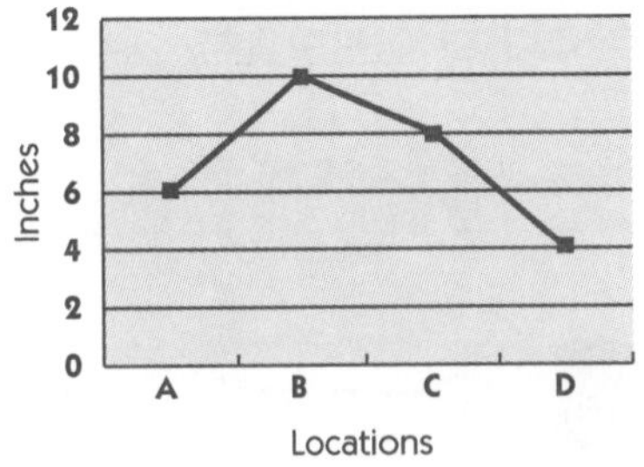

(B.) **Snowfall in Four Locations in Snowville**

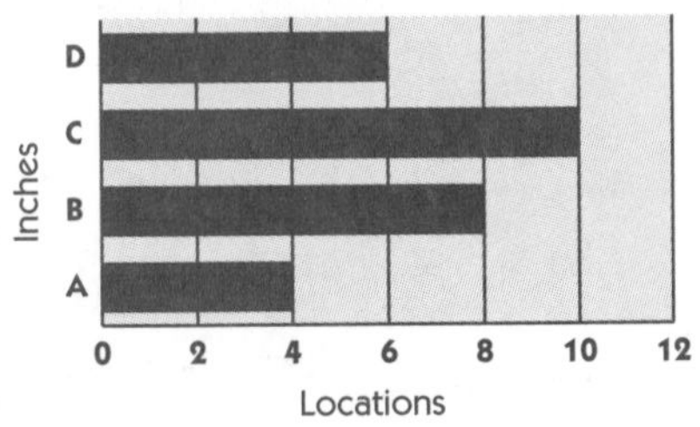

C. **Snowfall in Four Locations in Snowville**

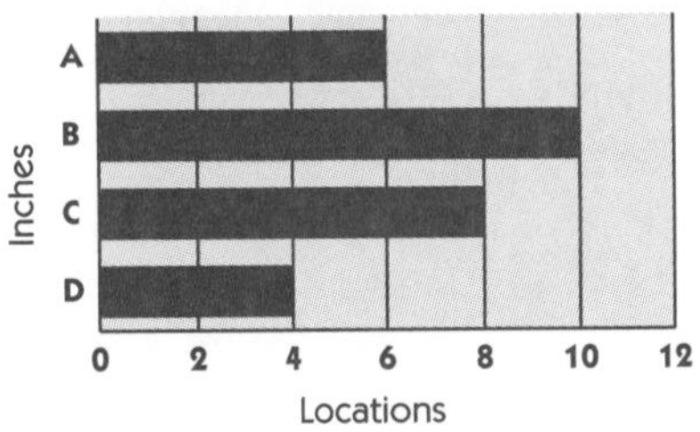

D. **Snowfall in Four Locations in Snowville**

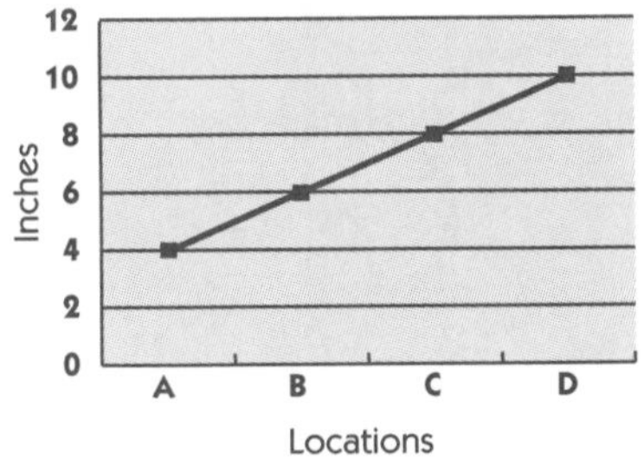

Anno's Math Games: Chapter 4

Connections to Mathematics Assessment: Check for Understanding III

126

Circle the best answer to the question.

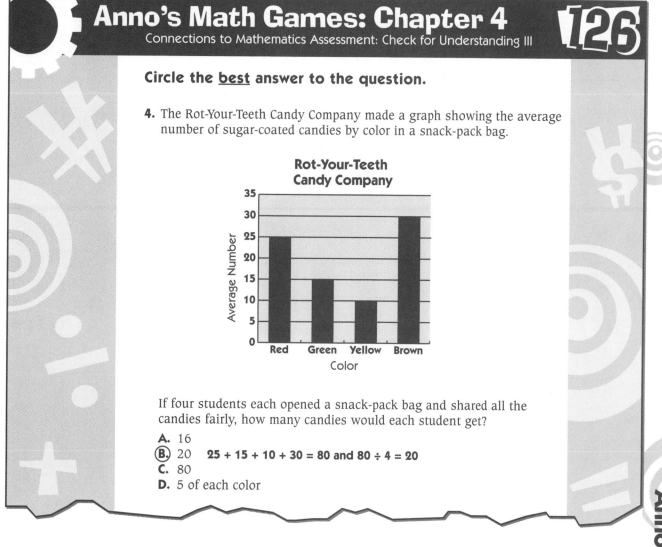

4. The Rot-Your-Teeth Candy Company made a graph showing the average number of sugar-coated candies by color in a snack-pack bag.

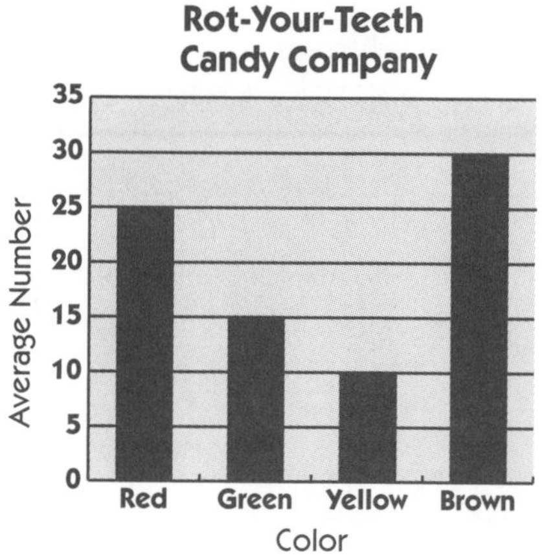

If four students each opened a snack-pack bag and shared all the candies fairly, how many candies would each student get?

A. 16
(B.) 20 **25 + 15 + 10 + 30 = 80 and 80 ÷ 4 = 20**
C. 80
D. 5 of each color

Anno's Math Games: Chapter 4

Connections to Mathematics Assessment: Check for Understanding IV

127

Circle the best answer to the question.

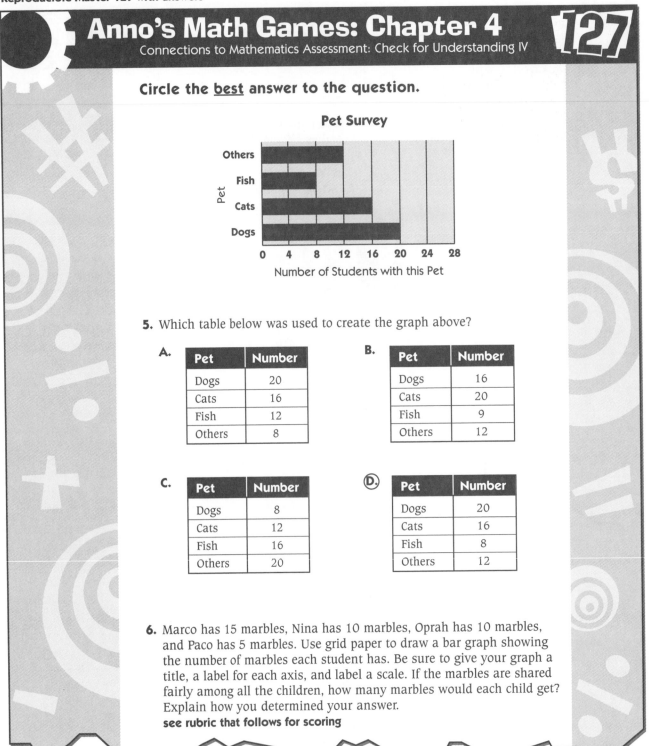

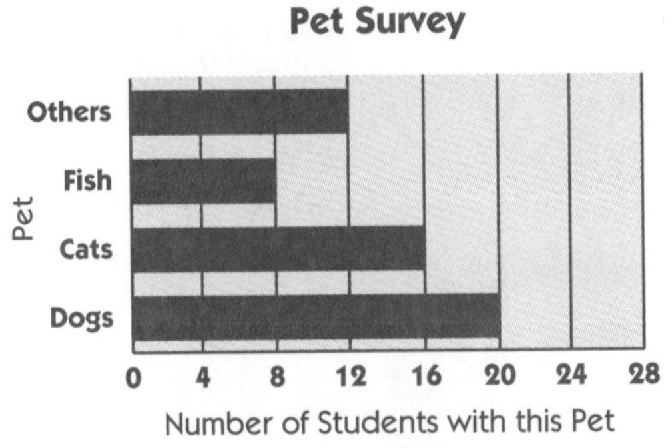

5. Which table below was used to create the graph above?

A.

Pet	Number
Dogs	20
Cats	16
Fish	12
Others	8

B.

Pet	Number
Dogs	16
Cats	20
Fish	9
Others	12

C.

Pet	Number
Dogs	8
Cats	12
Fish	16
Others	20

(D.)

Pet	Number
Dogs	20
Cats	16
Fish	8
Others	12

6. Marco has 15 marbles, Nina has 10 marbles, Oprah has 10 marbles, and Paco has 5 marbles. Use grid paper to draw a bar graph showing the number of marbles each student has. Be sure to give your graph a title, a label for each axis, and label a scale. If the marbles are shared fairly among all the children, how many marbles would each child get? Explain how you determined your answer.
see rubric that follows for scoring

RUBRIC FOR SCORING
Problem 6

An effective response will need to:
- show a bar graph with the correct data.
- state that each student will get 10 marbles.
- give a clear explanation.

POINTS	CRITERIA
3	Student shows the correct graph with appropriate title, labels, and scale. 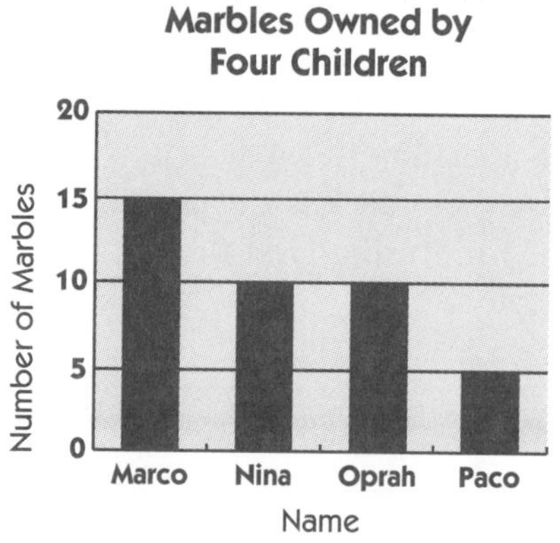 Student also provides a clear explanation of why each child would receive 10 marbles. Possible responses: *Each child would receive 10 marbles because Nina and Oprah already have 10 marbles, so Marco just needs to give 5 of his 15 to Paco. This way Marco and Paco also would have 10.* OR *Each child would get 10 marbles because it is the average, which is the sum of all the marbles divided by 4.*
2	Student shows the correct graph with an appropriate explanation for the average being 10 marbles, but has some errors in the graph. OR Student shows the correct graph and gives the correct average, but no explanation or an unclear explanation is given. OR Student shows the correct graph and gives an incorrect average, but provides an explanation that demonstrates an understanding of the concept. OR Student has some of the data graphed incorrectly, but has appropriate labels and gives the correct average with an appropriate explanation.
1	Student shows the correct graph with identifying parts missing and gives the correct average but with an unclear explanation. OR Student has some data incorrect on the graph with an incorrect average, but shows evidence of some understanding of the concepts.
0	Student shows no understanding of the problem.

Composition Connection

WRITING A POST-READING COMPOSITION

Materials

Copies of the book (focus on illustration on page 69), **Connection to Writing Assessment: Post-Reading Composition** (Reproducible Master 128), **Have I...? Checklist** (Reproducible Master 2), **Rubric for Scoring First Drafts** (Reproducible Master 3)

To practice skills in "using writing to interpret text," have students complete the following activity.

Give students the **Connection to Writing Assessment: Post-Reading Composition** along with a copy of the **Have I...? Checklist**.

Give students about 25 minutes in which to write the composition and edit/revise it based on the checklist.

Collect and score the students' compositions using the **Rubric for Scoring First Drafts**. Students may also be encouraged to put their scored drafts into a folder of "works in progress," which can be further edited and revised for sharing with an audience at some later date.

Reproducible Master 128

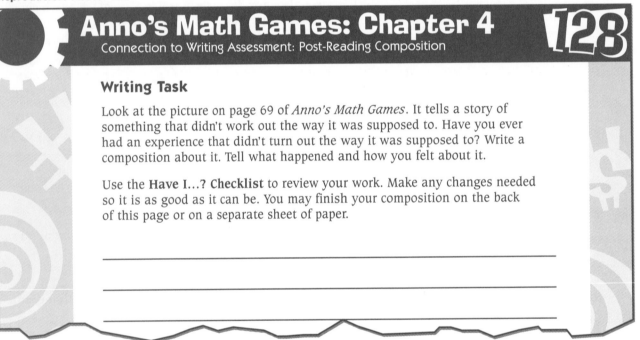

Anno's Math Games: Chapter 4

Connection to Writing Assessment: Post-Reading Composition

128

Writing Task

Look at the picture on page 69 of *Anno's Math Games*. It tells a story of something that didn't work out the way it was supposed to. Have you ever had an experience that didn't turn out the way it was supposed to? Write a composition about it. Tell what happened and how you felt about it.

Use the **Have I...? Checklist** to review your work. Make any changes needed so it is as good as it can be. You may finish your composition on the back of this page or on a separate sheet of paper.

Extending the Connections

DEVELOPING SKILL IN WRITING DESCRIPTIONS AND DETAILS ABOUT PEOPLE

Materials
Copies of the book

Have the students select a picture of one or more people from pages 71–73. (The same person may be pictured more than once). Have them write a detailed description of that person. They may also choose to "tell the person's story," describing where they live and what has happened to them.

Before they write their own descriptions, you may want to use a class writing activity to model writing a vivid description. There are many rich options, since the pictures are generally clear and direct.

Have students read their descriptions to one another and keep them in their "works in progress" folder. (See page *xxii* for a description of this device.) They may choose to develop this description into a full story or composition, or they may use it to remind themselves about using descriptive techniques. Finally, they may choose to incorporate the description into another writing piece that they develop later.

MAKE YOUR OWN GRAPHS

Present the following project ideas. Have students choose one and research the data to make a graph.

- Look up data on the 10 longest tunnels and make a bar graph to compare the distances.
- Look up data on the 10 longest bridges in the United States and make a bar graph to compare the distances.
- Use the Internet to research the "Top 10" most popular movies, sporting events, or music albums this year. Graph the results.

Teacher Notes

Anno's Math Games II

Written and illustrated by
Mitsumasa Anno

Overview of the Connections

The book *Anno's Math Games II* consists of five distinct chapters, each of which is explored in a separate lesson. Each chapter of *Anno's Math Games II* includes a sequenced set of vivid pictures and activities. The book presents opportunities for students to conceptually investigate and explore various mathematical topics that are embedded in the national standards. Because the individual chapters are each equal in size to a typical trade book, they are treated as separate lessons with unique activities and assessments.

The five chapters can be used independently or in various combinations. Each chapter addresses specific mathematical concepts.

Chapter	Anno's Math Games pages	Lesson pages	Math Concepts
CHAPTER 1 The Magic Machine	2 – 19	301 – 312	Mathematical functions and inverse properties
CHAPTER 2 Compare and Find Out	20 – 35	313 – 318	Searching for similarities and differences, sorting and classifying
CHAPTER 3 Dots, Dots, and More Dots	36 – 53	319 – 326	Density, infinity, and the concept of coordinates
CHAPTER 4 Counting With Circles	54 – 77	327– 338	Numerical representation, place value, and variables
CHAPTER 5 Counting Water	78 – 97	339 – 346	Largeness, volume, and standard and non-standard measure

Although *Anno's Math Games II* is not a traditional storybook, for language arts instruction, this book offers many opportunities for writing both longer and shorter compositions, as well as implementing a writing workshop in your class. There are no Listening Connections in these lessons, but a variety of other language arts activities are presented throughout. *Anno's Math Games II* is an especially good resource for sparking students' own ideas for writing. To read more about helping students find their own writing topics, see the "Writing Workshop" discussion on page *xxii* of this manual.

MATERIALS FOR THE CONNECTIONS

Anno's Math Games II • ISBN 0-698-11672-0
Written and illustrated by Mitsumasa Anno. New York: Putnam & Grosset Group, 1997.

Note: Additional materials are listed under the individual lessons for each chapter.

Anno's Math Games II

Chapter 1

The Magic Machine

Overview of the Connections

Chapter 1: The Magic Machines (pages 2–19) presents the concept of functions and function machines. Students apply logic and pattern recognition as they informally explore the concepts of inverse functions and variables. These ideas can be extended to promote a conceptual understanding of addition and subtraction of whole numbers and of mathematical sentences.

The illustrations tell nonverbal stories or otherwise present vivid illustrations perfect for study and observation. As students learn to "read" visual presentations, their skills in interpreting text grow. They come to recognize the importance of specificity in describing elements important to a story.

MATERIALS FOR THE CONNECTIONS

Anno's Math Games II • ISBN 0-698-11672-0

Written and illustrated by Mitsumasa Anno. New York: Putnam & Grosset Group, 1997.

Language Arts

~ Copies of the book (1 for each group of 2–4 students)

~ Optional: **Connection to Viewing Assessment: Writing About a Picture Prompt** (Reproducible Master 1)

~ **Have I...? Checklist** (Reproducible Master 2), a self-monitoring checklist for student writers

~ **Rubric for Scoring First Drafts** (Reproducible Master 3)

~ **Connection to Writing Assessment: Post-Reading Composition** (Reproducible Master 134)

Mathematics

~ **Function Machines I, II, and III** (Reproducible Masters 129–131)

~ **Connection to Mathematics Assessment: Check for Understanding I and II** (Reproducible Masters 132–134)

Viewing Connection

INTRODUCING THE LESSON WITH A PICTURE PROMPT AND WRITING

Materials

One or more copies of the book (pages 4–5), **Connection to Viewing Assessment: Writing About a Picture Prompt** (Reproducible Master 1), **Have I...? Checklist** (Reproducible Master 2), **Rubric for Scoring First Drafts** (Reproducible Master 3)

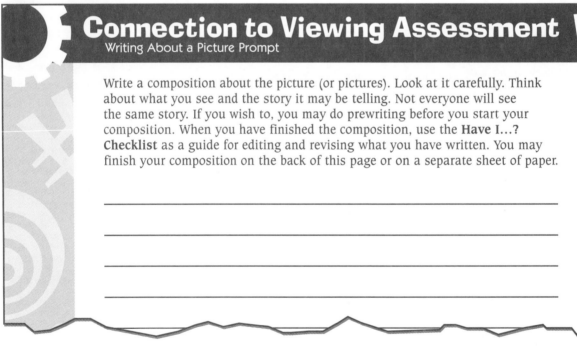

Show the class the pictures on pages 4–5 with the text covered up. These pages show the characters, Kriss and Kross, with a number of tools and a device that says "ANNO." If possible, allow students to continue to look at the picture throughout the writing session. You may distribute a copy of **Connection to Viewing Assessment: Writing About a Picture Prompt** to each student, or they may use notebook paper for their work. Also distribute a copy of the **Have I...? Checklist**.

Read these directions to the class:

"You are going to write a composition about this picture. Look at it carefully. Think about what you see and the story it may be telling. It is OK that not everyone will see the same story. If you wish to, you may do prewriting before you start your composition. When you have finished the composition, use the **Have I...? Checklist** as a guide for editing and revising what you have written."

Give the students 20–30 minutes to write their compositions and do initial editing.

Collect and score the students' compositions using the **Rubric for Scoring First Drafts**. Teach students how to compare their scored compositions to the rubric and to make notes about how to improve their compositions. Students also may be taught to use the rubric to score their own work or that of other students.

Reproducible Master 1

Connection to Viewing Assessment 1

Writing About a Picture Prompt

Write a composition about the picture (or pictures). Look at it carefully. Think about what you see and the story it may be telling. Not everyone will see the same story. If you wish to, you may do prewriting before you start your composition. When you have finished the composition, use the **Have I...? Checklist** as a guide for editing and revising what you have written. You may finish your composition on the back of this page or on a separate sheet of paper.

Mathematics Connection

DEVELOPING UNDERSTANDING

Before reading *Chapter 1: The Magic Machine* to students, play several rounds of the game "What's My Rule?"

To play the game, tell the class that you are thinking of a rule that can be applied to a number. The object of the game is for students to guess the rule.

Have a student give you a number. Then apply your rule—a mathematical function—to the student's number and tell the class the result. Discuss how the game is like a machine: You put a number in the machine, the machine does something to it and then produces a new number.

As students think they know the rule, have them raise their hands. Remind them not to say the rule out loud. Test if they really know the rule by giving them a number and having them respond with the new number that results when the rule is applied.

When most of the children seem to have the rule, have them write a journal entry describing the rule.

EXAMPLE 1

Suppose you have decided to use the rule of doubling. If a student said *3*, your response would be *6*. If another student said *9*, you would say *18*. When students think they know the rule, give them a number, and if they reply with the double, confirm that they, indeed, know the rule. When all students have indicated that they know the rule, have them write journal entries describing what the machine does. [Answer: This machine always doubles the number.]

Note: Use caution when using a rule that involves subtraction because it might introduce negative numbers. For example, if the rule were "subtract 8," and a student gave you the number 5, the result would be –3. To avoid this confusion with subtraction, tell students that for this game, your machine will accept only numbers greater than 10 and adjust the subtrahend in your rule accordingly.

ACTIVE READING

Materials
Copies of the book (1 for each group of 2–4 students), **Function Machines I, II, and II** (Reproducible Masters 129–131)

Once students are confident with the idea of figuring out what rules have been applied to numbers, tell them that you are going to read them a story about machines that have rules in them. When they look at the pictures, they must decide what the machine does. In some cases, they must figure out what happens if the machine works in reverse.

The reproducible masters **Function Machines I, II, and III** require students to answer questions about different machines shown on the pages in *Anno's Math Games II: Chapter 1*. The activity works best if each group of 2–4 students has a copy of the book.

You can proceed with this activity in different ways. You can:

- read Chapter 1 all the way through, and then return to the beginning for students to answer questions on **Function Machines I, II, and III.**
- read one two-page spread at a time, stopping after each one to have students complete the questions about those pages.

Distribute **Function Machines I, II and III** to students. Have them record and apply their findings.

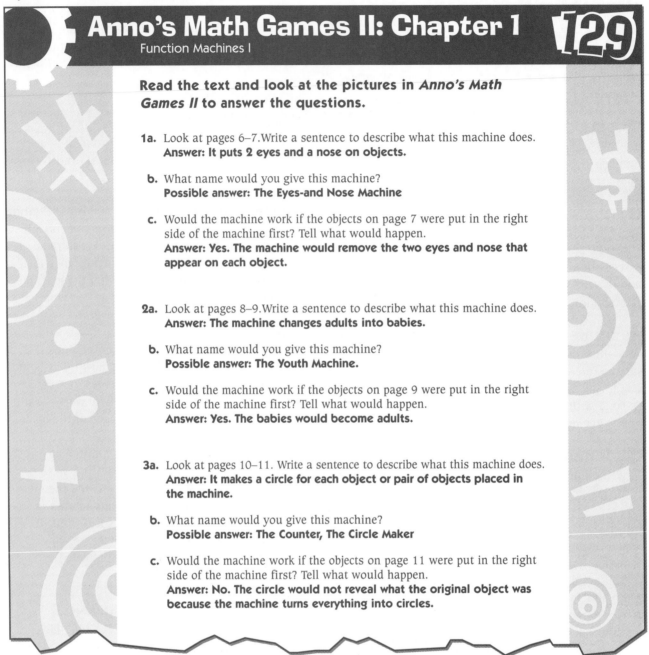

Anno's Math Games II: Chapter 1

129

Function Machines I

Read the text and look at the pictures in *Anno's Math Games II* to answer the questions.

1a. Look at pages 6–7.Write a sentence to describe what this machine does.
Answer: It puts 2 eyes and a nose on objects.

b. What name would you give this machine?
Possible answer: The Eyes-and Nose Machine

c. Would the machine work if the objects on page 7 were put in the right side of the machine first? Tell what would happen.
Answer: Yes. The machine would remove the two eyes and nose that appear on each object.

2a. Look at pages 8–9.Write a sentence to describe what this machine does.
Answer: The machine changes adults into babies.

b. What name would you give this machine?
Possible answer: The Youth Machine.

c. Would the machine work if the objects on page 9 were put in the right side of the machine first? Tell what would happen.
Answer: Yes. The babies would become adults.

3a. Look at pages 10–11. Write a sentence to describe what this machine does.
Answer: It makes a circle for each object or pair of objects placed in the machine.

b. What name would you give this machine?
Possible answer: The Counter, The Circle Maker

c. Would the machine work if the objects on page 11 were put in the right side of the machine first? Tell what would happen.
Answer: No. The circle would not reveal what the original object was because the machine turns everything into circles.

Anno's Math Games II: Chapter 1 130

Function Machines II

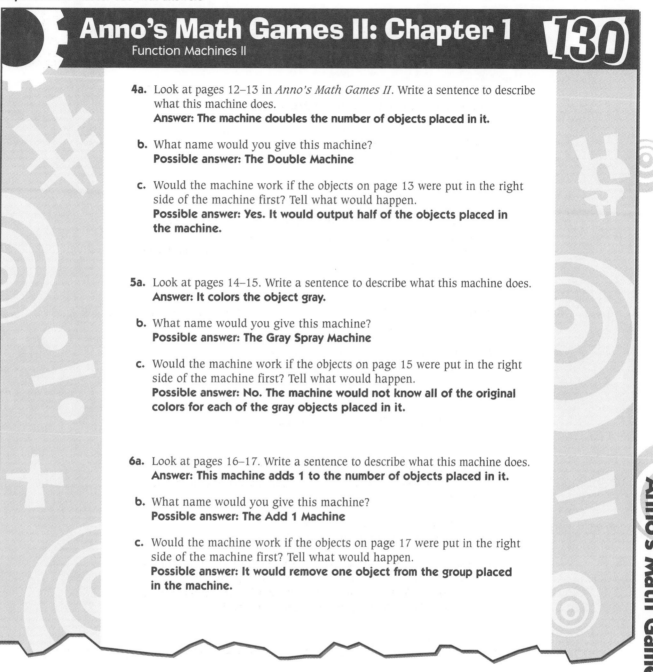

4a. Look at pages 12–13 in *Anno's Math Games II*. Write a sentence to describe what this machine does.
Answer: The machine doubles the number of objects placed in it.

b. What name would you give this machine?
Possible answer: The Double Machine

c. Would the machine work if the objects on page 13 were put in the right side of the machine first? Tell what would happen.
Possible answer: Yes. It would output half of the objects placed in the machine.

5a. Look at pages 14–15. Write a sentence to describe what this machine does.
Answer: It colors the object gray.

b. What name would you give this machine?
Possible answer: The Gray Spray Machine

c. Would the machine work if the objects on page 15 were put in the right side of the machine first? Tell what would happen.
Possible answer: No. The machine would not know all of the original colors for each of the gray objects placed in it.

6a. Look at pages 16–17. Write a sentence to describe what this machine does.
Answer: This machine adds 1 to the number of objects placed in it.

b. What name would you give this machine?
Possible answer: The Add 1 Machine

c. Would the machine work if the objects on page 17 were put in the right side of the machine first? Tell what would happen.
Possible answer: It would remove one object from the group placed in the machine.

Anno's Math Games II: Chapter 1

131

Function Machines III

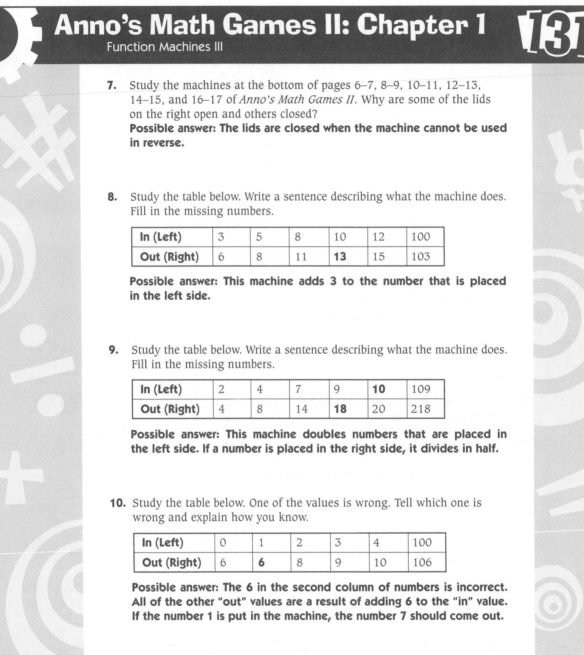

7. Study the machines at the bottom of pages 6–7, 8–9, 10–11, 12–13, 14–15, and 16–17 of *Anno's Math Games II*. Why are some of the lids on the right open and others closed?
Possible answer: The lids are closed when the machine cannot be used in reverse.

8. Study the table below. Write a sentence describing what the machine does. Fill in the missing numbers.

In (Left)	3	5	8	10	12	100
Out (Right)	6	8	11	**13**	15	103

Possible answer: This machine adds 3 to the number that is placed in the left side.

9. Study the table below. Write a sentence describing what the machine does. Fill in the missing numbers.

In (Left)	2	4	7	9	**10**	109
Out (Right)	4	8	14	**18**	20	218

Possible answer: This machine doubles numbers that are placed in the left side. If a number is placed in the right side, it divides in half.

10. Study the table below. One of the values is wrong. Tell which one is wrong and explain how you know.

In (Left)	0	1	2	3	4	100
Out (Right)	6	**6**	8	9	10	106

Possible answer: The 6 in the second column of numbers is incorrect. All of the other "out" values are a result of adding 6 to the "in" value. If the number 1 is put in the machine, the number 7 should come out.

CLOSURE

Make up your own function machines, and use a table to display several examples of what happens when you put a number in the left side. (See the tables in Problems 8–10 in **Function Machines III** for examples.)

Ask follow-up questions for the machines, such as:

- ***What would happen if I put a ____ in the left side of the machine?***
- ***What will happen if I put a ____ in the right side of the machine?***

Have students study the pictures on page 18–19. Ask:

Why did the author say the machine was broken? **[Answer: The pieces that were put together don't make sense. They don't match or they're put in the wrong place.]**

MATHEMATICS ASSESSMENT

Materials

Connection to Mathematics Assessment: Check for Understanding I and II (Reproducible Masters 132–133)

Distribute the worksheets with multiple-choice and open-ended questions called **Connection to Mathematics Assessment: Check for Understanding I and II**. This activity can be used to check students' understanding of the mathematics concepts covered in this lesson.

Collect and score the students' work using the answers and rubric that follow.

Reproducible Master 132 with answers

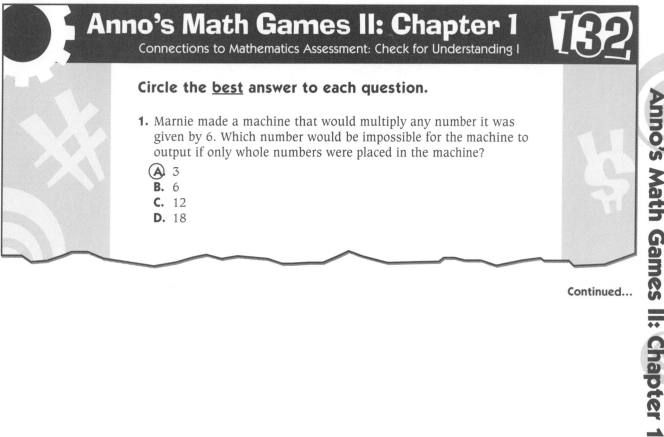

Anno's Math Games II: Chapter 1 — 132

Connections to Mathematics Assessment: Check for Understanding I

Circle the best answer to each question.

1. Marnie made a machine that would multiply any number it was given by 6. Which number would be impossible for the machine to output if only whole numbers were placed in the machine?
   - (A) 3 [circled]
   - **B.** 6
   - **C.** 12
   - **D.** 18

Continued...

2. If each set of objects on the left is placed in a machine, the machine outputs the quantities shown on the right.

Input	Output
✏✏✏✏✏	✏✏✏✏✏✏✏✏✏✏
👓👓👓👓👓👓	👓👓👓👓👓👓👓👓👓👓👓👓
☺☺	☺☺☺☺
✈✈✈✈✈✈✈	✈✈✈✈✈✈✈✈✈✈✈✈✈✈
✂	✂✂

Based on the inputs and outputs shown above, which of the following best describes what the machine does?

A. It adds two to every set of objects.
B. It divides each set of objects in half.
(C.) It doubles the objects.
D. It subtracts the same amount as put in.

3. If the machine in Problem 2 output ♠♠♠♠♠♠, what was the input?

A. ♠♠♠♠♠♠♠♠♠♠♠♠
(B.) ♠♠♠
C. ♠♠♠♠♠♠♠♠♠
D. ♠♠♠♠♠♠♠♠♠♠♠♠♠♠♠♠♠♠

Reproducible Master 133 with answers

Anno's Math Games II: Chapter 1

Connections to Mathematics Assessment: Check for Understanding II

133

4. Look at the table below. If the same rule was used to calculate each of the output values, which output value must be incorrect?

Input	2	3	5	7	8	10	100
Output	6	7	9	**10**	12	14	104

A. 6
B. 7
C. 9
(D.) 10

5. Which of the following is incorrect if the rule is to add 3 to the input number?

Input	Output
A. ✸✸✸✸✸	✸✸✸✸✸✸✸✸
(B.) ✿✿✿✿✿✿	✿✿✿✿✿✿✿✿
C. ◆◆	◆◆◆◆◆
D. ★★★★	★★★★★★★

6.

Input	Output
	■■■■■■■■
	■■■■
	■■■■■■
	■■■

Explain what the machine does to the input objects to get the output. Can this machine can be used in reverse? Why or why not? (For example, what would the input be if the output were the nine objects below?) **see rubric that follows for scoring**

■■■■■■■■■

Anno's Math Games II: Chapter 1

RUBRIC FOR SCORING

Problem 6

An effective response will need to:

- explain that the machine outputs one black square for each object that is input.
- explain that the machine cannot be used in reverse because it would not know what the original object was.
- be clearly presented.

POINTS	CRITERIA
3	The student correctly explains what the machine does and indicates and explains why the machine cannot be used in reverse. Example: *This machine outputs one black square for each object that is placed in the input side. The machine cannot be used in reverse because the machine would not know what the original object was. In the example given, the machine would know that nine objects have to come out, but it would not know what kinds of objects they should be changed to.*
2	The student correctly explains what the machine does and indicates that it cannot be used in reverse, but the supporting explanation is unclear or does not show understanding of the concept of a variable or function machine. OR The student demonstrates an understanding of the concepts at hand, but does not explain the answer in a clear manner; however, the student does indicate and explain clearly why the machine will not work in reverse.
1	The student tells what the machine does and that it does not work in reverse, but provides no explanation. OR The student shows some understanding of both parts of the question, but both parts contain gaps or unclear explanations. OR One part of the answer is correct and clearly explained, but the other part is incorrect with no explanation or an explanation that is unclear.
0	The student shows no understanding of the concept or leaves the problem blank.

Composition Connection

WRITING A POST-READING COMPOSITION

Materials

Copies of the book for each small group (focus on illustrations on page 8), **Connection to Writing Assessment: Post-Reading Composition** (Reproducible Master 134), **Have I...? Checklist** (Reproducible Master 2), **Rubric for Scoring First Drafts** (Reproducible Master 3)

Have students complete the following activity after finishing Chapter 1 of *Anno's Math Games II*.

Give students the **Connection to Writing Assessment: Post-Reading Composition** along with a copy of the **Have I...? Checklist**.

Give students about 20 minutes in which to write the composition and edit/revise it based on the checklist.

Collect and **score** the students' compositions using the **Rubric for Scoring First Drafts**. Students may also be encouraged to put their scored drafts into a folder of "works in progress," which can be further edited and revised for sharing with an audience at some later date.

Reproducible Master 134

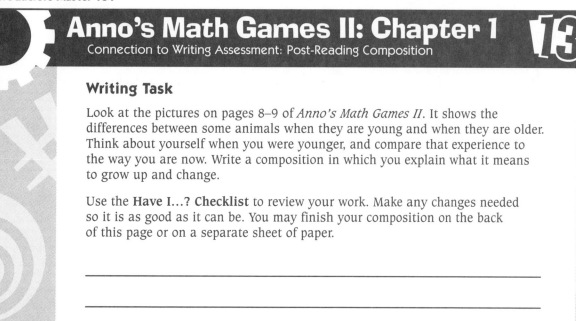

Anno's Math Games II: Chapter 1 134

Connection to Writing Assessment: Post-Reading Composition

Writing Task

Look at the pictures on pages 8–9 of *Anno's Math Games II*. It shows the differences between some animals when they are young and when they are older. Think about yourself when you were younger, and compare that experience to the way you are now. Write a composition in which you explain what it means to grow up and change.

Use the **Have I...? Checklist** to review your work. Make any changes needed so it is as good as it can be. You may finish your composition on the back of this page or on a separate sheet of paper.

____

____

____

Extending the Connections

CALCULATOR FUNCTION MACHINES

Materials
Calculators

To make a calculator into a function machine, choose a number and enter it in the calculator. Next press an operation sign and then the equals button. Now enter any number and repeatedly press the equals button. Each time the equals button is pressed, it will display an answer that has applied the number and operation that you entered into the machine previously.

EXAMPLE 1

Press the 4 button, the + button, and the = button. (The rule "add 4 to any number" has been entered in the calculator.) Press the 0 button, then the = button. The calculator will display 4. Press the = button again. Now the calculator displays 8. Press the = key again. This time the calculator displays 12, etc.

EXAMPLE 2

Press the 3 button, the + button, and the = button. Press the 4 button, and the = button. The calculator will display 7. Press the = button again. This time the calculator displays a 10, etc.

Once students understand how to make the calculator into a function machine, have them play a variation of "What's My Rule?" Students enter a rule in the calculator, then exchange calculators with friends, who try to guess their rule.

PROJECT

Materials
Very large box

Use a box large enough for a student to fit in. Have the student inside make up a rule. Students on the outside give a number to the "machine" and the student inside applies the rule and gives out a paper with the correct answer on it. Students must guess the rule.

ADDITIONAL RESOURCES

Windows on Math, Volume 4 Videodisc, Unit 1, "Freddie's Fabulous Function Machine." Atlanta: Optical Data Corporation, 1996. Call 1-800-524-2481.

Anno's Math Games II

Chapter 2

Compare and Find Out

Overview of the Connections

Chapter 2: Compare and Find Out (pages 21–35) presents opportunities for students to apply logic, pattern recognition, and classification skills while building a foundation for understanding partitioning, change, similarity, and paths. This chapter builds foundational skills, so it does not provide a Mathematics Assessment.

The illustrations tell nonverbal stories and present vivid illustrations perfect for study and observation. As students learn to "read" visual presentations, their skills in interpreting text grow. They come to recognize the importance of specificity in describing elements that are important to a story.

MATERIALS FOR THE CONNECTIONS

Anno's Math Games II • ISBN 0-698-11672-0
Written and illustrated by Mitsumasa Anno. New York: Putnam & Grosset Group, 1997.

Language Arts

~ Copies of the book (1 for each group of 2–4 students)

~ Optional: **Connection to Viewing Assessment: Writing About a Picture Prompt** (Reproducible Master 1)

~ **Have I...? Checklist** (Reproducible Master 2), a self-monitoring tool for student writers

~ **Rubric for Scoring First Drafts** (Reproducible Master 3)

~ **Connection to Writing Assessment: Post-Reading Composition** (Reproducible Master 135)

Mathematics

~ Transparencies or tracing paper

Viewing Connection

INTRODUCING THE LESSON WITH A PICTURE PROMPT AND WRITING

Materials

Copy of the book (pages 22–25), **Connection to Viewing Assessment: Writing About a Picture Prompt** (Reproducible Master 1), **Have I...? Checklist** (Reproducible Master 2), **Rubric for Scoring First Drafts** (Reproducible Master 3)

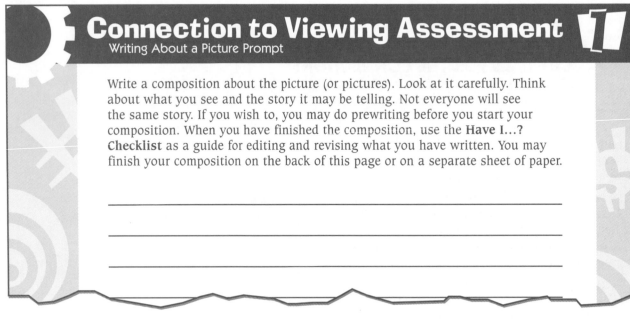

Show the class the pictures on pages 22–25 of *Anno's Math Games II*. Have students select one or more of the pictures to use in developing their compositions. If possible, allow students to continue to look at the picture throughout the writing session. You may distribute a copy of **Connection to Viewing Assessment: Writing About a Picture Prompt** to each student, or they may use notebook paper for their work. Also distribute copies of the **Have I...? Checklist**.

Read these directions to the class:

"You are going to write a composition about one or more of these pictures. Look at them carefully. Think about what you see and the story they may be telling. It is OK that not everyone will see the same story. If you wish to, you may do prewriting before you start your composition. When you have finished the composition, use the **Have I...? Checklist** as a guide for editing and revising what you have written."

Give the students 20–30 minutes to write their compositions and do initial editing.

Collect and score the students' compositions using the **Rubric for Scoring First Drafts**. Teach students how to compare their scored compositions to the rubric and to make notes about how to improve their compositions. Students also may be taught to use the rubric to score their own work or that of other students.

Reproducible Master 1

Connection to Viewing Assessment 1

Writing About a Picture Prompt

Write a composition about the picture (or pictures). Look at it carefully. Think about what you see and the story it may be telling. Not everyone will see the same story. If you wish to, you may do prewriting before you start your composition. When you have finished the composition, use the **Have I...? Checklist** as a guide for editing and revising what you have written. You may finish your composition on the back of this page or on a separate sheet of paper.

Mathematics Connection

INTRODUCTION AND ACTIVE READING

Materials

Several copies of the book (ideally, 1 for each group of 2–4 students)

As you read Chapter 2, pose questions and conduct activities as described in the book and in the guide below. Encourage students to practice active reading skills, such as asking questions, thinking to themselves, and discussing their ideas. Ensure that they understand that practicing effective reading means asking themselves questions while they read. You might choose to do some or all of the activities provided here.

The Chapter 2 exercises allow students to discover the importance of clearly defining attributes when sorting and classifying objects. These activities also build a foundation for understanding the concepts of *similarity* and *congruency*. In comparing pictures, students find out that two things can seem similar at first glance, but upon further inspection are found to be very different. For example, the mazes on pages 30 and 31 seem the same at first glance. They are both mazes, and the mice are in the same positions in each. Upon closer inspection, however, the reader discovers that the maze paths are not the same. The maze on the left has a pathway starting on the left. The maze on the right has a pathway starting on the right.

This concept can be transferred to geometric shapes. All triangles have similarities, yet they can have various classifications based on slight differences. When two shapes are congruent there are <u>no</u> differences. One shape may be in a different location from the other, but when corresponding sides and angles are matched, the shapes fit exactly, one on top of the other.

Read and discuss the illustrations on pages 22–35. Have students study the pairs of pictures that are presented. Be sure they note the page numbers with their descriptions. For each pair, ask students to write a description of the similarities and differences between the pictures. Use a pair-share discussion activity to compare student responses. Suggested responses for each pair of pages are provided.

PAGES 22–23: Dolls

Materials

Transparency sheet or tracing paper

These two pages provide a three-dimensional look at *congruency*. That is, they ask the question: Are the two dolls the same size and same shape?

ACTIVITY

Use a transparency and pen to outline the doll on the left page. Then place the outline over the doll on the right page. Ask:

Even though they are probably the same size, why don't they match exactly? **[Answer: The clothes and hair are different.]**

SIMILARITIES

The dolls are the same size and shape. The arms and feet are in the same position. The facial expressions are exactly the same.

DIFFERENCES

One has a hat, the other doesn't. One has pants on; the other has a skirt. One has a coat; the other a vest. One has straight hair; the other has pigtails. One has boots; the other doesn't.

PAGES 24–25: Dogs

SIMILARITIES

Both are dogs. Both have tails, two eyes, a nose, four legs, two ears, and fur.

DIFFERENCES

They are two different dog breeds. One has droopy ears; the other dog's ears stand up. One has a tail that stands straight up; the other has a tail that curls. One face is long and narrow; the other is full. One is brown and black; the other is white and gray.

PAGES 26–27: Red Riding Hood and the Wolf

SIMILARITIES

The objects are in exactly the same place in both pictures. The images in the pictures are the same. They both have frames around them.

DIFFERENCES

The picture on the right is slightly smaller than the picture on the left.

PAGES 28–29: Blocks

SIMILARITIES

Exactly the same number of each block shape is used in both pictures.

DIFFERENCES

The blocks are arranged differently so that they form two different objects.

PAGES 30–31: Mazes

SIMILARITIES

The same numbers of mice are in the same locations in both pictures. Both have mazes through which the mice can start and finish. If the line segments in both mazes were placed end-to-end, they would be equal in length.

DIFFERENCES

To travel the maze on the left, the mouse must go to the left first. To travel the maze on the right, the mouse must go to the right first.

PAGES 32–33: Farms

SIMILARITIES

Both are pictures of a farm scene with children playing hide-and-seek. The three trees are in the same positions. The houses are in the same positions. The cows in the top right corners are the same.

DIFFERENCES

There is a boy in a green shirt at the bottom left corner of the right-hand page, but not on the left-hand page. The chicken and watering can have reversed positions between the left-hand page and the right-hand page. The right-hand page has one more crow than the left-hand page. The left-hand page has a boy hiding behind the top-most tree. The left-hand page has a dog chasing a cat, but in the right-hand page the cat is chasing the dog.

PAGES 34–35: Color Pixels

SIMILARITIES

The designs have the same color arrangements and the same numbers of rectangles. Both designs are squares. Each row and column follows the same color pattern.

DIFFERENCES

The pixels in the picture on the left are all squares that are the same size. The pixels in the picture on the right get larger in the center and smaller at the edges.

CLOSURE

After completing these exercises, you may want to have students find similarities and differences among triangles or quadrilaterals. See the lesson on *Grandfather Tang's Story* for more activities in comparing and classifying quadrilaterals.

Describe how finding similarities and differences in these pictures are analogous to classifying quadrilaterals. All quadrilaterals have similarities, but they also can have differences.

Composition Connection

WRITING A POST-READING COMPOSITION

Materials

Copy of the book (focus on illustrations on pages 32–33), **Connection to Writing Assessment: Post-Reading Composition** (Reproducible Master 135), **Have I...? Checklist** (Reproducible Master 2), **Rubric for Scoring First Drafts** (Reproducible Master 3)

Have students complete the following activity after finishing Chapter 2 of *Anno's Math Games II*.

Give students the **Connection to Writing Assessment: Post-Reading Composition** along with a copy of the **Have I...? Checklist**.

Give students about 20 minutes in which to write the composition and edit and revise it based on the checklist.

Collect and **score** the students' compositions using the **Rubric for Scoring First Drafts**. Students may also be encouraged to put their scored drafts into a folder of "works in progress," which can be further edited and revised for sharing with an audience at some later date.

Reproducible Master 135

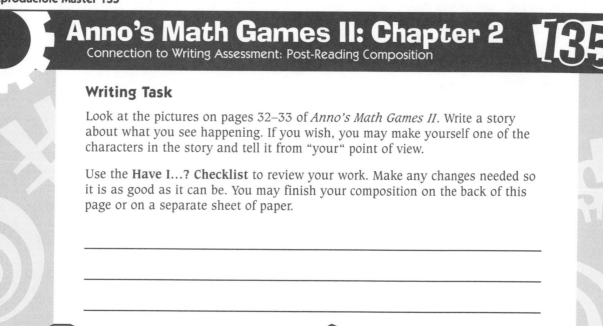

Anno's Math Games II: Chapter 2 135

Connection to Writing Assessment: Post-Reading Composition

Writing Task

Look at the pictures on pages 32–33 of *Anno's Math Games II*. Write a story about what you see happening. If you wish, you may make yourself one of the characters in the story and tell it from "your" point of view.

Use the **Have I...? Checklist** to review your work. Make any changes needed so it is as good as it can be. You may finish your composition on the back of this page or on a separate sheet of paper.

____

____

____

Extending the Connections

LANGUAGE ARTS ACTIVITY: Using Details to Describe

Talk to the class about the two pictures on pages 32–33. Ask students if they've ever played hide-and-seek. If so, ask:

What is the person who is wearing red shorts, a white shirt, and a yellow hat and leaning against the tree doing?

- ***How far into the game do you think this is?***
- ***How high has the person who is "it" counted?***
- ***How many different hiding places are being used?***
- ***What do you think is the best hiding place?***
- ***What details help you answer these questions?***

There are no single correct answers to the questions, but this is an opportunity for students to use details as evidence to support something they believe to be true. This is an important verbal skill. You also can ask students to explain the strategies that various children in the picture are using to avoid being found. They also can speculate about whether or not the strategies are good. Ask the class to think about when strategies can be useful in everyday life.

Anno's Math Games II

Overview of the Connections

Chapter 3: *Dots, Dots, and More Dots* (pages 36–53) uses sets of pictures and examples from real-life situations to develop the concept of density and infinity, as well as building a foundational understanding for coordinates.

The pictures in this section offer students an opportunity to reason out a story from the details presented.

Chapter 3

Dots, Dots, and More Dots

MATERIALS FOR THE CONNECTIONS

Anno's Math Games II • ISBN 0-698-11672-0

Written and illustrated by Mitsumasa Anno. New York: Putnam & Grosset Group, 1997.

Language Arts

~ Copies of the book (1 for each group of 2–4 students)

~ Optional: **Connection to Viewing Assessment: Writing About a Picture Prompt** (Reproducible Master 1)

~ **Have I...? Checklist** (Reproducible Master 2), a self-monitoring tool for student writers

~ **Rubric for Scoring First Drafts** (Reproducible Master 3)

~ **Connection to Writing Assessment: Post-Reading Composition** (Reproducible Master 137)

Mathematics

~ **Connections to Mathematics Assessment: Check for Understanding** (Reproducible Master 136)

~ Math journals

Viewing Connection

INTRODUCING THE LESSON WITH A PICTURE PROMPT AND WRITING

Materials

Copies of the book (page 37), **Connection to Viewing Assessment: Writing About a Picture Prompt** (Reproducible Master 1), **Have I...? Checklist** (Reproducible Master 2), **Rubric for Scoring First Drafts** (Reproducible Master 3)

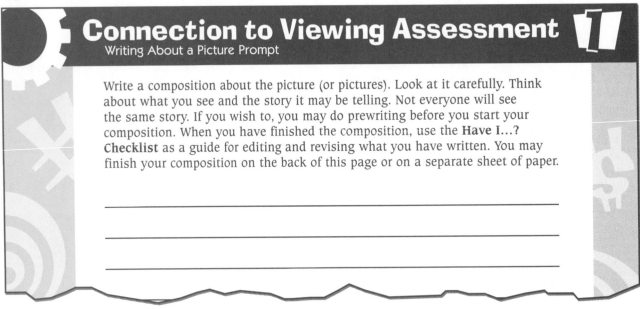

Show the class the pictures on page 37 with the text covered up. This page shows the characters, Kriss and Kross, tearing down a sign. If possible, allow students to continue to look at the picture throughout the writing session. You may distribute a copy of **Connection to Viewing Assessment: Writing About a Picture Prompt** to each student, or they may use notebook paper for their work. Also distribute copies of the **Have I...? Checklist**.

Read these directions to the class:

"You are going to write a composition about these pictures. Look at them carefully. Think about what you see and the story they may be telling. It is OK that not everyone will see the same story. If you wish to, you may do prewriting before you start your composition. When you have finished the composition, use the **Have I...? Checklist** as a guide for editing and revising what you have written."

Give the students 20–30 minutes to write their compositions and do initial editing.

Collect and score the students' compositions using the **Rubric for Scoring First Drafts**. Teach students how to compare their scored compositions to the rubric and to make notes about how to improve their compositions. Students also may be taught to use the rubric to score their own work or that of other students.

Reproducible Master 1

Connection to Viewing Assessment 1

Writing About a Picture Prompt

Write a composition about the picture (or pictures). Look at it carefully. Think about what you see and the story it may be telling. Not everyone will see the same story. If you wish to, you may do prewriting before you start your composition. When you have finished the composition, use the **Have I...? Checklist** as a guide for editing and revising what you have written. You may finish your composition on the back of this page or on a separate sheet of paper.

____

____

____

Mathematics Connection

DEVELOPING UNDERSTANDING OF DENSITY

You may wish to use this activity to introduce the concept of density before reading the book with the class.

Ask students if they have ever heard the terms *dot matrix printer* or *dots per inch*. Hold a discussion about what these terms mean in relationship to the clarity of the printing or scanning of a picture, or the clarity of a picture that one sees on a television or computer monitor. Establish that the more dots, or "pixels," in a given area — on their TV screen, a photo, a printed document, or an electronic computer image — the clearer the image.

Extend this idea into an informal discussion about the huge number of dots or points that exist.

Ask students how many dots it takes to make a line, and if it would be practical to count every dot? [No] Explain that an estimate of the dots is usually used because there are too many to count one at a time. (There are an infinite number of points because, in theory, you can always place one more dot or point between each pair of dots that already exists.)

ACTIVE READING

Materials

Several copies of the book (ideally, 1 for each group of 2–4 students), math journals

Read Chapter 3 of *Anno's Math Games II*, posing questions and discussing the text and illustrations. Encourage students to practice active reading skills, such as asking questions, thinking to themselves, and discussing their ideas. Ensure that they understand that practicing effective reading means asking themselves questions while they read.

After showing all the pages in this section, have students write a journal entry in response to the following prompt:

John used beads that were $\frac{1}{8}$ of an inch in diameter to make a picture of a barn, the sky, and clouds. Sally stitched exactly the same scene using yarn that was $\frac{1}{16}$ of an inch round. Which picture do you think would be clearer and why? [Answer: Sally's picture would probably be clearer because her thread is half the size of the beads and, therefore, would show more detail.]

PAGES 52–53: Developing the Concept of Coordinates

Use the pictures on page 52–53 to begin the idea of using numbers and letters to locate various objects. If the letters on the right of the page started with "A" on the bottom and continued in alphabetical order to label each row until the letter "M" was reached at the top, it would be easy to describe which tile was being copied by giving the number and the letter of the tile.

Based on this premise, ask the following questions:

- ***Describe the tile located by the number 5 and the letter A. (5,A).*** **[Answer: A border tile made of an orange square standing on one corner in the center and blue triangles around it.]**
- ***Describe the tile located by the number 10 and the letter L (10,L).*** **[Answer: Part of the skull of the pirate flag.]**
- ***At what location is the orange crow's nest on the mast of the ship?*** **[Answer: (9,I)]**

Extend the discussion of coordinates by explaining that every dot or pixel on a TV screen or a computer screen has a location name just like the tiles. Usually two numbers are used to identify the location rather than a number and a letter. These pairs of numbers are called *coordinates*. The first number always tells the numbers going across (the columns); the second number always tells the numbers up and down (rows).

So in the picture example above, if the letters A–M were replaced by the numbers 1–13, the location for (5,M) would be known as (5,13) The location of (10,L) would be called (10,12). Ask:

What is pictured at the location called (9,11)? **[Answer: It is where the mast and the boom cross. There is a black mark showing how they are connected.]**

- ***Describe the figure made from tiles (3,K), (4,K), (3,J) and (4,J).*** **[Answer: part of the sun]**

- ***Describe the figure made from tiles (11,7), (11,6), (11,5), (12,5), (12,6), (12,7), (13, 7), (13,6), and (13,5). [Answer: It is the sailor with the yellow cap on.]***

- ***Describe the tiles that would be used to make the pirate.*** **[Answer: (6,9), (6,8), (6,7), (6,6), (6,5) (7,5), (7,6), (7,7), (7,8), (7,9), (8,5), (8,6), (8,7), (8,8), (8,9), (9,8)]**

MATHEMATICS ASSESSMENT

Materials

Connection to Mathematics Assessment: Check for Understanding (Reproducible Masters 136)

Distribute the worksheet with multiple-choice and open-ended questions called **Connection to Mathematics Assessment: Check for Understanding**. This activity can be used to check students' understanding of the mathematics concepts covered in this lesson.

Collect and score the students' work using the answers and rubric that follow.

Reproducible Master 136 with answers

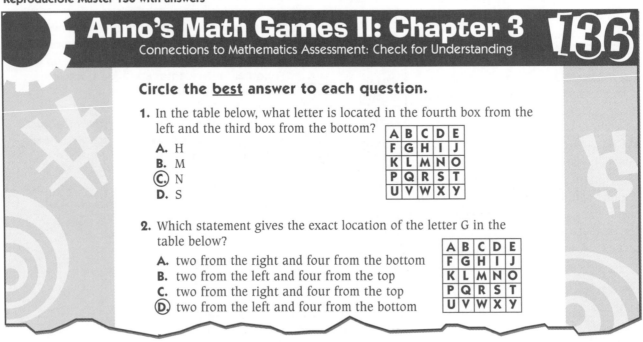

Anno's Math Games II: Chapter 3

Connections to Mathematics Assessment: Check for Understanding

136

Circle the best answer to each question.

1. In the table below, what letter is located in the fourth box from the left and the third box from the bottom?

A. H
B. M
(C.) N
D. S

A	B	C	D	E
F	G	H	I	J
K	L	M	N	O
P	Q	R	S	T
U	V	W	X	Y

2. Which statement gives the exact location of the letter G in the table below?

A. two from the right and four from the bottom
B. two from the left and four from the top
C. two from the right and four from the top
(D.) two from the left and four from the bottom

A	B	C	D	E
F	G	H	I	J
K	L	M	N	O
P	Q	R	S	T
U	V	W	X	Y

Continued...

3. Which camera should Roberto buy if he wants a digital camera that will produce the clearest, most detailed picture? A camera that records...

A. 300 dots per inch
B. 600 dots per inch
C. 900 dots per inch
(D) 1,200 dots per inch

4. Betsy is going to sew beads to make an image of an American flag. Assuming there are no gaps between the beads, which will give the clearest image of the flag?

(A) $\frac{1}{16}$-inch-round beads
B. $\frac{1}{8}$-inch-round beads
C. $\frac{1}{2}$-inch-round beads
D. $\frac{3}{4}$-inch-round beads

5. If the same size jar were filled to the top with the following objects, which would have the most objects? The jar filled with ...

A. marbles
(B) grains of sand
C. pebbles
D. grapes

6. If you wanted to count the number of objects in a pound, which of the following would be the most difficult to count: a pound of salt, a pound of grapes, a pound of peas, or a pound of coffee? Tell why.
see rubric that follows for scoring

RUBRIC FOR SCORING
Problem 6

An effective response will need to:
- identify a choice that would be very difficult to count (salt or coffee).
- give a logical explanation.
- present the answer clearly.

POINTS	CRITERIA
3	The student gives a clear, logical explanation for the item identified as hardest to count. Example: *The pound of salt would be hardest to count because the grains are so small. The others would be hard to count, but the salt has the smallest individual pieces.*
2	The student identifies an object, but the explanation is unclear.
1	The student identifies an object, but the explanation has gaps or is missing.
0	The student shows no understanding of the problem.

Composition Connection

WRITING A POST-READING COMPOSITION

Materials

☑ **Copies of the book for each group of 2–4** students (focus on pages 44–45), **Connection to Writing Assessment: Post-Reading Composition** (Reproducible Master 137), **Have I…? Checklist** (Reproducible Master 2)

Have students complete the following activity after finishing Chapter 3 of *Anno's Math Games II*.

Distribute the **Connection** to **Writing Assessment: Post-Reading Composition** along with a copy of the **Have I…? Checklist**.

Give students about 20 minutes in which to write the composition and edit/revise it based on the checklist.

Collect and score the students' compositions using the rubric below.

Students may also be encouraged to put their scored drafts into a folder of "works in progress," which can be further edited and revised for sharing with an audience at some later date.

Reproducible Master 137

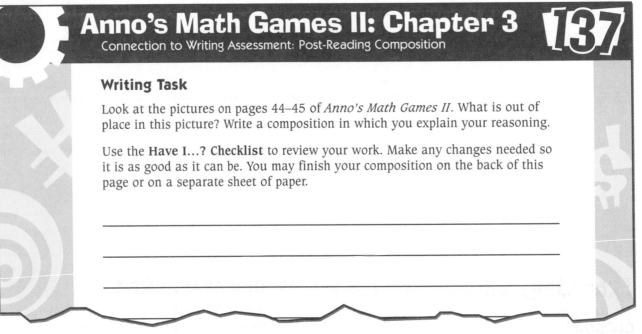

Anno's Math Games II: Chapter 3 137

Connection to Writing Assessment: Post-Reading Composition

Writing Task

Look at the pictures on pages 44–45 of *Anno's Math Games II*. What is out of place in this picture? Write a composition in which you explain your reasoning.

Use the **Have I…? Checklist** to review your work. Make any changes needed so it is as good as it can be. You may finish your composition on the back of this page or on a separate sheet of paper.

____

____

____

RUBRIC FOR SCORING

Open-ended Viewing Task

An effective response will need to:

- reflect knowledge of the story.
- justify ideas from the text.
- be logical in its reasoning.
- be well written and clearly presented.

POINTS	CRITERIA
4	Recognizes that relative size is the key difference and that the car is the wrong size unless it is a small toy. The person's hand drawing the strawberries gives a fairly consistent frame of reference to work from. The answer is well written, complete, and generally accurate in linguistic conventions, as well as logical in its reasoning.
3	Answer is generally well written and presents a logical response, but support may be weak or a key detail may be missing.
2	Doesn't understand the concept of "out of place" or misses a logical point and/or the ideas are accurate but sketchy and poorly developed. Writing may show weaknesses
1	States a conclusion, which may or may not be accurate, but provides no elaboration. Shows minimal or no understanding of the selection presented. Composition is generally poor.
0	Doesn't respond or doesn't deal with the task.

Extending the Connections

CLOSURE

Have students respond to the following prompt:

Name something that would be almost impossible to count and discuss how you would be able to describe and compare various quantities of this item. [Possible answer: Seeds are often very small, and they are often sold by the ounce or pound.]

ADDITIONAL RESOURCES

Windows on Math, Volume 4 Videodisc, Unit 9, "Judith's Juice Joint." Atlanta: Optical Data Corporation, 1996. Call 1-800-524-2481.

Lawrence, Paul. *ESPA^3 Book 3: "Tile Month."* Iowa City, Iowa: Tutor Tools, 1998.Call 1-800-776-3454.

Teacher Notes

Anno's Math Games II

Overview of the Connections

Chapter 4: Counting With Circles (pages 54–77) develops the concepts of variables (representing ideas using algebra), one-to-one correspondence, missing addends (which can be extended to basic equations and their solutions), the base-ten number system, and data organization and representation.

In language arts, students have opportunities to write about text that is presented in a visual fashion.

Chapter 4

Counting With Circles

MATERIALS FOR THE CONNECTIONS

Anno's Math Games II • ISBN 0-698-11672-0

Written and illustrated by Mitsumasa Anno. New York: Putnam & Grosset Group, 1997.

Language Arts

~ Copies of the book (1 for each group of 2–4 students)

~ Optional: **Connection to Viewing Assessment: Writing About a Picture Prompt** (Reproducible Master 1)

~ **Have I...? Checklist** (Reproducible Master 2), a self-monitoring tool for student writers

~ **Rubric for Scoring First Drafts** (Reproducible Master 3)

~ **Connection to Writing Assessment: Post-Reading Composition** (Reproducible Master 142)

Mathematics

~ Connecting cubes or beans (about 100 per group of 2–4 students)

~ Base-ten models

~ **Making Number Sentences I and II** (Reproducible Masters 138–139)

~ **The Number Sentence Game** (Reproducible Master 140)

~ **Connection to Mathematics Assessment: Check for Understanding** (Reproducible Master 141)

Viewing Connection

INTRODUCING THE LESSON WITH A PICTURE PROMPT AND WRITING

Materials

Copy of the book (pages 66–67), **Connection to Viewing Assessment: Writing About a Picture Prompt** (Reproducible Master 1), **Have I...? Checklist** (Reproducible Master 2), **Rubric for Scoring First Drafts** (Reproducible Master 3)

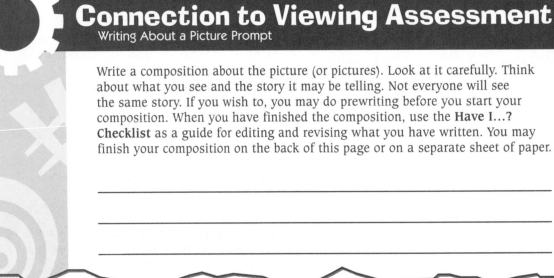

Show the class the pictures on pages 66–67 with the text covered up. This page shows a farm scene. If possible, allow students to continue to look at the picture throughout the writing session. You may distribute a copy of **Connection to Viewing Assessment: Writing About a Picture Prompt** to each student, or they may use notebook paper for their work. Also distribute copies of the **Have I...? Checklist**.

Read these directions to the class:

"You are going to write a composition about this picture. Look at it carefully. Think about what you see and the story it may be telling. It is OK that not everyone will see the same story. If you wish to, you may do prewriting before you start your composition. When you have finished the composition, use the **Have I...? Checklist** as a guide for editing and revising what you have written."

Give the students 20–30 minutes to write their compositions and do initial editing.

Collect and score the students' compositions using the **Rubric for Scoring First Drafts**. Teach students how to compare their scored compositions to the rubric and to make notes about how to improve their compositions. Students also may be taught to use the rubric to score their own work or that of other students.

Reproducible Master 1

Connection to Viewing Assessment 1

Writing About a Picture Prompt

Write a composition about the picture (or pictures). Look at it carefully. Think about what you see and the story it may be telling. Not everyone will see the same story. If you wish to, you may do prewriting before you start your composition. When you have finished the composition, use the **Have I...? Checklist** as a guide for editing and revising what you have written. You may finish your composition on the back of this page or on a separate sheet of paper.

____

____

____

Mathematics Connection

INTRODUCTION AND ACTIVE READING

Materials

Several copies of the book (ideally, 1 for each group of 2–4 students),

As you read Chapter 4, pose questions and conduct activities as described in the book and in the guide below. Encourage them to practice active reading skills, such as asking questions, thinking to themselves, and discussing their ideas. Ensure that they understand that practicing effective reading means asking themselves questions while they read. You might choose to do some or all of the activities provided here.

Read the story and show the pictures to the class. Suggestions for questions and extensions to each of the pages are provided below.

PAGES 56–57: Children

What does each circle stand for? **[Answer: A child.]**

PAGE 58: Horses

What does each circle stand for? **[Answer: A horse.]**

PAGE 59: Horses with Riders

What does each circle stand for? **[Answer: A horse and a rider.]**

PAGES 60–61: Elephants and Ants

After studying the picture, how do you know that the circles can stand for anything? **[Answer: The sets all look the same. The words above the boxes tell what the circles represent.]**

- ***Why would it be necessary to tell someone what the circles represent?*** **[Answer: So the circles have a meaning.]**
- ***Instead of the sets of five circles, what else could be used to identify these sets of objects?*** **[Answer: Use the symbol 5.]**

PAGES 62–63: Birds in Cages

Materials

Connecting cubes

Have students use different color connecting cubes to act out each of the problems from left to right on pages 62 and 63. Let green represent the birds outside of the cage and red represent the birds inside the cage. Once they have acted out the problems, check for understanding by modeling situations using the cubes and then translating each of the models to symbols. Ask questions, such as:

If the following sentences describe each of the pictures from left to right, what does the n stand for?

$n + 5 = 5$	$n + 4 = 5$	$n + 3 = 5$
$n + 2 = 5$	$n + 1 = 5$	$n + 0 = 5$

[Answer: The *n* stands for the birds out of cage.]

- ***Based on this idea, describe what n + 9 = 12 means.*** **[Answer: This sentence means that there are 3 birds outside of the cage.]**

PAGES 64–65: Goats and Crows

Match each of the sets shown below with an item in the picture. How do you know your answers are correct? [Possible answer: I counted 2 circles and there are 2 flowers. The amounts match so I know I'm right.]

● [Answer: The sun.]

●● [Answer: The flowers.]

●●● [Answer: The goats.]

●●●● [Answer: The crows or sets of four leaves.]

●●●●● [Answer: The apples.]

PAGES 66–67: Farm

●● [Answer: two trucks]

●●●●●●● [Answer: seven people]

●●● [Answer: three pigs]

●●●●●● [Answer: six houses]

●●●●●●●●● [Answer: nine cows]

PAGES 68–73: Circles to Cubes to Numbers

Materials

☑ Base–ten models

Have students use base-ten *units* and *tens* to model the "house" constructions in the book on pages 70–73.

PAGES 74–77: Comparing Scenes of Plants, Animals, and People

Materials

☑ **Making Number Sentences I and II** (Reproducible Masters 138–139), copies of the book (for 2–4 students per group)

To develop the concept of number sentences and variables, review the pictures and charts on pages 74–77. Model a few examples for the class before allowing the students to work in pairs or small groups.

Distribute Making Number Sentences I and II to groups of 2–4 students. Tell students to count the numbers of each animal and record the data in the appropriate columns on the activity sheet.

Making Number Sentences

Explain the examples below using the reproducible masters as a guide. Tell students that one way to represent the total number of like animals in the scenes on pages 74–75 and 76–77 is to use letters and numbers.

EXAMPLE 1

There are 3 horses in the scene on pages 74–75 and 4 horses in the scene on pages 76–77. This means there is a total of 7 horses altogether. If H stands for horses, then: $3H + 4H = 7H$.

EXAMPLE 2

There are 8 butterflies in the scene on pages 74–75 and 9 butterflies in the scene on pages 76–77. There is at total of 17 butterflies altogether. If B stands for butterflies, then $8B + 9B = 17B$.

EXAMPLE 3

There is 1 fox in the scene on pages 74–75 and 2 foxes in the scene on pages 76–77. There is a total of 3 foxes altogether. If F stands for fox, then $1F + 2F = 3F$.

Present the following additional problems to students.

What do you think the following sentences stand for?

- ***7M + 10M = 17M*** **[Answer: There is a total of 17 mice altogether.]**
- ***12L + 10L = 22L*** **[Answer: There is a total of 22 little birds altogether.]**

Have students finish the "Number Sentences" column as appropriate.

Building Number Sentences with Variables

Making Number Sentences II shows number sentences with variables based on the pictures from the book. Review the discussion given in **Making Number Sentences II** with the class. To help students understand the concept of variables, explain that there are times when sentences can help us find the missing numbers. Present the following examples:

EXAMPLE 1

If we know the total number of an animal in both scenes, and we know the number of the animal in one scene, we can find out how many of the animal there are in the other scene.

EXAMPLE 2

There are a total of 11 children in both scenes. Let C stand for the number of children in the first scene. Given the sentence $C + 6 = 11$, what does C stand for? [Answer: 5 children] What does the sentence mean? [Answer: The number of children in the first scene plus 6 equals the total number of children, which is 11.]

EXAMPLE 3

There are a total of 17 mice in both scenes. Let M equal the number of mice in the first scene. Given the sentence $M + 7 = 17$, what does M stand for? [Answer: 11 mice]

What does the number mean? [Answer: There were 11 mice in the first scene.]

What does the sentence mean? [Answer: The number of mice in the first scene plus 7 equals the total number of mice, which is 17.]

Have children write explanations for each of the remaining sentences in **Making Number Sentences II**.

Anno's Math Games II: Chapter 4

138

Making Number Sentences I

Use the first two columns in the chart below to record the numbers of each animal on pages 74–77 of *Anno's Math Games II*.

Animal	Pages 74–75	Pages 76–77	Number Sentences	Sentences with Unknown Variables
Horses	3	4	$3H + 4H = 7H$	$H + 4 = 7$
Butterflies	8	2	$8B + 2B = 10B$	$B + 2 = 10$
Foxes	1	9	$1F + 9F = 10F$	$1 + F = 10$
Snails	6	5	$6S + 5S = 11S$	$6 + S = 11$
Flowers	9	8	$9f + 8f = 17f$	$f + 8 = 17$
Children	5	9	$5C + 9C = 14C$	$C + 9 = 14$
Mice	7	10	$7M + 10M = 17M$	$7 + M = 17$
Squirrels	2	1	$2s + 1s = 3s$	$2 + s = 3$
Trees	4	4	$4T + 4T = 8T$	$4 + T = 8$
Little birds	10	12	$10L + 12L = 22L$	$L + 12 = 8$

Look at the information you recorded in the chart so far. Make a list of the types of plants and animals in order from smallest to largest amount.

Answer: fox, squirrel, horses, trees, children, snails, mice, butterflies, flowers, little birds

Anno's Math Games II: Chapter 4

139

Making Number Sentences II

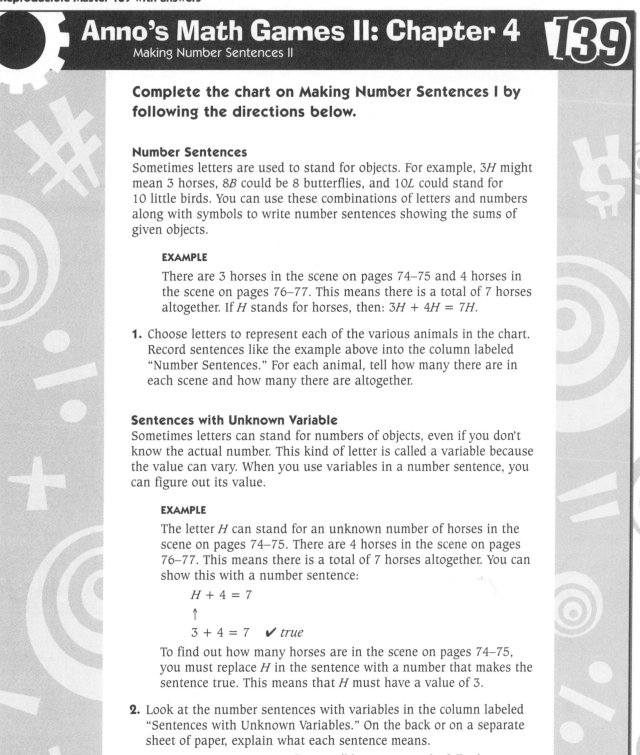

Complete the chart on Making Number Sentences I by following the directions below.

Number Sentences

Sometimes letters are used to stand for objects. For example, *3H* might mean 3 horses, *8B* could be 8 butterflies, and 10*L* could stand for 10 little birds. You can use these combinations of letters and numbers along with symbols to write number sentences showing the sums of given objects.

EXAMPLE

There are 3 horses in the scene on pages 74–75 and 4 horses in the scene on pages 76–77. This means there is a total of 7 horses altogether. If *H* stands for horses, then: $3H + 4H = 7H$.

1. Choose letters to represent each of the various animals in the chart. Record sentences like the example above into the column labeled "Number Sentences." For each animal, tell how many there are in each scene and how many there are altogether.

Sentences with Unknown Variable

Sometimes letters can stand for numbers of objects, even if you don't know the actual number. This kind of letter is called a variable because the value can vary. When you use variables in a number sentence, you can figure out its value.

EXAMPLE

The letter *H* can stand for an unknown number of horses in the scene on pages 74–75. There are 4 horses in the scene on pages 76–77. This means there is a total of 7 horses altogether. You can show this with a number sentence:

$H + 4 = 7$

↑

$3 + 4 = 7$ ✔ *true*

To find out how many horses are in the scene on pages 74–75, you must replace *H* in the sentence with a number that makes the sentence true. This means that *H* must have a value of 3.

2. Look at the number sentences with variables in the column labeled "Sentences with Unknown Variables." On the back or on a separate sheet of paper, explain what each sentence means.

See possible answers on the following page.

Possible answers:

- $H + 4 = 7$: The number of horses on pages 74–75 plus the 4 horses on pages 76–77 equals 7 horses altogether.
- $B + 2 = 10$: The number of butterflies on pages 74–75 plus the 2 butterflies on pages 76–77 equals 10 butterflies altogether.
- $1 + F = 10$: The fox on pages 74–75 added to the number of foxes on pages 76–77 equals 10 foxes altogether
- $6 + S = 11$: The 6 snails on pages 74–75 added to the number of snails on pages 76–77 equal 11 snails altogether.
- $f + 8 = 17$: The number of flowers on pages 74–75 added to the 8 flowers on pages 76–77 equals 17 flowers altogether.
- $C + 9 = 14$: The number of children on pages 74–75 added to the 9 children on pages 76–77 equals 13 children altogether.
- $7 + M = 17$: The 7 mice on pages 74–75 added to the number of mice on pages 76–77 equals 17 mice altogether.
- $2 + s = 3$: The 2 squirrels on pages 74–75 added to the number of squirrels on pages 76–77 equals 3 squirrels altogether.
- $4 + T = 8$: The 4 trees on pages 75–75 added to the number of trees on pages 76–77 equals 8 trees altogether.
- $L + 12 = 22$: The number of little trees on pages 75–75 added to the 12 little trees on pages 76–77 equals 22 little trees altogether.

PROVIDING PRACTICE

Materials

The Number Sentence Game (Reproducible Master 140), deck of playing cards, connecting cubes or beans (about 100 per group of 2–4 students)

Distribute copies of **The Number Sentence Game** to groups of 2–4 students. Encourage students to use the cubes to help them solve the number sentences. Once the sentences are established, students can use different color cubes for the unknowns and other colors to form the rest of the number sentence.

As an extension you may want to write sentences on the board and have students model the solutions using cubes.

Reproducible Master 140

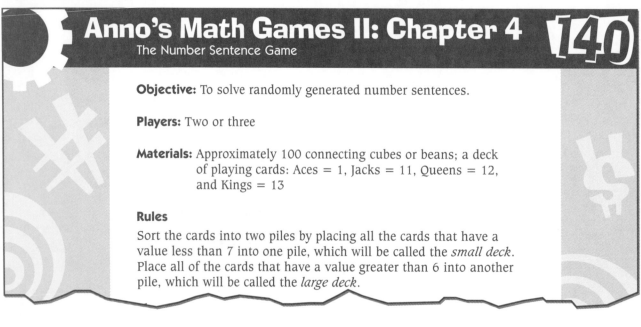

Anno's Math Games II: Chapter 4 — 140

The Number Sentence Game

Objective: To solve randomly generated number sentences.

Players: Two or three

Materials: Approximately 100 connecting cubes or beans; a deck of playing cards: Aces = 1, Jacks = 11, Queens = 12, and Kings = 13

Rules

Sort the cards into two piles by placing all the cards that have a value less than 7 into one pile, which will be called the *small deck*. Place all of the cards that have a value greater than 6 into another pile, which will be called the *large deck*.

Players take turns forming number sentences by following the steps below.

1. Take two cards from the *small deck*. These cards are used to make the part of the sentence on the left side of the equal sign. The first card is placed face down and it represents the *n*, or unknown, in the sentence. The second card is placed face up and it represents the number that is added to the unknown.
2. Take one card from the *large deck*. This card is used to make the part of the sentence on the right side of the equal sign. It represents the sum in the number sentence. Place it face up.
3. Tell what the value of the card that is face down should be to make the number sentence true. (Do not turn this card over. It's only a placeholder.)
4. Another player checks your answer by acting out the problem using cubes.

The player with the most number of cubes at the end of the game wins.

EXAMPLE PLAY

John takes two cards from the small deck. He places one card facedown and places a 3 of hearts face-up. From the large deck, he chooses a king of clubs. His number sentence is $n + 3 = 13$. *He says that* n *should be 10. Sue checks his answer by taking 10 cubes and 3 cubes and combining them to see if, in fact, they add to 13. John is correct! He takes 10 cubes.*

MATHEMATICS ASSESSMENT

Materials

Connection to Mathematics Assessment: Check for Understanding (Reproducible Master 141)

Distribute the worksheets with multiple-choice and open-ended questions called **Connection to Mathematics Assessment: Check for Understanding**. This activity can be used to check students' understanding of the mathematics concepts covered in this lesson.

Collect and **score** the students' work using the answers and rubric that follow.

Reproducible Master 141 with answers

Anno's Math Games II: Chapter 4

Connections to Mathematics Assessment: Check for Understanding

141

Circle the best answer to each question.

1. Let B stand for one baseball (B = ). Which of the following would best stand for $8B$?

   A. 
   B. 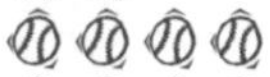
   C. 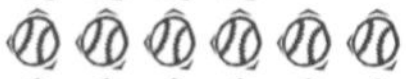
   (D) 

2. Let A stand for one paper airplane (A = ). Which of the following would stand for the two sets shown below combined together?

   A. 4A
   B. 6A
   (C) 10A **6 + 4**
   D. 24A

3. What is the value of N in the sentence: $N + 4 = 12$?

   A. 3
   B. 4
   (C) 8 **8 + 4 = 12**
   D. 12

4. You want to use different color chips to represent the objects below. Which of the following sets would be best represented by 6 yellow chips?

   A. 
   B. 
   C. 
   (D) 

Continued...

5. Let M stands for one moon (M = ☾). Which of the following best represents the total of $5M + 3M$?

A. ☾ ☾

B. ☾ ☾ ☾

C. ☾ ☾ ☾ ☾ ☾

(D.) ☾ ☾ ☾ ☾ ☾ ☾ ☾ ☾ **5 + 3 = 8**

6. Why can't you tell which of the following sets represents $4C$?

Set A: ♣ ♣ ♣ ♣

Set B:  **see rubric that follows for scoring**

RUBRIC FOR SCORING

Problem 6

An effective response will need to:

- show that the *C* has not been defined.
- give a clear explanation.

POINTS	CRITERIA
3	The student indicates a correct response with a clear explanation that reflects understanding of the concept. Example *You cannot tell what the 4*C *stands for because the* C *is not defined. In this case, the* C *might stand for* clover *but it also could stand for* cats. *The other reason* C *cannot be determined is because both sets A and B have the same number of elements.*
2	The student states that 4C cannot be determined showing some understanding of the concepts, but the explanation is unclear.
1	The student states that 4C cannot be determined, but the explanation has gaps and/or does not indicate understanding of the concept of a variable.
0	The student shows no understanding of the problem or leaves it blank.

Composition Connection

WRITING A POST-READING COMPOSITION

Materials

Copy of the book (focus on illustrations on page 59), **Connection to Writing Assessment: Post-Reading Composition** (Reproducible Master 142), **Have I...? Checklist** (Reproducible Master 2), **Rubric for Scoring First Drafts** (Reproducible Master 3)

Have students complete the following activity after finishing Chapter 4 of *Anno's Math Games II*.

Give students the **Connection to Writing Assessment: Post-Reading Composition** along with a copy of the **Have I...? Checklist**.

Give students about 20 minutes in which to write the composition and edit/revise it based on the checklist.

Collect and **score** the students' compositions using the **Rubric for Scoring First Drafts**. Students may also be encouraged to put their scored drafts into a folder of "works in progress," which can be further edited and revised for sharing with an audience at some later date.

Reproducible Master 142

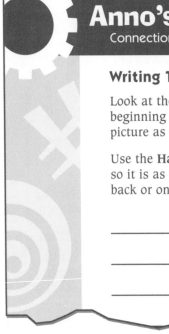

Anno's Math Games II: Chapter 4

142

Connection to Writing Assessment: Post-Reading Composition

Writing Task

Look at the pictures on page 59 of *Anno's Math Games*. It could be either the beginning of a story or the end of a story. Write a story in which you use this picture as either the beginning or the end of the story.

Use the **Have I...? Checklist** to review your work. Make any changes needed so it is as good as it can be. You may wish to continue your composition on the back or on another sheet of paper.

____

____

____

Anno's Math Games II

Chapter 5

Counting Water

Overview of the Connections

Chapter 5: Counting Water (pages 79–97) develops the concept of largeness, standard and non-standard measure, comparison, and base ten by discussing and showing situations that can occur when trying to measure and compare various amounts of water.

Both the pictures from this section and the writing activities based upon them are challenging and appropriate for students with more advanced language arts skills.

MATERIALS FOR THE CONNECTIONS

Anno's Math Games II • ISBN 0-698-11672-0
Written and illustrated by Mitsumasa Anno. New York: Putnam & Grosset Group, 1997.

Language Arts

~ Copies of the book (1 for each group of 2–4 students)

~ Optional: **Connection to Viewing Assessment: Writing About a Picture Prompt** (Reproducible Master 1)

~ **Have I...? Checklist** (Reproducible Master 2), a self-monitoring tool for student writers

~ **Rubric for Scoring First Drafts** (Reproducible Master 3)

~ **Connection to Writing Assessment: Post-Reading Composition** (Reproducible Master 144)

Mathematics

~ Two different-shaped containers that each hold about 2 quarts of water. (See pages 82–83 in the book for reference.)

~ Clear cylinders or beakers (quantity sufficient to hold 4 quarts of liquid) with ounce, cup, and quart markings

~ Ten 8-oz cups

~ **Connection to Mathematics Assessment: Check for Understanding** (Reproducible Master 143)

Viewing Connection

INTRODUCING THE LESSON WITH A PICTURE PROMPT AND WRITING

Materials

Copy of the book (page 81), **Connection to Viewing Assessment: Writing About a Picture Prompt** (Reproducible Master 1), **Have I...? Checklist** (Reproducible Master 2), **Rubric for Scoring First Drafts** (Reproducible Master 3)

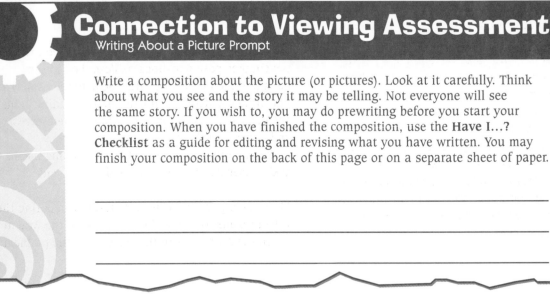

Show the class the pictures on page 81 with the text covered up. This page shows the character Kriss floating in a teacup. If possible, allow students to continue to look at the picture throughout the writing session. You may distribute a copy of **Connection to Viewing Assessment: Writing About a Picture Prompt** to each student, or they may use notebook paper for their work. Also distribute the **Have I...? Checklist**.

Read these directions to the class:

"You are going to write a composition about this picture. Look at it carefully. Think about what you see and the story it may be telling. It is OK that not everyone will see the same story. If you wish to, you may do prewriting before you start your composition. When you have finished the composition, use the **Have I...? Checklist** as a guide for editing and revising what you have written."

Give the students 20–30 minutes to write their compositions and do initial editing.

Collect and score the students' compositions using the **Rubric for Scoring First Drafts**. Teach students how to compare their scored compositions to the rubric and to make notes about how to improve their compositions. Students also may be taught to use the rubric to score their own work or that of other students.

Reproducible Master 1

Connection to Viewing Assessment 1

Writing About a Picture Prompt

Write a composition about the picture (or pictures). Look at it carefully. Think about what you see and the story it may be telling. Not everyone will see the same story. If you wish to, you may do prewriting before you start your composition. When you have finished the composition, use the **Have I...? Checklist** as a guide for editing and revising what you have written. You may finish your composition on the back of this page or on a separate sheet of paper.

____

____

____

Mathematics Connection

DEVELOPING UNDERSTANDING

Materials

Copies of the book (Chapter 3 pages 38–49 for review)

In the lesson for Chapter 3 of *Anno's Math Games II*, the class talked about dots, or *pixels*. Review with the class how sometimes there were so many dots that it would take a long time to count them and the job would be extremely boring. The beads in the design on page 49 could be counted, but it would take a long time. We could even count the stitches that the sewing machine made or the holes between the stamps (pages 38–39), but how about the sesame seeds used in the design on page 43?

As homework or a group assignment, have students write a plan describing how they could determine the quantity of beads, stitches, holes, and sesame seeds quickly, while still being reasonably accurate. Have each student or group evaluate the plan of another student or group. [Possible answers: To count all the beads, you could count the number of packages of beads that were used and then multiply by the number of beads that were in each package. Or you could weigh the beads to determine the number of beads in 1 ounce, then weigh the total amount of beads used. Multiply the total weight by the number of beads in 1 ounce to estimate the total number of beads. Using weight for the sesame seeds might also work, but even a half ounce of sesame seeds would be a lot of seeds to count. You could count the number of stitches in an inch and then multiply that by the number of inches in the entire length of stitches.]

INTRODUCTION AND ACTIVE READING

Materials

Several copies of the book (ideally, 1 for each group of 2–4 students), two different-shaped containers that each hold about 2 quarts of water, clear cylinders or beakers with ounce, cup, and quart markings (quantity sufficient to hold 4 quarts of liquid); ten 8-oz cups; rulers

Tell the students that you are going to read them a story about counting water! Discuss the difficulty this could present by connecting it to the idea of counting the dots in the pictures on page 44–45. Ask students if they have ever tried to count grains of salt or sand and why that would be very difficult.

Before you read Chapter 5 to the class, display two different-shaped containers, one filled with 6 cups of water, the other with 4 cups of water. (Refer to page 82–83 of *Anno's Math Games II* for container ideas.)

Ask students to suggest plans for determining which container is holding the most water. Discuss their various solutions.

Read pages 79–97 to the class. As you read the chapter, pose questions as described in the book and then follow up with the activities below. Encourage students to practice active reading skills, such as asking questions, thinking to themselves, and discussing their ideas. Ensure that they understand that practicing effective reading means asking themselves questions while they read.

After reading, hold a class discussion comparing the student plans for "counting water" with the way in which the characters in the story solve the problem.

PAGES 84–85: Measuring Water

Act out the scenes on pages 84–85. First empty each of the containers into uniform cylinders or beakers. (For now, ignore any measurement markings on the cylinders.) Discuss how you can visually determine which container held more water.

Then empty the contents of the cylinders into individual 8-oz cups. Discuss how many cups each of the original containers held. Ask how this "measuring" is different from the visual comparison in the beakers. [Possible answer: You know exactly how many cups filled each container instead of just knowing which had more water.]

PAGES 86–91: Using Nonstandard Measures

Re-read, discuss, and, where possible, model scenes on pages 86–91.

Have students study the containers on pages 90–91. Ask:

- ***Why weren't the other containers as good as the tall cylinder at measuring the water?*** **[Possible answer: Water can spill too easily or all the compartments might not all be filled to the same level.]**

PAGES 92–96: Using Standard Measures

Have students study the pictures and amounts on page 94. Ask:

- ***Why are these easy to count?*** **[Possible answer: You can count by 10s and then add on.]**
- ***How are they like base ten blocks?*** **[Possible answer: Ten cups look like a base ten rod and individual cups look like units.]**

Have students study page 95. Ask:

- ***What is wrong with the way Kriss and Kross measured the water on page 95?*** **[Answer: The units of measure are not the same.]**

If students have difficulty seeing the difference between the containers that Kriss used and those that Kross used, encourage them to use centimeter rulers to measure the bases of the two sets of cylinders.

Discuss the fact that most of the world uses liters and milliliters to measure liquids.

- ***In the United States, what units of measure are used for liquids?*** **[Answer: ounces, quarts, cups, gallons, etc.]**

ESTABLISHING EQUIVALENCIES

Fill the two 2-quart containers from the original "Counting Water" experiment into individual cup containers. Then pour the cups into a quart container to compare further. Establish cup, quart, and gallon equivalencies.

MATHEMATICS ASSESSMENT

Materials

Connection to Mathematics Assessment: Check for Understanding (Reproducible Master 143)

Distribute the worksheet with multiple-choice and open-ended questions called **Connection to Mathematics Assessment: Check for Understanding.** This activity can be used to check students' understanding of the mathematics concepts covered in this lesson.

Collect and score the students' work using the answers and rubric that follow.

Anno's Math Games II: Chapter 5

Connection to Mathematics Assessment: Check for Understanding

143

Circle the best answer to each question.

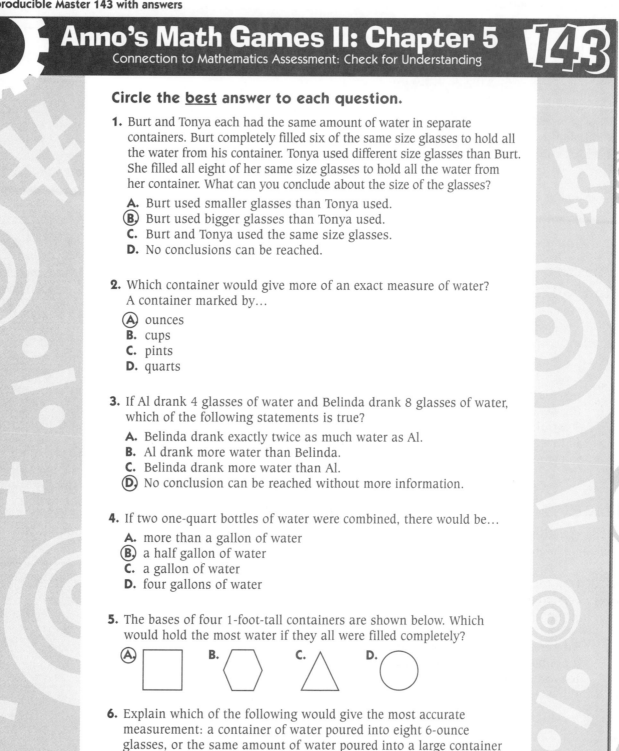

1. Burt and Tonya each had the same amount of water in separate containers. Burt completely filled six of the same size glasses to hold all the water from his container. Tonya used different size glasses than Burt. She filled all eight of her same size glasses to hold all the water from her container. What can you conclude about the size of the glasses?

A. Burt used smaller glasses than Tonya used.
(B.) Burt used bigger glasses than Tonya used.
C. Burt and Tonya used the same size glasses.
D. No conclusions can be reached.

2. Which container would give more of an exact measure of water? A container marked by...

(A.) ounces
B. cups
C. pints
D. quarts

3. If Al drank 4 glasses of water and Belinda drank 8 glasses of water, which of the following statements is true?

A. Belinda drank exactly twice as much water as Al.
B. Al drank more water than Belinda.
C. Belinda drank more water than Al.
(D.) No conclusion can be reached without more information.

4. If two one-quart bottles of water were combined, there would be...

A. more than a gallon of water
(B.) a half gallon of water
C. a gallon of water
D. four gallons of water

5. The bases of four 1-foot-tall containers are shown below. Which would hold the most water if they all were filled completely?

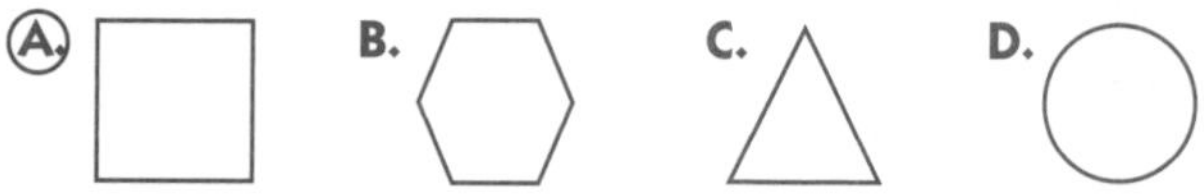

6. Explain which of the following would give the most accurate measurement: a container of water poured into eight 6-ounce glasses, or the same amount of water poured into a large container with ounce markings on the side. **see rubric that follows for scoring**

RUBRIC FOR SCORING
Problem 6

An effective response will need to:

- demonstrate understanding of the concepts of measurement systems, estimation, and precision or accuracy.
- present a clear and logical explanation.

POINTS	CRITERIA
3	The explanation of the answer demonstrates a clear understanding of the concepts of measurement systems, estimation, and precision or accuracy. Example 1: *The large container with the ounce markings would be the best way to measure because there might be spillage or inaccuracy in filling eight 6-ounce glasses with exactly the same amount of water. If the last glass was not completely filled and the glass did not have ounce markings on it, only an estimate could be made of how much water was in the last glass.* Example 2: *Pouring all the water into one container and then reading the amount to the nearest ounce would be more accurate than pouring the amounts into 8 different glasses because there would be more consistency in measuring and more precision because of the markings on the side of the container.*
2	The student indicates which method should be used to measure the water, but some of the measurement concepts are not addressed in the answer.
1	The student indicates which method would be used to measure the water, but there are gaps in the explanation or the explanation is missing. OR The student does not indicate which method should be used to measure, but the explanation shows some understanding of the essential concepts of accuracy in measurement.
0	The student shows no understanding of the problem or leaves the answer blank.

Composition Connection

WRITING A POST-READING COMPOSITION

Materials

Copies of the book (focus on illustrations on cover), **Connection to Writing Assessment: Post-Reading Composition** (Reproducible Master 144), **Have I...? Checklist** (Reproducible Master 2), **Rubric for Scoring First Drafts** (Reproducible Master 3)

Have students complete the following activity after finishing Chapter 5 of *Anno's Math Games II*.

Distribute the **Connection to Writing Assessment: Post-Reading Composition** along with a copy of the **Have I...? Checklist**.

Give students about 20 minutes in which to write the composition and edit/revise it based on the checklist.

Collect and score the students' compositions using the **Rubric for Scoring First Drafts**. Students also may be encouraged to put their scored drafts into a folder of "works in progress," which can be further edited and revised for sharing with an audience at some later date.

Reproducible Master 144

Anno's Math Games II: Chapter 5 — 144

Connection to Writing Assessment: Post-Reading Composition

Writing Task

Look at the pictures on the cover of *Anno's Math Games II*. Think about what you have learned from studying the pictures and talking about the ideas presented in this book. Imagine that the children pictured on the front of the book are in your class. Write a story telling what the children have learned and how they have learned it.

Use the **Have I...? Checklist** to review your work. Make any changes needed so it is as good as it can be. You may finish your composition on the back of this page or on a separate sheet of paper.

____

____

Extending the Connections

DAILY ACTIVITY

Each day for a week bring in a different container filled with water or sand and have the students guess how many ounces, quarts, etc., are in the container. Measure the amounts first into cups, then into quart, half-gallon, and gallon containers.

ADDITIONAL RESOURCES

Windows on Math, Volume 4 Videodisc, Unit 9, "Judith's Juice Joint." Atlanta: Optical Data Corporation, 1996. Call 1-800-524-2481.

ESPA^3 Book 3 "Tile Month." Iowa City, Iowa: Tutor Tools. Call 1-800-776-3454.

Appendix

Reproducible Masters List

1. Connection to Viewing Assessment: Writing About a Picture Prompt
2. Have I...? Checklist
3. Rubric for Scoring First Drafts

Alexander, Who Used to be Rich Last Sunday

4. Connection to Listening Assessment: Listening to a Story
5. Keeping Records for Alexander
6. 100 Pennies
7. Coin Combination Table
8. Connection to Mathematics Assessment: Check for Understanding I
9. Connection to Mathematics Assessment: Check for Understanding II
10. Connection to Writing Assessment: Post-Reading Composition

A Cloak for the Dreamer

11. Connection to Listening Assessment: Listening to Part of a Story
12. Understanding Line Symmetry I
13. Understanding Line Symmetry II
14. Pattern-Block Design I
15. Pattern-Block Design II
16. Connection to Mathematics Assessment: Check for Understanding I
17. Connection to Mathematics Assessment: Check for Understanding II
18. Connection to Writing Assessment: Post-Reading Composition

Counting On Frank

19. Connection to Listening Assessment: Listening to Part of a Story
20. Evaluating Estimates I
21. Evaluating Estimates II
22. Research Data
23. Checklist for Evaluating Plans and Solutions
24. Connection to Mathematics Assessment: Check for Understanding
25. Connection to Writing Assessment: Post-Reading Composition

The Doorbell Rang

26. Connection to Listening Assessment: Listening to Part of a Story
27. Circles
28. Fraction Circles
29. Models of Base Ten Blocks
30. Connection to Mathematics Assessment: Check for Understanding
31. Connection to Writing Assessment: Post-Reading Composition

Gator Pie

32. Connection to Listening Assessment: Listening to Part of a Story
33. Hundredths Grid
34. Connection to Mathematics Assessment: Check for Understanding I
35. Connection to Mathematics Assessment: Check for Understanding II
36. Connection to Writing Assessment: Post-Reading Composition

Meet the Authors

PAUL R. LAWRENCE

Driven by the belief that *all* students can learn mathematics, Paul Lawrence is widely known for his lively workshops for teachers of kindergarten through college and for the innovative teaching materials he has developed. His hallmarks are practical ideas and lessons that can be implemented in all classrooms.

Paul has been involved in mathematics education for the past 34 years. He taught high school mathematics and was a supervisor of mathematics for K–12. He has been a visiting part-time lecturer at Rutgers University and is past president of the Association of Math Teachers of New Jersey. In addition, he has been a member of committees involved with New Jersey's state tests in mathematics and currently serves as a member of the Board of Governors of the New Jersey Mathematics Coalition. He has been active with the New Jersey Standards Dissemination Project and has been a staff member of the New and Experienced Teacher Institutes for Excellence in Teaching Mathematics since their inception in 1986. He is often a presenter at local, state, and national conferences and has conducted hundreds of workshops throughout New Jersey.

Recent Publications

Windows on Math is a basal series with connecting video segments and a discovery approach to K–5 mathematics. Available from Optical Data Corporation, a division of McGraw-Hill Companies, 1-800-248-8478.

Mastering the Math SAT I and PSAT is a set of hands-on, discovery-based lessons and SAT-related problems that provide the conceptual understanding for students to complete SAT problems. Because 85% of the skills on the SAT are taught in middle school, this book has a 75% correlation to many states' middle-school mathematics standards. Available from Great Source Education Group, Houghton Mifflin, 1-800-289-4490.

ESPA^3 is a set of nine booklets, each of which features a different manipulative. Experiments, warms-ups, and daily activities build conceptual understanding and long-term retention that prepare students for New Jersey's fourth-grade test in mathematics. For more information, contact Tutor Tools, Inc., Iowa City, Iowa, 1-800-776-3454.

Continued...

ANN M. LAWRENCE

Ann Lawrence worked in public schools for more 30 years as a classroom teacher of English/language arts, a supervisor, and an administrator. She served as the director of basic skills, testing, and special programs in Edison, N.J., and retired as superintendent of schools in Saddle Brook, N.J. She currently serves as a consultant and teacher trainer while managing LLTeach, the Lawrences' consulting firm. Her passion is to help teachers find the most effective ways to empower students to excel in the language arts, to love reading and writing, and to be able to demonstrate their power whenever needed, especially on high-stakes tests.

Based on her practical experience, Ann is convinced that test preparation can and should be an integral part of meaningful classroom instruction. By using classroom assessments that mirror high-stakes tests and by focusing on meaningful, standards-based instruction, teachers will empower students with a broad range of knowledge and skills. As a result, the students will be able to achieve high scores in the testing/assessment setting and retain this knowledge as a basis for future learning.

These ideas guide Ann as she consults with districts on their curriculum, offers in-district staff-development workshops, and presents programs at state and national seminars and conferences. The topics of these workshops include writing as process, reading and writing across the curriculum, improving SAT scores, and improving student performance on statewide and norm-referenced assessments in the language arts. In addition, she works with teachers to help them prepare better classroom tests and assessments, and she works with districts to develop comprehensive testing and assessment programs.

Ann has written reviews for the *Journal of Adolescent and Adult Literacy*, a publication of the International Reading Association. Her article "The Superintendent Takes the SAT" was published in *Education Week*.